Taxing
America

CRITICAL AMERICA

General Editors: *Richard Delgado* and *Jean Stefancic*

White by Law: The Legal Construction of Race
  Ian Haney López

Cultivating Intelligence: Power, Law, and the Politics
of Teaching
  Louise Harmon and *Deborah W. Post*

Privilege Revealed: How Invisible Preference Undermines America
  Stephanie M. Wildman with *Margalynne Armstrong,*
  Adrienne D. Davis, and *Trina Grillo*

Does the Law Morally Bind the Poor? or What Good's the
Constitution When You Can't Afford a Loaf of Bread
  R. George Wright

Hybrid: Bisexuals, Multiracials, and Other Misfits
under American Law
  Ruth Colker

Critical Race Feminism: A Reader
  Edited by *Adrien Katherine Wing*

Immigrants Out! The New Nativism and the Anti-Immigrant
Impulse in the United States
  Edited by *Juan F. Perea*

Taxing America
  Edited by *Karen B. Brown* and *Mary Louise Fellows*

Taxing America

Edited by

KAREN B. BROWN

and

MARY LOUISE FELLOWS

NEW YORK UNIVERSITY PRESS

New York & London

NEW YORK UNIVERSITY PRESS
New York & London

Library of Congress Cataloging-in-Publication Data
Taxing America / edited by Karen B. Brown and Mary Louise Fellows.
    p.   cm.
    Papers presented at a conference held Nov. 3–5, 1995, at the
University of Minnesota.
    Includes index.
    ISBN 0-8147-2661-5 (pbk.) — ISBN 0-8147-2648-8 (clothbound)
    1. Taxation—United States—Congresses. 2. Taxation—Law and
legislation—United States—Congresses. 3. Income tax—United States—
Congresses. 4. United States—Economic policy—1993—Congresses.
I. Brown, Karen B., 1954– . II. Fellows, Mary Louise.
HJ2381.T396   1996
336.2'00973—dc20   96-25302
                            CIP

Manufactured in the United States of America

10 9 8 7 6 5 4 3 2 1

CONTENTS

PREFACE

This anthology is a product of the vibrancy and intellectual excitement found in a remarkable community of scholars. As a result of some earlier personal interchanges and a long-standing interest in each other's work, Professors Richard Delgado and Jean Stefancic invited us to consider participating in the Critical America series by challenging the current political tax discourse and many of the tax reform proposals generated by the 1994 election of a Republican Congress and the "Contract with America." That invitation was most timely because we had spent the previous six months working on a collaborative project rethinking tax theory to consider how it might operate to strip the tax law of its claim to objectivity and hold it accountable for its social and economic impact on traditionally subordinated groups.

That reconceptualization itself had been inspired by Professor Beverly Moran. Her earlier formal lectures and patient informal encouragement over the last several years had convinced us that working to develop an analytical framework would both uncover biases in the tax law and reveal antisubordination strategies to keep the tax law from maintaining and perpetuating marketplace discrimination. That early thinking had been advanced by discussions with other tax academics who attended a series of teaching conferences sponsored by the Society of American Law Teachers (SALT) in which working groups were organized according to subject areas. (Tax Working Group at the SALT Teaching Conference (SALT): Diversity in the Law School Curriculum (Minneapolis, Minn. Sept. 23–24, 1994); Tax, Trusts, and Estates Working Group at the 1993 SALT Teaching Conference: Reimagining Traditional Law School Courses: Workshops Integrating Class, Disability, Gender, Race, and Sexual Preference and Other Issues of Social Concern into Teaching and Course Materials (Santa Clara, Calif., Oct. 29–30, 1993); Tax Working Group at the SALT Teaching Conference: Reimagining Traditional Law School Courses: Workshops Integrating Class, Disability, Gender, Race, and Sexual Preference into Our Teaching and Course Materials (New York, N.Y., May 22–23, 1993)). The tax working groups at the SALT conferences, however, did more: they brought together a group of tax scholars in which each of us who previously had felt isolat-ed by the traditional tax analysis that dominated the legal literature and tax conferences now had found intellectual kinship.

The project of integrating traditional tax theory and antisubordina-tion principles was advanced even further at Critical Tax Theory: A Workshop organized by Professor Nancy Staudt at the State University of New York at Buffalo in the fall of 1995. Staudt had attended the SALT conference in Minnesota and wanted to create another forum to bring together scholars with a common interest in challenging traditional tax discourse and its claim to objectivity. That successful workshop, which identified yet more scholars interested in the project and new paths of inquiry, encouraged us to organize a conference for the contributors to this anthology to present the drafts of their essays to each other. Taxing America: A Conference on the Social and Economic Implications of Tax Reform, held November 3–5, 1995, at the University of Minnesota, was made possible by the generous support of Dean E. Thomas Sullivan and the Center for Legal Studies. After three days of creative interchange leading to new ideas and research projects, each of us left feeling that this anthology represents a significant step toward rethink-ing tax theory.

The various gatherings, conversations in hotel lobbies, and long con-versations over the telephone and by e-mail suggest that the group of tax critics is several dozen strong. It is our hope that this anthology will be a catalyst for encouraging others, who also feel traditional tax analy-sis is inadequate to address issues of discrimination and economic exploitation, to join in our conversation. For whatever else the antholo-gy accomplishes, it provides evidence that connection and interchange within a community of scholars are essential.

We especially thank Michael Voran and Renae Welder, 1996 gradu-ates of the University of Minnesota, who assisted us in the preparation of the manuscript and at the Taxing America conference. Further, we are grateful for the research support provided by the reference librari-ans of the University of Minnesota Law Library, especially Marci Hoffman, George Jackson, and Suzanne Thorpe. We thank Martha Heidt, a 1996 graduate of the University of Minnesota, for her willing-ness to assist us before and during the conference. Patricia Buenzle, Andrea Sheets, and Liz Steblay helped us remain organized, complete the manuscript, and make arrangements for the Taxing America conference. Finally, we thank Niko Pfund, the editor in chief of New York University Press, for his enthusiasm and support throughout the publication process.

As always, our friends and families maintained our spirits by asking about our progress and caring about our answers. Although somewhat skeptical that a book on taxation could be interesting, they were willing to listen long enough to believe it might be true.

KAREN B. BROWN
MARY LOUISE FELLOWS

INTRODUCTION

KAREN B. BROWN AND
MARY LOUISE FELLOWS

We find ourselves in a political moment when the clamor for tax reform has, once again, reached a high pitch. Yet, although questions about how the tax law can contribute to a strong economy abound, what has been entirely lost in the discussion is the role of tax law as a gatekeeper to the American Dream.

Most recently, the current fascination with tax reform was best embodied by the 1996 presidential candidacy of Steven Forbes, publisher of *Forbes* magazine, multimillionaire, and son of Malcolm S. Forbes. On the basis of little more than a flat tax mantra and his personal fortune, Forbes briefly captured the imagination of the media, policy wonks, and the body politic. Explicit in his political proposal was a repudiation of big government and a ratification and reification of private enterprise. Forbes claimed to want to level the tax playing field by eliminating notable loopholes, such as the home-mortgage interest deduction, but he failed to reconcile his fairness claim with the fact that his proposal overtaxed workers and undertaxed owners of financial capital.

Beyond Forbes's message, most people and parties, regardless of their location on the political spectrum, seem to agree on a few basics about taxes: (1) the lower they are, the better; and (2) if well designed, they can contribute to economic growth in the United States, assuring a share of the American Dream to every hardworking, taxpaying individual. Although one side of the political spectrum may emphasize reducing the burden on the middle class and the other may prefer to focus on lessening the tax burden on businesses, both leave unexamined how the current tax law may be reinforcing market failures that deny some individuals an opportunity to achieve economic security.

What is missing from both the political and the academic debate about taxes is a serious consideration of how the tax system exacerbates marketplace discrimination against traditionally subordinated groups. With dramatic and far-reaching tax reform always a possibility, the purpose of this anthology is to change the tax discourse to include issues of disability discrimination, economic exploitation, heterosexism, sexism, and racism. In a political environment in which the Contract with America and the Republican agenda put forth politically viable proposals that benefit the haves at the cost of the have-nots, a perspective that emphasizes the exploitive and discriminatory aspects of the tax code becomes critically important.

We have long felt uneasy about the assumption that the tax law only minimally contributes to social injustice and has little potential for advancing social justice. That uneasiness was reinforced by Beverly Moran's pathbreaking approach separating issues of class from those of gender and race when analyzing a tax rule, so that marketplace discrimination based on gender and race can be uncovered *across income levels*.[1]

Most of the essays in this anthology address class issues and their implications in designing a fair tax base and rate structure. Jonathan B. Forman and George K. Yin consider class issues by exploring the politically controversial earned income tax credit (EITC) and its appropriate role in the income tax system. Both essays start from the proposition that the EITC is a welfare transfer to low-income workers and not integral to the income tax structure.

In contrast, Jennifer J. S. Brooks, Charlotte Crane, Gwen Thayer Handelman, Mary L. Heen, and Denise D. J. Roy investigate how traditional tax analysis masks the ways the tax rules overestimate the productive contributions of entrepreneurs and underestimate them for workers, leading to an overtaxation of workers. Regina T. Jefferson extends the entrepreneur/worker discussion to consider the relationship between employers and employees regarding the federal tax policy on retirement savings. She focuses on the congressional proposal to establish American Dream Savings Accounts (ADSA) and concludes that they are likely to operate in a regressive manner against low- and middle-income workers, leaving many of them without sufficient funds for their retirement. Beverly I. Moran also considers the tax bias toward business by looking beyond the federal income tax and critiquing how governmental units compete for businesses to locate in their regions, using tax incentives. LaBrenda Garrett-Nelson, on the other hand, argues that current international tax policy unfairly taxes U.S. multinational corporations, making it difficult for them to compete effectively in the world economy. In addition to raising issues of class, the essays by Dorothy A. Brown, Karen B. Brown, Lily Kahng, Mary L. Heen and john a. powell make significant progress toward uncovering issues of gender, race and their intersection in the tax law, both domestic and international. An important contribution made by all the essays is that they identify how much more work needs to be done both with regard to economic exploitation, sexism, and racism against African Americans, which are addressed in this collection; and with regard to disability discrimination, heterosexism, and racism against other groups, which have been left largely unaddressed in the anthology and in the tax literature in general.[2]

Any examination of whether the tax law reinforces the subordination of persons based on their physical and mental abilities, class, gender, race, and sexual orientation follows from two propositions. The first is that economic arrangements can contribute significantly to creating social hierarchies and perpetuating discrimination. The second is that the federal tax law should further the policy goal of nondiscrimination by including rules designed to disrupt discriminatory practices.[3]

Within tax policy discourse, the analysis that we are advocating— interjecting social justice concerns into tax law—should be viewed as quite unremarkable. It is widely accepted that the federal tax law should be designed to meet the goals of equity, administrability, and economic rationality. These three goals are embedded in American political values, which include respect for individual autonomy, privacy, and free enterprise. For example, a tax rule that requires a taxpayer to reveal information generally viewed as personal, or subjects a taxpayer to government inspection of such information, is considered unadministrable because it would lack public support. Freedom from governmental intervention in an individual's private life is a strong American political value that, if not consistently reflected in existing tax laws, carries considerable weight in debates about current tax law and proposed reforms of it. Another strongly held American value reflected in these goals is a commitment against discrimination on the basis of class, gender, and race. (The same, however, cannot be said with any conviction regarding discrimination based on physical and mental abilities or sexual orientation.) No one would argue, for example, for tax rules that explicitly taxed the working class more than capitalists, women more than men, or persons of color more than whites. Although some would argue that legal remedies to reduce discrimination are ineffective and lead to economic inefficiencies,[4] no one argues that the law should be designed to exacerbate marketplace discrimination.[5] Any proposal to do so would be vigorously opposed as inconsistent with all three goals of the federal tax system that are based on the American belief in assuring individual dignity and equal opportunity. Therefore, although much of current tax discourse is carried on without reference to concerns about physical and mental abilities, class, gender, race, or sexual orientation, the candid introduction of nondiscrimination issues should be viewed as wholly consistent with the values underlying traditional tax analysis.

A social justice critique of tax policy discourse is merely an extension of the current tradition to integrate analysis of tax concepts with social policies regarding redistribution of income. Although the issue of progressivity remains unsettled, any particular tax provision or proposed reform is evaluated in terms of its impact on the distribution of income. What we are advocating is to modify tax policy discourse to embrace other issues of social justice in addition to the progressivity principle.

The first step in pursuing a social justice inquiry into tax—a step taken in many of the essays found in this anthology—is the dismantling of the conceptual tools that constrain traditional tax analysis from considering issues of discrimination and economic exploitation. Traditional tax analysis treats as goals of sound tax policy the following three principles: economic neutrality, objectivity, and progressivity. As a number of the essays show, each of these principles is more usefully understood as fiction. The goal of economic neutrality is a goal of minimizing the effect of income taxes on economic decision making, which assumes that an ideal marketplace is one that is untainted by tax considerations. The goal of objectivity is accomplished through the assumption that the tax base can, and should, be defined objectively without consideration of other governmental and social goals. An ideal income tax base is defined as one that is deduced from logically connected propositions that are free from any social and cultural underpinnings. The final goal, progressivity, assumes that, if we accurately define the ideal income tax base, income is an appropriate and sufficient measure of ability to pay. The exclusive focus on income implies that acquired wealth, which makes that level of income possible and creates opportunities for future income, should be irrelevant in determining a taxpayer's ability to pay.

The role of economic neutrality is explored here extensively by K. B. Brown, Crane, Garrett-Nelson, and Handelman. The principle of economic neutrality establishes the market as the ideal. Economic activity easily escapes scrutiny within tax policy discussions because it is understood only as something to be protected from interference by the tax law. Therefore, academic and political commentators comfortably ignore market failures in pursuit of the widely accepted goal of creating a set of tax rules that have a neutral effect on the economy. In fact, the principle of economic neutrality is used in tax discourse as a reason to reject correction of market distortions through the tax law and a reason to defend a tax rule that exacerbates market distortions. Disconnected from the realities of the marketplace, the principle of tax neutrality is converted into a fiction.

The one exception to the principle of economic neutrality and nonrecognition of marketplace failures is the widespread agreement that the tax law should be used to encourage savings and investment for the purpose of promoting economic prosperity. The savings bias accounts for much of the current attention being paid to proposals to overhaul the current income tax and replace it with some form of consumption tax. The implications of a shift to a consumption tax are explored by Brooks, Crane, Handelman, and Roy, with each raising a range of problems that will arise under a consumption tax, including the problems created if the distinction between the productivity of entrepreneurs and that of workers continues to prevail.

The second fiction, tax objectivity, allows the participants in tax discourse to claim a position of innocence and avoid accountability for the role the tax law may play in perpetuating social injustices. Tax objectivity is achieved by relying on the ideal income tax base developed by Robert Haig and refined by Henry Simons as a starting point for analysis. The ideal tax base is defined to be the algebraic sum of "(1) the market value of rights exercised in consumption and (2) the change in value of the store of property rights between the beginning and end of the period in question."[6] To apply this definition requires "distinguishing between consumption and expense."[7] An expense, meaning investment or savings, is to be taken into account in the second part of the algebraic sum when determining the change in value of accumulations. X dollars expended, for instance, for inventory that is later sold for Y dollars would result in Y-X income being subject to tax during the period. In contrast, X dollars spent during the taxable period for comfort or pleasure, such as for heating a home or going to a movie, represents an amount to be taken into account in the first part of the algebraic sum. The expenditure for heat or a movie is understood as producing no increase in the taxpayer's store of property rights and therefore is not deductible in part two of the algebraic sum. Instead, it is included in part one as an amount used for consumption for the purpose of determining the total amount of income earned by the taxpayer during the taxable period. Perhaps a more complete description of the tax treatment of a personal expenditure would recognize that X dollars spent for heat or a movie was first earned and taxed as an increase in accumulations for the period in accordance with the second part of the algebraic formula. Once expended for consumption purposes, the amount of accumulations is reduced by X dollars while the amount of consumption is increased by the same amount. The net effect of both explanations is that the ideal tax base for any period remains the same regardless of whether the increase in accumulations is saved or consumed.

The difficulty, of course, and the reason why tax objectivity is a mere fiction, is the inherent problem with Simons's definition. He himself recognized that "[a] thoroughly precise and objective distinction [between personal and business expense] is inconceivable."[8] Simons conceded that, however "unwelcome [the] criterion of intention," it is "inescapable."[9] Without the possibility of an objective basis to make the distinction between personal and business expenses, reliance on the ideal income tax base serves only to obscure biases in the tax law. Brooks, Crane, Handelman, and Roy extensively explore the personal/ business and the consumption/investment distinctions to uncover with particularity how the Haig-Simons model produces the appearance of tax objectivity and the reality that the tax system is thoroughly implicated in the discriminatory practices of the marketplace.

In more recent years the fiction of objectivity has been perpetuated in what has come to be known as the tax expenditure budget. The essays by Handelman, Heen, and Roy include excellent discussions of the tax expenditure concept, demonstrating how it cannot withstand scrutiny as well as how it distorts tax policy analysis. In 1967 Stanley Surrey in his capacity as assistant secretary of the treasury for tax policy made a speech in which he developed the concepts of *tax expenditures* and the *tax expenditure budget*.[10] Surrey understood the federal income tax system as consisting of two types of provisions. One type is the "structural provisions necessary to implement the income tax on individual and corporate net income,"[11] which are determined by reference to Simons's ideal income tax base. The other type is those provisions that "comprise[] a system of tax expenditures under which the Governmental financial assistance programs are carried out through special tax provisions rather than through direct Government expenditures."[12] The term *tax expenditures* was chosen to indicate that these provisions are the equivalent of direct government subsidies, the only difference being that they are accomplished through the federal income tax system. Surrey's purpose for classifying tax provisions as either structural or tax expenditures was to expose the relationship between tax reform and government subsidies and to suggest "new pathways to tax reform." For him tax reform meant grappling with questions such as "[I]s tax assistance the preferred route, or should the assistance be given directly? Which method comes closest to the targeted goal of the assistance and does so with fairness and efficiency?"[13]

The tax expenditure model, of course, did not obviate the need to address the personal/business distinction. On the contrary, the distinction is incorporated into the tax expenditure model. As Surrey acknowledges, there are, in considering the tax expenditure budget, "difficulties in the application of agreed income tax structural concepts, such as the proper line between allowable expenses incurred in trade or business or in the acquisition of income and nondeductible personal consumption expenses."[14] That acknowledgment, however, did not lead him or others to account for the difficulties in developing the tax expenditure budget. Instead, the tax expenditure budget has become the primary arbiter of which tax provisions are considered structural and free from scrutiny and which provisions are considered tax subsidies and subject to continuing reexamination for modification or repeal. The problem is not only that the tax expenditure budget falsely claims objectivity, but also that the fiction of objectivity, achieved through reference to the ideal income tax base and the tax expenditure budget, ultimately becomes an excuse for omitting social justice goals from tax analysis.

Another way that the tax law maintains its claim to objectivity is through the use of choice, a subject addressed by Crane, Handelman, Heen, powell, and Roy. Their work demonstrates in a variety of contexts how the concept of choice does more to inhibit than to encourage sound tax analysis. The definition of taxable income, which depends on the personal/business distinction, relies on assumptions about the taxpayer's ability to choose. An expenditure is deductible if it is deemed "necessary" to the production of income.[15] Once the taxpayer is identified as an entrepreneur, most expenses are regarded as necessary because the tax law defers to and respects the entrepreneur's business judgment. It is not that the tax law assumes the entrepreneur is not making choices about expenditures. It is that the tax law treats those choices as sufficiently constrained by the profit-making motive as to make choice irrelevant. In contrast, the tax law assumes that most expenditures incurred by nonentrepreneurs (workers inside and outside the marketplace) are the product of unlimited choice, and it is that ability to choose that justifies the conclusion that those expenditures are personal in nature and nondeductible.

Tax law has appropriated the idea of choice to perpetuate the perception that the tax law is objective. Once a taxpayer is deemed to have *chosen* to enter into an economic transaction, the tax law becomes an innocent bystander. Choice serves the dual goal of emphasizing the taxpayer's responsibility for the consequences of the choice and minimizing the tax law's complicity in perpetuating marketplace distortions. Choice can only perform this function, however, if it remains unexamined. Choice loses its analytical power once the ability to choose is understood as operating along a continuum. The more privileged societal position a person enjoys, the greater and more meaningful the choices. Choice and the absence of choice are used in the tax law to reflect the experiences of those who enjoy power by virtue of the dominant social positions they hold.

An example demonstrating the choice continuum, the fiction of objectivity, and the obfuscation of social injustice is found in the tax law's treatment of commuting expenses. This example builds on john a. powell's discussion of the federal government's tax and housing policy. Section 162 has been interpreted to deny a taxpayer a deduction for the cost of commuting between home and work.[16] The rationale traditionally given for denying commuting expenses is that where one lives relative to where one works is a matter of personal choice. powell shows that the choice of where one lives and works is structurally and systemically limited depending on one's race and class. Specifically, the denial of commuting expenses has a demonstrated disparate impact on African Americans because their choice of where to live and work is limited by the degree of housing and employment discrimination in the region. The absence of, or at least restriction on, choice suggests that commuting expenses are more work related than personal in nature. Denial of a deduction, therefore, perpetuates racial discrimination rather than disrupting it. Furthermore, providing no relief for commuting expenses adds yet more costs to the housing and employment discrimination already experienced by the taxpayer in the marketplace. powell's essay reveals the inadequacy of an analysis that depends on choice when it is unaccompanied by a consideration of market failures. With biases in seemingly objective rules uncovered, the challenge remains to establish a framework that integrates a social justice critique into the definition of an ideal income tax base.

The third fiction, progressivity, depends on a series of contestable propositions. One proposition is that redistribution of wealth can be achieved through a progressive income tax rate structure. The redistributive goal is undermined, however, by the exclusive focus of the tax law on marketplace income. It treats as irrelevant that the greater a person's wealth, the greater that person's opportunity for increased income. No one denies that wealth ownership allows people to generate the kind of income that can avoid taxation, that is to say, nonmarketplace productivity that is traditionally referred to in the tax law as *imputed income* and nonmarketplace accretions to wealth that are traditionally referred to in the tax law as *unrealized income*. The search for a workable income tax base, however, generally proceeds on the assumption that imputed and unrealized income are beyond practical reach. Without a serious commitment to reevaluating the regressive aspects of the tax base by considering the effect of acquired wealth on income, a progressive rate structure will remain an inadequate tool for redistribution. The importance of wealth is considered by Brooks, Jefferson, and powell as they evaluate questions involving the tax base and ability to pay.

A second contestable proposition regarding progressivity is that the tax law is socially just because it strives to tax according to ability to pay. The progressivity principle considers issues of class by adjusting tax rates to ameliorate the effects of income disparities; that is to say, the tax system injects progressivity predominantly through the rate structure rather than through the tax base. What remains unexamined and outside traditional tax discourse is how the marketplace produces income disparity and how the tax law contributes to that disparity. If the tax system is going to be used to further social justice, it must address the question of how the tax base can be defined in a manner that prevents, or at least discourages, economic exploitation leading to income disparity. Brooks, Crane, Handelman, Heen, Jefferson, powell, and Roy make tax base issues the central focus of their essays. Handelman, in particular, identifies the relationship of the tax base to marketplace distortions, how the tax base definition has been used to further economic exploitation, and how it could be used to ameliorate marketplace distortions.

The essays in this anthology establish the parameters of a theory of tax social justice and its operation within tax policy discourse. They also can be read as emphatic statements about the need for the theory to be further elaborated, explored, and tested. The contributors' commitment to this multifaceted project is reflected in the anthology's four parts, which identify the variety of ways traditional tax analysis can be challenged and social justice critiques can be injected into tax policy discussions.

In part 1, "Expanding the Tax Discourse: New Ways to Think about Wealth, Income, Race, and Gender," Kahng and D. A. Brown focus on tax rates and the effect of marital status, whereas Brooks and powell treat specific tax base issues of human capital and home ownership. These seemingly disparate topics are joined to introduce the reader to different approaches that can be used to integrate traditional tax and social justice theories. All the essays challenge basic tenets of the tax system generally thought to be unassailable and demonstrate how seemingly objective rules and principles play significant roles in the tax law of obscuring and thereby perpetuating social injustices.

Because so much has been written about the income and transfer tax treatment of married couples over the last fifty years, common wisdom holds that all of the issues relating to the subject have been, if not fully resolved, at least articulated. Kahng and D. A. Brown not only demonstrate the inadequacies in conventional discussions of tax and marital status but also provide two distinct approaches for reconsidering a wide range of tax issues. Kahng, in exploring the tax fiction of marital unity, shows how fictions in tax (both the income and the transfer tax) mask biases and cause harm when those relying upon them fail to recognize their fictional nature. She acknowledges that marital unity—the fiction that a married couple is an indivisible unit—served important administrative goals, but she questions why those benefits were not weighed against the substantial costs of embracing the fiction. She shows how the fiction itself was used to trivialize the costs of ignoring the differing economic rights allocated to husbands and to wives under differing state property law regimes (community- versus common-law property states) and reducing the incentive for common-law property states to provide married women with greater rights to the marital estate. As she says, the proclaimed benefits of treating all married couples, wherever resident, the same for tax purposes "would be an independent benefit . . . only if husbands and wives had the same rights, wherever resident." By exposing the principle of equal taxes for equal-income or equally wealthy married couples as a "fiction that masquerades as a first principle," Kahng not only changes the nature of tax policy discussions regarding tax and marital status but also charts new paths of inquiry to determine how other fictions in the tax law may be masking bias and causing harm.

D. A. Brown further explores the fiction of marital unity by looking at its racial as well as its gender implications. It is commonly known that two married spouses who earn roughly equal incomes suffer the highest marriage penalty, meaning that the couple would pay lower taxes if each earner were single and filed individual returns. Conversely, it is commonly known that a couple in which only one spouse has taxable income enjoys a marriage bonus, meaning that the couple would pay higher taxes if they had not married and had filed individual returns. By looking at working patterns of black and white women, D. A. Brown shows that, when gender and race wage discrimination are considered, black couples are more likely to pay a marriage penalty tax, whereas white couples are more likely to enjoy a marriage bonus. She does this by providing data showing that marriage tends to reduce the labor force participation rate of white women but to increase the participation rate among black women and that black wives contribute significantly more toward household income than white wives. By challenging the convention of referring to *all* married women as "secondary earners" and by showing how current income tax rate schedules exacerbate gender and race wage discrimination, D. A. Brown not only changes the nature of discussions regarding income taxation of married couples by injecting the interlocking issues of gender and racial justice, but she also provides a model for how to study race and class issues across income levels.

In Brooks's investigation of the proper taxation of human capital, she ultimately challenges the Haig-Simons ideal income tax definition. She shows how it has been used and misused to provide a theoretical justification for a consumption tax. The key to Brooks's analysis is her refusal, unlike other tax theorists, to ignore the "disproportionate distribution throughout society of material wealth, cash income, opportunity, and choice." Her commitment to the issue of redistribution of wealth allowed her to see the improbability of the claim that labor income was undertaxed, which in turn led her to make an incisive critique demonstrating that leisure, choice, and opportunity generally associated with human capital are, in fact, related to material capital. Having injected a social context into the consideration of taxation of human and material capital, Brooks has set the stage for a quite different theoretical debate about the "ideal" tax base.

powell's essay on tax and home ownership also emphasizes the relationship between wealth and income. The essay is based on two propositions: (1) "home ownership and equity are the most important sources of wealth to the individual American" and (2) housing, especially the placement and location of housing, is racialized. powell demonstrates how the federal government, through a variety of programs and policies, including formally neutral tax policies, "has contributed to racial separation and perpetuated this separation." Just as D. A. Brown shows that the marriage bonus is most likely to inure to the benefit of white couples, powell shows how tax rules "benefiting home owners have operated to the disproportionate benefit of whites." Equally important, he goes on to reveal how the tax law's role in facilitating the ownership of homes for whites indirectly facilitates whites' access to employment, good schools, safety, public services, recreational opportunities, and support for child development, all of which operate to improve their quality of life. The nexus between wealth and income that is explored in Brooks's essay is examined with particularity by powell when he links black families' inability to tap into home equity wealth with housing discrimination. He shows how perpetuation of that discrimination through the tax law contributes to the vast economic inequalities between blacks and whites in the United States.

In part 2, "Challenging Tax Traditions: The Bias of the Investment/ Consumption Dichotomy," Handelman, Crane, and Roy scrutinize the tax law distinction between investment (business) and consumption (personal) expenses and demonstrate its inadequacies and its business bias. Specifically, they show how the distinction underestimates the productive contributions of workers, leading to a misapprehension of how to analyze worker health care costs, an undervaluation of investment in education, and an inappropriate characterization of business's environmental cleanup costs as productive and accessibility expenses of workers who have or whose spouse or dependents have disabilities as nonproductive.

Handelman makes a forceful case for "acknowledging in our tax policy the individual lives and collective role of working people in American society." She demonstrates that tax policy on the one hand adopts the perspective of property owners, who, as a result, are under-taxed on income or benefits derived from property, and on the other hand ignores the perspective of workers, who are not provided equivalent opportunities for income exclusion and tax deferral. Thus, nontaxation of pension or health benefits traditionally is viewed as a major subsidy of workers, whereas nontaxation of the value of the use of property, gifts, and unrealized appreciation enjoyed by property owners traditionally is not seen as a subsidy but, instead, as consistent with the overall tax structure. Handelman goes on to show that the tax law's failure to acknowledge worker productivity would be exacerbated by current tax reform proposals that would replace the income tax with a consumption tax. The reason is that the consumption tax ignores "the production of wage labor" by characterizing all worker expenditures as consumption. Her essay focuses particularly on health care and maintains that tax law, whether through a consumption- or an income-based tax, should account for the productivity of workers by reasoning that "[i]f maintenance expenses on a manufacturer's capital equipment or the utility bills of a shopkeeper can offset these entrepreneurs' business income, it seems logical that the cost of medical care to maintain a worker's fitness ought to offset that worker's earnings from labor."

Crane also addresses the consumption tax proposals and demonstrates why the tax treatment of expenditures for education will be more problematic under a consumption tax than under the income tax. Crane begins by providing a critical analysis of the income tax in which she explains the attraction of its tax logic and its aspiration for economic neutrality. She shows how and why the income tax depends on various presumptions that produce tolerable errors, ultimately making the salient point that, although the errors under the income tax are unavoidable, that does not mean that errors are not made. Turning to the consumption tax, Crane provides a critical analysis of why the errors produced from presumptions regarding investment in human potential—errors that were tolerable under the income tax—are exacerbated under the consumption tax. She ultimately shows how, under the consumption tax, "investment in our own, or our family's, human potential would become the only investment that we must make in after-tax values" and why that might have a substantial impact on human behavior regarding investment in human potential. Crane's thesis is not to show how and when to identify a particular expenditure as investment (business) or consumption (personal) but to show that "[t]ax logic tells us nothing about whether the tax law should favor investment in human potential or investment in financial capital. The desirability of additional investment in human potential and the form that investment takes are policy decisions that we should make independent of tax logic."

Roy also makes an important contribution to the debate over the inadequacy of the tax law's personal/business dichotomy in her analysis of the tax treatment of environmental cleanup costs and disability access costs. Current law allows an immediate deduction for cleanup costs but requires a portion of access costs to be capitalized to the extent that it causes an increase in the value of property. The excess portion is deductible, if at all, only as a personal medical expense. Roy examines the differential treatment and finds it unjustified because the cleanup costs reflect consumption activity by businesses and the access costs reflect income production by the individual taxpayer. She goes on to explain that the personal/business dichotomy produces unsupportable tax results because it creates a hierarchy between personal and business categories through its "unquestioning association of personal with consumption expenditures and business with investment expenditures." Noting that her critique of the personal/business dichotomy is pertinent to the various consumption tax proposals that Congress is currently considering, she concludes by advocating a tax analysis that "begin[s] with the question whether the expenditure at issue is for consumption or for the production of income, without regard to whether the expenditure is personal or business." Only by starting there, Roy argues, can the tax law "acknowledge and value both the productive functions of the personal realm and the consumption functions of the business realm."

Part 3, "Rethinking Development: Old Practices, Old Rules, New World," includes essays by Moran, who investigates the use by local governments of tax incentives to encourage economic development, and by K. B. Brown and Garrett-Nelson, who each consider different aspects of U.S. international tax policy and its effect on economic development. Although all the contributors write in the context of a global economy and favor economic growth within that global perspective, their attention to and sympathies with the various economic players vary widely.

Moran focuses on the relationships between local U.S. governmental units and the businesses they attempt to attract or do attract to their regions as well as the relationships among governmental units who are competing against one another for economic development opportunities. After looking at the past and current history of localities attempting to attract businesses through tax incentives, the essay underscores the irony that the very qualities of the community that attracted the business in the first place (transportation arteries, skilled labor, and other infrastructure items, such as sewers) are the "things . . . that companies avoid paying for by negotiating special tax deals." It then explores the paradox of the governmental units competing for businesses to locate in their areas with tax incentives even though historically the cost of attracting and supporting those businesses frequently outweighs the economic benefits ultimately enjoyed by the region. Moran's primary interest is to investigate possible solutions for governmental units to disrupt their "race to the bottom" to provide tax incentives when businesses use their economically powerful position to fuel unhealthy competition among governmental units.

K. B. Brown investigates a similar dynamic that occurs when developing nations compete for business investment. Her primary attention is on U.S. tax treaty policy and how it has served to undermine the interests of developing nations as well as its own interests when those interests are, contrary to conventional international tax policy, broadly defined. K. B. Brown identifies the United States as a major player in the global economy who has failed to use its leadership to be an internationalist in tax matters rather than a unilateralist. Notwithstanding the dramatic changes in the post–World War II global economy, the United States has continued its unilateralist policy of entering into tax treaties with individual countries to advance its own interests by taking hegemonic stances, including maintaining that the treaty may be changed unilaterally by subsequent legislation, by revocation of the treaty, or by promulgation of administrative regulations. After demonstrating the "enormous promise" that developing nations consisting of significant populations of color hold "for substantial contribution to world economic growth," K. B. Brown challenges the United States to stop neglecting these countries and to act as an internationalist by forming alliances and acting in partnership with them. Current tax policy leaves these developing nations with little ability to attract business through tax incentives; instead it forces them to compete by allowing businesses to exploit their labor force and their other natural resources. Wise multilateral tax treaty making, according to K. B. Brown, can become a crucial ingredient in creating good working conditions for workers, preserving the environment, and assuring healthy economic growth.

In contrast to Moran and K. B. Brown, Garrett-Nelson focuses on how current international tax policy unfairly taxes U.S. multinational corporations, creating the risk that they will not be able to compete effectively in the world economy. Her probusiness stance, viewed as the key to world economic growth, provides an important contrast to the views found in the Moran and the K. B. Brown essays. Garrett-Nelson believes that the 1994 election of a Republican-controlled Congress, along with the growing interest in a consumption-based tax, will result in a serious reexamination of the current U.S. international tax policy. Most especially, she focuses on the antideferral policies of current tax law and how the question of deferral is currently being contested in a variety of tax reform proposals. Deferral in this context refers to the general policy of the United States not to tax a U.S. shareholder of a controlled foreign corporation (CFC) until the foreign-source income is repatriated to the shareholder as a dividend or the shareholder disposes of the CFC for a gain. This policy is accomplished through foreign tax credits (FTC). Garrett-Nelson recognizes that the general rule allowing deferral has the potential to "impair the domestic tax base," but she is critical of the "plethora of exceptions to deferral and the awful complexity of the current rules limiting the use of FTCs." Garrett-Nelson concludes that current proposals attempting to curtail the historical antideferral bias are welcomed and are as good as can be expected under current budgetary constraints. She also believes that fundamental tax reform leading to a consumption tax is possible and that this change creates a significant opportunity for reconsidering the CFC tax regime.

Finally, in part 4, "Implementing Subsidies: Tax Relief for Savers and for Workers," the contributors examine the law's progressivity principle and the ability-to-pay concept. Jefferson and Heen deal with these questions by looking at tax base issues; Forman and Yin concentrate more on what can be achieved through the tax system's rate structure. Jefferson demonstrates that the proposed ADSA, widely touted as an incentive for savings and a benefit for all Americans, in fact, is detrimental to low- and middle-income taxpayers. Heen details the ways in which current tax allowances for child care costs advantage middle- and upper-income women and disadvantage low-income women. Forman and Yin argue for reforms in federal income tax provisions relating to low-income workers. Forman urges simplification of the income tax system, and Yin contends that reform in the way the EITC is delivered to workers is needed.

Jefferson challenges the current tax reform proposal establishing the

ADSA, which is a retirement savings account that, unlike the traditional individual retirement account (IRA), allows no tax deduction when funded but permits tax-free withdrawals for expenditures other than for retirement. Her central criticism of the ADSA is that it is inconsistent with this country's policy of encouraging savings for retirement. She believes that the expansion of the use of retirement savings through ADSAs for purchase of a first-time home and educational or medical expenses may operate to the disadvantage of middle- and low-income taxpayers and subsidize current consumption for high-income taxpayers. Moreover, the ADSA would encourage middle- and low-income taxpayers to shift from traditional retirement savings arrangements to nonretirement uses, a dangerous shift that may result in inadequate savings for retirement. Low- or middle-income taxpayers might prefer an ADSA over a traditional retirement plan such as a section 401(k) plan, in order to have earlier access to the funds free of penalty. The resulting abandonment of traditional plans by lower-paid employees could cause employers to forgo establishment of plans that may provide "greater retirement security" than the ADSA. Rejecting the contrary claims of the ADSA's promoters, Jefferson demonstrates that the rate of savings is not likely to increase and that the greatest benefits would inure to high-income taxpayers. The disproportionate benefits to high-income taxpayers result from the progressive rate structure that enhances the advantages of tax deferral for those taxpayers at the higher marginal rates and from the subsidy for home-buying that is available only to those who can afford to own homes. Moreover, self-funded mechanisms like the ADSA to provide for medical and health expenses are likely to benefit only the wealthy because only they will have sufficient disposable income to take advantage of the tax benefits offered by ADSAs.

In an alternative approach to the issue of progressivity, Forman argues for simplification of the federal income tax system for low-income individuals, and Yin critiques current proposals for reform of the EITC, a twenty-year-old tax provision aimed at workers who live in poverty. Both view the EITC as a mechanism for the delivery of benefits to low-income individuals, akin to a welfare program, because it not only offsets the social security and federal income tax liabilities of many workers earning wages at the poverty level but also provides a modest refund in excess of those tax obligations. They depart from the view of some observers that the EITC ameliorates the market exploitation of workers resulting from discrimination on the basis of physical and mental abilities, class, gender, race, and sexual orientation. They also do not embrace the view that the EITC is not a subsidy to workers but a structural correction of a tax system that undertaxes entrepreneurs (by overvaluing their production and ignoring the income opportunities provided by wealth) and overtaxes workers by undervaluing their production. Notwithstanding their common view that the EITC is a subsidy, both Forman and Yin support the credit and argue that it should be strengthened. They may disagree, however, on the appropriate delivery mechanism.

Forman primarily critiques the undue complexity of the federal income tax system, including the EITC, for low-income individuals. He offers a range of proposals to achieve simplification. In addition to proposals to streamline the current return-filing process, Forman advocates alternatively either simplification of rules qualifying an individual for the EITC, in order to reach a larger group and to minimize administrative costs; or replacement of the EITC with a simpler social security tax exemption or with a worker credit to employers that would pass through to wage earners in the form of higher wages. Forman's proposals culminate in a call for revamping the current system either by integrating the income and social security taxes or by moving to a flat tax on income or consumption. If a major overhaul of the system is rejected, Forman would urge a move to a return-free system in which the IRS would compute liabilities for low-income taxpayers, or a final withholding system, in which most taxes would be collected by employers through wage withholding.

Yin concludes that the most beneficial reform of the EITC would involve a move to a transfer system. He details the problems resulting from delivery of the EITC through the tax system. These include complexity leading to less-than-full participation by eligible individuals and inadvertent error and fraud. Yin questions whether the EITC provides a work incentive, because the refund typically is recovered only once a year, and there is little evidence that a taxpayer connects the refund with work effort. These observations and a fear that a move to a consumption tax would reduce administrability of the EITC lead Yin to propose that the primary portion of earned income benefits be delivered through a welfare-type system. He urges use of money otherwise provided through a credit to workers to finance government-supervised work programs.

Heen's essay, like Forman's and Yin's, also examines the tax system's treatment of low-income workers. She, however, focuses on the tax base issues concerning child care. Heen critiques the tax law's treatment of child care expenses as it impacts low-, middle-, and high-income women differently. She notes that the historical failure of welfare and labor policies to support affordable child care, coupled with tax provisions that do not tax imputed income from services provided to the family, have encouraged women to provide services in the home. Those incentives have operated to the advantage of middle- and upper-income women who can afford to remain at home. This has established a race- and class-based double standard; the result is that low-income mothers have insufficient access to adequate child care for their own children because they have insufficient resources. Moreover, although the tax law has recognized the work-related nature of child care and has allowed a credit for expenses or an exclusion for employer-provided coverage, these provisions typically do not benefit low-income women. Heen rejects current tax analysis that views child care allowances as a subsidy and argues that child care costs are a legitimate income production expense. Even if allowances for child care costs are properly viewed as a subsidy, she favors them as necessary to offset the tax law's preferred treatment of household labor over waged work. Heen concludes by supporting tax allowances for child care costs for all taxpayers, including upper-income taxpayers, without the limits currently imposed, but she would expand allowances for low-income women either by increasing the maximum credit and making it refundable so that it would be of benefit to low-income workers or by mandating employer-provided programs for all workers.

The wide range of approaches taken and the various topics treated in the essays suggest both the breadth of a social justice theory in tax law and the need to explore the parameters of that theory by looking at particular provisions and rules. The essays are as important in suggesting new paths of tax research as they are in disrupting old ways of thinking about the tax law. Taken together, they represent a unique contribution both to tax scholarship and to the political debate about how, what, and whom we should tax. For those interested in joining in this project, the challenge of unlearning comfortable assumptions about the tax law will be as great as uncovering bias and discrimination in the tax law. What makes our efforts essential is that how America taxes itself today will determine what America will *be* tomorrow.[17]

NOTES

1. Beverly I. Moran, *Black Critique of the Internal Revenue Code*, Presentation at Critical Tax Theory: A Workshop, State University of New York at Buffalo Law School (Sept. 8–9, 1995); Beverly I. Moran, *Gender Bias in the Internal Revenue Code*, Presentation at the Symposium on Gender Bias in the Law, University of Chicago Law School (Dec. 2, 1994); Beverly I Moran, *Race Conscious Scholarship: Theory, Method, and Practice*, Presentation at the Conference on Minorities and Law Teaching of the Association of American Law Schools (Oct. 1992).

2. *But see*, in this volume, Dorothy A. Brown, *The Marriage Bonus/Penalty in Black and White* (indicating that the joint tax return is available only to legally married couples); Lily Kahng, *Fiction in Tax* (exploring the marital unit fiction and its application in the income and transfer taxes only to legally married couples); Karen B. Brown, *Transforming the Unilateralist into the Internationalist: New Tax Treaty Policy toward Developing Countries* (examining the effect of current international tax policy on developing countries with predominantly populations of color); Denise D. J. Roy, *Consumption in Business/Investment at Home: Environmental Cleanup Costs versus Disability Access Costs* (comparing the tax treatment of cleanup costs incurred by businesses that pollute with the treatment of access costs accorded individual taxpayers who are themselves disabled or who have a spouse or a dependent who is); *see also* Patricia A. Cain, *Same-Sex Couples and the Federal Tax Laws*, 1 Law & Sexuality 97 (1991) (analyzing the tax treatment of same-sex couples); Karen B. Brown, *How Does Tax Law Reinforce Subordination of Workers on the Basis of Race or Gender? Employment Discrimination Damage Awards* (unpublished manuscript) (analyzing the tax treatment of I.R.C. § 104, having to do with compensation for injuries and sickness).

3. *See* Mary Louise Fellows, *The Antisubordination Principle in Tax Policy: A Case Study on the Tax Treatment of Child Care Expenses* (unpublished manuscript) (showing why the antisubordination principle needs to be integrated into traditional tax analysis and how its consideration makes a difference in the consideration of tax issues).

4. *See* Richard A. Epstein, Forbidden Grounds: The Case against Employment Discrimination Laws (1992); Daniel R. Fischel & Edward P. Lazear, *Comparable Worth and Discrimination in Labor Markets*, 53 U. Chi. L. Rev. 891 (1986); Richard A. Posner, *An Economic Analysis of Sex Discrimination Laws*, 56 U. Chi. L. Rev. 1311 (1989). For examples of arguments favoring legal intervention, see Mary E. Becker, *Barriers Facing Women in the Wage-Labor Market and the Need for Additional Remedies: A Reply to Fischel and Lazear*, 53 U. Chi. L. Rev. 934 (1986); John J. Donohue III, *Prohibiting Sex Discrimination in the Workplace: An Economic Perspective*, 56 U. Chi. L. Rev. 1337 (1989).

5. *See* Edward J. McCaffery, *Slouching towards Equality: Gender Discrimination, Market Efficiency, and Social Change*, 103 Yale L.J. 595 (1993).

6. The definition of income in an ideal accretion tax system was first stated by Robert Haig as "the money value of the net accretion to one's economic power between two points in time." Robert M. Haig, *The Concept of Income—Economic and Legal Aspects*, *in* The Federal Income Tax 1, 7 (Robert M. Haig ed., 1921). It was later refined by Henry Simons. Henry C. Simons, Personal Income Taxation 50 (1938).

7. *Id.* at 54.

8. *Id.*

9. *Id.*

10. Stanley S. Surrey, Pathways to Tax Reform: The Concept of Tax Expenditures 3 (1973).

11. *Id.* at 6.

12. *Id.*

13. *Id.* at viii–ix.

14. *Id.* at 19.

15. I.R.C. § 162(a).

16. *See Commissioner v. Flowers,* 326 U.S. 465 (1946); *McCabe v. Commissioner,* 688 F.2d 102 (2d Cir. 1982).

17. The essays in this anthology were completed in April 1996 and do not reflect tax law changes after that date.

PART I

EXPANDING THE TAX DISCOURSE: NEW WAYS TO THINK ABOUT WEALTH, INCOME, RACE, AND GENDER

I

LILY KAHNG

Fiction in Tax

Legal fictions have long made us uneasy.[1] Jeremy
Bentham, perhaps legal fiction's most vociferous critic, described it as a
"syphilis, which runs in every vein, and carries into every part of the
system the principle of rottenness."[2] What is a legal fiction? Although
scholars have disagreed over its precise definition, generally speaking, a
legal fiction is a false statement of fact or a false factual construct used
to serve a legal end. For example, in medieval times, English common-
law courts had jurisdiction only over causes of action arising within
England. However, a court could acquire jurisdiction over a foreign
cause of action if the parties to the action made a false assertion that
the foreign place giving rise to the action was in England.[3] A more
modern example of a legal fiction is the tax doctrine of constructive
receipt, under which a cash method taxpayer is deemed to have
received income when in fact she has not.[4]

Legal fictions have been defended as providing a creative way to
reach equitable results.[5] Thus, for example, the doctrine of constructive
receipt prevents a cash method taxpayer from artificially deferring
income from one year to the next by manipulating the timing of its
receipt. However, legal fictions historically have been criticized for a
variety of reasons. Bentham abhorred them because, among other rea-

sons, he believed that they, along with the rest of the common law, made the law inaccessible to the people.[6] Henry Maine criticized legal fictions for obscuring the law to lawyers, thereby hindering their function.[7] John Chipman Gray thought legal fictions were "dangerous tools" when used to change the law rather than merely to classify established rules.[8] Gray also thought it important that the user of a fiction be aware of its fictional nature. He said, "One should always be ready to recognize that the fictions are fictions, and be able to state the real doctrine for which they stand."[9] Lon Fuller, like Gray, emphasized the importance of recognizing that fictions are fictions and warned that the danger of a legal fiction lay in its user's unawareness of its fictional nature.[10]

In tax, fictions abound. A taxpayer can be in "constructive receipt" of income;[11] foreign taxes can be "deemed paid" by a foreign corporation's U.S. shareholder;[12] "transitory" corporations can be "disregarded" in a corporate reorganization.[13] Each of these fictions serves to achieve a desired policy result and appears to avoid the dangers described by Bentham, Maine, Gray, and Fuller. However, tax fictions can be dangerous. They can mask underlying motives and biases and they can cause unforeseen harms. This essay will illustrate the dangers of fictions in tax by tracing the emergence of one such fiction, that of marital unity, the notion that a married couple is an indivisible unit rather than two individuals with separate and distinct rights in income and wealth.

THE GENESIS OF THE FICTION OF MARITAL UNITY

As recently as 1942, all taxpayers were taxed as individuals. However, not all married individuals were taxed in the same way. Married individuals residing in community-property states received certain tax advantages over married individuals residing in common-law states. Under the Supreme Court's 1930 decision in *Poe v. Seaborn*,[14] income earned by a husband in a community-property state was taxed half to him and half to his wife. (This essay refers to men as earners and wealth holders because men were the dominant earners of income and holders of wealth during this time period.)[15] In contrast, income earned by a husband in a common-law state was taxed completely to him. *Poe v. Seaborn*'s income-splitting rule allowed husbands in community-property states to pay less tax than husbands in common-law states, because income splitting mitigated the effect of progressive tax rates. In *Lucas v. Earl*[16] the Supreme Court denied husbands in common-law states the ability to reduce tax liability by shifting personal service income to their wives through contractual assignment. Husbands in common-law states could shift income to their spouses through other devices, however, such as family partnerships and trusts. The Internal Revenue Service (IRS) often challenged these devices as sham transactions and heavily litigated the issue.[17]

Husbands in community-property states also enjoyed favorable estate and gift tax treatment. (For the sake of simplicity, this essay will discuss only the estate tax and not the gift tax. The gift tax, however, has a parallel history and raises similar issues with respect to married individuals.) For example, if a decedent bequeathed his entire estate to his widow, he was taxed only on half of the community property transferred to her because of a presumption that the wife already owned the other half.[18] In contrast, a common-law decedent who bequeathed his entire estate to his widow was taxed on it all.[19]

The disparate treatment of community-property and common-law married residents caused much disgruntlement, and the first federal attempt to redress the disparity came in 1942. The Revenue Act of 1942 (1942 Act) increased the estate tax on decedents in community-property states to equalize their tax liability with decedents in common-law states. The equalization was achieved by requiring most community property to be taxed entirely in the estate of the first spouse to die. The 1942 Act, of course, provided for exceptions. Two types of community property, that derived originally from the surviving spouse's separate property and that derived from personal service income of the surviving spouse, continued to be taxed one-half in each spouse's estate.[20]

Obviously, married residents of community-property states were not pleased by the increase in their estate taxes. They complained that the increase caused hardships and inequities.[21] In the meantime, married residents of common-law states continued to be unhappy with their heavier income tax burden. Pressure mounted on state legislatures in common-law jurisdictions to adopt community-property systems in order to obtain favorable income tax treatment for their constituents. Several states (Oklahoma, Oregon, Michigan, Nebraska, Pennsylvania, and the Territory of Hawaii) succumbed to the pressure by enacting community-property regimes.[22] (All repealed their community-property laws after the federal legislation of 1948 discussed below.)

In 1948 Congress resolved the turmoil in both the income tax and the estate tax. For the income tax, the Revenue Act of 1948 (1948 Act) created an income-splitting scheme, under which all husbands could shift half of their income to their wives for tax purposes.[23] For the estate tax, the 1948 Act repealed the 1942 provisions that had increased the estate tax on residents of community-property states and in its place created a marital deduction. The new marital deduction permitted common-law decedents to transfer up to one-half of their property to their surviving spouses tax free, thus lightening the estate tax burden on common-law residents and equalizing it with that of community-property residents.[24]

The adoption of income-splitting introduced one element of the fiction of marital unity: all married couples were treated *as if* they shared their income whether or not they *actually* did. Stated another way, married couples with equal amounts of income were deemed to be equal for tax purposes despite the fact that husbands and wives had differing rights to the income depending on whether they resided in community-property or common-law states. For example, a husband living in a common-law state, who had complete control over his earnings, was taxed at the same rate as a husband living in a community-property state, who by law had a right to only half of his earnings.

Clearly, the immediate political goal in adopting this fiction was to reduce tax liability for husbands residing in common-law states.[25] Less clear is whether the fiction furthered some independent policy goal and, if so, what deliberative process Congress undertook in determining that goal. The deliberative process should have weighed the costs of income splitting against its benefits. Income splitting had certain administrative benefits. It eliminated the incentive for common-law states to switch to community-property regimes and thereby eliminated the cost of shifting from one system to the other. It also removed the incentive for residents of common-law states to use devices, such as partnerships and trusts, to shift income to their spouses, which eliminated the cost of creating and policing such devices. Both the Report of the House Committee on Ways and Means and the Report of the Senate Committee on Finance cite these two administrative benefits as the reasons for adopting income splitting.[26] Neither report, however, mentions the costs of income splitting. One cost was that income splitting mismeasured income to the extent that it ignored the differing economic rights allocated to husbands and wives under differing state property law regimes. Another cost was its effect on married women's property rights. Income splitting eliminated the political pressure on common-law states to provide married women with the stronger property rights of a community-property regime.

The Special Tax Study Committee, which recommended that the Ways and Means Committee adopt income splitting, at least mentioned the differing rights of married women in different states. Its report explicitly stated that uniformity in the taxation of married couples among common-law and community-property states was the desired policy goal and that the differing rights of married women in different jurisdictions were not significant for tax purposes: "The fact that the legal rights of [a man's] wife under the State law may differ ... does not seem to justify the significant differences in Federal income taxes payable. There has come to be rather, general agreement that spouses with similar incomes should pay similar Federal taxes, no matter where they live."[27]

This conclusion of the Special Tax Study Committee, however, does not reflect a reasoned policy analysis. Instead, the committee fell prey to the danger of which both Gray and Fuller warned: it failed to recognize the fictional nature of the fiction. Rather than recognizing the fictional nature of treating all married couples as if they shared their income, the committee relied upon the fiction to trivialize the differing allocations of rights between husband and wife under common law and community property. The committee defined the policy goal as "equal treatment of married couples with equal income," thereby assigning uniformity a value independent of its real administrative benefits.

The Special Tax Study Committee demonstrated the error in its logic through its treatment of other alternatives. The committee viewed nonuniform alternatives—those that would have recognized the differing rights accorded to married women in different states—as inferior, not only because of the administrative costs the alternatives would have entailed but also because of their nonuniformity. For example, the committee considered taxing all earned income to the earner, even in community-property states, and all community-property income to the spouse who exercised management and control of the property. As an alternative proposal, the committee considered reversing *Lucas v. Earl* so that married couples in common-law states could enter into sharing agreements that would be recognized for tax purposes. The committee rejected these alternatives as inferior to income splitting,[28] in part because they believed the income-splitting scheme would be easier to administer. However, the Special Committee cited uniform taxation as the most important benefit of income splitting:

> [Income splitting] eliminates the legal and administrative problems which now arise from the many attempts to divide income between spouses. . . . It avoids the serious questions which would arise in the interpretation and construction of contracts between spouses. *Most important, [income splitting] puts the incomes of husbands and wives, wherever resident, on a like basis for Federal tax purposes.*[29]

Uniform treatment of husbands and wives, wherever resident, would be an independent benefit of income splitting only if husbands and wives had the same rights, wherever resident. Husbands and wives had different property rights, however, depending on where they lived.

The fiction that all married couples share their income did not serve a valid policy goal. Rather, it served to obscure the costs of taxing married couples uniformly and transformed uniformity into an independent benefit. The fiction did not implement a policy determination that took account of all the costs and benefits of uniform taxation of married couples. Rather, the fiction substituted itself for such a policy determination.

As a political matter, how could the costs of income splitting, particularly its effect on married women's property rights, have been overlooked? There appears to have been a great deal of support for stronger married women's property rights. No women testified in the 1948 congressional hearings leading to the enactment of income splitting, but the General Federation of Women's Clubs submitted an article stating their views during the 1947 congressional hearings:

> Instead of penalizing the community property system, . . . the Congress should encourage its spread. By its recognition of the contribution of the wife to the marital partnership earnings, the community property system is

far in advance of any common-law State. Services are recognized to be rendered by the marital community, and income as earned by husband and wife alike. . . . Recognition is given to the fact that the wife is entitled to something more than food, clothing, and a place to sleep, and it ought to be the law everywhere.[30]

Men from community-property states also expressed support for the stronger rights given to married women under their systems during the 1947 hearings. They expounded on the superiority of the community-property system in recognizing married women's contribution to the production of income and suggested that common-law states would do well to adopt this superior system.[31] They argued that the favorable treatment accorded to community-property residents did not discriminate unduly against common-law residents but rather reflected real differences in the economic rights of husbands and wives.[32] They criticized the income-splitting proposal for giving common-law husbands the tax benefits of a property system intended to protect married women without requiring husbands to bear any of the burdens of such a system.[33]

These statements of support for stronger married women's property rights, however, masked a hidden motive among residents of community-property states. At the time of the 1947 hearings, Congress was considering several options to equalize the income tax treatment of community-property and common-law residents. Some of these options would have repealed the income splitting prescribed for community-property residents by *Poe v. Seaborn* and would have *increased* their income tax burden, for example, by taxing earned income exclusively to the earner rather than taxing half to each spouse.[34] In championing the community-property regime, community-property residents were at least partly motivated by the desire to preserve their favorable tax treatment.

A year later, in 1948, the only income tax proposal under consideration was income splitting for all married couples, a proposal that *decreased* the tax burden on common-law residents but left the tax burden on community-property residents unchanged. At this point residents of community-property states were predictably silent about the adverse effect of income splitting on married women's property rights.

The 1948 congressional hearings contain only one statement, by a Chicago accountant, that refers explicitly to married women's property rights, and it is distinctly unsympathetic:

> Every time the mandatory joint return issue has been raised, hosts of gold-plated suffragettes have descended upon Congress to reenact their epic drama regarding married women's rights, and claim that all will be lost if ever a wife must file a joint return with her husband and thereby again be "relegated to economic slavery." The real issues being thereby muddled, various moralists and misled church groups joined the battle and a deafening thunder of cries about marriage, morals, economic serfdom, and the like killed any further relevant determinations or any action.[35]

Professor Carolyn Jones has argued that sentiments like those voiced by the Chicago accountant played a central role in the enactment of income splitting. She argues that income splitting was attractive not only because it reduced taxes for common-law residents but also because it halted the community-property movement, thereby preserving traditional gender roles and power relationships.[36] Whether Congress was motivated simply by the desire for lower taxes or by a more complex set of motives that included preserving traditional gender roles and power relationships, the fiction of marital unity was the vehicle by which Congress could both justify its goals and obscure the social costs of achieving these goals.

The estate tax story is more tortuous than the income tax story but is equally imbued with the fiction of marital unity. Like the 1948 income tax amendments, the 1948 estate tax amendments were motivated by the desire for lower taxes.[37] Also like the 1948 income tax amendments, the 1948 estate tax amendments' stated goal was to equalize the estate tax treatment of married residents of community-property and common-law states.[38] This alleged goal, however, was even less plausible in the estate and gift tax context than in the income tax context, given that the 1942 Act equalized the estate and gift tax burden on community-property residents.[39]

The 1948 Act permitted all husbands, whether residing in community-property or common-law states, to transfer one-half of their wealth to their wives tax free. The deduction was tailored to mimic community-property treatment for husbands in common-law states making outright transfers to their wives.[40] Accordingly, transfers in trust—those in which the wife had an income interest that would terminate after some period of time—generally did not qualify for the deduction.[41] A transfer in trust was deductible only if it met the requirements of a power of appointment trust. The most significant of these requirements was that the wife be given control over the ultimate disposition of the trust property.[42] Significantly, dower transfers—those in which the wife received only an income interest for life, whereas the decedent designated the ultimate recipients of the trust property upon his wife's death—did not meet this requirement and were not deductible.

The estate tax marital deduction was premised on an assumption that parallels the fiction underlying income splitting. Income splitting was premised on the fiction that husbands and wives shared their incomes. The estate tax marital deduction was premised on the assumption that husbands and wives wanted to share, and actually did share, their wealth. A husband *actually* had to transfer half his wealth to his wife in order to be treated for tax purposes as if he shared that wealth. In contrast, under the income tax joint return, husband and wife were treated *as if* they shared his income, whether or not they actually did share it.

The assumption underlying the marital deduction was mistaken in a crucial respect: husbands did not *want* to share their wealth with their wives. They wanted to retain control over their wealth through dower transfers, but dower transfers did not qualify for the marital deduction. Estate planners and their clients were chagrined to find that the 1948 Act provided tax reduction at what they considered an exorbitant price: women had to be given control of the property. The extreme distress caused by this prospect is evidenced in the practical literature of the time:

> The wife must be given absolute control, either during her life or by her will; in either event she may (foolishly perhaps) cut off the objects of his bounty and leave his estate to a gigolo second husband.[43]

> Even where the [power of appointment trust] (rather than outright bequest) is used, the wife's unrestricted power of appointment can be a source of great personal power. The [husband's designated beneficiaries] can be cut off by a stroke of mother's testamentary pen.[44]

> There are few men in common law states who are willing to grant their wid-

ows more than a life estate where there are surviving children. The tax law should not offer a premium to a husband who ignores his better judgment and grants his widow a general power of appointment leaving his children at the mercy of any charlatan who has his widow's ear.[45]

In general, property relieved of taxation in the estate of the first to die will be taxed in the estate of the survivor—and will be subject to the unfettered disposition of the survivor in the meantime. For many people this power of disposition will be too high a price to pay.[46]

How could a provision as disruptive as the 1948 marital deduction have been enacted? Two factors offer an explanation. First, the 1948 marital deduction simply was not well thought out. It sailed through on the wave of support for the income-splitting plan, and its implications were not carefully scrutinized. Stanley Surrey, Tax Legislative Counsel for the Treasury Department during enactment of the 1948 amendments, observed:

[T]he splitting of estates and gifts simply rode in unheralded and uninspected on the coattails of splitting of income. . . . The impact upon estate planning, upon the disposition of property within the family, is immediate and startling. Yet on passage of the Act, only a relative handful of attorneys close to the theater of operations even approached awareness of what these provisions involve, and it will be many months or even years before operative understanding of all of their ramifications is achieved by tax practitioners.[47]

In addition to an incomplete understanding of the 1948 marital deduction and its consequences, Congress also may have had a strategic reason for downplaying the antidower incentive created by the marital deduction. President Truman and the Treasury Department opposed the marital deduction as well as the income-splitting scheme primarily because of the revenue losses they would cause. In opposing the marital deduction, Treasury Secretary John W. Snyder pointed out that it would disrupt the customary pattern of dower transfers, because dower transfers would be taxed relatively unfavorably under the marital deduction:

Since it is a frequent practice in common law States for a wealthy husband to give his wife a life interest in his estate with remainders to his children or other beneficiaries, equality of treatment [between community-property and common-law residents] would be achieved only by interfering to a large extent with this long-established pattern of family dispositions.[48]

Fearing that it might add fuel to this attack on the marital deduction, Congress may have been reluctant to call too much attention to the antidower incentive of the marital deduction. Perhaps they believed that the antidower incentive was a small price to pay for the marital deduction. Perhaps they believed that they could fight and win the antidower battle another day (as they eventually did).

The 1948 marital deduction was flawed in the eyes of practitioners and their clients, not because it was based on a fiction but because it required too much reality. In order to be taxed as if he shared his wealth with his wife, a husband actually had to cede control of his wealth to her. Completely inadvertently, the marital deduction strengthened married women's property rights by providing a tax incentive for husbands to transfer wealth to their wives.

The fiction of marital unity ultimately provided the solution to this "sorry mess," as Professor Surrey described it.[49] The first seeds of the fiction were planted by Allan H. W. Higgins, chairman of the American Bar Association, Section of Taxation, Committee on Equalization of Taxes in Community-Property and Common-Law States, and an enthusiastic proponent of the marital deduction. He argued that even dower transfers—transfers in trust in which the decedent designated the ultimate beneficiaries of the trust property upon his widow's death—should qualify for the marital deduction in the decedent's estate. He further proposed that the trust property be taxed to the widow upon her death, even though she had no control over disposition of the trust property. He noted "[i]t has long been the custom to protect wives by placing property in trust. As long as the trust property is taxed at the death of the surviving spouse, the marital deduction should apply irrespective of the varying provisions of the trust."[50] Higgins's claim, that transfers by a married couple to third parties should be taxed only once, no matter which spouse controls the transfer, was based on the fiction of marital unity. Again, the fiction provided a basis for disregarding the allocation of property rights between husband and wife for tax purposes. Higgins's proposal tracked the logic of income splitting. Transfers made by husbands would be deemed to be made by their wives as well. In this fashion, the fiction served to justify favorable tax treatment for transfers in which husbands retained control even after death of the ultimate disposition of their property.

Soon after the 1948 Act was passed, tax scholars began to invoke the fiction as the palliative for their anxiety that married women might acquire control of their husbands' property. In a 1948 article, Professor Surrey reiterated Higgins's proposal, clothing it in the fiction of marital unity:

> Husband and wife are regarded as a unit for income tax purposes, and I would similarly regard them as a unit for transfer tax purposes. There would be no tax as long as the enjoyment of property shifted from one to the other within this unit. The transfer tax would apply only when property left this unit and passed to the children or others. The unit would cease to exist on death of the surviving spouse.[51]

Professor Surrey stated his view in neutral, if conclusory, terms: the married couple is a unit, and property should be taxed only upon transfer from the unit to a third party. However, in a 1950 article, Professor Surrey expressed his true concerns:

> Basically the sorry mess we now face resulted from the illicit alliance in 1948 of transfer tax reduction and community property concepts. . . . The husband has to choose between tax savings through releasing his hand from the control of the property on his wife's death and the risk that when she dies some alien hand will be guiding her actions.[52]

Surrey uses the fiction of marital unity to disguise his real fear that women would acquire control of wealth and his opinion that women were too untrustworthy or incompetent to be wealth holders.

Surrey's vision for the estate tax finally was realized by the Economic Recovery Tax Act of 1981 (ERTA).[53] ERTA made two major changes to the marital deduction. First, the deduction was made unlimited in amount,[54] which eliminated the 1948 restriction that limited the deduction to half of the decedent's wealth. Second, dower transfers were made deductible in the decedent's estate under a new deduction for a qualified terminable interest in property (QTIP).[55] The QTIP rules further provided that property in a QTIP trust would be taxed in the widow's estate, even though she had no control over the disposition of the trust property upon her death.[56]

The legislative history of these provisions explains them by reference to the notion of the married couple as the taxpaying unit: all transfers within the unit should be exempt, without any limitation on the amount of transfers.[57] Transfers by the marital unit to others should be taxed only once, when the property leaves the marital unit.[58] ERTA engrafted the fiction of marital unity effortlessly from the income tax to the estate tax: "The committee believes that a husband and wife should be treated as one economic unit for purposes of estate and gift taxes, as they generally are for income tax purposes. Accordingly, no tax should be imposed on transfers between a husband and wife."[59]

After ERTA, the estate tax fiction of marital unity quickly became orthodoxy among tax academics:

> All quantitative limitations on the marital deduction were limited because "a husband and wife should be treated as one economic unit for purposes of the estate and gift taxes." . . . The QTIP provision is a natural extension of the [marital deduction] . . . given the shift in emphasis from mimicking community property to taxing property only once each generation.[60]

> Viewed broadly, the unlimited marital deduction has the effect of treating spouses as a single taxpayer with a lifetime equal to the survivor's. In this light, the *transfer* of a life interest from one spouse to the other can be regarded as the *retention* of a life interest by this notional taxpayer.[61]

> The substantive effect of [the 1981] changes is to treat the marital unit as a separate transfer tax unit with respect to interspousal transfers.[62]

The fiction of marital unity, however, camouflages the true purpose of the QTIP rules. The QTIP rules eliminated the antidower incentive inadvertently created by the 1948 marital deduction, which enabled husbands to reap the benefit of the marital deduction while retaining dead hand control of their wealth. Practitioners were quick to point out this benefit:

> [E]liminated is the nagging anxiety that the surviving spouse will remarry and . . . divert the marital deduction property from the natural objects of the decedent's bounty.[63]

> [T]he QTIP trust is attractive to many clients who want to "handcuff" the surviving spouse while at the same time qualifying for the marital deduction.[64]

It is no longer necessary for a testator to make the difficult decision of whether to take advantage of the marital deduction for his estate and give up control over the final disposition of his property or forego the marital deduction and maintain control. Formerly, . . . and a more painful prospect, it was not possible for a testator to ensure that the marital deduction property would not end up in the hands of his successor, if the surviving spouse decided to remarry.[65]

As the practical literature demonstrates, the principal attraction of the QTIP rules is that a husband can retain control over the ultimate disposition of his wealth even after his death, while enjoying the benefits of the marital deduction. The husband's desire to handcuff his wife is disguised by invoking the fiction of marital unity. Under the fiction, as long as wealth transfers by the married couple to third parties are taxed only once, the appropriate result has been reached. The fact that the husband controls the transfer, even after his death, is obscured by the fiction.

THE LEGACY OF THE FICTION OF MARITAL UNITY

From its ignoble origins as a means to procure a tax reduction for married men in common-law states, the fiction of marital unity has been elevated to a first principle of taxation. In 1976 Professor Boris Bittker, one of the most influential tax scholars of the twentieth century, observed that "the 1948 statutory principle of equal taxes for equal-income married couples has been 'almost universally accepted' by tax theorists."[66] This fiction is difficult to challenge because of its status as a first principle. Those who object to the harms inflicted on women by the fiction bear the burden of establishing that these harms are serious enough to require abandoning this fiction that masquerades as a first principle.

Income tax scholars, for example, have noted that the income taxation of married couples as units causes labor inefficiencies and biases against women in the workforce to the extent that individuals and not couples make labor decisions. Married women tend to be secondary earners and to have high labor supply elasticity relative to that of married men. As a consequence, married women tend to be marginalized in the workforce. Taxing married couples as units only can exacerbate this marginalization. The consequence is that couples may view the first dollar earned by a secondary worker as taxed at the marginal rate of the primary worker. Because it is more likely that secondary workers are married women, it is more likely that the incidence of this high marginal tax rate falls on them. This high rate of taxation, in conjunction with the relatively high labor supply elasticity of married women, helps to create barriers to the entry of married women into the workforce and thereby serves to perpetuate their marginalized status as workers.[67]

Despite the uncontrovertible evidence of the marginalization of women in the workplace caused by taxation of married couples as units, scholars who have challenged the current system of joint taxation have tended to approach the fiction with deference. Professor Pamela B. Gann, for example, argues that we should abandon joint taxation in part because of the costs to women in the workplace.[68] However, she treats the fiction of marital unity cautiously and pays obeisance to it as an established principle of taxation by carefully marshaling all of her arguments against it.[69] Professor Marjorie Kornhauser, who advocates that married people be taxed individually, has studied empirically the assumption underlying the fiction that married couples share their income.[70] It seems the fiction has become so powerful that only scientific evidence can debunk it.

In the estate tax, the fiction of marital unity has given rise to the principle that as long as wealth transfers by the marital unit are taxed only once, the allocation of property rights within the marital unit is irrelevant. Under the aegis of the QTIP rules, the dower transfer has reascended to perpetuate the customary pattern of wealth transmission under which men retain control of the ultimate disposition of wealth and women not only lack control, but are viewed as undeserving or incapable wealth holders.[71]

I have argued elsewhere that the QTIP rules, along with other estate tax provisions built upon the fiction of marital unity, undermine the prospect of women's achieving equal status with men as wealth holders.[72] Curiously, the empirical evidence, however, appears to indicate the opposite. Internal Revenue Service (IRS) data appear to indicate that women have become wealthier in recent years. In 1969 the IRS reported that approximately 38 percent of the top 9 million wealth holders were women.[73] In 1989 the IRS reported that approximately 42 percent of the top 3.4 million wealth holders were women.[74] The idea that women are increasingly wealthy has permeated the popular press.[75] The data, however, are misleading. They obscure the true wealth holdings of men and women because they are based on estate tax returns. On these returns, QTIP property is now included in her estate and accounted for as her wealth. The effect of this decision is to inflate the wealth holdings of women artificially. (Women are more likely to be beneficiaries of QTIP trusts, because women have a longer life expectancy than men and tend to be younger than their husbands.) At the same time, property transferred *to* a QTIP trust by a male decedent is excluded from his estate, even though he may retain control of the ultimate disposition of the property. The effect of this is to understate the wealth holdings of men. To the uninitiated, women appear to be gaining ground. In reality, we simply do not know. The fiction of marital unity has eliminated our ability to measure.[76] Through the QTIP trust, the fiction has created an illusory class of women wealth holders.

The purpose of this essay was to trace the development of the fiction of marital unity in tax and to demonstrate its dangers. As Bentham and Maine might have predicted, the fiction of marital unity has obscured the costs of implementing the fiction and has hindered an appropriate policy analysis. Once married men were deemed to share their income with their wives for income tax purposes, there no longer was an incentive for them actually to share either by contract or pursuant to state property laws. Once transfers made by either husband or wife were treated as a transfer by the marital unit, it no longer mattered for tax purposes that the husband would control the transfers.

As Gray and Fuller warned, much of the danger of the fiction arises from the failure of those relying upon it to recognize its fictional nature. On some level, policymakers and academics seemed to believe that the fiction was true, that all equal income couples were equal for tax purposes, no matter how the rights to that income were allocated between husband and wife. They seemed to believe that taxing the wealth transfers by the married couple should be the same no matter how control of that wealth was allocated between husband and wife.

The fiction of marital unity continues to exert its influence today in perpetuating the dominance of men as earners and wealth holders. In describing the medieval fiction of marital unity, a Charles Dickens character said, "[I]f the law supposes that . . . then the law is an ass."[77] Modern tax law continues to embrace this fiction, which not only attests to its remarkable ability to endure but also stands as a reminder that our law, like that referred to by Dickens, sometimes deserves to be called what it is.

NOTES

I am grateful to Stephen Garvey, Michael Klausner, and the participants in the University of Minnesota Law School's Taxing America conference for their helpful comments on earlier versions of this essay. I also thank Christine Chase for her research assistance.

1. *See* Louise Harmon, *Falling Off the Vine: Legal Fictions and the Doctrine of Substituted Judgment*, 100 Yale L.J. 1 (1990) (describing the history of the legal fiction debate); *see also* Theodore Silver, *One Hundred Years of Harmful Error: The Historical Jurisprudence of Medical Malpractice*, 1992 Wis. L. Rev. 1193 n.20; Note, *Expounding the Constitution: Legal Fictions and the Ninth Amendment*, 78 Cornell L. Rev. 139, 140–47 (1992).

2. 5 Jeremy Bentham, *Elements of Packing As Applied to Juries, in* The Works of Jeremy Bentham 92 (John Bowring ed., 1843) [hereinafter Bentham].

3. John Hamilton Baker, An Introduction to English Legal History 141 (3d ed. 1990).

4. Treas. Reg. § 1.451-2.

5. *See, e.g.,* William Blackstone, Commentaries on the Law of England 43 (1768).

6. 1 Jeremy Bentham, *A Fragment on Government, in* Bentham, *supra* note 2, at 235 n.s.

7. Henry Maine, *Ancient Law, in* The Problems of Jurisprudence 371 (Lon Fuller ed., 1946).

8. John C. Gray, The Nature and Sources of the Law 37 (1921).

9. *Id.*

10. Lon Fuller, Legal Fictions 10–11 (1967).

11. Treas. Reg. § 1.451–52.

12. I.R.C. § 902.

13. *E.g.,* Rev. Rul. 67–448, 1967-2 C.B. 144.

14. *Poe v. Seaborn*, 282 U.S. 101 (1930).

15. *See generally* Paula England, *Households, Employment and Gender: A Social, Economic, and Demographic View* (1986); Victor R. Fuchs, *Women's Quest for Economic Equality* (1988); Juanita M. Kreps, *Sex in the Marketplace: American Women at Work* (1971); Robert J. Lampman, *The Share of Top Wealthholders in National Wealth* (1962); Phyllis M. Palmer, *Domesticity and Dirt: Housewives and Domestic Servants in the United States, 1920–1945* (1989).

16. *Lucas v. Earl*, 281 U.S. 111 (1930).

17. *See* Division of Tax Research, Dept. of Treasury, The Tax Treatment of Family Income, *in* Revenue Revisions 1947–48: Hearings Before the Comm. on Ways and Means on Community Property and Family Partnerships, 80th Cong., 1st Sess. 846, 867–69 (1947).

18. *See, e.g., Estate of Lee v. Commissioner,* 11 T.C. 141, 144–45 (1948).

19. *See* Reduction of Individual Income Taxes: Hearings on H.R. 4790 Before the Senate Comm. on Finance, 80th Cong., 2d Sess. 26 (1948) [hereinafter Senate Hearings] (statement of John W. Snyder, secretary of the treasury).

20. Revenue Act of 1942, Pub. L. No. 77-753, § 402(b), 56 Stat. 798, 942 (amending § 118(e) of the 1939 Code; repealed 1948).

21. *See, e.g.,* Revenue Revisions, 1947–48: Hearings Before the Comm. on Ways and Means on Community Property and Family Partnerships, 80th Cong., 1st Sess. 776–93 (1947) [hereinafter 1947 Hearings] (statements of Charles E. Dunbar, Jr., and John G. Wisdom, attorneys for the Louisiana Community Property Taxpayers Committee); Senate Hearings, *supra* note 19, at 337 (statement of J. P. Jackson, representing State Rights Association of Houston, Texas).

22. *See* Revenue Revisions, 1947–48: Majority Report of the Special Tax Study Comm. Report to the Comm. on Ways and Means 1, 12 (1947) [hereinafter Special Report].

23. *See* Revenue Act of 1948, ch. 168, §§ 301–5, 62 Stat. 110, 114 (codified as amended in scattered sections of 26 U.S.C.).

24. *Id.* at § 351(b), 62 Stat. at 116.

25. *See* Revenue Revisions, 1947–48: Minority Report of the Special Tax Study Comm. to the Comm. on Ways and Means 35, 40 (1947) [hereinafter Minority Report] (describing the joint return as a "poorly disguised measure[]" to relieve high-income groups).

26. H.R. Rep. No. 1274, 80th Cong., 2d Sess. 22–23 (1948); S. Rep. No. 1013, 80th Cong., 2d Sess. 23–24 (1948).

27. Special Report, *supra* note 22, at 12.

28. *See id.*

29. *Id.* (emphasis added).

30. 1947 Hearings, *supra* note 21, at 914 (statement of Sen. Tom Connally of Texas).

31. *See, e.g., id.* at 834–35 (statement of Wesley E. Disney, representing the Governor and the Tax Commission of the state of Oklahoma).

32. *See, e.g., id.* at 775 (statement of Charles E. Dunbar, Jr., attorney for the Louisiana Community Property Taxpayers Committee).

33. *See, e.g., id.* at 797 (memorandum of James B. Howe, attorney, Seattle, Washington).

34. *See id.* at 11 (statement of John W. Snyder, secretary of the treasury).

35. Senate Hearings, *supra* note 19, at 276 (statement of Paul J. Foley, attorney, CPA).

36. *See* Carolyn C. Jones, *Split Income and Separate Spheres: Tax Law and Gender in the 1940s,* 6 Law & Hist. Rev. 259 (1988).

37. *See* Message from the President of the United States Returning Without Approval H.R. 4790, 80th Cong., 2d Sess. 4 (1948) [hereinafter Message from the President]; Senate Hearings, *supra* note 19, at 25 (statement of John W. Snyder, secretary of the treasury); Minority Report, *supra* note 25, at 59.

38. *See* Special Report, *supra* note 22, at 30.

39. *See* Message from the President, *supra* note 37, at 5; Minority Report, *supra* note 25, at 59.

40. *See* S. Rep. No. 1013, *supra* note 26, at 27–28.

41. I.R.C. § 2056(b)(1).

42. *Id.* at § 2056(b)(5).

43. Charles Looker, *The Impact of Estate and Gift Taxes on Property Disposition,* 38 Cal. L. Rev. 44, 62 (1950).

44. *Id.* at 67.

45. John W. Beveridge, *The Estate Tax Marital Deduction—Beneficent Intent, Baneful Result,* 44 Taxes 284 (1966).

46. John J. Waldron, *Implications of the Marital Deduction,* 87 Tr. & Est. 523, 523 (1948).

47. Stanley S. Surrey, *Federal Taxation of the Family—The Revenue Act of 1948,* 61 Harv. L. Rev. 1097, 1117 (1948).

48. Senate Hearings, *supra* note 19, at 26 (statement of John W. Snyder).

49. Stanley S. Surrey, *An Introduction to Revision of the Federal Estate and Gift Taxes*, 38 Cal. L. Rev. 1, 14 (1950).

50. Senate Hearings, *supra* note 19, at 316 (statement of Allan H. W. Higgins, chairman, American Bar Association, Tax Section, Committee on Equalization of Taxes in Community-Property and Common-Law States).

51. Surrey, *supra* note 47, at 1162.

52. Surrey, *supra* note 49, at 14.

53. Economic Recovery Tax Act of 1981, Pub. L. No. 97-34, 95 Stat. 172.

54. I.R.C. § 2056(a).

55. *Id.* at § 2056(b)(7).

56. *Id.* at § 2044.

57. S. Rep. No. 144, 97th Cong., 1st Sess. 127 (1981), 1981-2 C.B. 412; H.R. Rep. No. 201, 97th Cong., 1st Sess. 159 (1981), 1981-2 C.B. 352; Staff of Joint Comm. on Taxation, General Explanation of the Economic Recovery Tax Act of 1981, 233 (Comm. Print 1981).

58. *See, e.g.*, H.R. Rep. No. 201, *supra* note 57 at 160; Staff of Joint Comm. on Taxation, *supra* note 57, at 234.

59. S. Rep. No. 144, *supra* note 57, at 127.

60. Howard E. Abrams, *A Reevaluation of the Terminable Interest Rule*, 39 Tax L. Rev. 1, 12–13 (1983).

61. Joseph Isenbergh, *Simplifying Retained Life Interests, Revocable Transfers, and the Marital Deduction*, 51 U. Chi. L. Rev. 1, 32 (1984).

62. Harry L. Gutman, *Reforming Federal Wealth Transfers after ERTA*, 69 Va. L. Rev. 1183, 1220–21 (1983).

63. *Estate Tax Marital Deduction*, 239–4th Tax Mgmt. Portfolio (BNA), at A-58(3) (1990).

64. *Id.* at A-42 (1990).

65. *The Uses of a QTIP Trust*, 1 Tax Ideas ¶ 422 (1990).

66. Boris I. Bittker, *Federal Income Taxation and the Family*, 27 Stan. L. Rev. 1389, 1395 (1974) (citation omitted).

67. *See* Edward J. McCaffery, *Taxation and the Family: A Fresh Look at Behavioral Gender Biases in the Code*, 40 UCLA L. Rev. 983 (1993); *see also* Edward J. McCaffery, *Slouching towards Equality: Gender Discrimination, Market Efficiency, and Social Change*, 103 Yale L.J. 595, 600–35 (1993).

68. Pamela B. Gann, *Abandoning Marital Status as a Factor in Allocating Income Tax Burdens*, 59 Tex. L. Rev. 1, 39–46, 67 (1980).

69. *Id.* at 7, 25.

70. Marjorie E. Kornhauser, *Love, Money, and the IRS: Family, Income-Sharing, and the Joint Income Tax Return*, 45 Hastings L.J. 63 (1993).

71. *See* Mary Louise Fellows, *Wills and Trusts: The Kingdom of the Fathers*, 10 Law & Ineq. J. 137 (1991); Wendy C. Gerzog, *The Marital Deduction QTIP Provisions: Illogical and Degrading to Women*, 5 UCLA Women's L.J. 301 (1995).

72. Lily Kahng, *Gender Inequality and the Marital Deduction* (unpublished manuscript on file with author).

73. *See* Internal Revenue Service, U.S. Treasury Department, Supplemental Statistics of Income—1969: Personal Wealth, tables 2, 3 (of the top 9 million wealth holders in 1969, 5.6 million were men and 3.4 million were women).

74. Barry W. Johnson & Marvin Schwartz, Internal Revenue Service, Personal Wealth, 1989, 12 Stat. Inc. Bull. 105 (Spring 1993).

75. *See, e.g.*, Gary Belsky, *The Five Ways Women Are Often Smarter Than Men about Money*, Money, June 1992, at 75; Anne Matthews, *Alma Maters Court Their Daughters*, N.Y. Times, Apr. 7,

1991, at § 6, at 40; Penelope Wang, *Brokers Still Treat Men Better Than Women*, Money, June 1994, at 108; *Women: Financial Planners Turn to Untapped Market*, Chi. Sun-Times, July 2, 1995, at 37.

76. *See* Telephone Interview with Barry Johnson (Oct. 10, 1995) (noting that the IRS statistics do not reflect distortions caused by the QTIP rules); *but see* Johnson & Schwartz, *supra* note 74, at 111 n.11 (noting that the 1981 changes in the estate tax laws may affect patterns of wealth dispositions).

77. Charles Dickens, Oliver Twist 354 (Kathleen Tillotson ed., 1966).

2

DOROTHY A. BROWN

The Marriage Bonus/Penalty in Black and White

A marriage penalty occurs whenever a couple pays higher federal income taxes as a result of their marriage than they would pay if they remained single and filed individual returns. A marriage bonus occurs whenever a couple pays lower federal income taxes as a result of marriage than they would pay if they remained single and filed individual returns. Marriage penalties are the greatest where there are two wage earners; marriage bonuses are the greatest where there is only one wage earner. Although numerous articles have been written about the marriage penalty, this essay provides a different perspective.[1]

Here I will discuss the differences between black and white households and will show how the tax consequences of marriage tend to differ for taxpayers of different races. Black taxpayers are more likely to pay a marriage tax, whereas white taxpayers are more likely to receive a marriage bonus.[2] I will examine the tax consequences of the marital decision in the context of current law as well as in the context of the Contract with America Tax Relief Act of 1995 (H.R. 1215), as of this writing the most recent legislative proposal to address the marriage penalty.

The first section describes how the marriage penalty currently operates under the Internal Revenue Code. It then explains how H.R. 1215 would change current law. The second section, "The Tax Implications of the Marriage Decision," examines current data showing several differences observed in black and white households. It then analyzes that data to show the differing effects of the decision to marry on black and white households. The last section offers a method for eliminating the penalty associated with the decision to marry.

THE MARRIAGE BONUS/PENALTY

Empirical evidence suggests that economic factors, including tax liabilities, play a role in the decision to marry.[3] Accordingly, it is important to examine the circumstances under which a couple's tax liabilities can increase or decrease as a result of their decision to marry.

Operation of the Marriage Bonus/Penalty

The Internal Revenue Code is not marriage neutral. This is an unavoidable consequence, given the Code's current structure. No income tax system that both is progressive and permits joint filing by married couples can be marriage neutral.[4] All unmarried couples (both same-sex and opposite-sex) must file as two single persons. They cannot take advantage of the marriage bonus, nor can they suffer any marriage penalty.[5]

The operation of the marriage bonus/penalty is set forth in the chart below.[6] The calculations for the chart were made in the following manner. The income tax is computed for two taxpayers filing as single persons and then as a married couple filing jointly. The difference between the tax liabilities is the marriage penalty or bonus indicated in the chart. For the computations, the taxpayers were assumed to have no dependents or excess itemized deductions and to be under the age of sixty-five.[7] As noted in the chart, the marriage penalty is greatest where total household income is split equally between the spouses.[8] The marriage bonus is greatest where total household income is earned by only one wage earner.[9] However, these bonuses or penalties are not distributed evenly across the chart. For example, the marriage penalty does not begin until one spouse earns 20 percent of what the other spouse earns.[10] In addition, lower-income taxpayers otherwise eligible for the earned income tax credit get a smaller credit amount or no credit amount as a result of the decision to marry. The earned income tax credit aggregates the incomes of husband and wife, which reduces benefits and thereby produces a marriage penalty.[11] For certain low-income families, the marriage penalty can exceed $3,000.[12]

THE MARRIAGE TAX (PENALTY)/BONUS BY INCOME & ALLOCATION BETWEEN SPOUSES/SINGLES (1993)

	INCOME ALLOCATION					
Income	0%/100%	10%/90%	20%/80%	30%/70%	40%/60%	50%/50%
$10,000						(612)
$20,000	728	428	128	(173)	(180)	(180)
$30,000	968	278	(173)	(180)	(180)	(180)
$40,000	2,268	1,148	321	(180)	(180)	(180)
$50,000	3,282	1,882	1,075	425	(226)	(466)
$60,000	3,296	1,602	815	35	(746)	(1,285)
$70,000	3,596	1,568	555	(356)	(1,266)	(1,285)
$80,000	3,896	1,708	428	(746)	(1,285)	(1,285)
$90,000	4,196	1,848	408	(1,032)	(1,285)	(1,285)
$100,000	4,497	1,990	390	(970)	(1,270)	(1,284)
$125,000	4,695	1,590	(411)	(1,195)	(1,570)	(1,857)
$150,000	5,945	1,887	(970)	(1,420)	(1,857)	(1,859)
$200,000	5,990	882	(84)	(3,364)	(4,312)	(4,312)
$500,000	6,164	(4,203)	(8,789)	(11,642)	(13,442)	(15,024)

To summarize, there is always a marriage penalty for two-wage-earner couples who earn roughly equal amounts. There is always a marriage bonus for single-wage-earner couples.

Marriage Penalty Relief under H.R. 1215

H.R. 1215 includes a marriage penalty relief provision. Section 102 of the bill would provide taxpayers with a nonrefundable credit up to $145, which they could use to offset any marriage penalty incurred from both spouses working.[13] The stated reason for the change is a concern "about the inequities of the marriage penalty and the potential work disincentive it causes."[14] An additional stated reason is that "marriage penalties in the tax laws undermine respect for the family and may discourage family formation."[15] A quick review of the chart above will establish that a $145 tax credit will reduce substantially the marriage penalty for most couples earning less than $50,000.[16]

The proposed credit is limited to married taxpayers filing a joint return who are subject to the marriage penalty. The credit is designed to assist only those taxpayers subject to the marriage penalty in two-wage-earner households. Not every couple subject to the marriage penalty will receive a credit of $145. The legislative history does not discuss how Congress arrived at this figure other than by noting a desire to limit the cost to the Treasury to four billion dollars per year.[17]

Initially it was thought that taxpayers would be required to make several calculations in order to determine what portion, if any, of the tax credit was available to them.[18] The House, however, recently included in the relief provision a directive to the secretary of the treasury to provide a table that includes those calculations to assist taxpayers in determining the portion, if any, of the $145 nonrefundable credit for which they would be eligible.[19] As a result, taxpayers could simply look at the table to find the appropriate figure. However, the secretary of the treasury has not announced how the department will address the difficult issue of allocating deductions paid for by the husband and wife in those table calculations.[20]

THE TAX IMPLICATIONS OF THE MARRIAGE DECISION

This section considers the effects of the marriage decision by examining the differences between white and black households. The evidence suggests that there is a difference in the impact of both the marriage bonus and the marriage penalty based upon race. Black families are more likely to pay a marriage penalty; white families are more likely to receive a marriage bonus.

My analysis is limited to an investigation of the differences between black and white households. Without question, a richer, more complete examination ultimately must include Hispanic, Asian, Native American, and other racial or ethnic groups. In that regard this essay is intended only as a first step in considering the racial and gender implications of the rate structure. This essay also makes the simplifying assumption that there are no racially mixed households. That assumption does not distort the picture much, given that in 1985, 98.9 percent of black married women and 96.6 percent of black married men had a black spouse.[21]

The Internal Revenue Service does not keep statistical information according to race, but the Census Bureau and the Bureau of Labor Statistics do. Relying on their data, this section will begin by describing how married black women participate in the workforce at higher rates than married white women. It also will show that married black women contribute a higher percentage of total household income than married white women and that wage discrimination results in white men's earning more than white women, black men, or black women. Finally, this section will demonstrate that because of the marriage rate for black women relative to that for white women, a disproportionate number of black women are single heads of household, which suggests yet another path of inquiry.

One commentator estimated that in 1994 the average marriage penalty paid by American couples would be $1,244 and the average marriage bonus received by American couples would be $1,399.[22] Those figures mask the racial and gender implications of the joint tax return. Further analysis of the data indicates that black couples are more likely to pay a marriage penalty, whereas white couples are more likely to receive a marriage bonus.

Labor Force Participation Rates Based upon Gender and Race

Black women historically have entered the workforce in larger numbers than white women and have stayed there longer.[23] A 1990 study showed that 73 percent of married black women were in the waged labor force, compared to 64 percent for married white women.[24] If the marriage penalty exists only in households of two-wage-earner couples, married black couples, with a higher percentage of two wage earners, are more likely to pay a marriage penalty than white couples. Conversely, married white couples are more likely to receive a marriage bonus.

A recent study found that married black women contribute approximately 40 percent of their household's income. Married white women contribute only 29 percent of their household's income.[25] These statistics suggest that black couples not only are more likely to suffer a marriage penalty, but also that they will tend to pay more in marriage penalties than their white counterparts with equal household income.[26]

That study is valuable not only for revealing that women's rates of contribution to household income vary across race but also for highlighting gender essentialism in the tax literature. Married black women contribute a significant portion of total household income. Assuming that 40 percent is the average household contribution of married black women, it is possible, perhaps even probable, that certain married black women contribute more than 40 percent of total household income. Accordingly, married black women cannot unequivocally be considered a marginal second wage earner in the way that current tax literature treats all married women.[27] For example, Professor McCaffery recently described working married women as follows: "[H]istorically, of course, wives have usually been the marginal earners. . . . [M]arried working women earn, on average, forty-six percent of what their husbands do."[28] McCaffery's statistics may be more appropriate when applied to white married women, although he did not so limit his analysis. If a significant portion of married black women earn more than 50 percent of household income, however, they cannot be considered marginal earners. Given the vast differences between black and white women's working experiences, averages of the sort McCaffery used are wholly inadequate in understanding the operation of the joint tax return and suggest a path for future inquiry.

If any group is likely to view themselves and be viewed as marginal wage earners, it is married white women, who on average contribute 29 percent of total household income. Although black couples are more likely to suffer a marriage penalty, within the marital unit it is white women as marginal wage earners who are more likely to feel the greater impact of the marriage penalty. This is so because as a marginal earner, the couple may understand the wife's wages as taxed at the highest marginal tax rate.[29] In addition, if the marginal wage earner is a mother of young children, the couple also may view the increased child care costs as an added cost of her working.[30] Of course, this understanding of child care costs erroneously assumes that they are the costs of the working mother and not of the working father.[31] The Code treats a family member's performance of household services, including child care, as nontaxable imputed income. To the extent that married white couples are more likely to have only one wage earner, with the wife staying home and providing unwaged labor, the Code is more likely to reward them doubly. Not only are white couples more likely to enjoy a marriage bonus because of their household arrangement; they are more likely to enjoy an imputed income bonus from it as well.

Another important aspect of the concept of the marginal wage earner concerns nontaxable imputed income. These tax bonuses may explain in part the differing labor participation rates between married black and white women. Married white women, as a result of their status as marginal wage earners, are more likely to support their families by providing nontaxed labor, such as child care.

Given that black men may contribute less than 50 percent of household income, any analysis of the marginal wage earner in married black households would seem suspect. However, such an analysis surprisingly might reveal that black men, as secondary wage earners, are more affected by the marriage penalty than black women. This sort of analysis might provide one explanation for the declining labor participation rates of black men in recent years.[32]

Workforce participation for all men, however, has declined over the past two decades, although this decline is more dramatic for black men than for white men.[33] Among younger white men, extended education has been the primary cause for the decline in their labor force participation. That explanation does not hold for black men, however, whose educational enrollments have declined.[34]

The decline in labor participation rates among black men also may affect black women's waged labor participation. Black women, who contribute 40 percent of their households' income, are less likely than white women to be able to afford to stay at home and raise their children while their husbands provide all of the family's waged income.

The differences in waged labor participation between black and white families just described should not be viewed as static. Recent trends indicate that more married white women are entering the labor force. Those trends are attributable partially to the growing need for both spouses to work for the couple to maintain the wage growth previously enjoyed by traditional white, one-wage-earner households.[35] Moreover, as a consequence of continuing efforts toward wage equality in the workforce across gender and race lines, it may be that more white couples in the future will suffer the marriage penalty at rates similar to those historically experienced by married black couples.

Wage Rates Based upon Gender and Race

A more complete picture of the racial implications of the marriage bonus/penalty requires an investigation of the differences in taxable income between black and white households.[36] As noted above, black families are more likely to pay a marriage penalty than white families because black women tend to contribute a larger portion of their households' income than white women. One reason behind that phenomenon is employment discrimination.

On average, black women's earnings are closer to black men's earnings than white women's earnings are to white men's earnings.[37] For every dollar earned by a white man, a white woman earned 78¢,[38] a black man earned 74.8¢,[39] and a black woman earned 66¢.[40] Therefore, due to wage discrimination, even if all married women participated in the labor force at the same rates, black families still would be more likely than white families to pay a marriage penalty. Wage discrimination causes black men and women to earn roughly equal amounts, or at least amounts more equal than the amounts earned by white men and women.

Wage discrimination, of course, is not the only factor that tends to equalize earnings between spouses in black families. High labor participation rates by black women also tend to equalize spousal earnings. The combination of wage discrimination and the higher incidence of two-wage-earner households means that black men and women tend to contribute nearly equal amounts to total household income. Within the U.S. tax rate structure, that means that black families are more likely to pay the highest marriage penalty, which occurs when total household income is split equally between the two spouses.

Although wage discrimination penalizes black families, it benefits white families. White men are more likely than black men to earn an income on which their families can live. This allows white women the opportunity to remain at home and gives the opportunity for the couple to enjoy untaxed imputed income. Wage discrimination, then, helps to explain the differing rates of contribution to total household income between black and white married women. It also helps to explain the differing labor participation rates of black and white married women. Given white men's wages, the low wages of white women relative to those of white men, and the tax treatment of imputed income, white married women's decisions to work outside the home are less likely to be related to economic survival than to personal preference. Thus, marriage acts to reduce the labor force participation rates of white women, but not of black women.[41]

Although the impact of the marriage penalty is felt most severely by black families, as more white families have second earners in the labor force, it will become a problem for white families as well. Given the decreased labor participation rates of white men and the fact that white women are being employed in areas that once were the province only of white men, white families are more likely to have two wage earners. That means that in the forseeable future more white families may suffer the marriage penalty.

Head of Household Rate Differences Based upon Race

Married-couple families are much more economically prosperous than families headed by women. As a result, the increasing numbers of black single-parent households has caused the black poverty rates to soar.[42] Although one study found that 55 percent of families headed by white women were either poor or very poor, it also found that 80 percent of families headed by black women were in poverty.[43] That percentage for black women takes on special significance because only 36 percent of black women were in married-couple households.[44] Thus, a substantial number of black women are heads of household. These statistics intensify the urgency for scrutinizing federal income tax laws that penalize black women for marrying.

The experience of black women in the labor market has been different from that of white women and must be viewed separately.[45] Black female heads of household experience extreme poverty in part because of the wage discrimination that black women face. Unlike black women, white women have entered middle-income jobs,[46] and during the 1980s they were more successful than black women in breaking the glass ceiling.[47] Most of black women's gains in the employment sector have come in low-wage jobs, which helps to account for the disproportionate number of black female heads of household in pover-ty.[48] Black women have been concentrated in a few occupations with a very narrow wage range.[49] Even controlling for the effects of education, black women suffer wage discrimination in areas where white women do not.[50]

ENDING THE MARRIAGE BONUS/PENALTY

In 1986, when the marriage penalty deduction was eliminated, the marriage tax penalty had a remarkably low profile.[51] Perhaps if the pro-file of the issue were raised, alternative proposals could be considered. Given the rhetoric of family values, if the marriage penalty is contribut-ing to the disintegration of the family, whether it is black or white fami-lies, it should be eliminated once and for all.

Since the marriage penalty occurs whenever there is a progressive tax system that permits joint filing, there are three ways to eliminate the marriage bonus/penalty. The first is by abolishing the progressive tax system and replacing it with a flat tax system. Under a flat tax, neither spouse would be penalized by paying taxes at a higher rate than the other. The second is through abolishing the joint return. If tax returns were calculated for everyone on a single return basis, there would be no marriage bonus/penalty because liability for an individual taxpayer would not change upon his or her decision to marry.

A third and less drastic alternative would be to target the marriage penalty relief better to those who pay the highest penalty, namely to those couples whose incomes are equal. In addition, some considera-tion should be given to eliminating the marriage bonus, at least for couples in high-income brackets. By eliminating or reducing the mar-riage bonus/penalty, the tax law would be acknowledging and counter-acting marketplace wage discrimination based on gender and race. In contrast, to leave the marriage bonus/penalty intact serves to exacer-bate marketplace wage discrimination. Understood from this perspec-tive, the choice is clear.

NOTES

I would like to thank the participants at the University of Minnesota's Taxing America conference for their helpful comments on an earlier draft. A special thanks to Jerome McCristal Culp, whose earlier challenge inspired this essay. I would also like to thank Mr. Rick Goheen and the Institute for Policy Research for their research assistance.

1. *See, e.g.,* Boris I. Bittker, *Federal Income Taxation and the Family,* 27 Stan. L. Rev. 1389 (1975); Marjorie E. Kornhauser, *Love, Money, and the IRS: Family, Income-Sharing, and the Joint Income Tax Return,* 45 Hastings L.J. 63 (1993); Edward J. McCaffery, *Taxation and the Family: A Fresh Look at Behavioral Gender Biases in the Code,* 40 UCLA L. Rev. 983 (1993); Lawrence Zelenak, *Marriage and the Income Tax,* 67 S. Cal. L. Rev. 339 (1994).

2. *See* Nancy Staudt, *Taxing Housework,* 84 Geo. L.J. 1571 (1996) (discussing differences between black and white women that previously have been ignored by tax scholars). Since submitting this essay for the anthology, I have come to understand that Professor Beverly Moran of the University of Wisconsin Law School is engaged in a long-term project exploring issues of class, race, and gender in the tax law that considers the operation of the joint tax return as well as many other issues.

3. *See* James Alm & Leslie A. Whittington, *Marriage and the Marriage Tax, in* 1992 Nat'l Tax Ass'n. Proc. 200 (1992).

4. *See* Bittker, *supra* note 1, at 1395–96.

5. *See* 4 Boris I. Bittker & Lawrence Lokken, Federal Taxation of Income, Estates and Gifts §111.3.6 (1992); Patricia A. Cain, *Same-Sex Couples and the Federal Tax Laws,* 1 Law & Sexuality 97 (1991); Toni Robinson & Mary Moers Wenig, *Marry in Haste, Repent at Tax Time: Marital Status as a Tax Determinant,* 8 Va. Tax Rev. 773, 792–95 (1989).

6. *See* John Brozovsky & A. J. Cataldo II, *The Marriage Tax Penalty: Inequities and Tax Planning Opportunities,* 52 Ohio CPA J. 21, 22 (Dec. 1993) (chart in text reprinted with permission of publisher).

7. *Id.* at 21.

8. *See* John Brozovsky & A. J. Cataldo II, *An Historical Analysis of the Marriage Tax Penalty,* 21 Acct. Historians J. 163, 166 (1994).

9. *Cf.* Laura Ann Davis, Note, *A Feminist Justification for the Adoption of a Joint Filing System,* 62 S. Cal. L. Rev. 197, 205 (1988) (pointing out that at the adoption of the joint filing requirement in 1948, 80 to 85 percent of married couples had only one wage earner).

10. *See* McCaffery, *supra* note 1, at 1016.

11. *See id.* at 1015.

12. *See* Daniel R. Feenberg & Harvey S. Rosen, National Bureau of Economic Research, Inc., Recent Developments in the Marriage Tax 6–7 (Working Paper No. 4075) (1995).

13. H.R. Rep. No. 1215, 104th Cong., 1st Sess. 12–13 (1995).

14. *Id.*

15. *Id.* at 13.

16. *See* Feenberg & Rosen, *supra* note 12, at 11.

17. H.R. Rep. No. 1215, *supra* note 13, at 280.

18. *See* Hearing on Middle-Income Tax Cut Proposals Before the Senate Comm. on Finance, 104th Cong., 1st Sess. 10, 11–12, 45, 47–49 (1995) (statement of Deborah H. Schenk, AAA-Olincy Professor of Law, New York University School of Law) [hereinafter Schenk].

19. H.R. Rep. No. 1215, *supra* note 13, at 13.

20. *See* Schenk, *supra* note 18.

21. Robert G. Wood, *Marriage Rates and Marriageable Men: A Test of the Wilson Hypotheses*, 30 J. Hum. Resources 163, 172 (1995).

22. Feenberg & Rosen, *supra* note 12, at 11.

23. *See* Bette Woody, Black Women in the Workplace 37 (1992).

24. U.S. Comm'n on Civil Rights, Staff Report on the Economic Status of Black Women: An Exploratory Investigation 105 (1990); Staudt, *supra* note 2, at 1612.

25. U.S. Comm'n on Civil Rights, *supra* note 24, at 100, table 8.6.

26. *See* Chart *supra.*

27. *See, e.g.,* McCaffery, *supra* note 1, at 994.

28. *See id.*

29. *See* Zelenak, *supra* note 1, at 365–66.

30. *See id.* at 372–75.

31. For further discussion of child care costs, see Mary L. Heen, *Welfare Reform, the Child Care Dilemma, and the Tax Code: Family Values, the Wage Labor Market, and the Race- and Class-Based Double Standard,* this volume.

32. *See* Woody, *supra* note 23, at 147.

33. *See id.*

34. *See id.*

35. *See id.* at 9.

36. *Cf.* Abigail Thernstrom, *Two Nations, Separate and Hostile?* N.Y. Times, Oct. 12, 1995, at A15 ("The median income of black married couples with children is now only slightly lower than that for all American families.").

37. *See* Steven A. Holmes, *Census Finds Little Change in Income Gap between Races,* N.Y. Times, Feb. 23, 1995, at A10.

38. *See* Gary Belsky & Susan Berger, *Women Could Be Big Losers If Affirmative Action Falls,* Money, Aug. 1995, at 20.

39. *See Proponents, Opponents of Affirmative Action Point to Statistics,* Daily Rep. for Exec. (BNA), Aug. 2, 1995, *available in* WESTLAW, at § C; *see also* Reynolds Farley, *The Common Destiny of Blacks and Whites: Observations about the Social and Economic Status of the Races, in* Race in America 197, 206–7 (Herbert Hill & James E. Jones, Jr., eds., 1993) ("overall, fully employed black men in 1988 earned about three-quarters as much as white men").

40. *See* Belsky & Berger, *supra* note 38, at 20.

41. *See* Woody, *supra* note 23, at 41.

42. *See* Farley, *supra* note 39, at 213.

43. *See id.* at 213–17.

44. *See* Felicity Barringer, *Marriage Study That Caused Furor Is Revised to Omit Impact of Career,* N.Y. Times, Nov. 11, 1989, at A10; Farley, *supra* note 39, at 212.

45. *See* Annette Bernhardt et al., *Women's Gains or Men's Losses? A Closer Look at the Shrinking Gender Gap in Earnings,* 101 Am. J. Soc. 302, 325 (1995).

46. *See id.* at 320.

47. *See id.* at 324. *Cf.* Belsky & Berger, *supra* note 38, at 20 ("Largely overlooked in the debate about 'equal opportunity' vs. 'preferential treatment' is that women, particularly *white women,* have been among the biggest *beneficiaries* of 30 years' worth of affirmative action."); Sherry Bebitch Jeffe, *The State; Civil Rights; Don't Count on the Chief Beneficiaries of Affirmative Action to Rescue It,* L.A. Times, Mar. 26, 1995, at 6 ("Another report, issued by the Glass Ceiling Commission, a federal panel established four years ago to monitor the progress of women and minorities in business and industry, adds punch to the contention that white women have been the principal beneficiaries of affirmative-action programs. White women now account for 40% of

the nation's work force . . . and hold almost 40% of middle-management jobs. African American women and men are still greatly underrepresented in these positions.").

48. *See* Bernhardt et al., *supra* note 45, at 321.

49. *See* Woody, *supra* note 23, at 37.

50. *See id.* at 26.

51. *See* Harvey S. Rosen, *Thinking about the Tax Consequences of Marriage*, 41 Nat'l Tax J. 259, 260 (1988).

3

JENNIFER J. S. BROOKS

Taxation and
Human Capital

This essay explores how to measure and tax income from human capital. Human capital income is thought to include the value of leisure, services performed for oneself, choice, and opportunity, as well as cash income from wages. In our current tax system, wages are taxable when received. The other values, sometimes referred to as psychic income, are set aside in conventional applications of income theory as too murky, too difficult, and too impractical to measure and to include in real-life taxable income.[1] The question of the tax treatment of human capital income has new relevance as Congress debates switching from income taxation to taxation of consumption. Some theorists, most notably Louis Kaplow, seeking to apply a definition of ideal income to human capital, contend that individuals are endowed at birth with a stock of wealth equal to the present value of their future wage stream and that the receipt of this wealth is income at birth.[2] That interpretation, which this essay rejects, leads to the assertion that human capital is seriously undertaxed—an assertion that, if accepted, has important consequences for the design of the tax system.

If the distinction between waged and nonwaged human capital is to be useful, we must face the difficult problem of definition. The common usage in the tax literature of the terms *human capital, psychic income*, and *leisure* often is imprecise. This essay limits the term *psychic income* to the consumer surplus arising from enjoyment and confines the term *leisure* to include both rest and activities chosen for the enjoyment that they confer upon the individual engaging in them, for instance, reading a novel. A careful definition of human capital is the central task of this essay.

The ideal income/human capital argument is simple. Variously referred to as ideal income or the accretion model, the 1938 Haig-Simons definition of income includes in annual income the value of personal consumption *plus* net savings, which can be either an increase or a decrease in wealth.[3] Under the Haig-Simons definition of income, the right to receive future income is discounted to present value. This present value is includable in the year the right is established. Under Kaplow's interpretation of ideal income, the present value of an individual's future wage stream is includable as income at birth. He argues that this treatment taxes human capital in a manner identical with material capital, which he claims to be an appropriate result.

Why bother thinking about this highly rarefied theoretical definition of income? No one argues that it is feasible to predict at birth an individual's future wage stream, although Kaplow has described a computation that increases (supercounts) actual wages by a factor reflecting deferral.[4] There is, however, increasing congressional focus on the consumption tax, which treats receipts from material or human capital as income when consumed. In the past, critics have called this approach a naked wage tax that is unfair to those who consume their wage income and who cannot afford to own material capital.[5] Recently, Kaplow invoked the ideal income argument concerning wage income as a theoretical basis to disfavor ideal income taxation and to prefer consumption taxation. In an analysis resting on the Haig-Simons definition, he suggests that the current treatment of wages as income when received undertaxes human capital income by more than 40 percent when measured by the standard of the ideal income tax base. Kaplow argues that the Haig-Simons model requires human capital and material capital to be treated alike and both to be treated as wealth. His definition of wealth is based on the economic premise that all factors contributing to the production of wealth be included in the tax base. Arguing that the present value at birth of future wage income is equal to the stock of human capital at birth and, therefore, constitutes income at that time,

Kaplow concludes that income from labor is seriously undertaxed. He acknowledges the difficulty of collecting a tax on newborns by devising a system of proxy taxation, which uses a multiplier of 1.42 to tax wages when earned. Alternatively, he proposes that serious consideration be given to the consumption tax, which would tax wages when consumed. Consumption taxation, he contends, would leave the current treatment of wages unchanged for most taxpayers (those who consume their wages when received) and is logically preferable to the ideal income tax for anyone who favors taxing wages when received.

The argument that ideal income treatment of human capital properly includes in income-at-birth the present value of future wages raises interesting questions about the Haig-Simons definition and its application. The more important piece of Kaplow's argument, however, is the notion that the current income tax undertaxes human capital. Any sensible exploration of this assertion has to consider the definition of human capital as generally applied by income tax theorists. This essay concludes that significant values usually assumed to arise from human capital in fact attach to material capital. The association between these values and material capital not only supports current income tax treatment of receipts from material and human capital but also justifies modifications that would tax material capital more heavily in some circumstances. There is no basis to conclude that income from human capital is undertaxed by 40 percent or otherwise. Contrary to Kaplow's analysis, careful application of ideal income theory offers no basis for support of consumption taxation by those who favor taxing wages when received.

THE TASK OF DEFINING INCOME

A pure or ideal definition of income that consistently and fairly includes all value creation probably is not possible, even in theoretical terms.[6] Perfect measurement of an individual's lifetime income might be possible only in a Rawls-inspired prebirth auction, where individuals who had total foreknowledge of future events were able to bid for particular lives, including all the benefits and detriments of occupation, health, social status, and material wealth.[7] The prices set by the auction would be considered net income, and tax would be imposed and collected at birth. All other attempts at definition move very quickly from the all-inclusive theoretical to the far less inclusive practical. Economic historians interested in the theory of the state assert that the search for a perfect definition of income is irrelevant. They claim that what is relevant is the search for the definition of income that is least susceptible to manipulation, adverse selection, moral hazard, signaling, and other troublesome behavior by both citizens and the state—in other words, the construct that maximizes the well-being of the commonwealth.[8]

The task of defining income thus invokes two possibilities. The first is that even the most rigorous theoretical definition has an unacknowledged political component. The second is that a definition locally accepted as accurate may be applied consciously or unconsciously in accordance with conventions that violate the stipulated definition. The Haig-Simons definition itself, the competing consumption model, and any other definition offered as correct theory are influenced by the definer's point of view. Even the most widely approved theory of income may be found faulty in succeeding generations.

The "Common Meaning of Income"

What did the framers of the 1913 income tax law mean by income? There was no definition in the original legislation. Queried in debate on the House floor, a sponsor answered that "what is meant by 'income' is the common meaning of 'income'—the common understanding of the word."[9] It is not clear now, and probably was not then, exactly what people commonly understood the word *income* to mean. The most likely meaning is returns on capital received annually, especially interest, rents, and dividends. Novels of the time, which reveal common understandings to some extent, refer to income with this apparent meaning. Salaries and wages, too, were understood to be income, although the early income tax did not reach wages or most salaries. Irving Fisher, the great consumption-base proponent in economics, wrote some of his most compelling pieces at the turn of the century. His writings may have influenced people to think in terms of cash receipts rather than in terms of inchoate accruals. One fact seems certain: in 1913 the 1938 Haig-Simons definition of income was not within the "original intent" of the drafters of the income tax law.

We should not limit the definition of income to the common under-standing of the term in 1913. The world has changed too much to make that a sensible constraint. The modern securities market, with hun-dreds of innovative financial instruments created in only the last twen-ty years, bears little resemblance to the securities market of 1913. Not only have we embraced a variety of new forms of capital investment, but we have also accepted new interpretations of income to adapt to these new forms. The zero-coupon bond, breathtaking in its simplicity, demonstrated to tax policymakers the need to include in income the invisible annual accruals that we now are willing to call interest. Thus, it certainly is possible for an economic definition of income, articulated in 1938 and further developed by Kaplow and others, to influence our understanding of the term *income*. It also is possible that a particular definition may come to control our understanding. To some extent, this has already occurred.

Tax academics and tax policy economists have been trained to think in Haig-Simons terms. The so-called comprehensive income tax base rests on the Haig-Simons model.[10] The academic literature contains significant, powerful arguments for practical use of a pure accretion model, from the mark-to-market arguments of Slawson[11] and Shakow[12] to a variety of proposals, including Kaplow's.[13] A persistent minority view urged by Andrews[14] and Bradford[15] has been the con-sumed-income base, which drops the savings component of the Haig-Simons definition and treats consumption as the appropriate measure of income. Notice that last sentence: the words "drops the savings com-ponent of the Haig-Simons definition" demonstrate the dominance of the accretion theory, a dominance so pervasive that it is difficult to articulate the consumption model in any way other than as a truncated Haig-Simons definition.

The dominance of the Haig-Simons definition of income is puzzling given its analytical shortcomings. One of the weaknesses of the Haig-Simons definition is insistence on categorizing all expenditures either as savings or as consumption. Not all expenditures lend themselves eas-ily to this categorization. Is it clear, for example, that donations to a charity are consumption? Is an expenditure for medical care always, or only, consumption? Purchases of medical care seem in many ways to be an investment in human capital.[16]

Beyond the inherent problems with the Haig-Simons definition of

income is the question whether the description of income for tax purposes should be determined by a 1938 economic formulation. It is easy
to cede authority to a definition that presents itself in a neutral and scientific way. But the 1913 tax law was not derived from economic science. It was developed by people largely without training in economics
in an era not blessed with the Haig-Simons definition. The drafters of
the income tax conceived of it as an instrument of social policy. Many
of its terms and concepts are rooted in early twentieth-century understandings of social life. Some of these concepts—for example, the idea
that there is a bright line between income and property—no longer are
appropriate to describe contemporary market transactions. The definition of income and other important terms used in tax law ought to
evolve to meet changing circumstances and to serve changing social
needs. To some extent the Haig-Simons definition was a response to
changed circumstances and the need for a coherent economic description of income. Yet, a definition of income tied ineluctably to economics of sixty years ago offers too limited a vision of the relationship
between law and society. Even if we accept the Haig-Simons definition
as appropriate within the contemporary social context, we should
interpret and apply it according to the purposes of a modern income
tax.

The Purposes of an Income Tax

The U.S. income tax arose in the context of the turn-of-the-century
economy out of a populist, even Marxian, movement. Although a hundred years ago an antipopulist Supreme Court held in *Pollock v.
Farmers' Loan & Trust Co.*[17] that the income tax was unconstitutional,
Congress reenacted it in 1913 after a constitutional amendment.
Originally reaching only about the top 5 percent of income earners, the
tax was redistributive in its intent and application. The term *income*
was understood popularly as the accruals to material capital received in
the form of interest, dividends, and rents. Wages were taxed only in the
case of high-level salaried executives, who often were the owners of
material capital.

The expansion of the income tax to reach average and even lower
incomes, along with the increasing rates of taxation, suggests that the
needs and purposes of the income tax have evolved. But the notion that

tax rates should rise with income (vertical equity) continues to play a role in the American conception of an income tax. Even the general popularity of a flat tax probably is interpreted best as a reaction against the complexity of the current income tax rather than against the idea of vertical equity. In addition, another basic purpose of the income tax, to underwrite the spending choices of government, remains well accepted. Thus, a redistributive policy, however changed, still is an integral part of the structure of the current income tax.

At the turn of the century, the populist conception of owners of material capital, who derived their annual incomes from that capital, stood in stark contrast to that of wage earners, who were forced to labor for subsistence. In this picture of society, the owners of capital were identified as those with the ability to pay. It remains true that those with wealth are better able to pay taxes than those without it.

In an essay published posthumously, Joseph Pechman reported that the gap between rich and poor has been widening steadily over the last thirty years.[18] Although the twentieth century has seen the rise of a salaried middle class, in recent years both higher incomes and greater wealth have become concentrated in fewer hands. This picture of society, of the haves and the have-nots, is strikingly like the turn-of-the-century perceptions that led to the enactment of the income tax. Pechman argued for reinforcement of the income tax and for return to laws that carry out its original redistributive purposes. He described the brutal poverty that has developed in many urban areas and warned against the social consequences of perpetuating economic disenfranchisement. Society is different today, but it remains true that those with large amounts of material capital are better off than those who have little in the way of material capital.

The purposes of the income tax and the social context in which it operates should inform decisions about its design. If the income tax is to continue as a revenue source premised on the ability to pay, then we must undertake to define income with reference to actual circumstances that lead people to being more or less *able* to pay. We should not assume that increasing the tax burden on labor is appropriate without convincing evidence that labor is undertaxed. The assertion that labor is undertaxed is based on the contention that ideal income includes the present value, endowed at birth, of future wages. The validity of this assertion is inextricably linked to our understanding of social life and common economic circumstances.

Consider, for example, two identical twins, separated at birth, one adopted by a wealthy family and the other adopted by a family that immediately falls into straitened circumstances. The wealthy twin never needs to work for a living but enjoys the best society can offer in the way of food, shelter, education, and leisure. The poor twin, deprived from his most tender years of adequate food, shelter, education, and leisure, moves from one low-wage job to another. The availability of material capital has ensured to the wealthy twin an access to opportunities forever closed to the other. The absence of material capital has ensured to the poor twin the omnipresent, unrelenting necessity to work for survival. The poor twin's work produces cash wages that are taxable when paid. If the wealthy twin lives on an identical amount of taxable dividends and interest, are their incomes equal? Are material and human capital sufficiently identical that the income of each should be taxed in the same way, or is there significance to the difference between time spent in work and time spent in leisure? If so, should we take this difference into account when defining human capital, material capital, and income?

THE INEXACT PARALLEL BETWEEN MATERIAL AND HUMAN CAPITAL

Work

Much of the previous literature about taxation and human capital has dealt with issues like the deduction of educational expenses or the excludability of personal injury damage recoveries.[19] More recently, Kaplow has argued that wage-measured human capital, like material capital, is wealth. Seeking a unified concept of income that considers economic value and calling wage-measured human capital "the dominant component of most individuals' wealth,"[20] he concludes that ideal income includes this wealth in income-at-birth.[21] His proposal reaches a foundational question of the income tax: Are material and human capital enough alike to justify identical treatment under an income tax? The answer is no.

Even if future wages were absolutely foreseeable, their present value would not constitute an at-birth increase in wealth. Why? Because the work that will produce the wages remains to be performed. Newborns must one day perform the services that will entitle them to wages twenty years or more in the future. A comparison of a future prospect of wage income *if* services are performed and the future prospect of payment under a zero coupon bond is useful to understand why the requirement of work makes a difference. If both prospects are equally certain and if both have the same future payout, which is more valuable—the one that requires time and work, or the one that requires only time? The accretion model includes as income present-valued future sums that require merely time to mature. There is no reason to construe it to include sums that require time *and work*. If wage-measured value is to be included at birth, at a minimum there would seem to be some discount required for the comparatively lower value of an asset that cannot be transformed into money terms without labor. In most (but not all) cases, the future labor income is likely to be discounted to zero.

A Closer Look at the Definition of Human Capital

The familiar analysis of human capital income assumes that there are four aspects to human capital: leisure, choice, ability, and opportunity. Like others, Kaplow sets aside the value of leisure as inconvenient to tax, although he acknowledges it as a proper subject of income taxation.[22] He dismisses choice as irrelevant to the argument, because his analysis that labor is undertaxed applies only to wages actually received; supercounting wage income does not force people to work.[23] He treats ability as wealth only to the extent that it is used to produce wages.[24] Opportunity, he concludes, directly affects ideal income, because an investment in human capital has positive value only when the opportunity to earn income from that investment exists. It is, he says, "the availability of the opportunity rather than the investment itself [that] produces the change in wealth."[25] Thus, for Kaplow, opportunity is reflected in an increase in cash income.

If human capital comprises leisure, choice, ability, and opportunity, we should give some serious thought to how these four aspects are distributed among wage earners. Notwithstanding the emphasis of the income tax on ability-to-pay questions, one of the weaknesses of

Kaplow's analysis as well as of the accretion model is that both ignore this issue (as if every human had an equal share of these attributes). Before we accept the notion that the presence at birth of foreseeable or predictable future wages represents a present increase in wealth, it is useful to look at the context in which people exercise their so-called human capital.

It seems likely that ability is distributed throughout society without regard to ownership of material capital but that leisure, choice, and opportunity are linked closely to material wealth. A wage-measured definition of human capital sweeps aside any aspect of human capital that is not transformed into wages. But if an ideal concept of income is to include all economic value, it is necessary to reconsider excluding nonwage income generated from (and producing) human capital as inconvenient to measure. Is there economic value to *ability* that is never used to generate wages, to the *opportunity* to earn wages from human capital even though those wages are never generated, to the *leisure* that is the antithesis of wage production, or to the *choice* whether to use human capital to engage in waged work, when to do so, and for how long?

If these aspects of human capital have value not captured by future wages, perhaps they ought to be accounted for separately. The problem is not only that the ideal income model ignores them, but also that they are traditionally associated exclusively with human capital. If these values are distributed in direct relation to material wealth, then for purposes of income definition it is inappropriate to subsume them into human capital as psychic income. Instead, these values are more accurately described as conventionally uncounted income flowing from the ownership of material wealth.

How valid is the argument that noninnate human capital values— roughly defined as leisure, choice, and opportunity—are distributed in direct relation to material wealth? To answer this question it is useful to return to the example of the identical twins, separated at birth, who are raised in different material circumstances. Obviously, there is a leisure difference between the wealthy twin and the poor twin. Is there an opportunity difference between the two? An empirical approach to this problem might compare, for example, the incidence of early death among residents in areas with high property values with that among residents in areas with low property values. Do males under the age of twenty-one have the same death rate in Framingham as in New Haven? Recent studies have shown markedly higher death rates for young males, especially young black males, in poorer urban areas than in wealthy suburban districts.[26] If *not dying* is one prerequisite for having opportunities, then perhaps ownership of material wealth significantly increases opportunity.

It also appears that wealth creates opportunities that ability alone may never contemplate. Evidence is quite strong that people in poverty do not have the same chances for participation in society as those born into material wealth. Children in New York school districts experience a very different quality of education depending on the property values in each locale. Annual spending per pupil ranges from about $11,300 in districts with high property values to about $5,600 in districts with low property values. This difference, which is correlated to material wealth, translates into the difference between schools with eighteen-to-one student-teacher ratios, computers, music, drama, and art classes, and a 97 percent college admission rate, and schools with forty-five-to-one student-teacher ratios, plaster falling from the ceiling, not enough chairs or books to go around, and a dropout rate exceeding 50 percent.[27] These statistics leave little doubt that material capital makes a difference in the opportunities and choices available to the children in different schools. Material wealth gives one twin an opportunity edge.

The question whether there is a parallel between so-called human and material capital presses us to notice what society is like. Perhaps a guiding principle of the income tax—ability to pay—involves attention to differences between the lives of people who have enough material capital to guarantee them an adequate income stream, or access to an attractive career, and people who have no material capital and must work merely to subsist—the choice aspect often associated with human capital. No matter how much ideal income can be earned by someone committed to scrubbing the maximum number of floors humanly possible in a day, her life experience is not the same as that of someone who has the same ideal income from an annuity. The choice of whether to work, and under what conditions, more likely belongs to the annuity holder. Is the annuity-holder twin "significantly wealthier in a tax-relevant sense"[28] than the floor scrubber? If we *notice* that one works forty hours a week and the other lies in a hammock sipping margaritas, there is a difference. As Kaplow notes, a "true believer" in measuring income would include the value of leisure—an aspect of human capital closely linked to the ownership of material wealth.

The Inaccuracy of Relegating Leisure to Human Capital

It is tempting, when defining income, to exclude from consideration human capital that never is transformed into wages. But the existence of non-wage-measured human capital is relevant to the question of wealth, income, and the ability to pay. There are at least two obvious relationships between non-wage-measured human capital and income. First, there is the connection between the ownership of material capital and the power to spend human capital in ways that do not produce wages (leisure). Second, there is the connection between the absence of material capital and the requirement that human capital be spent in ways that do produce wages (work).

The traditional explanation of the failure to consider these connections is that psychic income is not easily taxed. Some income theorists say that it is inappropriate to include as income the value of leisure or of consumer surplus, which is the additional enjoyment or benefit that an individual obtains in excess of the price paid for a good or a service.[29] Others, Kaplow included, agree that the value of leisure properly is includable in income.

The inaccurate assumption that there is an equivalence between price and consumer value bears on the problem of human capital that never is transformed into wages. To ignore the presence of consumer values in *excess* of the uniform price for wages invites us to ignore the value of leisure—which we do—because it is convenient to do so. To ignore the *shortfall* of the uniform price for wages, compared to the real human cost of earning wages, invites us to ignore the additional cost of working—which we do—again, because it is convenient to do so. To ignore these important social facts (including economic circumstances) is to ignore the connection between the presence of material capital and the power to spend human capital in ways that do not produce wages (leisure) as well as the connection between the absence of material capital and the requirement that human capital be spent in ways that do produce wages (work).

The situation of a working single mother of a young child usefully demonstrates this point. In addition to the obvious inconvenience of working, she bears the cost of child care. Beyond the cash outlay for child care while working, she also bears additional costs, such as the loss of time that could be spent enjoying her child (for which the market price may not compensate her), the extra demands on her energy and physical strength that result from parenting after a long day at work, and in many cases, the additional loss of leisure that flows from the need to perform tasks involving manual labor in connection with child rearing. Even if she could afford to pay someone to do all the things included in her daily routine, the part of being a parent that requires engagement with children is something that good parents are not willing to purchase 100 percent of the time. In short, it is unlikely that a working single mother can enjoy the consumer benefits available to a nonworking single mother with equal money income.

The issues involved in this example go beyond those of imputed income from the performance of child care by a parent at home, which theoretically is includable under either an ideal income or an ideal consumption tax.[30] If the nonworking parent obtains child care for an equal amount of time, the difference between the two parents clearly is more than one of imputed income from services performed in the home, because they now have the same money costs and the same disposable cash income. Instead, the difference between the two is the leisure available to the nonworking parent.

It is impractical to measure in money terms the value gained in leisure and lost in working. This is why income tax theorists find it convenient to ignore leisure and other consumer surplus and costs. Kaplow acknowledges, however, that "a true believer in taxing ideal income— or consumption—would include leisure."[31] Despite this insight, his interpretation of ideal income to include the present value of future wages accepts the convention of disregarding the value of leisure. If the undeniable benefits of not working are to be excluded from income for convenience reasons alone, what can be done to compensate for the inaccuracy? An offsetting deduction for the real human costs of working is impractical and unlikely. If we are to arrive at an approach that achieves equivalence between material and human capital, it is appropriate to make some accommodation for the failure to count as income the leisure that ownership of material capital permits. The first step in this approach is to depict accurately the values conventionally associated with human capital.

A More Accurate Depiction of Human Capital

The values of leisure, choice, and opportunity should be stripped away from the definition of human capital and, at the very least, treated as independent values theoretically includable in income. Wage-measured human capital might be referred to as *labor capital* to distinguish it from the conventional use of the term *human capital*. But are leisure, choice, and opportunity truly independent? Ownership of material capital permits leisure, creates opportunities for personal development, and offers choices that are absent or foreclosed to the children of the poor. It takes a much greater amount of ability for a person born into poverty (where leisure, choice, and opportunity are in short supply) to earn the same income as a person born into material wealth. Material capital, then, includes a component that enhances the value of innate ability. The values of leisure, choice, and opportunity are more accurately depicted as attaching to material rather than to human capital.

The example of identical twins raised in different material circumstances emphasizes the connection between nonwage "human capital" values and material capital. The one twin's material wealth includes a set of choices and opportunities the other twin does not have. Surely these additional values are relevant for tax purposes. The ideal income argument describes labor as undertaxed if labor capital is omitted from income-at-birth and leads to Kaplow's description of a system to capture the omitted income by supercounting actual wages. But association of the values of leisure, choice, and opportunity with material capital raises the possibility that *material* capital is undertaxed. If we are serious about defining income, we ought to discover a method to measure these values.

The claim of an exact parallel between material and human capital is the foundation for Kaplow's system of supercounting wage income. Like treatment of like cases is the underlying theme of this argument. But there is not an identity between material and human capital. The distribution in society of noninnate values conventionally associated with human capital correlates closely with the ownership of material capital—so much so that equal treatment of material and human capital requires acknowledgment of their inherent inequality. Perhaps income from *material* capital should be supercounted to capture the additional value that material wealth creates. Perhaps that is what the income tax is about.

ALTERNATIVES

Defining income to include the values of leisure, choice, and opportunity is easier than measuring these values. Apart from discrete applications (imputed income from services, for example), actual measurement, if not impossible, is impractical. A more feasible approach is to identify surrogates for the values of leisure, choice, and opportunity. The suggestion that we could supercount income from material capital is a way to attack the measurement problem, but supercounting income presents a new problem of determining the correct multiplier.

Kaplow's analysis suggests a way to assign a multiplier. He assumes that the endowment of human capital equal to the present value of future wages earns interest and is consumed in annual amounts equal to a level payment annuity.[32] The level payment, which is equal to the amount of wages, is deemed to consist of both interest and capital. This means that in every year *except* the year of endowment, ideal income is *less than* the amount of wages. It is only his decision to treat wage-measured human capital as income-at-birth that leads Kaplow to supercount wage income (as a proxy for taxing income-at-birth). To adapt this system to an income definition that associates leisure, choice, and opportunity with material capital, we would ignore the initial endowment of wage-measured human capital. This suggestion is in line with conventional approaches to defining income, which ignore both at-birth labor capital and at-birth material capital, as well as the at-birth endowment of leisure, opportunity, and choice. This approach, in combination with the rest of Kaplow's analysis, would result in the discounting of wage income. Ideal income would be close to 100 percent of wages in the early years of work and would decline to about 10 percent of wages in later years. Although this approach may have the disadvantage of reducing the tax base, it would allow pure accretion treatment (economic depreciation) of labor capital. The result would be to increase the tax burden on material capital. This solution is implied by the work of Richard Goode,[33] who, Kaplow notes, does not include the present value of wage-measured human capital in at-birth income.[34]

A second way to capture the values of leisure, choice, and opportunity (with no promise of accuracy) is to modify the current income tax to eliminate some of the tax benefits associated with material capital or otherwise to impose a heavier tax burden on material capital. Use of a more carefully tailored rate structure, for example, might be a reasonable alternative. The rate structure might be altered in several ways:

- Expand the zero bracket amount
- Expand the zero bracket amount for taxpayers who live in property tax districts with low property values or with low per capita spending on education
- Increase the tax rate for taxpayers who live in property tax districts with high property values or with high spending on education
- Deny the property tax deduction
- Increase the tax rate on unearned income

The unintended incentive effects of these approaches would have to be evaluated carefully. Using per capita spending on education, for example, could discourage spending in wealthier districts. Amounts spent on private education would have to be counted. Use of local property values may be subject to manipulation as residents become aware of the federal tax consequences, thus raising compliance costs.

A third approach is to modify the current law's definition of income by allowing deductions for work-related costs of human capital. It may be difficult, however, to tailor the deduction appropriately. Already in the current law is the refundable earned income tax credit, which provides a deduction substitute (a credit rather than a deduction) to low-income workers. This provision serves some of the same purposes as a deduction for work-related costs of human capital.

A fourth tactic is to eliminate aspects of the current income definition that inappropriately shelter material capital from taxation. The following ideas have been proposed before and have obvious political problems:

- Eliminate the realization requirement
- Repeal section 1014 and make unrealized appreciation includable in income at death
- Integrate the corporate and individual income taxes but compensate for the lost corporate tax revenues by a windfall tax on old equity and a higher tax on unearned income

It is interesting to observe that these politically infeasible proposals typically have been justified as leading to more accurate measurements of income. All tend to increase the tax burden on material capital.

A fifth alternative, probably less feasible than the others, is to alter the tax system in more radical ways. The most dramatic of changes would be to enact the inverse of a consumption tax. The inverse tax would define income as returns on material capital. This definition does not attempt to measure the value of leisure, choice, and opportunity attached to material wealth but instead increases the burden on material capital by exemption of wage income from the tax base. This method indirectly captures non-wage-measured human capital values. But wage income is income, too, and not to count it distorts the tax base. Moreover, a capital base probably is too small to fund reasonable government spending needs. It seems likely, however, that this idea is consistent with the original conception of the income tax. Times change.

A less radical systemic change is to combine a traditional income tax with a consumption tax. This proposal would place most taxpayers on a cash-flow consumed income tax (with a substantial zero-bracket amount) and would reserve the accretion-model income tax for taxpayers with nonwage income above a substantial zero-bracket amount.[35] For example, a family of four with wages under $30,000 and minimal savings would pay no tax. A family of four with wage income above $30,000 but below $70,000 would pay tax under a consumption model. A family of four with income above $70,000 would pay tax on both wage and nonwage income at progressive rates, although perhaps scaled differently for the wage and nonwage income. The disadvantage of this system would be the increased complexity of using two rate schedules. The greater simplicity of the consumption tax for taxpayers subject only to it, however, might make the proposal as a whole attractive.

The difficulty with all of these alternatives to direct measurement and inclusion of the values of leisure, choice, and opportunity is their inaccuracy. To the extent that these surrogate approaches assume an association between the ownership of material capital and the economic values of leisure, choice, and opportunity, they may do rough justice. At a minimum, stripping these currently untaxed values away from the description of human capital and acknowledging their relationship to material capital offer a theoretical basis for the taxation of income from material capital, which a consumption tax would not reach.

If we begin by asking what the central problems are that the tax law addresses, we see both the need for revenue and an underlying concern for the distribution of the tax burden (if not a frankly redistributive spirit). Pechman's parting essay sounded a warning. He called for a restructuring of tax law to reverse the increasing gap between wage earners and the wealthy. This seems an unlikely social context in which to increase the tax burden on labor by 40 percent, which a system of supercounting wage income would do. The facts of social life should alert us to the improbability that labor income is undertaxed and cause us to examine carefully the assumptions that lead to this assertion and to its consequences for the design of the tax system.

If increasing the tax burden on labor is "not attractive," Kaplow says that the logical alternative to ideal income is a consumption tax. He suggests that people who dislike an ideal income analysis that increases the tax burden on labor should embrace an ideal consumption analysis that decreases the tax burden on capital. This is a false dichotomy. It is ironic that those reluctant to increase labor's tax burden directly should do so indirectly by embracing a model that eliminates the tax burden on capital. Moreover, there is no reason to accept the argument that material and labor capital should be treated as identical. Finally, there is a sound basis to interpret Haig-Simons income to exclude from income-at-birth the present value of future wages. As long as the work is still to be performed, there is no present increase in the newborn's wealth.

There are at least three implications of this exploration of taxation and human capital. The first implication is that the conventional definition of human capital is overinclusive. Values commonly associated with human capital may in fact be additional, untaxed values attached to material capital. This implication suggests that there is a trade-off between the untaxed at-birth present value of future wages and non-wage-measured "human capital" values. Further exploration of this hypothesis, drawing on empirical studies developed in other disciplines, is necessary to bolster the rough correlation suggested in this essay. If the hypothesis proves accurate, this critique offers a justification for taxing material capital more heavily than wage-producing human capital.

The second implication is that we should reject the asserted consequences of the ideal income argument for design of the tax system. Labor income is not currently undertaxed when compared to ideal income. Furthermore, the use of an ideal definition of income to provide theoretical support for a consumption tax is misleading. A consumption tax eliminates from the tax base material-capital income not spent for personal consumption. Although much of this income is currently untaxed or undertaxed when measured against the Haig-Simons definition,[36] shifting to a pure consumption tax would eliminate entirely the tax burden on unconsumed receipts from material capital. In light of the close connection between material wealth and untaxed values of leisure, choice, and opportunity, the consumption model as now articulated appears also to be an inaccurate description of income.

The third implication is that the community of tax academics must engage in a discussion of alternate definitions of income. Why have income tax theorists allowed the Haig-Simons definition to corner the market on income definitions? Although the connection between theoretical formulations and their underlying assumptions about society is nearly invisible, there is a connection. Tax policy has no more claim to neutrality than any other field of study created by human beings. *Weltanschauung* grips us all. It is time for tax academics to sever the bonds that limit our ability to think about income other than by reference to a stipulated definition that emerged from economic theory in 1938.

What aspects of the social and economic environment should we take into account in our alternative definitions of income? Pechman's final essay counsels us to look carefully at the disproportionate distribution throughout society of material wealth, cash income, opportunity, and choice. "What is income?" is a broader question than most of us have been willing to ask. To answer this question, we ought to notice who gets to participate in society and in economic life. We should identify the values that enable that participation. In the end, any definition we adopt reflects how we see the world. Perhaps it also shapes what that world might become.

NOTES

Earlier drafts of this article benefited from the comments of participants in the ABA Tax Section's Teaching Taxation Committee program on human capital held in August 1995, of participants in Taxing America: A Conference on the Social and Economic Implications of Tax Reform, University of Minnesota Law School (Nov. 3–5, 1995), and of participants in a December 1995 faculty workshop at George Mason University Law School. I am particularly grateful for the detailed comments of Glenn Coven of William and Mary Law School, Gwen Handelman of Washington & Lee Law School, and Louis Kaplow of Harvard Law School.

1. *See, e.g.,* Boris I. Bittker et al., A Comprehensive Tax Base? A Debate (1968); Comprehensive Income Taxation (Joseph A. Pechman ed., 1977); Nicholas Kaldor, An Expenditure Tax app. to ch. 1, at 58 n.9 (1954).

2. *See, e.g.,* Louis Kaplow, *Human Capital under an Ideal Income Tax,* 80 Va. L. Rev. 1477 (1994) (arguing that the initial endowment of human capital at birth constitutes income in an amount equal to the present value of the newborn's future wages [income-at-birth]).

3. *See* Robert M. Haig, *The Concept of Income—Economic and Legal Aspects, in* The Federal Income Tax 1, 7 (Robert M. Haig ed., 1921) (articulating the savings element); Henry C. Simons, Personal Income Taxation 50 (1938); *see also* Kaplow, *supra* note 2, at 1477 n.1 (noting that the ideal income definition usually is drawn from Simons's definition, but that the ideal income definition may not reflect Simons's intent).

4. *See* Kaplow, *supra* note 2, at 1507–12 (describing a system of supercounting wages as a proxy for taxing the endowment at birth of the present value of a future wage stream).

5. *See, e.g.,* Alvin Warren, *Would a Consumption Tax Be Fairer Than an Income Tax?* 89 Yale L.J. 1081 (1980); Alvin Warren, *Fairness and a Consumption-Type or Cash Flow Personal Income Tax,* 88 Harv. L. Rev. (1975) (replying to William D. Andrews, *Fairness and the Personal Income Tax: A Reply to Professor Warren,* 88 Harv. L. Rev. 947 (1975) [hereinafter Andrews 1975] and William D. Andrews, *A Consumption-Type or Cash Flow Personal Income Tax,* 87 Harv. L. Rev. 1113 (1974) [hereinafter Andrews 1974]).

6. *See* Kaldor, *supra* note 1, at 70 ("[T]he problem of defining individual Income, quite apart from any problem of practical measurement, appears in principle insoluble").

7. *See* John Rawls, A Theory of Justice (1977) (explaining the "original position" in which social rules are established prebirth with no one knowing what his or her position in society would be).

8. *See, e.g.,* Yoram Barzel, *An Alternative Approach to Analysis of Taxation,* 84 J. Pol. Econ. 1177 (1976).

9. 50 Cong. Rec. 502–14 (1913).

10. *See* sources cited *supra* note 1.

11. *See, e.g.,* W. David Slawson, *Taxing as Ordinary Income the Appreciation of Publicly Held Stock,* 76 Yale L.J. 623 (1967).

12. *See, e.g.*, David J. Shakow, *Taxation without Realization: A Proposal for Accrual Taxation*, 134 U. Pa. L. Rev. 1111 (1986).

13. *See, e.g.*, Noel B. Cunningham & Deborah H. Schenk, *Taxation without Realization: A "Revolutionary" Approach to Ownership*, 47 Tax L. Rev. 725 (1992); Mary Louise Fellows, *A Comprehensive Attack on Tax Deferral*, 88 Mich. L. Rev. 722 (1990).

14. *See* Andrews 1975, *supra* note 5; Andrews 1974, *supra* note 5.

15. *See* David F. Bradford & U.S. Treasury Tax Policy Staff, Blueprints for Basic Tax Reform (1977).

16. *See* Charlotte Crane, *Shifting from an Income Tax to a Consumption Tax: Effects on Expenditures for Education*, this volume; Gwen Thayer Handelman, *Acknowledging Workers in Definitions of* Consumption *and* Investment: *The Case of Health Care*, this volume; Denise D. Roy, *Consumption in Business/Investment at Home: Environmental Cleanup Costs versus Disability Access Costs*, this volume.

17. 157 U.S. 429, *aff'd. on reh'g*, 158 U.S. 601 (1895).

18. Joseph A. Pechman, *The Future of the Income Tax*, 80 Am. Econ. Rev. 1288 (1990).

19. *See, e.g.*, William S. Vickrey, Agenda for Progressive Taxation 123–26 (1947); Loretta C. Argrett, *Tax Treatment of Higher Education Expenditures: An Unfair Investment Disincentive*, 41 Syracuse L. Rev. 621 (1990); Evelyn Brody, *Paying Back Your Country through Income-Contingent Student Loans*, 31 San Diego L. Rev. 449 (1994); Jennifer J. S. Brooks, *Toward a Theory of Damage Recovery Taxation*, 14 Wm. Mitchell L. Rev. 759 (1988); David S. Davenport, *Education and Human Capital: Pursuing an Ideal Income Tax and a Sensible Tax Policy*, 42 Case W. Res. L. Rev. 793 (1992); David S. Davenport, *The "Proper" Taxation of Human Capital*, 52 Tax Notes 1401 (1991); Joseph M. Dodge, *Taxing Human Capital Acquisition Costs—Or Why Costs of Higher Education Should Not Be Deducted or Amortized*, 54 Ohio St. L.J. 927 (1993); Daniel I. Halperin, *Business Deductions for Personal Living Expenses: A Uniform Approach to an Unsolved Problem*, 122 U. Pa. L. Rev. 859 (1974); John K. McNulty, *Tax Policy and Tuition Credit Legislation: Federal Income Tax Allowances for Personal Costs of Higher Education*, 61 Cal. L. Rev. 1 (1973); Christopher R. J. Pace, *The Problem of High-Cost Education and the Potential Cure in Federal Tax Policy: "One Riot, One Ranger"*, 20 J.L. & Educ. 1 (1991); Bernard Wolfman, *The Cost of Education and the Federal Income Tax*, in Proceedings of the 29th Annual Judicial Conference, 42 F.R.D. 437, 535 (1966).

20. Kaplow, *supra* note 2, at 1500.

21. *See id.*

22. *See id.* at 1507 n.73.

23. *See id.* at 1506 (supercounting wages means multiplying wages by a factor that compensates for deferring taxation of human capital income-at-birth until wages are received).

24. *See id.* at 1496 n.31.

25. *Id.* at 1495–96 (discussing table 3, which shows an investment in human capital); *see also id.* at 1489, 1504 (asserting that opportunity affects ideal income).

26. *See generally* Andrew Hacker, Two Nations: Black and White, Separate, Hostile, Unequal 249–62 (Statistical Sources) (1995) (collecting statistics showing opportunity differences by race).

27. *See* Jonathan Kozol, Savage Inequalities 83–132 (1991).

28. Kaplow, *supra* note 2, at 1504.

29. *See id.* at 1504 n.61, 1507 n.73.

30. *See, e.g.*, William A. Klein & Joseph Bankman, Federal Income Taxation 121–22 (10th ed. 1994) (noting that the performance of services in the home often is described as a form of income, albeit administratively infeasible to tax); Kaplow, *supra* note 2, at 1507 n. 73. For a delightful exploration of imputed income issues, see Noel B. Cunningham & Deborah H. Schenk, *The House that Jack Built*, 43 Tax L. Rev. 447 (1988).

31. Kaplow, *supra* note 2, at 1507 n.73.

32. *See id.* at 1483, table 1.

33. *See* Richard B. Goode, The Individual Income Tax 93 (rev. ed. 1976).

34. *See* Kaplow, *supra* note 2, at 1499 n.48.

35. *See* Andrews 1974, *supra* note 5, at 1185–88 (suggesting a similar hybrid system).

36. *See* I.R.C. § 1014 (leads to untaxed income because it permanently excludes appreciation on property owned by a taxpayer at death from tax by increasing the property's basis to its fair market value as determined at the taxpayer's death).

4

JOHN A. POWELL

How Government Tax and Housing Policies Have Racially Segregated America

Because the spatial location and form of housing are important indicators of individual and collective access to social, economic, and political resources, the prevalence of racial segregation in the metropolitan United States and the patterns of home ownership tied to it are extremely problematic. Based upon its location and form, housing becomes "much more than shelter: it provides social status, access to jobs, education and other services, a framework for the conduct of household work, and a way of structuring economic, social and political relationships."[1] The location of one's housing signifies access to or denial of resources and social, political, and educational opportunity structures. Furthermore, home ownership and equity are the most important sources of wealth to the individual American. The racialization of home ownership and home equity, therefore, cements racial segregation across time and generations because wealth largely indicates "individual and family access to life chances . . . [as] it is used to create opportunities, secure a desired stature and standard of living, or pass class status along to one's children."[2]

The racialization of space in metropolitan America developed out of a need for new constructs to preserve racial hierarchy and hegemony. The concurrent demise of formal discrimination and rise of minority migration into metropolitan America created a new urban landscape in which the physical, social, economic, and political relations of the races were to be played out. Whereas once the marginalization of the racial Other was clearly implemented and evidenced through formal, legal separation, destruction of these formal implements of discrimination threatened the racial hierarchy and structures that facilitated this marginalization. White America responded to this threat with the concurrent signification of urban space along racial, political, and economic lines: "as urbanization of the colonized accelerated, so the more urgently were those racialized forced to occupy a space apart from their European(ized) masters."[3] Initially, racial minorities were segregated by neighborhoods within the metropolitan city. As the sheer magnitude of minority migration made this infeasible, whites fled the city for the suburbs, closing the door on minorities behind them. Thus, space became racialized along city and municipal lines rather than along neighborhood lines.

At the same time, politics and public policy were shaped around this new construction of racialized space. Political entities and tax structures were delineated by city and municipality under the ostensibly race neutral principle of "local solutions to local problems with local programs funded by taxes on local property."[4] In reality, the fragmentation of metropolitan politics and policies concretized the boundaries of racial space and ensured that resources and opportunity did not flow between them: "the racial poor were simultaneously rendered peripheral in terms of urban location and marginalized in terms of power."[5] This imposition of artificial local divisions upon metropolitan regions created a framework in which "the fate of the city becomes not a shared interest, but part of a battle over how resources will be distributed across political boundaries."[6]

The resiliency of this spatial arrangement over time and across generations was also strengthened through the public and private denial of home ownership to the marginalized minorities. Government-led lending policies ensured that minorities were denied the potential for social and economic advancement that adheres to home ownership by precluding wide-scale home ownership in the central city. Simultaneously, government zoning policy excluded minorities from the "lender-friendly" suburban areas and the opportunities for home ownership that abounded there.

Over time, racialized spatial lines have shifted outward to "accommodate" the continued growth of metropolitan areas and those minorities who have accumulated the economic ability to move out of the central city. Thus, suburban America has also become racialized. Blacks are little more integrated in the suburbs than they are in the cities, the biggest difference being the level of poverty in the neighborhood. Although Blacks have moved to the suburbs, they have largely moved into areas predominantly populated by minorities that are contiguous to large concentrations of poor minorities in the central cities.

The spatial divisions of metropolitan America and the exclusion and deprivation that accompany them have in turn created a dual reality for the white majority and the racial Other. Concentrating minorities in the inner city and excluding them from resources, power, and the potential for advancement has led to the concentration of poverty, crime, poor education, and other severe antisocial phenomena. Conversely, white suburbanites have been largely shielded from the effects of this deprivation and the public cost of confronting them. In essence, the racialization of space has subsidized white suburban America at the severe expense of minorities.

The deviant, antisocial traits found in the inner city have in turn provided white America with a justification for the exclusion and deprivation that have caused them: "The poverty of the inner city infrastructure provides a racial sign of complex social disorders, of their manifestation when in fact it is their cause; ... [I]dealized racial typifications [are] tied to notions of slumliness, physical and ideological pollution of the body politic, sanitation and health syndromes, lawlessness, addiction, and prostitution."[7] The role that social context and segregation play in the creation of these conditions is ignored as the inner city becomes viewed as the space in which these aberrant things happen rather than the intersection of conditions that cause these things to happen. The causal chain is reversed so that the effect is perceived to determine and justify the cause. In a self-perpetuating and obscuring manner, "the reinforcement of racial identities solidifies the boundaries between groups and makes existing societal rules for classifying people into racial groups appear natural and immutable."[8] Racial explanations based on segregative effects ignore not only the isolation and exclusion that have caused the realities of the inner city, but also the role that opportunities and resources directed exclusively at whites have played in the realities of the suburb. The inner city is perceived as the natural result of shiftless, criminal, antisocial Blacks, whereas the suburb is perceived as the natural result of honest, hardworking, self-sufficient whites.

The federal government is strongly implicated in the development and current reality of metropolitan America. The federal government, through a variety of programs and policies, has penalized the African American community and subsidized the white community by subsidizing and reifying racial segregation and racial inequality in the distribution of resources in the United States. Taxation is one vehicle through which the federal government has contributed to racial separation and perpetuated this separation via subsequent "neutral" policies. The government's tax policies, such as deductions for home mortgages and investment incentives for new businesses, have racialized space by encouraging and enabling widespread disinvestment from the central cities and communities of color. Furthermore, by denying minorities access to wealth via home ownership, and the benefits of suburban location, tax policies have solidified this segregation. Government housing policies and programs (including the federal home mortgage loan), public housing programs, land use policies, and federal highway construction have also exacted a tax from minority communities and delivered a benefit to white suburban enclaves. These policies overburden central cities with societal costs to the benefit of suburban communities, who avoid their share of these costs through the localized power model.

This essay will detail the racialization of American metropolitan space and the effects it has had upon the majority and minority areas. After charting the spatial development of metropolitan America and the effects of segregation within it, it will focus primarily upon the role of the federal government in these phenomena.

THE GROWTH OF METROPOLITAN AMERICA AND WHITE MIGRATION TO THE SUBURBS

In the mid–twentieth century, metropolitan America experienced a significant surge in population. A substantial portion of this urban influx was the migration of African Americans from the rural South to the urban North[9]; a smaller part resulted from the emigration of Latinos, Asians, and people from the Caribbean.[10] With this flood of newcomers, America's central cities reached their zenith in terms of housing the metropolitan population. A study of 168 metropolitan areas found that in 1950 70 percent of America's metropolitan population resided in central cities.[11] As this migration of minorities accumulated, white city residents responded by ensuring that minority population growth occurred within segregated neighborhoods, and "areas of acceptable black residence became more and more narrowly circumscribed."[12]

The sheer magnitude of minority migration caused minority enclaves to expand, threatening the borders of established racial neighborhoods, and so a second mass movement occurred in which white urban dwellers with economic means fled the central city for the suburbs. Following World War II the unsatisfied demand for housing and government funding for home mortgages fueled this flight.[13] By 1990 60 percent of the population of 320 metropolitan areas resided in the suburbs[14] as a result of this "racially motivated 'White Flight.'"[15] The Kerner Commission, established by President Lyndon B. Johnson to study the causes of racial tension in urban America in the wake of the riots of 1968, found that between 1950 and 1966 98 percent of African American population growth occurred within metropolitan areas, primarily within the central cities. Conversely, between 1960 and 1966 78 percent of white population growth occurred in suburban portions of metropolitan America.[16] Metropolitan America had been racialized along neighborhood lines, but it was now racialized along the borders of the city and the suburbs.

By 1970 metropolitan areas followed a general pattern: "a largely black central city surrounded by predominately white suburbs."[17] As of 1990 67.8 percent of African American metropolitan residents lived in central cities as opposed to a mere 33 percent of white metropolitan residents.[18] Although some middle-class Blacks have been able to move to the suburbs as well,[19] this has had little effect on the levels of black exclusion from wealth and white communities. Patterns of "tipping" (the phenomenon of whites tending to flee neighborhoods as Blacks move into them)[20] have carried into the suburbs to the point where black suburbanization is merely a sign of the expanding ghettos.[21] Whether located in the city or in the suburb, a neighborhood's distance from a black-identified neighborhood is highly predictive of its chances of white and black population gain and loss.[22] In fact suburbs with large black populations tend to be more like central cities than like other suburbs:

> [S]uburbs that attract black residents tend to be older areas with relatively low socioeconomic statuses and high population densities. Black suburban neighborhoods are typically adjacent to or near the central city and relatively unattractive to white renters and home buyers. Often they are older, manufacturing suburbs characterized by weak tax bases, poor municipal services and high degrees of debt. Black suburbs spend a disproportionate amount of their revenues on social services. In a less extreme fashion, therefore, black suburbs replicate the conditions of inner cities.[23]

Alongside the racialization of space in metropolitan America has been a signification of urban space economically. The physical confinement of Blacks to the central city has coincided with the economic confinement of Blacks to poverty. In 1944 87 percent of black families lived below the federal poverty line compared to 48 percent of white families, and per capita black income was 39 percent of per capita white income.[24] Although general levels of poverty diminished due to a period of economic growth beginning with World War II, in 1964 black families were still four times as likely as white families to be living in poverty.[25] This disparity has persisted to the present day. For example, in 1984 31 percent of black families lived in poverty compared to 11 percent of white families, and black family real income was only 57 percent of that for whites.[26] Relatedly, wealth disparities across metropolitan areas correlate with racial disparities. Controlling for education and occupation, a black person's net worth, measured in terms of home equity and financial assets, is, on average, $43,143 less than that of a white person.[27]

Accompanying and stimulating this shift in population and wealth has been a shift in production activities mirroring the movement of middle- and upper-class whites to the suburbs.[28] Manufacturers have left older, less efficient factories and moved to suburban locations.[29] This movement is inextricably linked to the racialization of metropolitan space: firms are lured to the suburbs because of the economic deprivation of the central city and the economic subsidization of the suburbs as manifested by the "inferior public services in central cities,

[and] weak household purchasing power of inner-city residents."[30] Retail and consumer services have also largely abandoned the central city as businesses "followed their traditional middle- and upper-income patrons to the suburbs."[31]

THE EFFECT OF METROPOLITAN SEGREGATION ON URBAN BLACKS

The racial and economic segregation of metropolitan America has severely adverse consequences for Blacks living in the central cities. This fact is tightly linked to the localization of metropolitan political and tax structures. State delegations of power have given local governments authority over basic public services, such as police and fire protection, sanitation, public health services, and schools; the power to finance these services through revenues generated from local property taxes; and the power to regulate land usage through zoning.[32] This fragmentation of power over issues of regional import has dammed the flow of metropolitan resources and created vast reservoirs of opportunity in the suburbs. It has created a set of "legal rules that permit and sustain the insulation of suburbs from regional problems,"[33] concentrating these problems in the central city.

One of the major effects of this racially and economically segregative system upon the central city is that it has led to erosion of the local tax base. This has had numerous negative effects upon the central city. One particularly injurious result is that little money is available for public services in the area where there is the greatest need for them. Because of the numerous social ills (discussed later) that accompany segregation, "the cost[s] of providing police and fire protection, judicial systems, public hospitals, and jails are much higher in low-income areas."[34] This weak tax base has also resulted in a poor quality of education being offered to central city children, given that education is funded primarily through local property taxes. Yet another effect is the neglect of infrastructure in central cities. With the exception of highways, most urban infrastructure, from transit systems to water and sewage treatment, is outdated and "well beyond [its] useful life."[35] Substantial reduction within the last few decades in the amount of federal grants for public works has exacerbated this problem.[36] The high cost of these public services and the departure of industry and commerce have led to the highest tax rates' falling upon that sector of the population least able to bear them, as well as to inadequacy in the services provided.[37]

A particularly troublesome effect of the chasm between central city tax revenue capacity and public service needs is that it has caused central cities to engage in debilitating bidding wars with one another in order to generate public revenue. This competition has led to a lowering of wages, health and safety standards, and environmental regulations as cities try to entice investment.[38] The result is that cities, and the minorities confined there, pay more of the hidden costs of the economy in the form of injuries, lost wages, and environmental harms. For example, minorities in the United States are more likely than whites to live near sources of pollution and in areas where levels of ambient pollutants, such as lead and carbon monoxide, are elevated.[39] In fact race is the factor most closely connected to proximity to these hazards, more than income or other socioeconomic factors.[40]

Severe social effects result from the concentration of race and poverty in central cities: "[I]n concentrating poverty, . . . segregation also concentrates conditions such as drug use, joblessness, welfare dependency, teenage childbearing, and unwed parenthood, producing a social context where these conditions are not only common, but the norm."[41] This "social context" has the tendency to perpetuate multigenerational poverty. Lacking peers with strong educational backgrounds and internalizing the perception of ghetto schools as inferior, inner city students tend to lose their sense of "destiny control" and develop a feeling of powerlessness, resigning themselves to their current situation.[42] A related phenomenon, caused by a lack of employment opportunities and a consequent lack of employed role models, is that inner city residents tend to develop a "weak labor force attachment" and a propensity for antisocial behavior.[43]

The adverse effects of segregation and concentrated poverty have proliferated. Segregation has led to an inadequate housing market for minorities. Given that segregation and discrimination limit housing options in the central city, an artificial housing market is created, in which demand exceeds supply. The declining stock of central city housing, coupled with discriminatory home mortgage lending practices, forces minorities to pay inordinately high prices for substandard housing.[44]

Metropolitan segregation has led to a dramatic increase in violent crime rates among Blacks, despite a decrease in crime rates for society as a whole. In fact, the degree of black-white segregation is the most important variable in determining levels of black crime, far more significant than income, poverty, education, occupation, age composition, population size, or region.[45] The relationship between racial segregation, concentrated poverty, and violence is dramatic and undeniable: "[B]y concentrating the persistently poor in certain neighborhoods, segregation has created a 'street orientation,' . . . a social world characterized by high levels of interpersonal hostility and aggression."[46] Furthermore, "to survive on the streets of segregated, inner-city America, one must learn, and to a significant extent internalize, the code of violence. In this way violent behavior is passed from person to person and parents to children in a self-feeding, escalating fashion."[47]

Segregation and the departure of commerce and industry for the suburbs have created what has been termed a "spatial mismatch," whereby most new job creation has occurred in areas inaccessible to low-income central city residents.[48] In particular, low-skilled job creation is occurring mainly in suburban factories and shopping malls, whereas the minority poor are concentrated in the central city.[49] Because most job information is disseminated via word of mouth, poor minorities are less likely than whites to learn of these opportunities.[50] Furthermore, these opportunities often are not viable for the minority poor because of their distance from the central city. Car ownership rates are low for central city residents, and public transportation is often designed so as not to make the suburbs accessible from the inner city. For those who do own cars, "these jobs often do not pay high enough wages to compensate for the cost of the commute."[51]

An inadequacy of health care in the central cities has resulted from segregation: "[N]early one in four blacks remains outside private health insurance or Medicaid coverage."[52] Even for those who can afford to pay, health care is still difficult to obtain because of an "overcrowding of public hospitals, clinic closures, and 'runaway hospitals' that have eliminated or reduced medical services in central cities, and a shortage of physicians and dentists willing to practice in urban minority neighborhoods."[53]

It is ironic, in view of the Herculean burden that segregation and the concentration of poverty place upon the central city, that segregation operates as a subsidy for exclusive suburbs. By concentrating the costly effects of poverty in the central cities, white suburbs are able to avoid their share of the "poor burden." Shielded by the moat of localized political and tax structures surrounding them, suburbs avoid the costs of confronting crime, poverty, and the numerous social ills of the central city. In other words, localization of policies allows the suburbs to exclude "undesirables" from residing within their bounds and absolves them of any responsibility once they have done so.[54]

FEDERAL POLICIES TO ENCOURAGE SUBURBAN MIGRATION OF POPULATION AND RESOURCES

Although the private, commercial, and industrial transition to suburbia is often considered to be the natural result of technological and market forces, in reality the movement has been subsidized by an array of federal policies.[55] All levels of government are implicated in the creation of urban segregation and the resultant concentration of race and poverty. Various government programs and policies, many of which continue today, through their instigation of discriminatory practices or their accommodation of discrimination and intentional segregation, have aided in the spatial racialization of metropolitan America. Significant among these practices are government policies about taxing and fund allocation, particularly government policies on mortgage assistance and home ownership, and government and judicial land zoning practices and policies.

Government subsidies for home mortgages and tax deductions connected to home ownership have played a large role in creating and maintaining racially segregated neighborhoods and perpetuating the racially discriminatory distribution of resources. In 1933 the federal government established the Home Owners' Loan Corporation (HOLC). As a result of the Great Depression, many home owners had defaulted on their home mortgages and many more were in danger of default. HOLC was created to refinance mortgages in danger of default and provide low-interest loans to those who had lost their homes to foreclosure.[56]

Redlining

One endeavor of the federal officials who administered HOLC was to promote uniformity among financial institutions, including uniform appraisal standards.[57] As they did so, the standards that HOLC officials implemented introduced the practice of redlining: racially or ethnically diverse central city neighborhoods were systematically undervalued and deemed too risky for investment.[58] Areas with even the smallest of black populations were given the worst possible rating to indicate a high risk of default.[59]

The effect of HOLC's racist practices was greatly increased by HOLC's influence on the underwriting practices of other government programs and private financial institutions. In particular, HOLC set the tone for the operation of the mortgage insurance program of the Federal Housing Administration (FHA). The FHA, established by Congress in 1934 "to bolster the economy and increase employment by aiding the ailing construction industry,"[60] was given the power to guarantee home loan mortgages. The impact of this program was enormous: "Lenders, jittery after years of high rates of loan defaults and foreclosures, could originate home loans free from the risk of loss. By 1972 the FHA had insured eleven million home purchase mortgage loans and twenty-two million home improvement loans."[61] The FHA followed the lead of HOLC's appraisal standards and discouraged lending in integrated and minority neighborhoods.[62] Its underwriting manual explicitly reflected this policy:

> Areas surrounding a location are [to be] investigated to determine whether incompatible racial and social groups are present, for the purpose of making a prediction regarding the probability of the location being invaded by such groups. If a neighborhood is to retain stability, it is necessary that properties shall continue to be occupied by the same social and racial classes.[63]

The FHA also encouraged municipalities to enact exclusionary zoning ordinances and racially restrictive covenants.[64]

The impact of the FHA's policies on metropolitan America cannot be overemphasized:

> Locked out of the greatest mass-based opportunity for wealth accumulation in American history, African Americans who desired and were able to

afford home ownership found themselves consigned to central-city communities where their investments were affected by the self-fulfilling prophecies of the FHA appraisers: cut off from sources of new investment their homes and communities deteriorated and lost value in comparison to those homes and communities that FHA appraisers deemed desirable.[65]

The Levittown, New York, housing development in Long Island provides a stark illustration of the FHA's role in racializing metropolitan space and home ownership. Mass scale affordable housing was built in Levittown as a result of FHA financing, making the American Dream accessible to thousands of middle-class Americans. However, as late as 1960, not one of Levittown's 82,000 residents was black.[66] By defining creditworthy neighborhoods by their "whiteness," HOLC and the FHA ensured that home ownership would occur solely in the suburbs and that it would be solely available to whites.

Redlining practices introduced by HOLC and continued by the FHA impacted the practices of private lenders as well. HOLC officials adopted the practice of circulating their redlined maps throughout the lending industry to assist private lenders in the identification of risky loan areas.[67] The actions of private lenders were also influenced by the refusal of the FHA to guarantee loans in minority neighborhoods and by its active advocacy of segregation.

The practice of redlining in the private lending industry has continued to the present day. Studies show that, controlling for factors such as education and financial resources, banks are less willing to lend to a prospective entrepreneur who locates in a central city community, particularly a person of color.[68] Furthermore, data obtained under the Home Mortgage Disclosure Act (HMDA)[69] reveals that lending discrimination is not restricted to minority neighborhoods but instead attaches to minorities wherever they may go. In general, people of color are two to three times more likely to be rejected for loans than similarly situated white applicants.[70] One study concluded that whites are accorded a "general presumption of creditworthiness" that has caused lenders to overlook flaws in their credit record, while minorities benefit from no such presumption.[71]

The effect of this widespread redlining in the home mortgage industry is that the opportunity for minorities to become home owners, and thus obtain home equity wealth, has been severely curtailed. A look at neighborhoods within metropolitan areas reveals that the proportion of the population that is black is highly determinative of home owner-ship rates.[72] As of 1960, when the FHA was in full stride, 60 percent of white households were home owners as compared to only 35 percent of black households.[73] The disparity between black and white home own-ership rates has remained virtually constant over time: as of 1989 69.4 percent of white households owned homes as compared to 43 percent of black households.[74]

The effect of this disparity upon minorities is particularly egregious given the significance of home ownership and home equity wealth to financial security and potential social advancement: "[H]ome equity is the key way that families accumulate wealth. As more families borrow against their homes for college tuition, new business capital, and other purposes, the ownership gap exacerbates black-white differences in access to capital."[75] Thus, not only has discrimination in the home mortgage industry helped to create segregated metropolitan areas by discouraging integration; it has also helped to perpetuate this segrega-tion and the dire economic conditions of central cities by denying minorities a primary vehicle for social advancement and economic stability.

When combined with other racist, wealth-denying practices tracing back to slavery and Jim Crow laws, the denial of home ownership to Blacks has caused what has been referred to as a "sedimentation of racial inequality": "the effect of this 'generation after generation' of poverty and economic scarcity for the accumulation of wealth has been to 'sediment' this kind of inequality into the social structure."[76] This inequality not only penalizes Blacks who are denied the benefits of home ownership, but it also subsidizes whites. Whereas "blacks have had 'cumulative disadvantage,' whites have had 'cumulative advan-tages.'"[77] Whites disproportionately reap the benefits of government fund allocation and are freed from competing for scarce resources with an entire sector of the population. Thus, "the accumulation of wealth for whites is intimately tied to the poverty of wealth for blacks."[78]

Tax Benefits of Home Ownership

The tax system as a whole has operated to the benefit of members of the upper income levels. The large and widening gap that exists between the lowest and highest income groupings expands even further after taxes. Between 1980 and 1995 the bottom two income deciles suffered pretax losses of 8.4 percent and 2.3 percent of income, whereas the top income decile experienced a 37.1 percent increase in income. After taxes, this gap widened as the bottom two deciles' losses increased to 10.3 percent and 3.4 percent, while the top income decile's gains increased to 41.1 percent.[79]

In particular, because home ownership is highly correlated with race, subsequent "neutral" tax deductions benefiting home owners have operated to the disproportionate benefit of whites, exacerbating the disparity between black and white opportunity structures.[80] Tax benefits for home owners include interest deductions for home mortgages, favorable capital gains treatment, tax-free imputed income, and deductions for local real estate taxes.

Home owners are permitted to deduct the interest on debt incurred to finance the acquisition of a home.[81] This deduction applies to both the acquisition of a principal residence and the acquisition of a vacation home[82] and is subject to the generous limitation that only the interest on $1 million of debt between the two homes is deductible.[83] Home owners are also able to deduct the interest on home equity indebtedness up to debt of $100,000.[84] These tax benefits serve to spread the gap between black and white opportunity structures. Given that the home equity loan was designed to assist parents sending their children to college, and that it applies to any expenditure, including business expenditures (for which there is no limit on the deductibility of interest),[85] it directly expands life-advancing opportunities for white home owners without any concurrent benefit to Blacks who have been denied home ownership opportunities.

Capital gains preferences benefit home owners in several ways. First, gains from the sale of a home are not recognized if reinvested in a home of equal or greater worth within two years.[86] Also, home owners over fifty-five years old may take a one-time exclusion of gain on the sale of a principal residence (i.e., a permanent deferral of capital gains) up to $125,000.[87] Furthermore, capital gains preferences pass generationally as the successive owner of a home, following a taxpayer's death, takes a basis in the home equal to its fair market value at the time of death.[88] Thus, a successive owner avoids taxes on any appreciation in the value of a home between the original owner's acquisition and the time of his or her death.

Home owners also benefit from Congress's failure to tax imputed income. Home owners who do not rent their homes receive imputed income in the form of the fair market value of the use of their home. The value of this use, the imputed income, is not subject to taxation. Renters also gain the fair market value use of the home that they rent. However, they pay taxes for this usage as their income devoted to rental payments is subject to taxation. In other words, whereas the home owner who chooses not to rent gives up only the fair market rental value of his or her home, the renter gives up the fair market rental value of the home (in the form of rental payments) plus the taxes paid on the income used to pay that rent. A final tax benefit that accrues for home owners is the tax deduction for local real property taxes.[89]

Given the magnitude of these tax breaks and the discriminatory distribution of home ownership, federal tax benefits for home owners have led to prodigious savings for upper-income taxpayers. Over half of the savings generated by these benefits accrue to people with incomes above the ninety-first percentile.[90] The home mortgage interest and property tax deductions alone amount to $54 billion, with about $20 billion of this going to the top 5 percent of taxpayers.[91] In 1993 $150.2 billion worth of capital gains were reported by taxpayers and 72 percent of this total was reported by the top 1 percent of tax filers, the remainder of the capital gains being reported by a scant 6 percent more of taxpayers (i.e., 93 percent of taxpayers received no benefit from capital gains preferences).[92] The priorities embedded in this tax structure become evident when one considers that, despite the great need for low-income housing, federal spending for low-income housing has consistently been only a fraction of the revenue forgone in favor of home owners. In 1993, for example, home owner tax preferences represented $72.8 billion in forgone revenue, while the federal government spent only $18 billion to subsidize low-income housing (a four-to-one ratio).[93] The federal government has opted to use the tax system to enhance the white suburban opportunity structure rather than to address the tremendous wealth differential that exists between Blacks and whites: "The effect of the tax code's 'fiscal welfare' is to limit the flow of tax relief to blacks and direct it to those who already have assets. This seemingly race-neutral tax code thus generates a racial effect that deepens the economic gulf between blacks and whites."[94]

Economists have long maintained that home ownership is oversubsidized.[95] Efforts to restrict availability of these tax deductions, however, have come at the expense of low- and moderate-income households and failed to address the disparity with which the benefit is distributed.[96] The Tax Reform Act of 1986 provides a case in point. Even though the act reduces the overall size of the home mortgage interest deduction, the top 12 percent of the home-owning population still receives 54 percent of the subsidy.[97] Furthermore, by raising the standard deduction and reducing the number and amount of non-housing expenses that may be itemized, the act reduces the value of the home mortgage interest deduction for those households, predominately low- and middle-income, that have a high ratio of loan to home value.[98]

Federal Funding of Infrastructure

Federal spending and policies in areas other than home mortgage programs have also racialized metropolitan America. The federal government, at the behest of suburbanizing, middle-class whites, has facilitated and hastened the flight to the suburbs through massive funds allocated for public highway construction.[99] The federal government has spent $123 billion for highway construction, as well as billions more on infrastructure expansion and maintenance for the developing suburban areas.[100] Coupled with "subsidized cheap fuel and mass-produced automobiles," massive highway construction has helped to make "living on the outer edges of cities both affordable and relatively convenient."[101]

The development of highways, in addition to aiding residential "white flight," has fueled industrial and commercial abandonment of the central cities. By the 1970s the ring of expressways encircling cities had generated new commercial and industrial centers.[102] Federal tax policies helped to get central city businesses on the road by making it economically advantageous for firms to relocate in the suburbs rather than make capital improvements on existing plants.[103] Thus, not only has the federal government contributed to the racial stratification of metropolitan America by facilitating "White Flight," it has also contributed significantly to the "spatial mismatch" that has caused most new job growth to occur in areas inaccessible to central city residents.[104] Government financing of highway construction without comparable funding for public transportation has created a metropolitan transportation system "designed to transport suburban households from their homes to the central business district, . . . not designed to move central households to suburban worksites."[105]

This lack of public transportation and the distance between home and potential employment have created a dependency upon automobiles for central city residents who desire such employment.[106] However, these largely low-paying jobs make it extremely difficult for would-be workers to cover the cost of owning a car: "[A]utomobile ownership in the core areas of these cities is so expensive relative to the actual or potential incomes of their disadvantaged residents that most cannot afford this increasingly essential means of securing and maintaining blue collar employment."[107]

Statistics on car ownership rates for black central city residents illustrate this conundrum. For example, in Philadelphia, 50.9 percent of black central city households are without cars, in Boston 51.3 percent are carless, and in New York a staggering 69.3 percent of black central city households do not have a car and the potential for suburban employment that comes with one.[108] Congress has done nothing to alleviate the great cost of car ownership for central city residents. The tax code consistently has been interpreted to deny taxpayers a deduction for the cost of commuting between home and work.[109] This denial is predicated upon the erroneous assumption that individuals *choose* where they live relative to their work place, ignoring the fact that segregation and discrimination deprive minorities of this choice.

The design of transportation systems to serve the interests of suburban residents is manifested in cement and steel throughout metropolitan America. In Detroit the highways built in the aftermath of the 1968 riots take commuters from downtown skyscrapers to the white suburbs, without providing any exits into black central city Detroit. In New York highway overpasses in some areas have been constructed so low as to prevent buses, and the central city residents that they carry, from passing beneath them. Portions of the public rail system in Chicago that once served affluent suburban neighborhoods have been torn down to prevent access for low-income central city residents. Consistent with governmental indifference to central city residents, the location of these highways has damaged minorities in another respect as urban neighborhoods have been destroyed or extremely devalued by the construction of overpasses. Furthermore, these highways have been used as physical barriers to separate racially identifiable neighbor-hoods.[110]

Federal spending on public housing and "urban renewal" projects has also contributed to segregation. The Housing Act of 1949[111] began the process of "urban renewal" through its Division of Slums and Urban Redevelopment. Urban renewal has razed entire neighborhoods of tenements and rowhouses and replaced them with large, high-density public housing projects,[112] creating an "institutional mechanism for concentrating large numbers of poor people in a small geographic space."[113] One of the major flaws of the Housing Act is that it gave local authorities, rather than federal authorities, the power to locate public housing sites, and in doing so gave suburban municipalities the option of not participating.[114] Consequently, public housing was concentrated in the central cities where land was more expensive. Because of "strong resistance to encroachment by white neighborhoods, a strict government unit-cost formula, shrinking federal slum clearance subsidies, and high land costs," high density "multistory elevator towers on slum sites" became the inevitable end of urban renewal.[115] Furthermore, within the inner cities, public housing was built in the least desirable and most segregated areas.[116] Thus, urban renewal "turned out to be nothing short of 'warehousing' the racially marginalized"[117] in order to keep them in discrete locations away from white neighborhoods and away from those areas of the city where suburban whites continued to work.

These public housing projects came to embody the racialized conception of black central cities. Congress introduced admissions criteria requiring that these projects be filled with only the extremely poor. Originally, residency was limited to those "who are in the lowest income group and who cannot afford to pay enough to cause private enterprise" to build adequate housing.[118] Currently, congressional mandates require that 75 percent of occupants of existing public housing and 85 percent of occupants of new public housing earn a maximum income of 50 percent of the area's median income.[119] In addition, Congress allocated no funds for the maintenance of newly created public housing, and rental payments were insufficient to cover maintenance costs. This caused the quality of public housing to decline rapidly.[120]

Urban renewal in the form of public housing "has fostered the concentration of poverty in inner-city neighborhoods, sometimes single-handedly creating massive ghettos."[121] Current statistics for public housing show that the median income of residents is $6,500, and three-fourths of nonelderly families living in public housing are below the poverty line.[122] Not surprisingly, public housing is also very racially segregated: two-thirds of the nonelderly residents are black and another one-fifth are Latino.[123]

STATE POLICY AND FEDERAL COMPLICITY IN DISCRIMINATORY ZONING PRACTICES

One of the major ways in which the racial and economic segregation of metropolitan America has been preserved is through the abuse of zoning power. The power to regulate land use is vested in the police power of the state.[124] This power has been delegated by the states to individual municipalities through zoning enabling acts under the auspices of the localized power model, which asserts that local governments are best able to serve the interests of their constituents. With the stratification of metropolitan America, individual municipalities have used this virtually unfettered delegation of power to enforce and maintain economic and racial segregation through the practice of exclusionary zoning. The only restriction on municipal zoning authority is that municipalities use it to benefit the "general welfare."[125] As will be discussed later, this generally has turned out to be no restriction at all.

Exclusionary zoning takes the form of land use requirements designed to prevent integration by precluding the development of housing for low- and moderate-income persons. The specific types of zoning provisions used to exclude minorities are many and various, although there are some common ones. One common method of exclusion is through overzoning for nonresidential purposes: zoning boards will zone portions of their municipality for commercial and industrial development to a degree that far exceeds projected growth in those areas.[126] Also, within those areas zoned for residential uses, exclusive municipalities will generally zone most, if not all, of the area for single-family, detached dwellings, partially or wholly prohibiting less expensive, multiunit housing.[127] Costs rise further within residential zones through minimum house size requirements that greatly exceed those considered necessary for health reasons[128] and through minimum lot size and frontage requirements.[129] Numerous other devices have been employed, for example, requiring unnecessary impact studies and application fees, restricting the number of bedrooms permitted, and mandating expensive housing adornments.[130]

Despite the requirement that municipalities use their zoning power to benefit the "general welfare," state and federal officials have failed to regulate municipal land use practices significantly enough to prevent discrimination:

> By delegating control over zoning and other land use powers to municipal officials, whose immediate loyalty is to the existing residents of a town, many state legislatures have permitted the emergence of a balkanized land use system that is so arbitrarily segregated by race, economic class and housing cost that it would surely be unconstitutional if it had been centrally designed.[131]

Attempts at gaining judicial redress have also been ineffective because the judiciary has been very accommodating of exclusive suburbs.

In 1917 the Supreme Court declared that land use restrictions based explicitly on race violated the Fourteenth Amendment.[132] It reconciled this decision with others that maintained segregation by emphasizing that the Fourteenth Amendment specifically protected property rights but did not protect so-called social rights.[133] Despite this longstanding declaration of de jure segregation as unconstitutional, the judiciary has done little to prevent de facto segregation in land use. The Supreme Court's 1926 decision in *Village of Euclid v. Ambler Realty Co.*[134] has set the tone for a history of deferential review of zoning ordinances that do not contain explicit racial classifications.

In *Euclid* the Court articulated the standard that the provisions of a zoning ordinance are unconstitutional only if "such provisions are clearly arbitrary and unreasonable, having no substantial relation to the public health, safety, morals or general welfare."[135] Although *Euclid* did not involve a segregation-related challenge, the Court's benign approach has eliminated the Fifth and Fourteenth Amendments as viable sources for redress of the injuries of exclusionary zoning. Two cases in particular, decided in the 1970s, made this a *fait accompli*: *Warth v. Seldin*[136] and *Village of Arlington Heights v. Metropolitan Housing Development Corp.*[137]

Warth was an attempt to gain low- and moderate-income housing in

Penfield, New York, an exclusive suburb of Rochester. The Court dismissed the plaintiffs' claims for lack of standing. Relying on the Constitution's "case or controversy" requirement and general concerns of justiciability, the Court stated that to have standing to bring a constitutional claim, a plaintiff "must allege a distinct and palpable injury to himself."[138] Because the plaintiffs were seeking relief based upon the generally exclusionary nature of Penfield's zoning ordinance rather than a particular, discrete action taken by the municipality, the Court concluded that "the facts alleged fail to support an actionable causal relationship between Penfield's zoning practices and petitioners' asserted injuries."[139] The Court concluded that the failure of the low-income plaintiffs to find housing in Penfield was "a consequence of the economics of the housing market, rather than of respondent's assertedly illegal actions."[140] It reached this conclusion despite knowledge that Penfield's zoning ordinance allocated 98 percent of the town's vacant land for single-family detached housing with substantial minimum lot and building requirements, and made 0.3 percent of the land available for multifamily structures.[141]

Two years later, in *Arlington Heights*, the Court again heard a constitutional challenge to exclusionary zoning. The plaintiffs in this case avoided the standing problems of *Warth* by proposing a low-income housing development, seeking a rezoning so that it could be built, and having their rezoning request denied. The Court rejected this case on the merits, however, based on its recently created principle that to establish a Fourteenth Amendment violation a plaintiff must show discriminatory intent on the part of the governmental entity being sued.[142] The Court went on to elucidate circumstantial evidence that may be regarded as showing discriminatory intent, including deviations from established procedure.[143] The sophistication of exclusionary zoning practices by 1977 guaranteed that no such deviations would be found.

The net effect of these two cases is that the Court has precluded constitutional challenges to exclusionary zoning. By requiring a narrowly focused, discrete injury, the Court misconstrues the nature of exclusionary zoning and ignores the discriminatory context in which seemingly neutral decisions take place. The racialization of space in metropolitan areas, combined with the localization of power, creates a lens of racism through which colorless decisions become colored. Focusing on the decision rather than its effect ignores this fact. In *Arlington Heights*, for example, the Court attributed no significance to the scant number of black residents resulting from the zoning practice, 27 out of 64,000, according to the 1970 census.[144]

The Court's remedial jurisprudence makes it improbable that, even if a successful claim were brought, significant redress could be had. In *Milliken v. Bradley*,[145] a school desegregation case, the Court stated that "the controlling principle consistently expounded in our holdings is that the scope of remedy is determined by the nature and extent of the constitutional violation."[146] In view of the Court's practice to narrowly define a violation, linking the remedy to the magnitude of the violation ensures that a systemic solution such as dismantling of the zoning scheme rarely will be gained. Thus, exclusionary zoning challenges brought under the Constitution are high-cost, high-risk, piecemeal weapons against a systemic problem.[147]

Congress's most significant attempt to confront exclusionary zoning and other forms of housing discrimination, the Fair Housing Act (FHA),[148] has also proved ineffective. This resulted from a weak statute created by legislative compromise and ineffective judicial enforcement. To facilitate passage of the FHA, Sen. Everett Dirksen of Illinois dramatically weakened its enforcement mechanisms by eliminating HUD's authority to hold hearings, issue complaints, and publish cease and desist orders. Senator Dirksen's amendment also reduced penalties for violations of the FHA.[149] Moreover, if HUD could not resolve a dispute, the FHA only allowed for referral of the case to the U.S. attorney general if there was evidence of a "pattern or practice" of discrimination or if the alleged discrimination raised an issue "of general importance."[150] Enforcement officials rarely determined that individual acts of discrimination satisfied these criteria.[151] According to a study by the U.S. Commission on Civil Rights, HUD referred only 10 percent of the cases it could not resolve to the attorney general. The attorney general pursued a very small percentage of the referrals.[152]

In an attempt to overcome the inadequacies of the FHA, Congress amended it in 1988. The amendments extended the time to file a housing discrimination complaint from 180 days to two years, allowed attorney's fees and court costs to be recovered by successful plaintiffs, and raised punitive awards to ten thousand dollars for a first offense. They also authorized the attorney general, the Department of Justice, and HUD to take a more aggressive approach to addressing housing discrimination.[153]

Courts have acted to strengthen the FHA's ability to confront exclusionary zoning. Appellate courts agree that exclusionary zoning challenges brought under the FHA do not require a showing of discriminatory intent.[154] These cases also take a broader view of the type of injury necessary to provide standing to sue. They find a legally cognizable injury in the "adverse impact on a particular minority group and harm to the community generally by the perpetuation of segregation."[155]

Despite these steps taken by Congress and the judiciary, the FHA continues to be an ineffective mechanism for eradicating segregation. The amended FHA continues to target discrete acts of discrimination in a larger race neutral framework. Yet the invidious effect of systemic and systematic discrimination continues to be ignored. Furthermore, the success of the FHA's piecemeal approach hinges largely upon the extent to which the attorney general, the Justice Department, HUD, and the president wish to advance its goals.[156] One election can reorient the antidiscrimination conviction of one or all of these offices and thus have a dramatic impact upon the efficacy of the FHA. The November 1994 congressional elections provide a case in point. The newly elected group is now attempting to eliminate, for example, the Justice Department's power to bring "pattern or practice" cases on its own initiative under the FHA.[157]

Litigation under the FHA has not been more effective than litigation under the Constitution in curtailing exclusionary zoning. The FHA continues to use the tort and criminal liability models that require identification of a violation, detection of a perpetrator, and proof at trial that the perpetrator's act constitutes a statutory violation. This standard of proof continues to make exclusionary zoning litigation time consuming. The requirements for standing make litigation expensive because a would-be plaintiff must propose an unsuccessful development in order to suffer the requisite injury.

The net result of these inadequacies is that only a few of the meritorious cases have been litigated, and even fewer have resulted in a favorable decision for the claimant.[158] Furthermore, remedies are modest because courts do not redress the systemic damage caused by individual acts. "[I]nstead of ordering a rezoning and invalidating the town's restriction on multi-family housing, the usual case will involve a remand to the trial court to weigh alternative sites. Remedies usually will be limited to one development in one jurisdiction rather than wholesale changes in zoning ordinances."[159] Thus, the case-by-case approach articulated by Congress in the FHA and practiced by the judiciary continues to accommodate the overarching system of residential segregation and racial inequality by misconstruing the nature of housing discrimination as an aggregation of discrete acts taken against individual minorities, rather than recognizing it as a systemic problem with broad ranging effects upon minorities as a group.

FEDERAL AND STATE POLICIES CREATE AND CONSTRAIN INDIVIDUAL CHOICE

The role of governmental policies in the segregation of metropolitan America refutes the accepted myth that segregation is the result of personal preferences and choice. Reasonable examination demonstrates that choice cannot explain segregated housing patterns in the United States. As this essay has evidenced, the purportedly "natural" process of suburbanization has been heavily subsidized and encouraged through taxing and spending policies, while the exclusion of minorities has been enabled through the delegation of zoning and property tax disbursement powers. Nonetheless, it is argued that, after nearly thirty years of integrationist efforts, if minorities remain spatially concentrated it is a reflection of their own preferences.[160] From this perspective, today's housing markets no longer reflect state-sponsored discrimination but instead signify the aggregated choices of millions of Americans to live in areas that contain their preferred racial balance.[161] Such an argument misapprehends the manner in which choice is informed and constrained by political policies and their consequences.

At a deeper level the choice argument ignores a substantial body of literature that helps us to ascertain when preferences are legitimately effectuated in a democracy.[162] Proponents of deliberative justice[163] and social choice[164] theory argue that the participation of affected individuals is essential to the legitimacy of decisions. From this perspective the preference of most whites, or for that matter of most Blacks, to live in same-race neighborhoods cannot be effectuated legitimately absent the meaningful participation of those injured by the disastrous effects of segregation. Put another way, even assuming that housing patterns merely reflect Americans' preferences, it does not necessarily follow that such preferences should be effectuated. As a society we constrain, coerce, and inform individual choice through public policy on fronts ranging from traffic regulation to drugs to antitrust. In this way policy contributes to construction of social meaning.[165] Given that segregation demonstrably exacts extreme costs on American society, and on black America in particular, public policy should address rather than accede to segregationist preferences.

However, public policy has opposed, not supported, integrationist choices. By contributing to a social meaning in which a black neighborhood signifies urban woes and a white neighborhood signifies social opportunity, federal and state policies have informed the segregationist decisions reached by individuals. Just as a residence is essentially linked to an opportunity structure, residential choices take place within a larger structure of opportunity. Indeed, federal and state policies have created individual "choices," by whites and Blacks, in significant and interrelated ways.

Federal and state policies have simultaneously created choice for and choices by whites. That is, by producing segregated housing markets, federal and state policies allow whites to select their preferred residential option, an all-white or mostly white neighborhood.[166] Moreover, by subsidizing suburbanization and sponsoring disinvestment in cities, federal and state policies have created whites' choices by ensuring that there is only one rational option.

For the white home seeker there is really no choice. The "option" of locating in the city is accompanied by a long refrain of burdens: higher taxes and inadequate government services, poor schools, negative investment consequences if the home-seeker is a buyer, higher crime rates, scarce and overpriced retail outlets and consumer services, and limited employment options. At the same time the "option" of suburban location reflects all the benefits of federal and state largesse. The decision is, in effect, already made.

Meanwhile minorities' choices are constrained and denied. Although the preferred neighborhood composition of all whites is all, or predominantly, white, the expressed preference of most Blacks is for a neighborhood that is half-black, half-white.[167] Black home-seekers do not have the option of selecting their preference because such neighborhoods are virtually nonexistent. Indeed, when the exercise of Blacks' choices results in a neighborhood whose composition even approaches their preferred balance, whites overwhelmingly elect to move to a more exclusive area. This phenomenon of tipping is well documented.[168] It is engendered and enabled by the existence of exclusive communities and rendered rational by the consequences that follow when space is racialized and identified as black.

However, it is argued that Blacks' behavior belies their expressed preference for integrated neighborhoods. It has also been asserted that arguments like that offered in this chapter denigrate non-whites by failing to respect minorities' decisions to live within their own communities.[169] Both arguments fail to perceive the extent to which minorities' residential choices are framed and limited by the opportunity structure in which they are made. Racial minorities effectively are denied choice.

For the racial poor, choice is foreclosed. By definition there is no economic access to exclusive neighborhoods. African Americans, in particular, live in poverty (deriving less than 30 percent of area median income) and have severely constrained housing options. In effect they are limited to subsidized housing, which is disproportionately located in neighborhoods with high concentrations of racialized poverty,[170] or the severely distressed surrounding areas. To the extent other options might be available, the racial poor lack the information and mobility to explore them. Economics and race constrain the housing choices of poor African Americans.[171] Although poor whites are more numerous than poor Blacks, they rarely live in areas of concentrated poverty.[172] It is clear that even though poor whites have some of the same economic constraints, they nonetheless have more access to credit and housing markets than middle-class Blacks.[173]

The limited success of the section 8 voucher and certificate programs (that provide low-cost housing for persons in poverty), which are intended to enhance choice for subsidized households, illustrates the conundrum for the racial poor. A number of studies have demonstrated the difficulties voucher and certificate holders have in finding suitable housing and the tendency of black recipients to remain in concentrated areas when they do locate housing.[174] Again, some might argue that these results reflect a preference to remain in black communities. However, a number of system features in the administration of section 8 operate to defeat the program's utility for enhancing choice.

In particular, the proliferation of public housing authorities organized at the smallest practical levels has created and sustained barriers for section 8 recipients seeking to move to a new neighborhood.[175] Within this fragmented structure, residency preferences and separate application procedures keep urban applicants on long waiting lists.[176] Once a household has obtained a voucher, it must locate housing within a limited time or lose it. Yet, no provision is made to assist families seeking residential locations outside of the issuing authority's jurisdiction. In fact the issuing authority will lose administrative fees if the household locates outside its jurisdiction.[177] Indeed, until 1987 subsidized households could not move outside of the issuing jurisdiction without losing their subsidy.[178]

The power of choice/no choice for the racial poor can be seen by the success of affirmative choice programs. Demonstration programs that correct some of these features have increased residential mobility.[179] Significantly, mobility counseling and provision of simple information, such as the availability and location of suitable units, are the most important factors in successful programs.[180] To date, such demonstration programs have reached only some twelve thousand households, whereas nearly six million African Americans live in neighborhoods with high concentrations of racialized poverty.[181]

Those who contend that racial concentration in poor neighborhoods merely reflects the preference of Blacks point to the concentration of middle- and upper-income Blacks in predominantly black suburbs. The availability of greater economic resources to this group, however, does not insure that it has the same freedom of housing choice enjoyed by whites. In the late 1960s, for example, 50 percent of affluent Blacks and 40 percent of middle-class Blacks moved into houses formerly occupied by whites.[182] These households did not choose to experience segregation. Their expectation of integration was defeated by the resegregation caused by white flight.

The context in which housing decisions are made, moreover, cannot be overemphasized. Survey data indicate that most African Americans are reluctant to be the first to cross the color line.[183] Entrenched segregation forecloses the choice of an integrated neighborhood within a significant black population. In the absence of integrated neighborhoods, African Americans tend to locate in primarily black areas, a choice constrained by an ongoing history of exclusion and rejection.

On the one hand, the black home-seeker may contend with the "steering" practices of discriminatory real estate agents, credit discrimination, hostility from new neighbors, the chain reaction of tipping, and other forms of discrimination. On the other hand they may relent and move into a predominantly black area. The choice is effectively preordained.

PROSPECTS FOR DE-RACIALIZING METROPOLITAN SPACE

It is clear from the preceding discussion of metropolitan segregation that any hope of de-racializing metropolitan space and promoting racial, social, and economic justice requires not so much that we remedy individual acts of discrimination, but that we deconstruct the fragmented localized model that perpetuates the systemic segregation plaguing metropolitan America. It is only through this that we can fuse the separate and disparate opportunity structures currently available to Blacks and whites into one just opportunity structure available to all. Although this has yet to happen in a systematic way, there are some isolated examples of change that we might hope to draw from in this endeavor.

One example is the New Jersey Supreme Court's attempt to promote regional "fair share" housing. This court's approach to housing discrimination, exclusionary zoning in particular, was unique in several ways. First, the court recognized that exclusionary zoning and the segregation it maintained were systemic problems that did not necessarily reveal themselves through discrete, discriminatory actions. Consequently, the court found that a municipality's action would violate the requirement that it zone for the general welfare if evidence of exclusionary zoning techniques were present.[184] Furthermore, the court recognized that housing segregation was a regional problem that transgressed local political boundaries. Consequently, it mandated that each municipality allow for low- and middle-income housing "at least to the extent of the regional need therefor."[185] Anticipating problems with noncompliance, the court went so far as to authorize lower courts to mandate zoning provisions and to approve specific projects.[186] As might be expected, the far-reaching, progressive nature of this doctrine was very controversial, and it led to the New Jersey legislature's passage of the Fair Housing Act,[187] which usurped oversight of the fair share doctrine and weakened its requirements and enforcement.

It is difficult to evaluate the individual success of the court's fair share doctrine apart from New Jersey's Fair Housing Act, but it is evident that much housing has been built as a result of the two. A study of fifty-four municipalities from 1983 to 1988 found that as of 1988 22,703 units were scheduled for production, 2,830 units had already been built, and 11,133 units were in the process of development.[188] The sheer magnitude of this remedy obviously eclipses any gains that one might hope to make through the piecemeal litigation available under Title VIII.

Despite its successes, New Jersey's approach to fair housing is flawed. First, the doctrine fails to incorporate race as a factor to determine the effects of, or remedies for, exclusionary zoning. Consequently, many municipalities were able to meet their fair share obligation through economic, but not racial, integration.[189] Second, the doctrine has not been successful in creating housing for the very poor. This shortcoming is due largely to the doctrine's reliance on the private market. Private developers building fair share units, given their profit-maximizing agenda, have priced their units so that they are affordable only to the very top of the eligible income groups.[190] A judicial order that this type of housing be built could not benefit the very poor, because only a legislature could provide the subsidy necessary to enable the very poor to acquire high-priced units.[191] Furthermore, because the fair share doctrine evaluated eligibility based upon current income, it failed to account for wealth disparities that lead to chronic poverty. Thus, many municipalities fulfilled their obligation by providing housing for "many persons who are income-poor only because of predictable, short-term life-cycle circumstances (e.g., students or young married couples)."[192]

John Charles Boger has proposed a National Fair Share Act that builds upon the successes of the fair share doctrine and remedies some of its weaknesses. Building upon New Jersey's regional fair share model, Boger has suggested a legislative remedy that creates financial incentives and disincentives for compliance and noncompliance: in addition to providing federal subsidies for those municipalities seeking to meet their fair share burden, Boger would corral noncompliant municipalities by progressively denying the home mortgage interest deduction and local property tax deduction for their constituents.[193] Boger would also incorporate racial calculations into the computation of a municipality's fair share need to insure integration and urban deconcentration.[194]

Michigan's reconstruction of school financing provides another example of the type of solution necessary to address regional problems. In 1993 Michigan revamped its funding of education in an attempt to shrink the gross disparity in educational funding caused by traditional funding based upon local property taxes. Under the old system, property taxes accounted for about 65 percent of Michigan's educational funding and created an educational system in which richer school districts spent as much as ten thousand dollars per student annually and poorer school districts spent as little as thirty-five hundred dollars.[195] Under the new Proposal A,[196] "the state controls the distribution of about 79% of education funds, while locally collected and distributed property taxes contribute 20% and federal aid supplies 1%."[197] Although the new plan does not create complete equality among school districts, it does significantly reduce the educational gap, and it ensures that every student receives a "basic foundation allowance" guaranteeing a minimal level of expenditure.[198]

Although neither New Jersey's fair share doctrine nor Michigan's Proposal A is sufficient to de-racialize metropolitan space and provide equal access to opportunity in a comprehensive way, they do provide glimpses of the kind of solution that must some day be proffered. The solution would deconstruct artificially created local power enclaves and address and rethink metropolitan segregation on a regional level. Such a broad-based solution is imperative if we ever hope to provide all metropolitan residents with real life choice and meaningful access to opportunity.

NOTES

john a. powell would like to thank Gavin Kearney, University of Minnesota Law School Class of 1997, for his outstanding research. His critical insight and hard work tremendously improved the quality of the essay.

1. John O. Calmore, *Spatial Equality and the Kerner Commission Report: A Back-to-the Future Essay*, 71 N.C. L. Rev. 1487, 1489 (1993) (citing Critical Perspectives on Housing xviii (Rachel G. Bratt et al. eds., 1986)).

2. Melvin L. Oliver & Thomas M. Shapiro, Black Wealth/ White Wealth: A New Perspective on Racial Inequality 2 (1995).

3. David Theo Goldberg, Racist Culture: Philosophy and the Politics of Meaning 187 (1993).

4. Richard Briffault, *Our Localism: Part II—Localism and Legal Theory*, 90 Colum. L. Rev. 346, 349 (1990).

5. Goldberg, *supra* note 3, at 188.

6. John O. Calmore, *Racialized Space and the Culture of Segregation: "Hewing a Stone of Hope from a Mountain of Despair*," 143 U. Penn. L. Rev. 1233, 1251 (1995) (citing Margaret Weir, *From Equal Opportunity to "The New Social Contract*," in Racism, the City, and the State 93, 104 (Malcolm Cross & Michael Keith eds., 1993)).

7. Goldberg, *supra* note 3, at198.

8. David R. James, *The Racial Ghetto as a Race-Making Situation: The Effects of Residential Segregation on Racial Inequalities and Racial Identity*, in Law & Social Inquiry, 407, 420 (Arthur F. McEvoy et al. eds., 1994).

9. John Charles Boger, *The Urban Crisis: The Kerner Commission Report Revisited*, 71 N.C. L. Rev. 1289, 1298 (1993).

10. Henry Cisneros, *Meeting the Challenge of Urban Revitalization*, 27 U. Mich. J.L. Ref. 633, 634 (1994); *see also* Keith Aoki, *Race, Space, Place: The Relation between Architectural Modernism, Post-Modernism, Urban Planning, and Gentrification*, 20 Fordham Urb. L.J. 699, 750–51 (1993).

11. David Rusk, Cities without Suburbs 5 (1993).

12. Douglas S. Massey & Nancy A. Denton, American Apartheid: Segregation and the Making of the Underclass 32 (1993).

13. *Id.* at 44.

14. *Id.*

15. Anthony Downs, New Visions for Metropolitan America 29 (1994).

16. Boger, *supra* note 9, at 1298 (citing Report of the National Advisory Commission on Civil Disorders 12–13 (Bantum Books 1968), which is known as the Kerner Commission Report).

17. Massey & Denton, *supra* note 12, at 61.

18. Boger, *supra* note 9, at 1310 (citing Bureau of the Census, U.S. Department of Commerce, Series P-60, No. 175 Poverty in the United States: 1990 Current Population Reports 77 (1990)).

19. Douglas S. Massey & Nancy A. Denton, *Suburbanization and Segregation in U.S. Metropolitan Areas*, 94 Am. J. Soc. 592, 593–94 (1988).

20. Oliver & Shapiro, *supra* note 2, at 40.

21. Massey & Denton, *supra* note 12, at 70.

22. *Id.* at 79 & table 3.5.

23. Massey & Denton, *supra* note 19, at 593.

24. Norman Krumholz, *The Kerner Commission Twenty Years Later*, in The Metropolis in Black and White: Place, Power, and Polarization 31 (George C. Galster and Edward W. Hill eds., 1992) [hereinafter Metropolis].

25. *Id.*

26. *Id.* at 32.

27. Oliver & Shapiro, *supra* note 2, at 8.

28. Donald A. Hicks, *Revitalizing Our Cities or Restoring Ties to Them?* 27 U. Mich. J.L. Ref. 813, 824–25.

29. *Id.*

30. George C. Galster & Edward C. Hill, *Place, Power, and Polarization: Introduction*, in Metropolis, *supra* note 24, at 1, 10.

31. John D. Kasarda, *Urban Change and Minority Opportunities, in* The New Urban Reality 33, 41 (Paul Peterson ed., 1985).

32. Richard Briffault, *Our Localism: Part I—The Structure of Local Government Law*, 90 Colum. L. Rev. 1, 19 (1990).

33. Briffault, *supra* note 4, at 349.

34. Downs, *supra* note 15, at 48.

35. Peter Dreier, *America's Urban Crisis: Symptoms, Causes, and Solutions*, 71 N.C. L. Rev. 1351, 1370 (1993).

36. *Id.* at 1317.

37. Downs, *supra* note 15, at 48; *see also* Boger, *supra* note 9, at 1299.

38. Dreier, *supra* note 35, at 1373.

39. Ken Saxton & Kenneth Olden, *Environmental Justice: The Central Role of Research in Establishing a Credible Scientific Foundation for Informed Decisionmaking*, 9 Toxicology & Indus. Health 685 (1993).

40. Robert Bullard & Beverly Wright, *Environmental Justice for All: Community Perspectives on Health and Research Needs*, 9 Toxicology & Indus. Health, 821, 824 (1993).

41. Boger, *supra* note 9, at 1317–18.

42. *Id.* at 1299 (citing James S. Coleman et. al., U.S. Department of Health, Educ., & Welfare, Equality of Educational Opportunity 23 (1966)).

43. William J. Wilson, The Truly Disadvantaged: The Inner City, the Underclass, and Public Policy 57–58 (1987).

44. Boger, *supra* note 9, at 1300.

45. Douglas S. Massey, *Getting Away with Murder: Segregation and Violent Crime in Urban America*, 143 U. Penn. L. Rev. 1203 (1995) (citing Ruth D. Petersen & Lauren J. Krivo, *Racial Segregation and Black Urban Homicide*, 71 Soc. Forces 1001, 1013 (1993)).

46. *Id.* at 1219 (citing Elijah Anderson, *The Code of the Streets*, Atlantic Monthly, May 1994, at 81, 83).

47. *Id.* at 1221.

48. Boger, *supra* note 9, at 1317–18.

49. Galster & Hill, *supra* note 30 at 4.

50. *Id.*

51. *Id.* at 5.

52. Oliver & Shapiro, *supra* note 2, at 24.

53. Boger, *supra* note 9, at 1329–30.

54. Briffault, *supra* note 4, at 355.

55. Dreier, *supra* note 35, at 1355.

56. Michael H. Schill & Susan M. Wachter, *The Spatial Bias of Federal Housing Law and Policy: Concentrated Poverty in Urban America*, 143 U. Penn. L. Rev. 1285, 1308 (1995).

57. *Id.* at 1309.

58. Massey & Denton, *supra* note 12, at 51.

59. Schill & Wachter, *supra* note 56, at 1309.

60. Oliver & Shapiro, *supra* note 2, at 17.

61. Schill & Wachter, *supra* note 56, at 1309.

62. *Id.* at 1310.

63. *Id.* (citing Dennis R. Judd, The Politics of American Cities: Private Power and Public Policy 281 (1979) (quoting FHA Underwriting Manual)).

64. Oliver & Shapiro, *supra* note 2, at 18.

65. *Id.*

66. *Id.*

67. Massey & Denton, *supra* note 12, at 52.

68. Timothy Bates, *Small Business Viability in the Urban Ghetto*, 29 J. Regional Sci. 625, 635–37 (1989).

69. Pub. L. No. 94-200, 84 Stat. 1125 (1975).

70. *See* Alicia H. Munnell et al., Mortgage Lending in Boston: Interpreting HMDA Data 1 (Federal Reserve Bank of Boston) (Oct. 1992).

71. *Id.*

72. Wilhelmina A. Leigh, *Home Ownership and Access to Credit* 10 (Dec. 3, 1993) (unpublished manuscript, on file with Institute on Race and Poverty, University of Minnesota Law School).

73. *Id.* at 11.

74. *Id.*

75. James Candill, *Racial Differences in Homeownership and Housing Wealth, 1970–1986*, 30 Econ. Inquiry 83, 99 (1992).

76. Oliver & Shapiro, *supra* note 2, at 51.

77. *Id.*

78. *Id.*

79. Thomas Edsall & Mary Edsall, Chain Reaction 219–20 (1991).

80. Oliver & Shapiro, *supra* note 2, at 42.

81. I.R.C. § 163(h)(3)(B).

82. *Id.* at § 163(h)(4)(A).

83. *Id.* at § 163(h)(3)(B)(ii).

84. *Id.* at § 163(h)(3)(C).

85. *Id.* at § 163(h)(2)(A).

86. *Id.* at § 1034.

87. *Id.* at § 121.

88. *Id.* at § 1014.

89. *Id.* at § 164(a)(1).

90. Peter J. Salsich, *A Decent Home for Every American: Can the 1949 Goal Be Met?* 71 N.C. L. Rev. 1619, 1627–28 (1993).

91. Oliver & Shapiro, *supra* note 2, at 44.

92. *Id.* at 43.

93. Salsich, *supra* note 90, at 1627–28.

94. Oliver & Shapiro, *supra* note 2, at 43.

95. *See* James R. Follain & David C. Ling, *The Federal Tax Subsidy to Housing and the Reduced Value of the Mortgage Interest Deduction*, 44 Nat'l Tax J. 147 (1991).

96. *Id.* at 157.

97. *Id.*

98. *Id.* at 149.

99. Massey & Denton, *supra* note 12, at 44.

100. Dennis Judd & Todd Swanstrom, City Politics: Private Power and Public Policy 180–81, 207–9, 392 (1994).

101. Oliver & Shapiro, *supra* note 2, at 16.

102. Aoki, *supra* note 10, at 793–94.

103. Oliver & Shapiro, *supra* note 2, at 16.

104. Dreier, *supra* note 35, at 1376–77.

105. Galster & Hill, *supra* note 30, at 10.

106. Kasarda, *supra* note 31, at 55.

107. *Id.*

108. *Id.* at 56.

109. *See, e.g., Commissioner v. Flowers*, 326 U.S. 465 (1946); *McCabe v. Commissioner*, 688 F.2d 102 (2nd Cir. 1982).

110. Dreier, *supra* note 35, at 1376–77.

111. Pub. L. No. 81-171, 63 Stat. 413 (1949).

112. Aoki, *supra* note 10, at 765–73.

113. Douglas S. Massey & Shawn Kanainveni, *Public Housing and Concentration of Poverty*, 74 Soc. Sci. Q. 109, 120 (1993).

114. Schill and Wachter, *supra* note 56, at 1292.

115. Goldberg, *supra* note 3, at 191.

116. Schill & Wachter, *supra* note 56, at 1295.

117. Goldberg, *supra* note 3, at 191.

118. Schill & Wachter, *supra* note 56, at 1295 (citing Pub. L. No. 74-412, § 2(1), 50 Stat. at 888 (1995)).

119. Cranston-Gonzalez National Affordable Housing Act, Pub. L. 101-625, § 511, 104 Stat. 4079, 4194 (1990).

120. Schill & Wachter, *supra* note 56, at 1296.

121. *Id.* at 1292.

122. *Id.* at 1299 (citing Connie Casey, Characteristics of HUD-Assisted Renters and Their Units in 1989 68 (1992)).

123. *Id.* (citing Casey, *supra* note 122, at 44).

124. Florence Wagman Roisman & Philip Tegeler, *Improving and Expanding Housing Opportunities for Poor People of Color: Recent Developments in Federal and State Courts*, 24 Clearinghouse Rev. 312, 343 (1990).

125. *See Village of Euclid v. Ambler Realty Co.*, 272 U.S. 365, 387 (1929).

126. *Southern Burlington Cty. NAACP v. Township of Mt. Laurel (Mount Laurel I)*, 67 N.J. 151, 202, 336 A.2d 713, 740 (1975)(Passman, J. concurring).

127. *Id.* at 200, 336 A. 2d at 739.

128. *Id.* at 197, 336 A. 2d at 737.

129. *Id.* at 199, 336 A. 2d at 738.

130. John M. Payne, *Title VIII and Mount Laurel: Is Affordable Housing Fair Housing?* 6 Yale Law & Pol'y Rev. 361, 365 (1988).

131. Roisman & Tegeler, *supra* note 124, at 343.

132. *Buchanan v. Warley*, 245 U.S. 60, 82 (1917).

133. *Id.* at 74; *see also Plessy v. Ferguson*, 163 U.S. 537, 550–51 (1896).

134. *Village of Euclid v. Ambler Realty Co.*, 272 U.S. 365 (1929).

135. *Id.* at 395.

136. *Warth v. Seldin*, 422 U.S. 490 (1975).

137. *Village of Arlington Heights v. Metropolitan Hous. Dev. Corp.*, 429 U.S. 252 (1977).

138. *Warth*, 422 U.S. at 501.

139. *Id.* at 507.

140. *Id.* at 506.

141. *Id.* at 495.

142. *Arlington Heights*, 429 U.S. at 264–65.

143. *Id.* at 267.

144. *Id.* at 255.

145. *Milliken v. Bradley,* 418 U.S. 717 (1974).

146. *Id.* at 744.

147. *Arlington Heights,* 429 U.S. at 262.

148. 42 U.S.C. § 3601 et seq. (1988 & Supp. I 1989, Supp. II 1990).

149. Massey & Denton, *supra* note 12 at 193.

150. George Metcalf, Fair Housing Comes of Age 3–14, 85–86 (1988).

151. *Id.*

152. Massey & Denton, *supra* note 12, at 197.

153. *Id.* at 210–11.

154. *See, e.g., Metropolitan Hous. Dev. Corp. v. Village of Arlington Heights,* 558 F.2d 1283 (7th Cir. 1977), *cert. denied,* 434 U.S. 1025 (1978); *Resident Advisory Brd. v. Rizzo,* 564 F.2d 26 (3rd Cir. 1977).

155. *Arlington Heights,* 558 F.2d at 1290.

156. Massey & Denton, *supra* note 12, at 212.

157. H.R. 1362, 104th Cong. 1st Sess. §§ 145, 147 (1995).

158. John Charles Boger, *Toward Ending Residential Segregation: A Fair Share Proposal for the Next Reconstruction,* 71 N.C. L. Rev. 1574, 1584 (1993).

159. Michael H. Schill, *Deconcentrating the Inner City Poor,* 67 Chi.-Kent L. Rev. 795, 836 (1991).

160. *See, e.g.,* David J. Armor, Forced Justice: School Desegregation and the Law 127–146 (1995).

161. *See id.*

162. *See, e.g.,* Jurgen Habermas, *Morality and Ethical Life, Does Hegel's Critique of Kant Apply to Discourse Ethics,* 83 Nw. U. L. Rev. 38 (1989); Lawrence Lessig, *The Regulation of Social Meaning,* 62 U. Chi. L. Rev. 943 (1995); Richard H. Pildas & Elizabeth S. Anderson, *Slinging Arrows at Democracy: Social Change Theory, Value Pluralism and Democratic Politics,* 90 Colum. L. Rev. 2121 (1990).

163. *See, e.g.,* Habermas, *supra* note 162.

164. *See, e.g.,* Frank I. Michelman, *Law's Republic,* 93 Yale L.J. 1013 (1984).

165. *See* Lessig, *supra* note 162, at 944–49.

166. *See* Armor, *supra* note 160, at 132–41; Massey & Denton, *supra* note 12, at 88–96.

167. Armor, *supra* note 160; Massey & Denton, *supra* note 112.

168. *See, e.g.,* Massey & Denton, *supra* note 12; Robert H. Sander, *Individual Rights and Demographic Realities: The Problem of Fair Housing,* 82 Nw. U. L. Rev. 874, 894–902 (1988).

169. *See, e.g.,* Michael R. Tein, *The Devaluation of Nonwhite Communities in Remedies for Subsidized Housing Discrimination,* 140 U. Penn. L. Rev. 1463 (1992).

170. Massey & Kanainveni, *supra* note 113, at 120; *see also* John Goering et al., The Location and Racial Composition of Public Housing in the United States 28–52 (HUD, Office of Policy Dev. and Research) (Dec. 1994); John Goering et al., Promoting Housing Choice in HUD's Rental Assistance Programs: A Report to Congress 6–12 (HUD, Office of Policy Dev. and Research) (Apr. 1995).

171. Massey & Denton, *supra* note 12, at 84–88; John Charles Boger, *Race and the American City: The Kerner Commission in Retrospect—An Introduction,* 71 N.C. L. Rev. 1289, 1336–37 (1993).

172. David T. Ellwood, Poor Support: Poverty in the American Family (1988).

173. *See id.;* George C. Galster, *Residential Segregation in American Cities: A Contrary Review,* 7 Population Res. & Pol'y Rev. 93, 103–8 (1988); Sander, *supra* note 168, at 886 nn.99–101.

174. *See, e.g.*, Housing Vouchers for the Poor: Lessons from a National Experiment (Raymond J. Struyk and Marc Bendick Jr. eds., 1981).

175. Phillip Tegeler et al., *Transforming Section 8: Using Federal Housing Subsidies to Promote Individual Housing Choice and Desegregation*, 30 Harv. Civ. R.- Civ. L. L. Rev. 451, 456–58 (1995).

176. *Id.*

177. *Id.*

178. *Id.*

179. *Id.* at 458.

180. *Id.* at 458–59; *see also* Paul B. Fisher, *Racial and Locational Patterns of Subsidized Housing in the Chicago Suburbs*, 1 Geo. J. on Fighting Poverty 384 (1994); Barbara Sard, *The Massachusetts Experience with Targeted Tenant Based Rental Assistance for the Homeless: Lessons on Housing Policy for Socially Disfavored Groups*, 1 Geo. J. on Fighting Poverty 16 (1994).

181. George E. Peterson & Kale Williams, *Housing Mobility: What Has It Accomplished and What Is Its Promise, in* Housing Mobility: Promise or Illusion (Alexander Polikoff ed., 1995) (citing Paul A. Jargowsky, *Ghetto Poverty among Blacks in the 1980s*, 13 J. Pol'y Analysis & Mgmt. 288–310 (1994)).

182. Sander, *supra* note 168, at 887.

183. Massey & Denton, *supra* note 12, at 89; Sander *supra* note 168, at 887–88.

184. *Mount Laurel I*, 67 N. J. at 180–181, 336 A.2d at 728.

185. *Id.* at 174, 336 A, 2d at 724.

186. *Southern Burlington Cty. N.A.A.C.P. v. Township of Mount Laurel (Mount Laurel II)*, 92 N.J. 158, 285–86, 456 A.2d 390, 455 (N.J. 1983).

187. N.J. Stat. Ann. § 52:27D-301–29 (West 1986).

188. Lamar et al., *Mount Laurel at Work: Affordable Housing in New Jersey, 1983–88*, 41 Rutgers L. Rev. 1197, 1210 (1989).

189. *Id.* at 1256.

190. *Id.* at 1261.

191. *Id.* at 1261-62.

192. Boger, *supra* note 158, at 1598–99.

193. *Id.* at 1608.

194. *Id.* at 1612.

195. *Recent Legislation*, 108 Harv. L. Rev. 1411 (1995).

196. Mich. Comp. Laws Ann. § 211.27a (West Supp. 1994).

197. *Recent Legislation, supra* note 195, at 1411–12.

198. *Id.* at 1412.

PART II

CHALLENGING TAX TRADITIONS: THE BIAS OF THE INVESTMENT/CONSUMPTION DICHOTOMY

5

GWEN THAYER HANDELMAN

Acknowledging Workers in Definitions of *Consumption* and *Investment*

The Case of Health Care

The income tax is billed as advantaging wage earners in various ways, from redistributing wealth through progressive rates to conferring government largesse in the form of tax subsidies. Heading the list of tax subsidies is the nontaxation of employer-paid health benefits, which the Joint Committee on Taxation identifies as the largest federal "subsidy" provided in the form of forgone tax revenue. These advantages are illusory.

The distribution of the tax burden ultimately is a function of the definition of terms. The income tax incorporates conceptions of income grounded not in the experiences of working people but in unrealistic assumptions of economists and abstractions of legal academics.[1] The result is a tax law that systematically disfavors earnings from labor. Entrepreneurs are taxed on net income, with deductions allowed for the costs of producing that income. In contrast, all living and family expenditures are defined as nondeductible consumption without regard to whether they facilitate work or leisure.[2] Distributional tables based on a definition of income that exaggerates wage earners' ability to pay give a distorted view of the allocation of the tax burden by failing to account for all of the costs of producing wage income. Tax subsidies that purportedly tilt the tax system in favor of working people actually only partly compensate for a biased definition of income.

Prosavings tax reform proposals would substitute a tax base even more unfavorable to people who generate social product through their labor. With grand appellations like "The Freedom and Fairness Restoration Act," an array of tax reform proposals sound the theme of encouraging saving and investment. It is a maxim of macroeconomic policy that only by increasing domestic saving will the nation be able to generate the investment revenues necessary to fuel national growth. Its corollary states that saving is favored; consumption is disfavored. However, the definition of the pivotal terms *consumption* and *investment* proceed from accounts of history and society that, at best, ignore the contributions and experience of workers and, at worst, betray hostility to workers, particularly to organized workers. As under current law, the proposals generally treat a worker's expenditures on mental or physical development and fitness as consumption, whereas for a business to deplete natural resources to produce virtually any product, whether with beneficial or harmful social and environmental effects, counts as investment.

These definitions have harsh consequences for working people who devote their resources primarily to employment-related expenses and to investment in their productive capacity. The prosavings proposals would magnify the significance of the definition of consumption because they would aim taxes at consumption in order to encourage individuals to turn over funds to entrepreneurs for investment. In essence, they seem to have less to do with encouraging investment and more to do with who is to make investment decisions. Thus, the likely primary beneficiaries of the prosavings proposals will not be worker-investors but entrepreneurs.

The Contractors with America did not invent these peculiar definitions of consumption and investment. Used in less evangelistic rhetoric, they have been around for some time and will prevail in this Congress and many more to come unless different accounts of American history and society are recognized. In Irving Howe's words, the productive role and experience of working people have been "block[ed] out of our national consciousness."[3] In his introduction to the visually powerful *Images of Labor*, Howe urged recognition "in our social arrangements and our cultural experience [of] the centrality of the American working class."[4] This essay argues for acknowledging in our tax policy the individual lives and collective role of working people in American society. Otherwise, tax reform will exacerbate the unfairness and the distortions existing under current law.

This essay explores ways that tax policy has "blocked out" workers and considers alternative approaches with a particular focus on the tax treatment of worker health care costs. Part 1 of the essay shows how the late Stanley Surrey's intellectually and politically influential tax expenditure analysis ignored the perspective of workers in accommodating theory to practice. Tax expenditure analysis is "firmly ensconced in the tax policy literature, in the law school curriculum, and, via the Congressional Budget Act, in federal law."[5] So, too, is the habit of blocking out workers from tax policy. Part 2 shows that the most prominent proposals for fundamental tax reform target wage earners out of disregard for their productive role. Part 3 shows that tax reform, rationalized by negative stereotypes of workers, would accelerate shifting of industrial production costs to them. Part 4 urges acknowledging the contributions and experience of workers by recognizing as investment many expenditures currently designated as consumption. This last part uses health care expenses to illustrate the approach.

Despite challenges by legal academics and economists of the stature of William Andrews,[6] Boris Bittker,[7] Joseph Pechman,[8] and David Bradford,[9] classification of health care expenditures as consumption has assumed the status of objective and unassailable fact in tax and health policy discourse and appears to constitute the official federal government position. This essay concludes that expenses of workers' necessary health care should not be treated as consumption and, accordingly, that employer-provided health care should not be subject to tax under either an income- or consumption-based tax. This conclusion would seem to bolster arguments for eliminating rules that prohibit discrimination in favor of highly compensated employees under employee benefit plans. If exclusion of employer-provided benefits is appropriate in calculating net economic income, then regulating the distribution of employee benefits under nondiscrimination rules would seem unjustified.[10]

However, elimination of nondiscrimination rules would be a mistake because, despite their shortcomings, they have facilitated broad, though far from universal, distribution of social insurance benefits through the private sector in the form of employer-paid medical and retirement programs and other benefit arrangements.[11] Absent the nondiscrimination requirements, many employers likely would drop coverage of rank-and-file workers under health and retirement programs. Market forces are inadequate to cause employers to assume the full social costs of their enterprises because of externalities and serious inequalities in bargaining power between labor and management. Therefore, employee benefit nondiscrimination requirements can be justified as an incentive for employers to internalize these enterprise costs. Requiring employers to internalize their costs will cause employers to assume responsibility for the social implications of their actions.

I . IGNORING THE PERSPECTIVE OF WORKERS UNDER TAX EXPENDITURE ANALYSIS

The tax expenditure concept begins with the ethical proposition that the public is entitled to a fair contribution from its members to finance public functions, based on their ability to pay as measured by income. People who have equal incomes are to pay equal tax (horizontal equity) and people who have more are to pay more (vertical equity). "Tax expenditure" is a term of art for tax rules that for reasons other than administrative feasibility do not accurately measure the ability to pay taxes. The term was chosen to connote that deviations from the ability-to-pay standard are the equivalent of a government subsidy in the form of tax relief rather than a direct payment.[12]

Generally, excusing taxpayers from paying their fair share by levying tax on less than their full economic income is a tax subsidy or tax expenditure. Nevertheless, one-time assistant secretary for tax policy Stanley Surrey, who introduced the concept of the tax expenditure budget, recognized that a tax system in the real world cannot be based on an entirely theoretical definition of income. Thus, under tax expenditure analysis, the practical definition of income employed is "somewhat less comprehensive than the economists' approach."[13]

One issue of administrative feasibility is the taxpaying public's perception of fairness. If the tax system seems arbitrary and alienating to taxpayers, the accuracy of self-assessments will suffer. Thus, if a receipt is not recognized in common understanding as increasing economic well-being, definitional adjustments may be justified even if, under economic theory, the amount should be counted as an increase in ability to pay. In adjusting for taxpayers' perceptions of fairness, however, tax expenditure analysis reflects unacknowledged, and surely unintentional, class bias. Higher-income taxpayers are the principal beneficiaries of these prudential adjustments to the definition of income. The experiences and perceptions of working people are not taken similarly into account.

On feasibility grounds, tax expenditure estimates do not include as income gifts, the rental value of the use of one's own property (imputed income), or unrealized appreciation in the value of property. Taxpayers do not perceive enjoyment of these economic benefits as income-producing events, even though they represent clear instances of increases in economic power. Those with income in this form enjoy substantial tax savings relative to those who have income in the form of wages. The former pay no tax on gifts or the value of their use of a residence or other consumer durables, whereas wage earners pay income tax on all wage income (without any compensating deduction if they rent property that they cannot afford to own). Further, deferral of tax on value acquired in the form of unrealized increases in the value of property (rather than in the form of taxable wages) allows an economic benefit to the owner of the property that is equal to the interest that can be earned on the amount not paid in tax currently. That benefit increases with the length of time between the point at which the value of the property increased (when a worker would have paid tax on a like amount paid in wages) and the time of sale when the gain is recognized for tax purposes. Wealthier taxpayers own more valuable consumer durables and investment property and give and receive more substantial lifetime and testamentary gifts than the less well-to-do. Consequently, upper-income households enjoy a much greater incidence of nontaxable income in the form of gifts, imputed income, and unrealized appreciation.

Tax expenditure analysis does not show a similar solicitude toward the perceptions of fairness of taxpayers who have much less wealth in property but who have employment-derived benefits. Nontaxation of pension accumulations is a prominent tax expenditure. Yet, pension savings, a form of wealth workers may have accumulated, is no more likely to be regarded by a taxpayer as income, prior to actual payment, than is unrealized appreciation. Similarly, it is doubtful that workers see payments to maintain physical or mental health as representing some sort of advance in economic well-being. Yet, nontaxation of employee-provided health care benefits is treated as a tax expenditure.

The bias in tax expenditure analysis reflects what Irving Howe described as the "dominant American myth of a nation of independent craftsmen, small farmers, sturdy businessmen, usually self-employed, sometimes hiring a few 'hands,' but mostly succeeding through their own industriousness and sobriety."[14] That myth has "disabled us from seeing what is there in front of our collective nose," that is, wage earners who actually perform the productive work.[15] A jolting example of erasing workers from accounts of American life appears in a property law hornbook, which explains that generally "personalty is created specifically for sale or use by the *creator* and clearly belongs to its *producer*. Thus, a new automobile is the property of the *manufacturer* . . . [!]"[16] The auto worker's contribution, even his or her existence, is not acknowledged. If workers are not recognized as producers, it follows, as Surrey vehemently insisted, that the costs of producing income from labor, such as health care expenditures, properly are treated differently from the costs of producing income from material and financial capital.

2. IGNORING THE PRODUCTIVE ROLE OF WORKERS UNDER TAX REFORM

Similarly, in the accounts of history and society propelling the prosavings proposals, the entrepreneur is ascribed central social value; the contributions of workers are not valued at all. The economic theory of Jean-Baptiste Say (1768–1832), who coined the word "entrepreneur," propels the supply-side economics behind much of prosavings tax reform.[17] Say's theory of the law of supply and demand posits that production opens demand for products. Say's Law often is summed up as "supply creates its own demand."

Say asserted that all goods produced by society are consumed either by the producer, or by another maker of goods, or by a third party who trades for current output with a promise to pay with equivalent amounts of future output. For example, producers of food and clothing will consume each other's production through trade. New entrepreneurs borrow food and clothing from already-established producers of those goods and promise to pay for the goods in the future with equivalent amounts of their output plus interest. According to Say's Law this means that the overall value of what people produce creates the wealth necessary to buy the goods and services that people make.

Say's account of growth makes suppliers the critical actors in the economy and leads supply-side economic policy to focus upon *producers* rather than *consumers*. Supply-side economists conclude that low rates of taxation on production will yield the greatest increases in productivity and growth. Producers will create and trade more goods if taxes are limited because lower taxes will increase the incentive to produce. Workers do not figure prominently in this story because supply-side economics implicitly equates production with entrepreneurial activity rather than with the labor of the invisible worker. It removes workers from the category of producer and categorizes expenditures by workers as disfavored consumption rather than as favored investment. As currently conceived, the three major proposed approaches to fundamental restructuring of the tax system—the flat tax, the value-added tax, and the consumed-income tax—ignore the production of wage labor.

The Flat Tax

Among the major tax reform proposals currently being debated are several variations on the flat-rate income tax. A flat-rate income tax would replace the graduated system with a single, low rate. In order for a flat-tax system to generate the same revenue as the current system, the tax base would have to be broadened. In other words, the tax system would have to tax a broader range of transactions.

The Freedom and Fairness Restoration Act of 1995,[18] sponsored by House Majority Leader Richard K. Armey and Sen. Richard Shelby,[19] is based on the flat tax proposed by economist Robert E. Hall and political scientist Alvin Rabushka, as described in *The Flat Tax*.[20] The tax would apply to business income and to wages. Income from interest, dividends, and capital gains would be nontaxable to individuals on the ground that they are taxed at the business level. Businesses would be taxed on total receipts minus payments the business makes to workers and suppliers. Thus, deductions for the cost of earning income generally would be allowed to reduce the business income subject to tax. The costs of employee benefits other than contributions to retirement plans, however, would not be deductible and therefore would be taxed at the employer level.

The wage tax would be imposed on wages in excess of an exempt amount. Wages equal total compensation, other than employee benefits taxed at the employer level, plus retirement plan distributions. Under the bill, single taxpayers would be allowed a $10,700 allowance, and head of household filers would be allowed $14,000. Married taxpayers would be allowed $21,400. The bill would allow an additional $5,000 deduction for each dependent. Proponents claim that the allowances make the system progressive, but other features of the flat tax have the opposite effect. Workers would not be allowed any deduction for the costs of earning income. Also, because of their weak bargaining position in the current labor market, employees likely would end up paying the tax on benefits in the form of reduced wages, even though the tax nominally is imposed on employers.[21] Employees also might end up paying an even greater portion of the business-level tax. Economists disagree as to whether investors, consumers, employees, or a combination would bear business-level taxes.[22] At the minimum, that consumers and employees might bear at least some of the business-level tax must be taken into account when evaluating the distributional effects of the flat tax.

In form the flat tax is not purely a consumption tax because of the tax on business income at the business level. However, the flat tax would operate as a consumption tax to the extent that consumers and employees would bear the business tax. Indeed, its authors acknowledge that the "logic" of the flat tax, "stripped to basics," is to tax consumption, measured as income minus investment. According to Hall and Rabushka, "[t]he public does one of two things with its income— spends it or invests it." Under this logic, businesses and shareholders invest, whereas workers spend.[23] For wage earners, nothing counts as investment.[24]

Consumption Tax Proposals

Various proposals more frankly directed to taxing personal consumption command considerable support as encouraging saving. Tax reformers who believe that it is fairer to tax what individuals take out of the economy (consumption) rather than what they put in (investment) favor consumption taxes. However, consumption taxes tend to be regressive because consumption falls as a percentage of income as income rises.[25] The regressivity may be alleviated by providing exemptions or lower rates for food, medicine, and other necessities. Moreover, if expenditures necessary to maintain and to develop worker fitness for employment were recognized as investment, taxing only consumption might not prove regressive.

The Value-Added Tax. A consumption-based value-added tax (VAT) that extends through the retail stage is essentially a multistage equivalent of a retail sales tax. The retail sales tax is a tax on sales to households, collected only at the retail level at the time of purchase by the ultimate consumer. In contrast, a VAT is collected as the goods move through the various stages of production and distribution. A VAT would tax the value of all goods and services consumed in the United States as that value is added in increments along the production and distribution chain, up to and including purchase by the ultimate consumer. Participants in the chain would pay the tax on the value that they add to the product. For example, a manufacturing business "adds value" to a product if the market value of its product is greater than the cost of the crude material required to manufacture that product. The manufacturer would pay tax on that "value added."[26]

VATs take two forms. Under the "credit method," there is actually no calculation of a firm's value added. Instead, the tax is collected on the firm's gross receipts from sales, with a credit allowed for the VAT paid by suppliers. This is the form of VAT favored by European Economic Community nations. Under the "subtraction method," the VAT is measured by calculating the difference between the firm's receipts from sales on one hand and outlays for equipment and inventory on the other. The United Savings Allowance Tax Act (USA Tax),[27] sponsored by Senators Nunn and Domenici, includes a "cashflow tax" on businesses, similar to a subtraction-method VAT. The USA Tax would impose an 11 percent tax on a business's net cash flow plus compensation, interest, and dividends paid, with a credit allowed for Social Security and Medicare taxes paid.[28]

The Consumed-Income Tax. A consumed-income tax is a tax on persons, not on sales. The intellectual architect of current consumed-income tax reform proposals is David Bradford, professor of economics at Princeton University, former economic advisor to President George Bush, and former deputy assistant secretary for tax policy under President Jimmy Carter. During the Carter administration Bradford authored *Blueprints for Basic Tax Reform.*[29] The original *Blueprints* and a 1984 revision[30] give the basic arguments in favor of overhauling the current income tax system and present several alternatives, one of which has evolved into a proposal under the USA Tax plan.

The Nunn-Domenici USA Tax includes a graduated consumption tax, at rates ranging from 8 to 40 percent. It would tax individuals on receipts in excess of personal exemption and standard deduction amounts. Additional deductions would be allowed for amounts invested in financial assets and for home mortgage interest, charitable contributions, and alimony. The proposal would allow a limited deduction for higher education tuition. To address regressivity associated with the consumption base, the USA tax would allow employees a credit for Social Security and Medicare taxes paid. Unlike the flat tax, the USA Tax is designed to have no effect on the current allocation of tax burdens across income classes. Its purpose is to simplify the current tax system and to encourage saving without sacrificing progressivity. However, the definitions of *savings, investment,* and *consumption* would further entrench the inequity and the distortion in the tax law that is attributable to disregarding workers as producers of economic growth.

3. SCAPEGOATING WORKERS IN TAX REFORM

Casting wage earners as choosing to consume rather than to save leads to allocating to workers primary responsibility for financing public functions. Characterizing all workers' expenditures as consumption also provides the rationale for using the tax law to impose on workers, rather than on entrepreneurs, the social costs of production. As I show below, tax law changes contemplated under the prosavings proposals likely would result in many employers' abandoning responsibility for maintenance of the welfare of their workforce and shifting to workers the cost of protection "against the common misfortunes of industrial society."[31] Since World War II employer-paid health, retirement, and other benefits have provided much of that protection. The employment relationship has served as the primary institutional mechanism through which the United States has provided income security, health care, and other determinants of well-being.[32]

The employment-based social welfare system grew out of postwar collective bargaining aimed at requiring employers to internalize the costs of maintaining and renewing the workforce. Unions addressed the anomaly that "[e]very well-operated company sets aside money for depreciation, repair, and replacement of machinery" but only infrequently makes "similar provisions for the care of its employees—human beings."[33] Speaking as general counsel for the Congress of Industrial Relations, Arthur Goldberg observed that "the provision of minimum insurance coverage for employees and their dependents [is] a responsibility of the employer of precisely the same character as the responsibility to provide safe working conditions, adequate lighting, reasonable safety devices, etc."[34] In short, employee benefits are part of every business's production costs. It is elementary economics that employers should bear the full costs of production in order that the market for their products function efficiently. Employee benefit plans are a means to achieve this end. Employers, however, are reluctant to pay for employee benefits; they balk at workers' and unions' attempts to gain employee benefits as unnecessarily driving up production costs. The recent tax reform proposals have adopted the employers' position. In consequence, antiworker and antiunion sentiments permeate the rhetoric of tax reform, obscuring and distorting the role of employee benefit programs in our economy and our society.

The Role of Employee Benefit Plans

An employment-based benefit system was a fallback option even for organized labor, which advanced it. Government programs such as those in Western Europe might have addressed social insurance needs better as an infrastructure expenditure to support private enterprise. However, powerful political opposition both to liberalizing Social Security and to national health insurance led the labor movement to hold employers and industries individually accountable for the welfare of the labor force from which they profit.

Although the tax treatment of employee benefit plans had little to do with their evolution or design,[35] the tax law has facilitated internalization of labor costs by employers through employee benefit programs. Contributions by a sponsoring employer to employee benefits are deductible business expenses for purposes of calculating tax liability.[36] The covered employee does not pay taxes on the value of retirement plan contributions,[37] health insurance coverage,[38] health benefits provided under self-insured plans,[39] and other welfare benefits.[40] To the extent that benefits are funded through a qualified trust, accumulations are not taxed.[41]

One important condition of obtaining favorable tax treatment for employee benefit plans is that, for nonunion workplaces, the plans may not discriminate in favor of "highly compensated employees."[42] The nondiscrimination rules serve to encourage employers to internalize the costs of maintaining the welfare of the rank and file, who might not otherwise have sufficient bargaining strength to obtain such employee benefits.[43]

The Effect of Proposed Tax Reform

Prosavings tax reform would encourage businesses to shift their production costs to workers. As under current law, retirement benefits would not be taxed until distribution under either the flat tax or a consumption tax, but the nondiscrimination rules that currently provide tax incentives to extend coverage under qualified retirement plans to rank-and-file workers would lose their force because employers and executives would be allowed expanded tax-free savings opportunities outside qualified plans. Other dramatic changes to employee benefit plans also would occur. Flat-rate income tax proposals would tax employer-paid health and life insurance, dependent care, and all other employee benefits except retirement contributions. A consumption-based system also would tax many employer-paid benefits such as health care.

Studies predict that changing the tax treatment of employee benefits "would significantly affect the comprehensiveness of employer-paid benefits."[44] For example, taxation is likely to add to health care costs for workers even if the tax is imposed at the employer level. Employers can be expected to follow already-established patterns of response to health care cost increases—raise deductibles and copayments or eliminate health benefits altogether. Thus, tax reform predictably will accelerate the recent trend in benefit structures to shift labor cost responsibilities and risks onto workers. Defined contribution savings plans that yield an uncertain retirement income have replaced defined benefit pensions.[45] Specified health coverage has given way to defined contribution spending accounts, which allow benefit cost increases to be allocated entirely to employees. The tax reform proposals exacerbate this pattern of cost-sharing without profit-sharing.

Although the effect of comprehensive reform proposals on the employment-based social welfare system is incidental, risk-shifting to workers is the purpose of the "Medical Savings Accounts" (MSAs) proposed by Ways and Means Committee chair William Archer and included in several legislative proposals. With MSAs, the force of the tax law would be added to the pressures shifting risks onto individual workers by encouraging employers to provide only catastrophic rather than comprehensive health coverage.

MSAs would use individual savings accounts similar to individual retirement accounts (IRAs) to address medical needs. Individuals covered only by a catastrophic health plan could make annual deductible contributions, or alternatively exclude contributions made by an employer, up to the lesser of the deductible under the catastrophic plan or $5,000 ($2,500 for individuals). An individual's contribution would not be treated as an itemized deduction but instead would be deductible to determine adjusted gross income. A catastrophic plan is defined as a health plan that has a deductible amount of at least $3,600 ($1,800 for individual coverage). MSAs would permit nontaxation of health care expenses only to the extent they are prefunded. Withdrawals from an MSA would be tax free if used for medical expenses for the individual, spouse, or dependents. Although earnings on accounts and withdrawals for nonmedical purposes would be taxable, deductible (or excludable) contributions to the account could be saved indefinitely for use for other purposes.

Stories about Workers

The rationale behind MSAs reveals misperceptions about the realities of workers' life experience and hostility toward workers seeking health care. Proponents of MSAs in effect blame workers for the country's health care cost crisis. In an analysis of the legislation, the Joint

Committee on Taxation staff reports that proponents argue that the current tax system, particularly the unlimited exclusion for employer-provided health benefits, encourages the overconsumption of health care.[46] A Congressional Budget Office report on health reform concurs:

> Because workers who receive health insurance as a fringe benefit are shielded from much of the cost of that insurance, they have been slow to switch to lower-cost providers of insurance and health maintenance organizations. People who are covered by more expensive (that is, more comprehensive) insurance are more concerned about the quality of care they receive and less concerned about its cost. As a result, the rapid growth in the consumption of medical services and in medical expenditures has been able to proceed relatively unchecked.[47]

These accounts scapegoat workers, in particular unionized workers who most successfully have bargained for comprehensive benefits fully financed by their employers. These accounts urge us to believe that fully insured employees have caused skyrocketing health care costs by their excessive demand for medical attention. Left unexplained is why having access to health benefits would encourage employees to obtain more medical care than they need when there is no advantage in excessive care. In fact there are disincentives (such as time, inconvenience, discomfort, and fear) to obtaining even needed care that are not necessarily apparent to those who view the lives of working people from a distance. Furthermore, there is little basis for believing that individuals effectively can supervise the medical decisions and charges of health care providers.

The arguments underlying MSAs make sense only to those who deny that worker health care costs are costs of producing labor income. Antiunion, antiworker attitudes are the premises for the conclusion that employment-based health coverage and nontaxation of health benefits are responsible for the country's health care cost crisis. If, however, health care costs were regarded as equivalent to an entrepreneur's costs of producing income, nontaxation of workers' health care costs would not be blamed so easily for rising health care costs.

4. INCLUDING WORKERS IN TAX REFORM

Acknowledging workers and their productive role in the American economy will lead to different conclusions about what constitutes a tax expenditure, consumption, and investment, which in turn will lead to different directions for tax reform. The need to acknowledge workers' contributions and experiences within tax policy becomes even more urgent as the new employment and political order shifts entrepreneurial risks (but not entrepreneurial profits) to workers. In this environment fairness demands that the concept of net income be applied evenhandedly to entrepreneurs and to wage earners.

A concept of income that relies exclusively on what comes in fails to account for differences in purchasing power. Traditional tax policy, therefore, has developed a concept of income that accounts for the uses of income and allows the system to tax income as a measure of what an individual can buy—that is, consumption or additions to wealth.[48] This comports with the ethical principle of the income tax system that tax liability should be apportioned according to ability to pay as measured by income net of the expenses of producing income rather than by gross receipts.

Most of tax policy builds upon the Haig-Simons definition of income in implementing the uses view of income. According to this model an individual's income is the sum of what the individual consumes during the year (consumption) and the increase in the individual's wealth (investment or saving). Professor Bradford observes:

> Most people are at first puzzled by [the Haig-Simons definition of income]. They not unreasonably think of income as something that comes in, such as wage or interest receipts. But the concept of income appropriate for tax purposes somehow must be related to the well-being of the person receiving it, and that depends on what the person obtains with purchasing power, not where he got it.[49]

The definition of consumption inevitably is an ethical and political matter.[50] Consumption is calculated by reference to specific transactions.[51] Although certain activities, such as attending a movie, can easily be recognized as consumption, other activities are not classified so easily.[52] As a result, their tax treatment is a function of policy and not predetermined under the Haig-Simons or any economic model.

Whether an activity should be classified as consumption depends upon what value is placed on that transaction within the larger system. The Haig-Simons model does not indicate whether medical expenses should be classified as consumption.[53] That classification depends upon what ethical and political perspectives are brought to bear on the construction of the tax rules.

Human capital includes value acquired through individual expenditures on education, health care, and other human-development activities. Henry Simons's "quite limited discussion of the practical application of an income tax" did not specify the tax treatment of these types of expenditures.[54] Contemporary tax policy analysts simply have assumed that expenditures by workers are consumption rather than investment. For example, Prof. Stephen Utz totally disregards investments in human capital in calculating "net product," which he defines as new wealth minus economic resources consumed. He recognizes that "[s]ome productive activities benefit more if the person performing them is equipped with an education, training, or muscle that has deliberately been acquired for productivity's sake."[55] Yet he asserts that, when labor alone is the source of new wealth, the new wealth "owes nothing to existing economic resources."[56]

The first step in acknowledging workers in tax reform is to reject the false dichotomy between investment and consumption. Individuals do not have "two personalities: one a seeker after profit who can deduct expenses in that search; the other a creature satisfying his needs as a human and those of his family but who cannot deduct such consumption and related expenditures."[57] In fact deduction of many employment-related expenditures and human capital investments has been disallowed on the ground of the impossibility of distinguishing between their personal and business elements.[58]

Of course, human capital is not identical to material capital, but the differences do not justify systematic disregard of lifelong investments for income production in ourselves and our children.[59] That human capital investments necessarily benefit the whole person does not justify such disregard. Studies indicate that for a majority of both full-time and part-time workers, work is their primary life activity. Thus, a working person's employment-related and human-capital expenditures may be regarded justifiably as primarily directed to the activity of work.

For entrepreneurs, expenses motivated primarily by a business purpose are allowed as a deduction from taxed income. For example, although personal gratification may be a substantial motivation or consequence, if the primary purpose is business, tax law allows deductions for costs such as travel, entertainment, or comfortable furnishings.[60] Limits on the deductibility of business expenses under standards of reasonableness, and inquiry into whether the expenditure is "lavish and extravagant," attempt to exclude outlays with only remote connection to producing income or no business purpose whatsoever.[61] Generally, however, the tax law defers to entrepreneurial judgment as to the appropriateness of an expenditure for business purposes. Workers' investment decisions are entitled to similar respect.

Current law recognizes that the cost of sustaining and renewing the labor force is a business cost. For example, employers are allowed to deduct their costs of recruiting, training, and retaining a workforce and can deduct through depreciation their investment in a "workforce in place."[62] When undertaken by the employer, many worker education and maintenance outlays are excluded from employee income, which is the equivalent of allowing the worker a deduction. Disallowing deductions for similar outlays that workers decide to invest in themselves indicates either distrust of workers' judgments, or an intent to advantage entrepreneurs over workers, or both.

The Case of Health Care

If maintenance expenses on a manufacturer's capital equipment or the utility bills of a shopkeeper can offset these entrepreneurs' business income, it seems logical that the cost of medical care to maintain a worker's fitness ought to offset that worker's earnings from labor. Business and investment outlays are entitled to a deduction because not doing so would result in double taxation of amounts taxed as income when originally received. For example, if $100 is taxed at a 15 percent rate, $85 remains. If the taxpayer uses the $85 to buy materials to produce a product that sells for $90, the taxpayer has taxable gain of only $5 ($90 in receipts minus $85 expenditures made to generate receipts). The taxpayer should not have to pay tax again on the $85. Income tax should be imposed only on net increases in wealth.

Under the Haig-Simons definition of income, any expenditure for medical care is a decrease in wealth and so should reduce income subject to tax unless it is consumption rather than investment. Just as tax law generally defers to an entrepreneur's business judgments as to what costs are appropriate to incur to produce income, a worker's medical expenses should be presumed "necessary" for work. Contrary to current law, health care costs should not need to be "extraordinary" to justify a deduction or exclusion from income.[63] An exception, of course, generally should be made for medical care expenditures that are lavish or extravagant, such as spa treatments or lavishly appointed health facilities.

Any expenditure to secure health insurance also represents a decline in wealth because it represents an immediate volitional loss for the purpose of averting a later potentially catastrophic one. Correspondingly, obtaining coverage through employment is not a gain transaction but merely serves to preserve the status quo. In this regard, acquisition of health insurance is no different from medical expenditures incurred to preserve or to restore health. In the absence of an increase in economic power, there should be no tax on coverage. Although health benefits provide access to money or services, they merely insulate the recipient from economic calamity. Indeed, the money or services may be accessed only in the rather narrow circumstance of seeking treatment for a medical condition. Coverage to *prevent* rather than to treat injuries or illness is no more an exercise of dominion and control. Instead, it is action taken under the duress of threat of harm. Thus, current law allowing workers to pay no income or employment taxes on the value of health coverage provided through employment is appropriate. Contrary to prevailing tax policy analysis, the deduction of health care costs and the exclusion of employment-provided health care benefits are not tax expenditures equivalent to a government outlay.

The Role of Nondiscrimination Rules

In the nonunion workplace, the favorable tax treatment accorded to employee benefit plans generally is conditioned on satisfying certain requirements, which include nondiscrimination rules circumscribing favoritism to highly compensated employees. Prof. Edward Zelinsky has argued that, if the current law's treatment of employee benefits is consistent with taxation of economic income rather than a tax subsidy, then regulation of the distribution of the subsidy through nondiscrimination rules unnecessarily and unjustifiably complicates the tax law.[64] What Professor Zelinsky may have failed to take into account is that the complexity of the nondiscrimination rules is attributable largely to employers' insistence on retaining flexibility in designing compensation packages. Simple means to comply with nondiscrimination rules are available under current law at the employer's option. The real failing of current nondiscrimination rules is that they allow too many workers, notably contingent workers, to be denied employer-paid benefits that higher-paid employees enjoy. This suggests an expanded, rather than a contracted, role for nondiscrimination conditions.

Professor Zelinsky also fails to consider how nondiscrimination rules operate to intervene in the market to require employers to bear the social costs of their activities. In theory an efficiently operating market would operate to internalize worker welfare costs. However, when the negative effects can be externalized and gross disparities in bargaining power exist, the labor market malfunctions. The nondiscrimination rules provide incentives for employers to bear their full labor costs in nonunion workplaces where market forces are the most likely to fail because of unequal bargaining power.

The portion of the workforce covered by collective bargaining agreements has declined, and "steadily declining union membership in this country contributes to growing inequality" between labor and management.[65] Employers are hiring reluctantly and are announcing layoffs. This affects the bargaining climate by intimidating employees from negotiating wage and benefit improvements, even at the bargaining table. With many people out of work and looking for jobs, job security is a bargaining priority. Employment relations have become further attenuated because of expansion of the use of independent contractors and other contingent employment arrangements.

The escalating cost of health care also has undercut workers' ability to bargain effectively over wages. Increased levels of funding have gone only to retaining and not to improving benefits. In some cases even retention of benefits has not been possible. "Job lock" resulting from an inability to replace employer-sponsored health coverage (because of a preexisting condition or the unavailability of affordable coverage through alternative employment or in the individual insurance market) has impaired worker mobility seriously and has underscored the dependent status of employees. Meanwhile, employers increasingly withdraw from responsibility for the well-being of their workers and shift labor cost responsibilities and risks onto workers.

The nondiscrimination rules are a recognition of the differences in bargaining power between highly compensated employees and the rank and file. The nondiscrimination requirements assure that the rank and file share the benefits of the bargaining power wielded by the highly compensated employees. If a plan fails to meet certain participation requirements, highly compensated employees will be taxed on the value of their plan benefits. Thus, employers are encouraged to assume the costs of maintaining the welfare of the rank and file to save on executive compensation costs. If the tax savings to highly compensated employees are sufficiently great, it will be in an employer's business interests to extend benefits broadly. Benefits to rank-and-file workers can be paid out of the "surplus generated to highly compensated employees and employers" by nontaxation.[66]

As the prosavings proposals recognize, tax law may be used productively to correct market inadequacies to generate appropriate levels of investment. In *Corporate Investments in Human Capital: How Financial Accounting Standards Undermine Public Policy*,[67] Russell Coff and Eric Flamholtz persuasively argue for an active government role in encouraging human capital investment because externalities or market failures justify governmental involvement with the economy. Markets fail to reach the socially optimal equilibrium when either "(1) the social cost of a given behavior exceeds the cost borne by the actor, or (2) the social benefit of a behavior exceeds the benefit realized by the actor."[68] Without governmental intervention, firms may underinvest in worker human capital for both of these reasons as well as because of the inefficiency of the labor market. Employers may not invest in workers because the firm may not realize a return on its investment in any particular worker or specific children supported by workers (who bear many of the costs of renewing the workforce). In addition, because the labor market is impaired seriously by inequalities in bargaining power, workers currently are not able to require employers to bear the full costs of their enterprise.

Given the risks that firms "may behave in a manner which consistently undermines the greater social good," the government must "guide investment policies with a keen understanding of how and why the market might be failing."[69] Human capital investment is the often ignored cornerstone of economic competitiveness, and public policy, particularly tax policy, ought to encourage businesses to invest in human capital acquisition and to recognize the value they have in their workforce. As Coff and Flamholtz note, "by ignoring human assets, policymakers have a skewed perception of the problem."[70]

Government might guide investment in human health best by mandating employers to provide health benefits to all employees. These should not be regarded as unfunded mandates; they are funded with employer returns on the labor of their employees. If the employer cannot make a profit while paying for employee health care, then the enterprise is costing society more than it is contributing.[71] However, the recent failure of health reform efforts indicates that employer mandates—or the alternative, national health insurance—will be long in coming. In the interim, nondiscrimination rules compensate for the unequal bargaining positions of labor and management and provide protections against socially irresponsible behavior that may result when businesses do not bear the full economic costs of their decisions.

Joseph Bankman has argued that nondiscrimination rules actually diminish worker welfare, and that wages would be higher in their absence.[72] The experience of the country's contingent workforce suggests otherwise. Eliminating nondiscrimination requirements does not result in higher wages if workers lack bargaining power. Nondiscrimination rules generally do not apply to part-time and temporary workers and to those classified as independent contractors. These workers generally receive no benefits and actually are paid at lower rates of cash compensation than their full-time counterparts. The reason is their weak bargaining position.

Prof. Arne Kalleberg's studies contradict the comfortable assumption that part-time employment has mushroomed to satisfy a demand generated by women's increasing participation in the workforce and their supposed preference for flexibility and a lesser work commitment.[73] Professor Kalleberg's data show that full-time and part-time workers are about equally committed to their employers and that part-time workers are just as likely to designate work as their most important life activity.[74] In fact, contingent work arrangements have not evolved to accommodate a less committed component of the workforce, but instead they have evolved to disadvantage unfairly many workers who have no other choice. Women are taking temporary work because of their "lack of bargaining power and limited employment alternatives."[75]

Professor Kalleberg's work shows that contingent employment is spawning an underclass of working Americans by contributing to polarization in income and benefits as well as in noneconomic job rewards. He reports that part-time workers earn roughly half the hourly cash wages of full-time workers.[76] A breakdown by occupational category showed the same 50 percent differential in wages.[77] Temporary workers are similarly disadvantaged. Temporary workers earn 20 percent less on average than permanent employees.[78] The inapplicability of nondiscrimination rules does not translate into higher wages for workers but only into denial of benefits.

Most part-time workers are not covered under employment-provided health or retirement income plans. Involuntary part-time workers are approximately three times as likely not to have health insurance than those who work part-time voluntarily.[79] For Professor Kalleberg, the "pattern of disadvantage for part-timers with regard to fringe benefits is clear: persons working part-time obtain fewer fringe benefits than full-timers, even after controlling for their education, age, race, length of experience with their employer, occupational level, authority position, employee or self-employed status, and the size of their employing establishment."[80] Although some part-time workers have health insurance under the family coverage provided through the employment of a spouse or other family member, studies show that close to half of part-time workers have no direct or indirect employment-based health coverage.[81] Among temporary employees, the Employee Benefits Research Institute has estimated that 30 percent lack any health insurance.[82]

The data show both that the contingent workforce lacks bargaining power and that ready resort by employers to contingent employment arrangements further undermines the bargaining power of full-time workers. In these circumstances the labor market cannot fulfill the function of allocating social costs to those who generate them, and government intervention is necessary. Given the preference of our political culture for economic pressure over legal mandates, accounting for the full human costs of enterprises and providing for investment in the productive capacity of workers must be achieved for the present through the tax incentive of nondiscrimination rules.

Irving Howe lamented that "[t]he working class, both as actuality and idea, has never been wholly accepted in American society or adequately reflected in American culture."[83] We too easily "slip into the cliches of 'individualist' nostalgia and bland denial, ignoring the reality of the American workers, pretending they have little or no shared experience."[84] U.S. tax policy has suffered as a result, and the prosavings proposals would perpetuate and magnify, rather than remedy, the economic and ethical distortions under current tax law. A remedy requires wholesale reconsideration of tax policy in light of working people's lives and contributions. This essay has begun to consider how acknowledging workers in the tax law might change the tax policy discussions of working people's health care costs. Other technical questions need to be explored before tax law changes based on this approach can be adopted. Issues that need investigation include whether the definition of medical care should be revised to limit nontaxation to medically necessary care; whether some portion of medically necessary care should be deemed personal consumption; whether the portion of medical care allocated to consumption should rise with income as the likelihood of unnecessary health care spending increases; and how to apply nondiscrimination rules to deductibility of medical expenses as well as to exclusion of employer-paid health benefits.

Acknowledgment of workers in tax law, of course, has implications beyond health care costs. It will affect analysis of other employment-related expenditures, such as those for child care, commuting, education, clothing, food, and housing. Acknowledging workers in tax policy also means reevaluating the treatment of child-rearing costs. Human productive capacity does not come cheap, let alone free.

Finally, acknowledging workers in tax policy should lead to a reconsideration of tax proposals designed to put economic pressure on workers to hand over their money to entrepreneurs to make American society's investment decisions. The economic choices of workers to develop their productive capacity and that of the future workforce deserve respect. This reconsideration seems crucial for a de-industrializing society that urgently requires investment in human potential.

NOTES

The author acknowledges with great appreciation the assistance of Rachel E. Berry of the Washington and Lee University law class of 1996; Jack Van Doren, professor of law, Florida State University; and editors Karen B. Brown and Mary Louise Fellows. The author also wishes to thank the other contributors to this anthology who participated in the conference *Taxing America: A Conference on the Social and Economic Implications of Tax Reform*, November 3–5, 1995, Minneapolis, Minnesota.

1. *See, e.g.*, Stephen G. Utz, Tax Policy: An Introduction and Survey of the Principal Debates 112 (1993); Jeanne M. Dennis, *The Lessons of Comparable Worth: A Feminist Vision of Law and Economic Theory*, 4 UCLA Women's L.J. 1 (1993).

2. *See* I.R.C. § 262(a).

3. Irving Howe, *Introduction* to Images of Labor 13 (Moe Foner ed., 1981).

4. *Id.* at 15.

5. Edward A. Zelinsky, *Qualified Plans and Identifying Tax Expenditures: A Rejoinder to Professor Stein*, 9 Am. J. Tax Pol'y 257, 261 (1991) (citations omitted).

6. *See, e.g.*, William Andrews, *Personal Deductions in an Ideal Income Tax*, 86 Harv. L. Rev. 309 (1972) (arguing that the cost of restoring one's good health reduces ability to pay taxes).

7. *See, e.g.*, Boris I. Bittker, *Accounting for Federal "Tax Subsidies" in the National Budget*, 22 Nat'l Tax J. 309 (1969) (arguing that nontaxation of health benefits may be treated as "'ability-to-pay' structural provisions rather than tax concessions").

8. *See, e.g.*, Joseph A. Pechman, Federal Tax Policy 92 (5th ed. 1987) (recognizing that "a medical deduction is needed to equalize 'ability to pay' an income tax between a family with an illness and a family without an illness").

9. *See, e.g.*, David F. Bradford, Untangling the Income Tax 20 (1986) (observing that "[t]wo taxpayers whose outlays would be the same except that one has larger medical bills than the other might reasonably be described as enjoying the same level of consumption").

10. *See, e.g.*, Edward A. Zelinsky, *The Tax Treatment of Qualified Plans: A Classic Defense of the Status Quo*, 66 N.C. L. Rev. 315 (1988).

11. *See generally* U.S. Dept. of Labor, Retirement Benefits of American Workers: New Findings from the September 1994 Current Population Survey (1995) (reporting findings of Bureau of Census Survey on retiree pension and health benefits).

12. *See* Congressional Budget and Impoundment Control Act of 1974, Pub. L. 93-344, § 3(a)(3), 88 Stat. 297, 299 (codified at 2 U.S.C.§ 622(3)).

13. Stanley S. Surrey, Pathways to Tax Reform: The Concept of Tax Expenditures 18 (1973).

14. Howe, *supra* note 3, at 12.

15. *Id.*

16. John E. Cribbet & Corwin W. Johnson, Principles of the Law of Property 11 (3d ed. 1989).

17. *See* Leonard Silk, *Economic Scene: Classical Laws Debated Anew*, N.Y. Times, Dec. 23, 1983, at D2; *Supply-Side for Beginners*, Invest. Bus. Daily, Feb. 3, 1995, at B1; *Voodoo Doctors*, Invest. Bus. Daily, June 8, 1995, at B1.

18. H.R. 2060, 104th Cong., 1st Sess. (1995); S. 1050, 104th Cong., 1st Sess. (1995).

19. *See, e.g.*, John Godfrey, *Flat Tax Backers Stress Simplicity, but Devil Remains in the Details*, 67 Tax Notes 167 (1995).

20. Robert E. Hall & Alvin Rabushka, The Flat Tax (2d ed. 1995).

21. *See, e.g.*, Bradford, *supra* note 9, at 134–35, 205–6; Service Employees Int'l Union, Out of Control, into Decline: The Devastating Twelve-Year Impact of Healthcare Costs on Worker Wages, Corporate Profits, and Government Budgets 1 (1992); Joseph Bankman, *The Effect of Anti-*

Discrimination Provisions on Rank-and-File Compensation, 72 Wash. U. L.Q. 597, 603–5 (1994). *But see* Norman P. Stein, *Qualified Plans and Retirement Policy: A Reply to Professor Zelinsky,* 9 Am. J. Tax Pol'y 225, 240–43 (hypothesizing circumstances in which tax would not be passed on to workers).

22. *See, e.g.,* Bradford, *supra* note 9, at 136–47.

23. Hall & Rabushka, *supra* note 20, at 55.

24. *Id.*

25. *See* U.S. Treasury Dep't, Tax Reform for Fairness, Simplicity, and Economic Growth— Value-Added Tax 19 (1984).

26. *See id.* at 5–11.

27. S. 722, 104th Cong., 1st Sess. (1995).

28. *See, e.g.,* Barbara Kirchheimer, *Nunn, Domenici Introduce "USA" Tax to Replace Income Tax,* 67 Tax Notes 592 (1995).

29. David F. Bradford & U.S. Treasury Tax Policy Staff, Blueprints for Basic Tax Reform (1977).

30. David F. Bradford & U.S. Treasury Tax Policy Staff, Blueprints for Basic Tax Reform (2d ed. rev. 1984).

31. Alan Derickson, *Health Security for All? Social Unionism and Universal Health Insurance, 1935–1958,* 80 J. Am. Hist. 1333, 1335 (1994).

32. *See, e.g.,* Mary E. O'Connell, *On the Fringe: Rethinking the Link between Wages and Benefits,* 67 Tul. L. Rev. 1421 (1993).

33. Derickson, *supra* note 31, at 1349; *see* Edmund F. Wehrle, *"For a Healthy America": Labor's Struggle for National Health Insurance, 1943–1949,* 5 Lab.'s Heritage 28 (1993).

34. 1 Stanley S. Surrey et al., Federal Income Taxation: Cases and Materials 139 (1972) (quoting a talk given by Arthur J. Goldberg).

35. *See* Association of Private Pension and Welfare Plans, Benefits Bargain: Why We Should Not Tax Employee Benefits 16–17 (1990) [hereinafter APPWP].

36. *See, e.g.,* I.R.C. §§ 162(a), 404, 419, 419A.

37. *See id.* at § 402.

38. *See id.* at § 106.

39. *See id.* at § 105.

40. *See, e.g., id.* at §§ 79 (excluding employer-provided group term life insurance up to $50,000), 125 (governing tax treatment of flexible benefit arrangements), 129 (excluding employer-paid dependent care).

41. *See id.* at § 501(a).

42. *See id.* at § 414(q).

43. *See* discussion *infra,* "The Role of Nondiscrimination Rules."

44. Deborah J. Chollet, *Background on the Tax Treatment of Employee Benefits: An Overview of the Issues, in* Employee Benefit Research Inst., Why Tax Benefits? 3, 14–21 (1984) [hereinafter EBRI]; *see* APPWP, *supra* note 35, at 57–64; Paul B. Ginsburg, *The Potential Effects of Changes in the Tax Treatment of Employers' Health Insurance Contributions, in* EBRI, *supra,* at 71, 71–72.

45. *See* Everett T. Allen, Jr., *Trends Resulting from the Current Tax Treatment of Employee Benefits, in* EBRI, *supra* note 44, at 25, 26; Harry G. Smith, *The Reasons Employers Provide Employee Benefits and the Influence of Tax Treatment on Employer Decisions, in id.* at 35, 37.

46. *See* Staff of Joint Comm. on Taxation, 104th Cong., 1st Sess., Description and Analysis of H.R. 1818 (The Family Medical Savings and Investment Act of 1995) (Comm. Print 1995).

47. Congressional Budget Office, The Tax Treatment of Employment-Based Health Insurance xi (1994).

48. *See* Bradford, *supra* note 9, at 15.

49. *See id.* at 16.

50. *See id.* at 20.

51. *See id.*

52. *See id.*

53. *See id.*

54. *See* Utz, *supra* note 1, at 113.

55. *Id.*

56. *Id.* at 91.

57. Stanley S. Surrey & William C. Warren, Cases on Federal Income Taxation 272 (1960) (quoted in *United States v. Gilmore,* 372 U.S. 39, 44 (1963)).

58. *See* Jennifer J. S. Brooks, *Developing a Theory of Damage Recovery Taxation,* 14 Wm. Mitchell L. Rev. 759 (1988).

59. *See, e.g.,* Brian E. Lebowitz, *The Mistaxation of Investment in Human Capital,* 52 Tax Notes 825 (1991).

60. *See* I.R.C. § 162(a).

61. *See, e.g., id.* at § 274.

62. *Id.* at § 197; *see Ithaca Industries, Inc. v. Commissioner,* 17 F.3d 684 (4th Cir. 1994), *cert. denied,* 115 S. Ct. 83 (1994) (explaining rationale for deduction for workforce in place).

63. I.R.C. § 213(a) (medical care expenses of the taxpayer, the taxpayer's spouse, or dependent, not otherwise compensated for, are deductible only if they exceed 7.5 percent of the taxpayer's adjusted gross income).

64. Zelinsky, *supra* note 10, at 315.

65. Bennett Harrison, Lean and Mean: The Changing Landscape of Corporate Power in the Age of Flexibility 195 (1994).

66. Bankman, *supra* note 21, at 597.

67. Russell W. Coff & Eric G. Flamholtz, *Corporate Investments in Human Capital: How Financial Accounting Standards Undermine Public Policy,* 5 Stan. L. & Pol'y Rev. 31 (1993).

68. *Id.*

69. *Id.*

70. *Id.*

71. *See, e.g.,* Harrison, *supra* note 65, at 20–26.

72. Bankman, *supra* note 21.

73. Arne L. Kalleberg, *Part-Time Work and Workers in the United States: Correlates and Policy Issues,* 52 Wash. & Lee L. Rev. 771 (1995).

74. *Id.* at 777–78.

75. Eileen Appelbaum, *Introduction: Structural Change and the Growth of Part-Time and Temporary Employment, in* Economic Policy Inst., New Policies for the Part-Time and Contingent Workforce 1, 4 (Virginia L. duRivage ed., 1992) [hereinafter EPI]; *see* Richard S. Belous, *The Rise of the Contingent Workforce: The Key Challenges and Opportunities,* 52 Wash. & Lee L. Rev. 863, 871 (1995).

76. Kalleberg, *supra* note 73, at 780–82.

77. Belous, *supra* note 75, at 874, table 5; *see* Jonathan P. Hiatt & Lynn Rhinehart, *The Growing Contingent Work Force: A Challenge for the Future,* 10 Lab. Law. 143, 148 (1994) (reporting that studies show that a part-time worker identical in industry, occupation, sex, age, and other characteristics to a full-time worker still earns an average of from 10 percent to 15 percent less per hour).

78. Hiatt & Rhinehart, *supra* note 77, at 148–49.

79. *Id.* at 149; *see* Kalleberg, *supra* note 73, at 782.

80. Kalleberg, *supra* note 73, at 782–83.

81. *See* Belous, *supra* note 75, at 875, table 6 (reporting that from 48 percent to 49.5 percent of part-time workers have no coverage under an employer plan); Chris Tilly, *Short Hours, Short Shrift: The Causes and Consequences of Part-Time Employment, in* EPI, *supra* note 75, at 15, 22 (citing the Employee Benefits Research Institute report that approximately 42 percent of part-time workers have no direct or indirect employment-based health coverage).

82. Francoise J. Carre, *Temporary Employment in the Eighties, in* EPI, *supra* note 75, at 45, 56.

83. Howe, *supra* note 3, at 12.

84. *Id.* at 13.

6

CHARLOTTE CRANE

Shifting from an Income Tax to a Consumption Tax

Effects on Expenditures for Education

The existing income tax system relies heavily upon an appearance of objectivity and upon its potential for economic neutrality. Neither would be possible if the tax law did not limit itself to values that normally are subject to market transactions and if it did not adhere to an internal logic that requires that all previously taxed investments be allowed as offsets to income derived from market activities. Concerns about economic neutrality, however, have led to calls to transform the income tax base to tax only consumption. Many proponents of the consumption base have observed that the income tax could identify consumption easily merely by allowing a deduction from the existing income tax base for all values received and directed toward anticipation of future market income, regardless of when that future income might be received. Thus, a consumption tax would allow a deduction for all personal savings and for all investment in plant and equipment. Only values not reinvested and therefore assumed to be consumed would be subject to tax.

Both the existing income tax and the proposed consumption tax rely on the distinction between expenditures that anticipate future market participation, commonly thought of as "business" or "investment," and expenditures that do not, usually denoted "personal consumption."

146

Taxpayers may deduct from the tax base only those investments that they expect to yield future taxable income. However, we cannot divide human activity so easily. This is especially true for activities relating to the development of individual human potential, which this essay loosely refers to as *education*. Thus, it is not surprising that the tax law has difficulty when it encounters investments in human potential.

Parts 1 and 2 of the essay outline the ways in which the traditional income tax relies on the presence of market activity and tax logic to ensure the appearance of objectivity and to pursue economic neutrality and the inherent limitations on the tax law's efforts to achieve this neutrality. Part 3 then explores the ways in which the traditional tax law has responded to educational activities undertaken in anticipation of both market and nonmarket transactions. Finally, parts 4 and 5 suggest ways in which the transformation of the income tax into a consumption tax, without further consideration of the appropriate taxation of expenditures for education, would fall far short of the goal of economic neutrality with respect to expenditures for education.

I. THE LOGIC OF THE INCOME TAX

The income tax has long enjoyed a considerable degree of popularity within the ranks of liberal academics, both inside law schools (at least among those who know anything at all about the income tax) and outside. One source of that popularity is its potential for income redistribution, especially in the absence of a broad-based federal wealth tax. The income tax, however, remains popular even with those who would prefer to de-emphasize its potential for wealth redistribution. One source of this intellectual popularity is the sense that, although it is far from perfect, the income tax is logical and thus perfectible. This sense of perfectibility derives in part from the assumption that the income tax, if it were defined properly, could be a rational tax implemented entirely through the rule of law. The ideal tax would take all values into account and would ascertain a person's tax liability with neither the arbitrariness inherent in particularized classifications, which is the bane of customs and excise taxes, nor the lack of precision and subjectivity inherent in assessment of values, which is the weakness of property tax schemes. Of course, the income tax has not avoided either pitfall, but reformers ordinarily see these problems as unfortunate details in the implementation of the tax that do not affect the soundness of the tax system.

This apparent perfectibility of the definition of the income tax in turn derives from the prevailing economic model for the tax base. The model, usually attributed to Henry Simons but not uniquely his contribution, insists that enhancements in wealth and all consumption be included in the tax base.[1] An income tax under that model is one in which all values relevant to the tax are taxed but are taxed only once. If taxpayers make investments that are likely to produce additional taxable income in the future, they must identify the investments so that they can offset them against later income to ensure that only new wealth is taxed. The model allows a logical reference point from which to define the base. Under it, the identification of the values, the timing of this identification, and accounting for values previously subject to tax are the critical issues. Within its logic the Simons model promises resolution of all uncertainties regarding base definition.

The model, within certain boundaries explored more fully below, allows the income tax to aspire to economic neutrality, in the sense of creating as little interference with productive economic activity as possible. It allows economic activity to take place on a level playing field without distortions resulting from the operation of the tax. What is more, partisan politics and the whim of the tax collector need play no role in the design or implementation of the tax. Government can impose the taxes needed for its support entirely through the operation of law.

Thus, the base-defining rules of the income tax provide it with a logical structure amenable to deductive legal reasoning. This logical structure generally is not available to sales taxes, which can operate only on arbitrarily limited bases, or property taxes, which not only operate on limited bases but also construct values where no market has operated to reveal them. The claim of income tax logic has allowed intricate tax rules to develop without (yet) collapsing entirely from their own weight. We can interpret the language of the Internal Revenue Code (Code) not just by looking at its inelegant prose but also by referring to its internal logic. However, regardless of whether any particular exegesis of the Code limits itself to the text, the logical structure of the Code remains available.

Tax logic also has provided a semblance of uniform enforcement because every transaction is analyzed in terms of the same logic. If we could gather enough facts to understand the true economic consequences of the transactions at hand, the logic would produce correct answers to any issue that arises. If the Code fails to achieve the correct answer for any given case, it is because Congress has enacted language that seems to reach a different result. If, however, Congress endorsed the economic model more fully and stopped trying to write detailed statutory language that intentionally or unintentionally invites exceptions to the logic, the Code could reach the correct answer.

Tax logic is not the sole reason for the success of the income tax as a source of revenue; certain nonlogical aspects of the income tax, including wage withholding, are equally important. However, we must have an appreciation of tax logic to understand the appeal of the income tax. It is no accident that the income tax has flourished during the same era in which the legal process movement has been most successful. Both phenomena rely upon a belief in the perfectibility of legal outcomes through the rational application of objective principles. Both allow reliance on a similar notion of the rule of law, which operates abstractly and without the need for subjective judgment, at least until the details must be considered.

2. THE MARKETPLACE LIMITATIONS

Several practical limitations prevent the achievement of economic neutrality. Perhaps the most commonly acknowledged limitation relates to the timing of income and the consequent offsets to that income that create a gap between the base defined under the constraints of realization and the base defined under a true accretion tax. The tax law strives to treat all returns on investment and effort in anticipation of market returns equally. However, the income tax cannot tax returns to investment and effort at the same rate unless it can identify with precision the time at which the returns occur.

There is a more fundamental limitation on economic neutrality and perfectibility of the income tax that proposals for reform less often address. The income tax base cannot be economically neutral regarding human behavior unless it includes all anticipated returns to that behavior. Generally, the traditional income tax accounts only for returns derived from participation in the marketplace. It taxes only values received in market transactions and counts as investments only those made in anticipation of market transactions. When we use market criteria as a sole referent for the values subject to tax, we overlook returns toward which we intentionally have made prior investments, which we may make inside or outside the marketplace. We overlook anticipated nonmarket or household returns. These overlooked returns include those self-created values commonly referred to as *imputed income,* such as the value of doing one's own laundry, of mowing one's lawn, or of entertaining oneself by playing a musical instrument. We also are likely to fail to account for investments in the *potential* to create nonmarket returns. The market criteria overlook the efforts of parents raising children, of the public formally educating children, and of individuals' own efforts to improve their personal potential in ways that do not anticipate immediate market returns.

There surely is nothing wrong with deciding to overlook these values. If we choose to do so, however, we no longer can pretend that the income tax has no impact on economic behavior. The effect on human behavior will depend upon whether taxpayers respond to these overlooked returns by investing more heavily in them than they would if these returns were not overlooked. But if we choose not to overlook these values, we must develop criteria outside of market transactions for identifying and for measuring them. If we do not use market criteria, implementation of the income tax will require subjective judgments, if only to determine what tangible things and intangible states we should count as taxable returns.

It is just at this point that the objective and economically neutral income tax founders. The income tax must measure and include *all* returns in the tax base if it is to affect *all* investment or return-seeking activity equally. There are, however, limits on what the income tax can count as returns and how it can measure those returns. The tax base, without sacrificing its purported objectivity, cannot include those things for which there is no independent measure. Independent measurement requires a system of commensurable values so that returns can be compared to each other.

Market transactions establishing prices allow for meaningful comparisons of the value of returns. The income tax simply cannot include those things that normally are not subject to market transactions or for which there are no ready market substitutes without losing its claim to objectivity. Comfort, companionship, pleasure, and entertainment, while all being susceptible to market transactions, are far more often enjoyed without participation in the market. Thus the nonmarket values toward which most human effort is expended are beyond the reach of an income tax that requires market transactions.

In truth, despite its aspiration to include all new wealth and all consumption, the income tax can identify and can measure only intermediate goods. It can include only the amounts that we choose to spend on things that we expect to make us comfortable and to entertain us. It must limit its scope to those items of commerce used as means toward nonmarket ends. The tax law presumes that there is no value except those values revealed through market transactions. The tax law thus is forced to ignore values produced and consumed entirely outside the marketplace. It does not count goods or services created and enjoyed without market participation, even when a market for those goods or services is identifiable.

Just as any investment property has no value except that which is derived from its anticipated cash flow, items of commerce have no inherent value except for their ultimate anticipated consumption value. The tax law presumes that intermediate values revealed through market transactions ultimately provide an equivalent amount of consumption value. It therefore ignores values lost or gained after taxpayers enter into market transactions by presuming that taxpayers realized all expected returns and no more than expected returns on investment in consumer goods.

This weakness in identifying the precise return included in the income tax need not be a fatal flaw. The income tax has survived and can continue to survive merely by finessing instances in which the determinations of more particularized value are the hardest and by substituting presumptions that minimize intolerable error. Simons himself was acutely aware of the limitations on the definition of income and hence on the need for presumptions. One of his major contributions to the ongoing debate about the income tax base was that he outlined those presumptions that we should use and identified criteria for evaluating whether the errors produced by the presumptions were tolerable given the public policy of income redistribution.[2]

These presumptions are implicit in most of the basic rules distinguishing consumption from investment. Thus, the tax law presumes that an employee who is required to accept lodging on the business premises acquires no consumption value. It does not presume that she experienced a negative return for her services, which might be the case, for instance, if she has young children and must pay someone else to care for them. It also does not presume a positive return, which might be the case if she has no family and the business premises are a fancy resort hotel. The tax law presumes that anyone purchasing durable consumer goods has extracted the anticipated return from the asset, at least in the absence of a casualty. Therefore, it presumes that an owner of a pleasure boat that succumbs to dry rot has extracted at least as much return from the boat as she anticipated when she paid for it, regardless of her actual use of the boat. The tax laws take the market price of the consumer good as an adequate substitute for returns on investment, regardless of the time period over which the consumer enjoys the good.[3]

A similar presumption is implicit in the notion that any investment, whether business or personal, that the taxpayer cannot show to produce a specific finite return or useful life produces an infinite return. The tax law presumes, for example, that investments in goodwill and related intangibles or in land used for waste disposal produce a limitless return, because taxpayers cannot establish a finite return. Although many of the hard cases in which this presumption might be invoked have been resolved or reversed by statute, the operation of the presumption to avoid an impossible factual determination about the duration of the return is common. For instance, the presumption denies recovery for the cost of landfills that will be filled someday and for skill-specific professional training that will produce income for many years. Through the use of these types of simplifying presumptions, the income tax has proved robust. The presumptions, however, result only in obfuscating the weak spots in tax logic; they do not resolve the conundrums.

Because the income tax always has been associated with at least a nominal degree of progressivity, we might assume that reliance on market transactions and the monetized values that accompany them simply is a function of its redistributive potential. The limitations inherent in reliance on market transactions, however, would be necessary even if the income tax abandoned all pretense of serving a redistributional purpose. Moreover, the income tax operates on the principle that it should measure only those returns that taxpayers can liquidate readily. Otherwise, the tax laws might lead to liabilities that taxpayers either could not pay, or could pay only if they engage in additional economic activity.

Despite the considerable attention given to the problems associated with the timing of income and returns from traditional financial transactions, commentators have given relatively little attention to the more profound inability of the income tax to take into account nonmarket values. It is not by accident that tax logic has downplayed certain aspects of the tax law's inability to treat all returns on investment and effort neutrally. Most of those theorists who devoted their time to questions of base definition likely made significant investments only where market values were a sufficient, if not the principal, return motivating their own investment. Like Mr. Banks in *Mary Poppins*,[4] these theorists were able to treat as inconsequential any investment that did not anticipate a return of values tradable in a market. Mr. Banks could not imagine a world in which it might be more important to feed the birds than to deposit twopence at interest. Similarly, most of those who have contributed to income tax theory have not imagined a world that includes significant choices between household and market production. The economic neutrality consequences of ignoring this aspect of human investment seemed, when noticed at all, to be just another clearly tolerable error.

3. THE DEVELOPMENT OF HUMAN POTENTIAL UNDER THE CURRENT INCOME TAX

Some education occurs in the context of regularized market transactions. People do buy through music lessons, yoga classes, and job skills training classes a significant amount of education. In many of the market contexts, the suppliers of education, taking into account the costs of providing the education, which include alternative uses for the resources devoted, set prices below which they will not provide the education. Prospective buyers of education make rational choices about whether to purchase education, by taking into account the costs of the education, both in terms of time and of after-tax investment, and the benefits of the education, both immediate and future, in achieving both intermediate market and ultimate personal values.

The great bulk of education, however, is provided outside the normal operation of competitive markets. This occurs as a result of the diversion to education of private resources within the family as well as of governmental resources. Parents do not as a general rule monitor their child-rearing efforts and resources to assure that they do not exceed the benefits received. Formal education outside the home is not likely to be subject to a competitive market. Public elementary and secondary schools are among the most suspect of institutions these days precisely because the rigors of the market economy only incompletely affect them. Even when private resources appear to be bidding openly for education, for instance, in the market for college education, the price charged rarely reflects the producers' costs, and the price actually paid by any purchaser is not likely to reflect ordinary competitive market forces.

Not only is investment in education often made in contexts that do not resemble competitive markets, but investment in education frequently is made without a clear sense of whether the return on that investment will result in taxable market activity or will result in a nonmarket, nontaxable return. Indeed, it frequently is difficult to classify education as an intermediate, rather than as an ultimate, good. Does a parent place a child in day care to allow the parent free time to earn wages (an intermediate good leading to taxable values), to enrich the child's future life (an intermediate good leading to nontaxable values), or to entertain the child (an ultimate nontaxable good)? Do those enrolled in adult-education computer courses expect to enhance their personal life (an intermediate good leading to nontaxable values), to improve their job skills (an intermediate good leading to taxable values), or simply to be entertained (an ultimate nontaxable good)?

When faced with questions about the creation and transfer of values concerning human potential, the income tax does not work well. It simply cannot account for activities that take place without any semblance of market activity, for example, activities entirely within the family. It accounts very poorly for those situations in which there are either expenditures to acquire education or other transfers of value associated with the acquisition of education that occur where markets likely do not operate, for example, in public and private formal education. Perhaps even more significantly, the tax laws rarely can identify investments in education as investments primarily directed toward future market activity or as investments primarily directed toward personal or household activity.

The presumptions made regarding the transfer of values concerning the development of human potential are among the least satisfactory of any of those adopted by the income tax. Although there are some deviations, the tax law treats virtually all investment made other than by employers in human potential as consumption. It treats all amounts expended by parents on behalf of their children as the parents' consumption. It attributes money paid to others to teach one's own children as consumption. It does not view the training and disciplining of children by parents and other family members as a taxable transfer. The law ignores parents' expenditures for their children as well as the children's receipt of the benefits of those expenditures. It does not allow a loss to parents, even in the face of a casualty, if they fail to realize a return on their investment in the upbringing and formal education of their children.

The tax law accounts for children by allowing parents a dependency exemption, but its operation bears little resemblance to accounting for the costs of raising a child as an investment.[5] It also allows a relatively small credit for child care purchased in the marketplace[6] or, alternatively, allows a relatively small exclusion for employer-provided child care.[7] Neither reflects the value given or received through the preschool education of children, whether it takes place in the home or elsewhere. Similarly, the accounting for costs of elementary and secondary education allowed through the deduction of local property and state income taxes is hardly an accurate surrogate for an accounting for the human potential value created or received.

The presumption that all development of human potential is consumption, rather than investment leading to taxable income, prevails in all but a very few limited contexts. In some instances it can be argued plausibly that the denial of a deduction for job-related education results not only from the presumption that the expenses are consumption but also from the presumption that they produce a yield of unlimited duration. Under the income tax, either presumption justifies a denial of an offset to income for the investment. The tax law does allow a few taxpayers to deduct the cost of investment in their own training. However, only taxpayers who are already employed may treat their personal investment in education as an investment in future market activity, and even then they may do so only if the anticipated effect on their productive lives is relatively minor.

In contrast, those who are employed and who receive training from their employer may exclude its value under the presumption that none of the training in fact amounts to consumption. This preference is not explicit in the rules as written. The rules purport to apply the same test to education expenses provided by employers and to education expenses paid for by employees.[8] Nevertheless, it is easy to find challenges to the claims for education expenses of individual employees in the reported cases, whereas challenges to education expenses of employers are rare.[9] Even if they were rigorously subject to the same standards, the tax laws allow employees to exclude education expenses paid by employers without regard to the constraints on itemized deductions, but those constraints do apply to deductible employee-paid expenses. For taxpayers who do not own their homes and therefore have limited itemized deductions, the deduction for itemized education expenses frequently is worthless.

The traditional notion that the tax laws should exclude scholarship income is a more significant exception to the presumption that all education is in fact consumption. Notably, however, this exclusion is treated under the tax expenditure budget as an expenditure, which indicates that it is unjustified under tax logic and represents a government subsidy to the taxpayer.[10] Since 1986 the Code has limited the exclusion to those expenses that clearly do not substitute for ordinary consumption expenses for housing and food. If others, whether the educational institution or third parties, are willing to subsidize an individual's education, that individual need not take those amounts into account when determining income. Perhaps the best explanation for the existence of this exception is the distinct possibility, given the market in which scholarships are used as subsidies, that the nominal value transferred in the name of the student does not represent its equivalent dollar value to the student if that value had been made available to the student for consumption. What students actually pay for an education at any given private institution does not indicate what they would have paid had there been open-market bidding for all educational opportunities. The stated tuition at any institution, whether public or private, simply is not a good surrogate either for the amount that any student would have been willing to pay for education at that institution or for the value she received from that education. In the absence of a scholarship, those at private institutions might well not have been willing to pay the full stated price, much less the actual price of producing the education they receive. Those at public institutions might well have been willing to pay more than the stated tuition price, given the large public subsidy many of the students enjoy.[11] This explanation means, however, that for scholarships the tax law abandons the presumption that amounts apparently spent for consumption actually have yielded an equivalent amount of consumption.

The tax law's current treatment of the development of human potential raises serious questions concerning economic neutrality. The Code ordinarily does not distinguish between personal investment in one's own ability to produce in anticipation of market activities and any other consumption value, despite the fact that only the former will subject the investor to tax at a later stage as well. Neither does the Code distinguish between those who contribute their own or family funds for higher education and those who benefit from the contribution of other taxpayers within their state, or those who benefit from the largesse of scholarship-providing foundations, even though only the former have included these values as consumption in their income. If taxpayers use their own funds, they may take a deduction for the amount spent on education only if they already have acquired sufficient skills to be employed, and then only when the enhancement in their education is incremental and is not likely to result in a change in job definition. Only if an employer has paid these expenditures directly are they likely to be fully honored as expenditures with no consumption component. These rules and presumptions, furthermore, embody a very restrictive view of human activity. They apply more easily to individuals with one set of skills who are likely to use those skills for production in one activity for one employer. Of course, the impossibility of distinguishing between development of human potential that creates marketplace values, which will be taxed, and the development of human potential that creates nontaxed values adequately explains these rules. Just because these errors are unavoidable does not mean they should not be acknowledged as errors.

4. PUSHING TAX LOGIC: THE ELIMINATION OF THE INVESTMENT COMPONENT OF INCOME

If we do not take the income tax too seriously, we need not see many of its logical dead ends, perhaps even those dealing with the development of human potential, as intolerable flaws. Tax logic serves the income tax well. The structure allows the tax law to remain internally coherent and therefore self-perpetuating. The logic allows for lawyers' arguments about the meaning of particular statutory language. We can prefer a particular reading of a statute because we think it produces the least tension with the overall logic of the tax law. The logic also provides a language useful for internal critiques. Reformers can promote a statutory change on the ground either that it is consistent with the tax logic and that it moves the tax base closer to the ideal, or that the proposed change, although not consistent with the tax logic, is a deviation made necessary by some other imperfection in current practice.

But we can take tax logic too far. It has led relatively friendly critics of the income tax to suggest that Congress could improve the income tax by eliminating the wealth enhancement or investment component of the traditional tax base. Several persistent proposals urge that only values deemed to have been consumed should be included in the tax base.[12] Congress could transform the traditional income tax into a consumption tax relatively easily by allowing deductions for all amounts devoted to business purposes or otherwise invested in contemplation of a future taxable return. Under a cash-flow consumption tax, taxpayers could deduct from the tax base any amount invested in a way that anticipated a taxable return, but they later must include the amount in the tax base when they realize the return. Business meals, computer purchases, and stock investments would be deductible, because they represent investments made with future taxable income in mind, regardless of when that income actually might be realized. Only consumption—that is, expenditures not recognized as investments in anticipation of future market production—would remain in the tax base.

The proponents of a consumption tax contend that it would allow the income tax to be economically neutral in its effect upon decisions between savings and consumption. Those with a preference for savings no longer would have that preference hindered by a tax on the return from savings. The flaw inherent in the income tax resulting from the disincentive to save, at least in the ways that count as savings for the purpose of the tax, would be eliminated. Proponents claim that another advantage of the consumption tax is that it would eliminate the myriad accounting problems that result from trying to determine when investments are made and when returns are realized. Less than perfect resolution of each of these timing problems inevitably detracts from the economic neutrality of the current income tax.

The disincentive to save inherent in the income tax derives from the prevailing presumption that whatever value results from a taxpayer's choice to accelerate consumption should not be included in the tax base. Unless the value of accelerated consumption is taxed, the income tax induces a potential saver to accelerate consumption, a component of which, if it has any value, remains untaxed. Since 1986, by including loan proceeds in the tax base without allowing a deduction for interest paid with respect to that debt, the value of some of this acceleration has been included in the income tax base, albeit incompletely. This treatment of loan proceeds still fails to tax those who accelerate consumption by consuming immediately upon realizing spendable values.

Indeed, the proponents of a cash-flow consumption tax contend that the current tax laws fail to account properly for the consumption value that is forgone when a realized value is not consumed but saved. Accordingly, they argue that the traditional income tax imposes a tax on the same value twice. For example, a taxpayer has income when she earns $1,000. Even though she is taxed upon earning the $1,000 because she is able to consume the $1,000 immediately, when she chooses to save these funds and to earn $100, the tax law takes the increase in her cash position into account but not the detriment resulting from her deferred consumption. She is in some senses no better off after the passage of time than she was before she decided to save, and yet she is taxed on the full amount of her interest earned. Two alternatives could rectify this situation and avoid the disincentive to save. First, the tax law could charge all those who realize values but who consume them immediately with the return they could have received—that is, impute interest forever on all values received. Second, the tax law could ignore the returns received by those who choose to delay consumption. The latter is the choice most often urged within academic circles and is the only one to emerge in any political proposal.

These proposals for altering the income tax base thus would eliminate the disincentive to save when that saving would produce values that later would be included in income. The consumption tax proposals would result in a substantial contraction of the tax base and a related increase in the rate to be applied to that contracted base. In addition, with only consumption left in the base, eliminating the disincentive to save would only place more pressure on the faulty means that have been developed for distinguishing investment from consumption.

5. APPLYING THE EXTENDED TAX LOGIC OF THE CONSUMPTION TAX TO THE DEVELOPMENT OF HUMAN POTENTIAL

Most proponents of a cash-flow consumption tax do not anticipate other substantial changes in the traditional approach to base-defining problems.[13] Several academic discussions have noted the problems but have not addressed them rigorously. Few of the current proposals even bother to mention issues relating to the distinction between consumption and investment. If anything, the proponents anticipate an overall simplifying effect. Thus, the presumption that all expenditures that do not anticipate a market return directly lead to consumption would likely survive these proposed changes.

The proponents of the move to a consumption tax appear not to have considered whether the resulting errors regarding the taxation of investments in human potential would remain tolerable. On the contrary, they cite the inability to account for human capital as an additional justification for the move to a consumption tax. In one exercise supporting the move to the consumption tax, Louis Kaplow demonstrates that, under his simplifying assumptions, the current income tax favors the returns on human capital over the returns on financial capital (used here to refer to tangible and intangible assets). He suggests that this favorable tax treatment prevails even though returns on most financial capital are subject to realization rules that tax them relatively late, whereas returns on human capital generally are taxed upon receipt.[14] He argues that human capital should be taxed as it accumulates because that treatment parallels the general tax treatment of the accumulation of financial capital. Thus, he concludes that the income tax should tax each individual in a way that acknowledges the presence of human capital at birth. Kaplow does not propose that the Code actually impose a tax at birth, but instead he proposes that the Code tax wages at a higher rate to compensate for the failure to tax the accumulation of human capital in a timely fashion. Kaplow's scheme does not account for any costs, market or otherwise, of that human capital except for the relatively trivial forgone wages and cash outlays that may occur at later stages in the wage earner's life. These outlays have a relatively small impact on the total value present at birth, because, in general, they represent only a relatively small shift in the timing of the consumption of the value received. Also problematic is Kaplow's assumption that human and financial capital are unrelated and easily distinguished. He does not consider, for instance, that taxpayers may transform the returns on their effort into returns on financial capital.

Kaplow's presentation is, in fact, only an elaboration on the arguments of others. The proponents of a cash-flow consumption tax frequently argue that current law already taxes returns to human capital on a consumption-tax basis; that is, it taxes wages as they are earned rather than when the potential to earn wages develops. Under this view returns to human potential are favored, because the tax law fails to tax the human capital from which wages arise. Some have suggested that the Code's failure to allow a deduction for the costs of human capital, at least in the case of tuition paid for formal education, compensates for the Code's failure to tax the acquisition of value in the form of human capital as the education occurs. They note that tax laws do not allow a deduction for the interest paid on loans to fund education.[15] These two offsetting errors may produce a tolerable result. Noteworthy is that the economic literature suggests that no definitive answer is possible regarding the question of bias against or in favor of investment in human capital.[16]

However, even on its own terms, there are flaws in the argument's logic. To the extent that we use human capital to contribute to the value of financial capital, returns to the combined investment enjoy some of the same benefits under the income tax that would be available under a consumption tax.[17] A failure to account for the acquisition of human capital justifies a move to a consumption tax only if we assume both that only relatively small additions to human potential are acquired with after-tax values and that wages and ultimate consumption values are the only return to human capital. Indeed, it is entirely possible that given the incentives present under the current income tax, the contribution of human capital to the value of financial capital and to returns on that combined capital is in the same order of magnitude as the wage return to human capital. Proponents of the consumption tax cannot justify a move to it in terms of the relative advantage enjoyed by human capital under the income tax without taking a more careful look at the effect of the move on behaviors remaining subject to tax. If only consumption is included in the tax base, the stakes involved in presuming that all expenditures seeking an increase in human potential reflect consumption would obviously be greater, if only because rate increases necessarily must accompany base narrowing.

The severity and undesirability of the tax base change would depend upon the identity of the particular taxpayers most severely affected. The greatest impact would likely fall on those who spend a relatively large portion of their after-tax income on education that seems most closely related to income production, for instance, night school tuition and child care. For a taxpayer earning $25,000 a year and spending $5,000 on night school tuition, the proposed change would increase the rate at which the taxpayer is taxed erroneously on 20 percent of her income. For a taxpayer earning $20,000 a year and paying $5,000 a year for child care, the proposed change would exacerbate an error affecting 25 percent of her income. Few of the proposals offer any features that would mitigate the effect of these errors.

Although the increased stakes for many taxpayers would lead to calls for further refinement of the lines between investment and consumption, the presumption that all ambiguous expenditures relating to human potential are consumption would take on particular importance under the consumption tax. Could the familiar presumption that virtually all individual taxpayer investment in human potential is not likely to result in a taxable return survive the pressure that the consumption tax would place upon it? Given the scholarly attention to the issue, one might think that the presumption was barely holding its own even under the traditional income tax.[18]

Any increased tendency to treat expenditures such as child care and tuition as investments in market wages might threaten to leave little tax base at all. At some level, child care and tuition differ from food and shelter only in that they are not shared by all taxpayers. It may not be easy to establish the degree to which any particular taxpayer purchases those items in anticipation of future income, nor may it be easy to distinguish those items from other costs that taxpayers would not incur except for the need to earn in the market. One writer has even used the impossibility of excluding investment in human potential under a consumption tax as proof of the inappropriateness of viewing it as investment under the income tax at all.[19]

Ignoring the income-related component of an education expenditure, however, is more difficult to justify under a consumption tax than under an income tax. Under the consumption tax, investments in human capital would be subject to tax, but all other investments would enjoy an immediate deduction. Investments in human capital no longer would share the same adverse tax treatment as other investments for which there appears to be no finite return. Instead, under the consumption tax, investment in our own, or our family's, human potential would become the only investment that we must make in after-tax values.

Expenditures for education that we can explain fully by their potential to produce taxable income and for which the consumption component appears trivial demonstrate most clearly why issues regarding investments in human capital would be exacerbated under the consumption tax. Tuition for an advanced degree in actuarial science achieved as a night student at a commuter campus might be an example of an educational expenditure having a negligible consumption component. The consumption tax, just like the present income tax, would allow a deduction for cash expenditures for the tuition, if the taxpayer spent the money in anticipation of immediate taxable income. However, the consumption tax should allow a deduction for any expenditure in anticipation of any future taxable income, not just those expenditures promising an immediate market return. If the taxpayer anticipates only future income, we can justify the failure to provide any amortization deduction for the tuition under the income tax on the grounds both that the appropriate amortization period is so long a period that the deductible amounts are trivial and that there is no decline in the value of the acquired potential over the taxpayer's life. On either ground any error inherent in not allowing amortization deductions is tolerable. No similar justifications are available for failure to allow a deduction under the consumption tax. Neither duration of return nor uncertainty of declining value should prevent a deduction for investment under a cash-flow consumption tax. Consequently, the error involved in invoking a presumption that all education is ultimately consumption would have far greater impact under the consumption tax.

Allowing an immediate deduction for a broad range of expenditures relating to education and other human development probably would not be satisfactory either. As is the case with the use of certain arguably excludable fringe benefits under the current income tax, such a deduction could entice taxpayers to construct transactions that appear to meet educational investment criteria to avoid taxation on its consumption component. Canny taxpayers easily could contrive returns on educational expenses that, in fact, include large, but hard to identify, consumption components. For example, executive retreats at business schools and parents' events at private colleges might well last weeks instead of days. The tendency under a consumption tax for taxpayers to seek cash investments that provide returns in the form of consumption might be a problem of relatively minor significance in defining the consumption tax base. This form of tax avoidance, however, would be available far more readily, as many fringe benefits are now, to those with relatively greater disposable incomes. The errors made in resolving these uncertainties could well have undesirable distributional consequences.

Perhaps the lack of attention to issues relating to education and other nonmarket values under a consumption tax comes from a general sense that inappropriate results would be too unsystematic to be worthy of attention. This perception is not surprising to the extent it is held by those analysts who rarely deal with the problems inherent in defining the individual tax base. Alternatively, perhaps the lack of attention is based on the assumption that the continuation of the familiar presumptions would have tolerable impacts. In some cases this may be true. The continued lack of deduction for tuition, for instance, in absolute dollar amounts, would affect most severely those who have the choice to pay high tuitions to private institutions. If the consumption tax retained any pretense to redistribution, this would be an acceptable result. However, looking exclusively at absolute dollar amounts obscures other redistributional issues. The continued presumption that all tuition payments should be treated as consumption would affect most keenly those who do not have the financial means to attend private colleges or universities, that is, those whose before-tax paycheck might have covered both community college tuition and housing, but whose after-tax paycheck clearly cannot.

The acceptability of the errors resulting from a continuation of the presumption that virtually all individual taxpayer spending for education is consumption would be even more questionable if its companion presumption, that all investment in human capital directed by employers is investment, also survived. The combined effect of these presumptions would be that those whose skills allowed them to obtain jobs in the first place could receive additional employer-provided or -funded training tax free, whereas those without jobs would suffer under the presumption that their expenditures were mere consumption and therefore must be made with after-tax dollars.

Although the proponents of a consumption tax acknowledge these problems, they do not acknowledge the consequences of the presumption in human terms. David Bradford, for example, considers the anticipated effects of a move to a consumption tax on incentives to invest in human potential.[20] His principal contention is that the move to a consumption tax would not change the "description of the taxation" of education, although it would change "the description of the taxation of interest," and that, consequently, it is not necessary to view the difficulties in developing this description as an obstacle to the move to the consumption tax. According to Bradford, the problems inherent in developing the description are present in both taxes and therefore, should not trouble the proponent of the consumption tax.

Bradford illustrates the problem in the income tax by outlining the mechanism by which the failure to allow a deduction for education under the income tax would result in more investments in human capital that can be made in pretax dollars. He demonstrates that the investment made in after-tax dollars clearly would be disfavored when compared to the investment in the form of forgone earnings. However, he does not tell us much about the mechanism by which the investment in forgone earnings would be accomplished. He simply asserts that the pretax investment of forgone earnings would "take the form of reduced earnings in my current job." Is the earnings reduction the result of an employer's decision to substitute training for cash wages or the result of the individual taxpayer's decision to invest her own pretax efforts outside the marketplace? Bradford does not tell us, but he assumes there to be no difference relevant to the choice of tax base. More importantly, he fails to note that the effect of the disparity between after-tax and pretax investment under the income tax would be exaggerated under the consumption tax. Investments in human potential would be the only after-tax investments under the consumption tax.

With a consumption tax that, like the traditional income tax, continued to rely on market transactions and the presumption that all individual investment in human potential is consumption, taxpayers likely would attempt to obtain tax-free consumption values using either of the two strategies just suggested. They could try to extract consumption values through cash investments that appear to anticipate marketplace returns, or they could invest in human potential using untaxed values, that is, investing effort entirely outside the marketplace. Nonmarket efforts likely mean investment in the family through nonmarket and household activities. Thus, the force of the logic behind the consumption tax, to eliminate the disincentive to save after realizing market returns, would inevitably exaggerate the disincentive to participate in market transactions at all.

Why earn a wage to pay for a child's lesson, rather than stay home and teach the lesson (albeit poorly) oneself, if the wage is to be so heavily taxed that the lesson cannot be afforded? For many of the proponents of the consumption tax, this disincentive to market participation, even when exaggerated under the consumption tax, is of little consequence, because the choice to participate in market activities seems hardly a choice to them. If marketplace participation is unavoidable, investment in marketplace participation will be made almost regardless of how adversely it is taxed. For some women, however, market participation still appears to be a choice that requires conscious investment to pursue. Unlike their male counterparts, some women constantly are reminded of how their decision to invest in marketplace returns is disfavored, even without an income tax bias. Inappropriately, heavy taxation of their investment in marketplace activities is far more likely to affect the level of their investment.

In summary, the enhanced preference under the consumption tax for investment in untaxed values that in turn yield nonmarket returns would be likely to induce even more nonmarket investment that probably would not lead to marketplace returns. Similarly, we could expect an increase in employer-provided education, which in effect would allow an investment of pretax values in human potential, because it would receive preferred tax treatment. In contrast, we could expect personal investment in education and in other forms of human capital to decline under the greater relative burden it would bear under the consumption tax.

Those who are not in a position to respond to this change in the incentive to participate in the marketplace, but for whom an increase in the relative price of investment in marketplace skills would affect the level of investment that is possible, would feel even worse effects. Many remain compelled to participate in market transactions for cash returns even though the tax law treats their investments in their ability to so participate as consumption and requires them to make that investment in after-tax values. These individuals may have very few choices for enhancing their earning capacity, but they are likely to find that the one choice that they do have, investing wages in education, would be the least favored use of their after-tax values under the consumption tax. Only these investments would remain subject to the double tax on investment that prompted the move to the consumption tax in the first place.

MORE MODEST ASPIRATIONS FOR THE INCOME TAX

Tax logic has served the income tax well, and, if employed only to answer those questions that arise within a tax base, the principal contours of which are established through external criteria, it can continue to serve a useful purpose. It simply is not useful in establishing the contours themselves. Tax logic tells us nothing about whether the tax law should favor investment in human potential or investment in financial capital. The desirability of additional investment in human potential and the form that investment takes are policy decisions that we should make independent of tax logic.

NOTES

1. *See* Henry C. Simons, Personal Income Taxation 50 (1938).
2. *See, e.g., id.* at 54 ("[the] drastic expedient of treating all outlays for augmenting personal

earning capacity as consumption" is a presumption that "has little more than empty, formal, legalistic justification"); *id.* at 120 (supporting the presumption that consumption must be measured by the dollar value of goods).

3. *See* Daniel I. Halperin, *Valuing Personal Consumption: Cost versus Value and the Impact of Insurance,* 1 Fla. Tax Rev. 1 (1992).

4. Pamela L. Travers, Mary Poppins (1934).

5. *See* I.R.C. § 151.

6. *See id.* at § 21.

7. *See id.* at § 129.

8. *See id.* at § 127 (allowing employers to provide both training and money to pay for education); *see also* S. Rep. No. 1263, 95th Cong., 2d Sess. 98 (1978) (explaining that §127 was enacted to avoid the difficulties of applying the standards of the treasury regulations to courses taken under the direction of and paid for by employers).

9. *See, e.g., Love Box Co., Inc. v. Commissioner,* 842 F.2d 1213 (10th Cir.), *cert. denied* 488 U.S. 820 (1988) (denying deduction for costs taxpayer incurred in sponsoring seminars on self-reliance attended by employees).

10. For further discussion of tax expenditures, see Gwen Thayer Handelman, *Acknowledging Workers in Definitions of* Consumption *and* Investment: *The Case of Health Care,* this volume.

11. *See* Charlotte Crane, *Scholarships and the Federal Income Tax Base,* 28 Harv. J. on Legis. 63, 69–74 (1991).

12. *See, e.g.,* Irving Fisher, The Spending Tax, 18–20 (Bulletin of the Nat'l Tax Ass'n 1921); Nicholas Kaldor, An Expenditure Tax (1955); William Vickery, Agenda for Progressive Taxation (1947); Irving Fisher, *Income in Theory and Practice and Income Taxation in Practice,* 5 Econometrica 1 (1937); *see also* David F. Bradford & U.S. Treasury Tax Policy Staff Reform, Blueprints for Basic Tax Reform (2d ed. Rev. 1984) (a more recent and influential contribution that includes analysis of the relationship of the consumption tax base to the traditional income tax base); Robert E. Hall & Alvin Rabushka, Low Tax, Simple Tax, Flat Tax (1983) (popularizing the concept of the flat tax); William D. Andrews, *A Consumption-Type or Cash Flow Personal Income Tax,* 87 Harv. L. Rev. 1113 (1974) (an influential contribution that, like Bradford's, includes analysis of the relationship of the consumption tax base to the traditional income tax base).

13. *See, e.g.,* Richard L. Doernberg, *A Workable Flat Rate Consumption Tax,* 70 Iowa L. Rev. 425, 456–57 (1985) (noting with approval the Hall-Rabushka proposal's failure to even mention the problem, although commenting upon the disparity between the likely treatment of employer investment and employee investment); Michael J. Graetz, *Implementing a Progressive Consumption Tax,* 92 Harv. L. Rev. 1575, 1589 (1979) (noting that education is more likely to be deductible under the consumption tax); George K. Yin, *Accommodating the "Low-Income" in a Cash-flow or Consumed Income Tax World,* 2 Fla. Tax. Rev. 445, 453 (1995) (noting the substantial stakes for low-income students).

14. *See* Louis Kaplow, *Human Capital under an Ideal Income Tax,* 80 Va. L. Rev. 1477 (1994).

15. *See, e.g.,* Mary Louise Fellows, *A Comprehensive Attack on Tax Deferral,* 88 Mich. L. Rev. 722, 780–83 (1990).

16. *See* George R. Zodrow & Charles E. McLure, *Direct Consumption Taxes,* 46 Tax L. Rev. 407, 449 n.130.

17. *See* Andrews, *supra* note 12, at 1145.

18. *See, e.g.,* Loretta C. Argrett, *Tax Treatment of Higher Education Expenditures: An Unfair Investment Disincentive,* 41 Syracuse L. Rev. 621 (1990); David S. Davenport, *Education and Human Capital: Pursuing an Ideal Income Tax and a Sensible Tax Policy,* 42 Case W. Res. L. Rev. 793 (1992); David S. Davenport, *The "Proper" Taxation of Human Capital,* 52 Tax Notes 1401 (1991);

Joseph Isenberg, *The End of Income Taxation*, 45 Tax L. Rev. 283, 310 (1990); Brian Lebowitz, On the Mistaxation of Investment in Human Capital, 52 Tax Notes 825 (1991); Christopher R. J. Pace, *The Problem of High-Cost Education and the Potential Cure in Federal Tax Policy: "One Riot, One Ranger,"* 20 J.L. & Educ. 1 (1991); Clifford Gross, Comment, *Tax Treatment of Education Expenses: Perspectives from Normative Theory*, 55 U. Chi. L. Rev. 916 (1988).

19. *See* Joseph M. Dodge, *Taxing Human Capital Acquisition Costs—Or Why Costs of Higher Education Should Not Be Deducted or Amortized*, 54 Ohio St. L.J. 927, 957–59 (1993).

20. *See* David F. Bradford, Untangling the Income Tax 205–6 (1986).

7

DENISE D. J. ROY

Consumption in Business/Investment at Home

Environmental Cleanup Costs versus Disability Access Costs

A recent Internal Revenue Service (IRS) ruling exposes the inadequacies of the personal/business dichotomy that is a mainstay in traditional tax analysis. On June 2, 1994, the IRS ruled that expenses of removing PCB-contaminated soil from a taxpayer's property and backfilling with uncontaminated soil may be currently deducted.[1] The public ruling ended a controversy that began when the IRS ruled privately that the cleanup costs should be capitalized.[2] Stunned by the capitalization ruling, taxpayers reacted swiftly and unanimously in arguing that capitalization (1) does not clearly reflect income and (2) would discourage cleanup efforts in contravention of U.S. environmental policy.[3] They reacted with indignation to a legislative proposal to allow rapid (three- to five-year) amortization of cleanup costs, a significant improvement over the IRS's initial position.[4]

After soliciting reactions from taxpayers and wrestling with the issue for more than a year, the IRS finally capitulated and issued Rev. Rul. 94-38. Framing the issue as one of timing, the IRS ruled that the cleanup expenses are analogous to "repair" expenditures that may be currently deducted rather than capitalized. In reaching the current deduction outcome, the IRS ignored a bifurcation approach that would have required capitalization of a portion of the expenditure. This bifurcation approach has been used when taxpayers, due to physical disabilities, renovate their homes to make them accessible.[5]

The different treatment of environmental cleanup costs and disability access costs is a function of different assumptions about the productivity of expenses incurred in the business and in the personal realms. In starting with the timing question, the traditional business deduction analysis assumes that all nonpersonal business expenses produce income, thereby sidestepping the fundamental question whether such expenditure should be deducted against income at all. According to economic definitions of income, that fundamental question requires an inquiry into whether the expense is for the production of income or for consumption. The personal/business dichotomy makes an inquiry about consumption in the business-expense context appear irrelevant.

This essay criticizes the personal/business dichtomy by showing how it contributes to the anomalous distinction between the treatment of certain expenditures relating to medical care and the treatment of environmental cleanup costs. It concludes that the personal/business dichotomy derives its strength from its reflection and promotion of certain myths underlying the public/private split in American jurisprudence. Of particular relevance to this discussion are the myth that productivity is, and should be, the only goal of the business realm and the myth that productivity is limited to the business realm. Our continued uninterrogated acceptance of the personal/business dichotomy as an objective principle of income measurement can be traced to our failure to appreciate its value-laden role in allocating power and conferring legitimacy. Uncovering the inadequacies of the dichotomy and the role it plays in taxation has broad policy implications. As this essay shows, the equation of business with productivity is as much embedded in the structure of consumption tax proposals as it is in the structure of our income tax rules. Whether we choose to move to a consumption base or continue to rely primarily on an income tax, the personal/business dichotomy will continue to mask political choices about the scope of our tax base.

THE PERSONAL/BUSINESS DICHOTOMY

The deduction analysis on which the Internal Revenue Code (Code) is premised generally holds (among other things) that to measure income accurately, business expenses, which produce income, must be deducted, while personal expenses, which reflect consumption, must not be deducted (the personal/business dichotomy). The dichotomy is incorporated into the Code through provisions like section 162, which allows a deduction for "all the ordinary and necessary expenses . . . in carrying on any trade or business," and section 262, which disallows any deduction for "personal, living, or family expenses."

The personal/business dichotomy is justified on income measurement grounds in virtually every introductory federal income tax textbook.[6] The textbook I assign to my students, *Federal Income Taxation* by William Klein and Joseph Bankman, has three chapters on the deductibility of expenditures: "Personal Deductions, Exemptions, and Credits, " "Allowances for Mixed Business and Personal Outlays," and "Deductions for the Costs of Earning Income."[7] As the authors describe it, the first chapter addresses allowances "associated with purely personal circumstances or objectives," the third addresses allowances "associated with purely business or investment circumstances or objectives," and the second examines "the somewhat perplexing intermediate ground."[8] Klein and Bankman explain the significance of the personal/business dichotomy in their section on "The Role of the Personal Deduction:"

> Personal deductions are those that have nothing to do with the production of income. . . . On the one hand, a deduction may be a proper allowance in arriving at a definition of income that accords with our sense of justice; it may be a proper refinement of the concept of income as a measure of ability to pay. On the other hand, a deduction may be intended not as a refinement of the concept of income so much as an express approval of, or encouragement to, particular kinds of expenditures, in which case the deduction can sensibly be analogized to a direct subsidy.[9]

From these readings my students learn that expenditures fall along a range between personal and business deductions, with business deductions being allowed as a matter of justice (if one accepts the ability-to-pay rationale for the income tax) and personal deductions being allowed, if at all, as a subsidy. The allowance for business expenses is based on objective, neutral (and therefore indisputable) principles of income measurement, whereas any allowance for personal expenses is based on subjective, value-laden (and therefore disputable) judgments of the legislature. Business deductions are allowed as a matter of right; personal deductions are allowed, if at all, only as a privilege. Business expenses are productive; personal expenses are not.

The personal/business dichotomy forms the basis for many of the items included in the tax expenditure budget, which is published annually by the Joint Committee on Taxation and by the Administration.[10] "The tax expenditure budget depends on the notion that there is a natural, neutral or normal income tax and that it is possible to identify departures without great difficulty or dissent."[11] According to the Joint Committee on Taxation's tax expenditure budget for 1995–99, "departures" from the "natural, neutral or normal" income tax include exclusions or deductions for health care (including the deduction for disability access costs) and other personal expenses, such as child care, but do not include environmental cleanup costs or other ordinary and necessary business expenses.[12] Although "there is much legitimate debate over and genuine uncertainty about the proper contours of an income tax, . . . there does seem to be substantial agreement that most of the items on the published lists deserve to be there—that they achieve some purpose . . . other than the measurement of net income."[13] Again, the message is that the personal deductions included on the list provide a "subsidy" equivalent to a cash transfer payment, whereas business deductions excluded from the list are allowed to arrive at the "natural, neutral or normal" net income base.

Despite its persistent and central rule in tax analysis, the personal/business dichotomy is both too narrow and too broad with respect to its apparent goal of accurate measurement of income. It is too narrow in its implication that personal expenses are never productive. It is too broad in presuming that business expenses are always productive. In either realm, it remains appropriate to inquire instead whether expenses are for consumption or for production of income. Economists, at least in their analysis of the individual income tax,[14] have recognized its inadequacies, but the dichotomy's inadequacies seem to be ignored in the deduction analysis that is commonly used by lawyers and policymakers. Moreover, there appears to be no room for consumption in economists' definition of taxable business income.[15]

The personal/business dichotomy is also misleading in suggesting that business expenses must be allowed as a matter of objective, neutral justice, but that personal deductions are ideologically based and therefore vulnerable to repeal and limitation. Again, some economists have recognized that income is subjective and that administrative convenience, rather than truth, justifies use of objective definitions.[16] Others have noted the philosophical and political issues raised in distinguishing between consumption and investment expenditures.[17] As the formulation of the tax expenditure budget demonstrates, however, tax policy analysts persist in treating income measurement as a matter of science rather than political choice.

This essay reveals and challenges the fundamental presumption that the personal/business dichotomy achieves objective income measurement by contrasting the tax treatment of two kinds of expenditures: (1) expenditures to remove PCB-contaminated soil from the taxpayer's property and replace it with uncontaminated soil (cleanup costs)[18] and (2) "expenditures for removing structural barriers in a personal residence for the purpose of accommodating it to the handicapped condition of the taxpayer, taxpayer's spouse, or dependents who reside there" (access costs).[19] By focusing on a business expense that does not have any personal element, this essay goes beyond the mixed personal/business expense critique to challenge the core presumption that all nonpersonal business expenditures are productive.

COMPARISON OF CLEANUP COSTS AND ACCESS COSTS

Working Example/Overview

Cleanup costs and access expenditures appear to be quite similar. In each case the tax policy problem is posed most sharply in the case of expenditures that increase the value of the property to which they relate (related property) but by less than the amount of the total expenditure. Each kind of expenditure can thus be broken down into two components: (1) the portion increasing the value of the related property (investment portion) and (2) the portion in excess of the value added to the related property (excess portion). For instance, for each type of expenditure, one thousand dollars spent may cause an increase in the value of the related property of, say, seven hundred dollars, so that the one thousand dollars can be broken into a seven-hundred-dollar investment portion and a three-hundred-dollar excess portion. In each case it appears the expense should be bifurcated, with the investment portion capitalized and the excess portion deducted if, and only if, there is some justification for allowing a deduction.

Nonetheless, only the access expenditures are treated in a bifurcated manner. The portion causing an increase in the value of the related property is capitalized, and the excess portion is deductible, if at all, only as a personal medical expense.[20] Cleanup costs, on the other hand, are fully deductible in the year paid or incurred.[21] Although policy staff studying the cleanup expense issue considered a similar bifurcation approach,[22] the IRS eventually sided with taxpayers in allowing a full deduction.

In the following sections I examine the so-called Haig-Simons definition of economic income. I apply this definition to cleanup costs and access costs to determine whether the results change if the deduction analysis begins, not with the personal/business dichotomy, but with the fundamental question whether an expenditure is for consumption or for production of income. I then consider whether environmental policy considerations justify the difference in treatment between cleanup and access costs.

Economic Income Measurement

Principles. According to the Haig-Simons definition, economic income of an individual equals the sum of consumption and savings (the net accretion in the value of the individual's store of property rights).[23] Under our income tax system, the Haig-Simons definition is modified in two major ways: by the annual accounting principle and by the realization doctrine.[24] That is, income is measured at the end of every taxable year, and net changes in wealth are taken into account as they are realized in market transactions rather than when they occur.

I am using the Haig-Simons definition of economic income, as modified by the realization doctrine and the annual accounting principle, as a basis for criticizing the personal/business dichotomy. By doing so I do not want to suggest, however, that these principles are any less value-laden and subjective than the personal/business dichotomy. The consumption/investment dichotomy is itself questionable,[25] as is the use of objective (e.g., market) rather than subjective measures of value.[26] Others have noted the artificial nature of the realization doctrine, questioned the need for it, and pointed out the benefit it provides to owners of capital over workers.[27] By holding other features of the income tax system constant, however, I can focus attention on the personal/business dichotomy to show that it cannot be justified by income measurement considerations even within the conventional framework of analysis.

According to the Haig-Simons understanding of economic income, as modified, wealth of the taxpayer can be expended in one of two ways. It either disappears in consumption, or it is converted to another form, sometimes for the purpose of creating additional wealth for the taxpayer. Although consumption expenditures cause a reduction in wealth, they cannot be deducted as losses because the taxpayer gets the benefit of the consumption. The expenditures also cannot be deducted against future income because the consumed wealth disappears, and therefore the future income cannot be a return of the consumption expenditure in a different form. In contrast, the economic income paradigm holds that expenditures that convert wealth from one form (e.g., cash) to another (e.g., stock) must eventually be deducted from total wealth to ensure that only net increases in wealth are treated as taxable income. To the extent new wealth is just old wealth converted to a different form, the taxpayer is no wealthier. Expenditures incurred converting existing wealth to a different form are deductible but, in accordance with realization rules, only when income from (or a loss of) the new form of wealth is realized. In sum, the paradigm denies a deduction at any time for consumption expenditures and permits a deduction for expenditures that convert one form of property right into another form of equal value, but allows that deduction only in the year the new investment yields realized income (or a realized loss).

Application to Two Costs. The relationship between personal expenses and the production of income, although not adequately reflected in our federal income tax system, has received some attention.

> In a broad sense a large fraction of what is called consumption may be considered a cost of production in that it is necessary in order to sustain an efficient labor force. The impossibility of distinguishing clearly between the part of household expenditure that serves to make possible further production and the part that constitutes, in Adam Smith's phrase, "the sole end and purpose of all production," raises philosophical questions.[28]

The question of uncovering the personal aspects of business expenses also has been addressed, as Klein and Bankman's chapter on "mixed" business and personal expenses reflects. The distinct (at least historically) question this section raises is whether certain business expenses may be neither personal nor for production of income. Are there nonpersonal business expenses that are actually for consumption?

Applying an economic understanding of income, as modified by the realization doctrine and the annual accounting principle, to cleanup and access expenses reveals that they are more difficult to distinguish than traditional deduction analysis would suggest. The following illustrations will facilitate the explanation of the distinction between the two types of expenses. On January 1, 1995, a calendar-year taxpayer spent one thousand dollars in cash to clean up land, causing the value of the land to increase by seven hundred dollars. On the same day, a calendar-year taxpayer with a weak heart spent one thousand dollars to install an elevator in her home at the direction of her doctor, causing the value of the home to increase by seven hundred dollars. The question in each case is whether the costs are for consumption or convert wealth from one form to another.

Investment Portion. In both instances, to the extent of the seven-hundred-dollar portion of the one-thousand-dollar expenditure, the taxpayers have converted wealth in the form of cash to wealth in another form. One converted cash for cleaner land and the other for an upgraded home. The value of each taxpayer's total store of property rights neither increased nor decreased in 1995, and neither taxpayer consumed any value in 1995. Where wealth is converted from one form to another, there is no need for a deduction unless and until the new wealth produces gross income, from which the earlier investment must be deducted to prevent double taxation or it is lost in a realization event. Instead, the expenditure should be capitalized and deducted only as the property produces realized income or loss. The mere investment of the seven hundred dollars does not warrant any positive (inclusion) or negative (deduction) adjustment to taxable income.

According to conventional capitalization analysis, there is one significant difference between the investment portion of cleanup costs and the investment portion of access costs. The investment portion of the cleanup expenditure restores value lost because of the pollution but does not increase the value of the land relative to its original prepollution state. In contrast, the investment portion of access costs increases the value of the home above its original predisability value. According to the test in *Plainfield-Union Water v. Commissioner,*[29] expenditures that merely restore value are to be deducted as repair expenditures, whereas expenditures that add new value are to be capitalized.

Does the distinction between restoration of lost value and creation of new value withstand scrutiny under our modified understanding of economic income? The answer is no for two reasons. First, as already noted, expenditures merely restoring value are nonetheless investment expenditures that convert wealth from one form to another. The expenditure itself does not add to or subtract from economic income. Allowing a deduction in the year of the expenditure because it restores value lost in a prior period effectively allows a deduction for the prior unrealized loss, contrary to the realization doctrine. Moreover, allowing it in a year other than the year in which the loss was realized contradicts the annual accounting principle.

The second reason the distinction fails is that the seven-hundred-dollar investment portion of the access expenditure appears to add new value to the taxpayer's home only by reference to an objective, market-based understanding of value. If the analysis instead focused on the subjective value of the home to the taxpayer with the weak heart, the expenditure would also be revealed to restore value lost to the taxpayer when she could no longer use the stairs in her home. From this standpoint, the home is no more valuable to her following installation of the elevator than it was before she contracted heart disease. Indeed, it may be *less* valuable to her because elevators are slower and less reliable than stairs. To the extent it does not increase the value of the house the seven-hundred-dollar portion of the expenditure should be analyzed in the same manner as the three-hundred-dollar excess portion.

The taxpayer incurring cleanup costs may also argue that cleanup costs do not produce any subjective increase in value because the property is no better suited for the taxpayer's use cleaned up than it was when contaminated. That observation does not lead inevitably to a deduction of the expense but should lead, instead, to the question whether the expenditure was for consumption or for production of income. In other words, if economic income principles are applied with reference to objective valuation, both kinds of expense convert wealth from one form to another and therefore should be capitalized. If subjective valuation is taken into account, both taxpayers may have experienced a loss, and the question remains whether the loss was for consumption or production of income.

Excess Portion. In considering the three-hundred-dollar portion of the cleanup expenditure that exceeds the increase in the value of the cleaned up land, the question, again, is whether the three hundred dollars is consumed or invested to produce income at some point in time. Given that the excess portion of the cleanup expenditure does not increase the value of the related property, it should avoid the consumption characterization only if the excess portion can be found reflected somewhere else in the taxpayer's store of property rights, even if only momentarily. In this regard it is revealing that attempts at applying traditional matching analysis are indeterminate with respect to these expenses.

The concept of matching is a corollary to the realization doctrine and the annual accounting principle.[30] It is used to identify (or justify) the proper period for reporting income and expenses. What is being matched to what usually goes unstated or unanalyzed, however, beyond a vague generalization.[31] The purpose of matching in the expense context is to determine what portion of the taxpayer's gross income should be deducted as a return of capital. This is the sense of the Supreme Court's long-term benefit test for capitalization—if an expense will generate income over more than one taxable year, the deduction for the expense must be allocated among the years of income production.[32] To allow a current deduction of the expenditure would understate income in the year of deduction and overstate income in the remaining years over which the expense continues to produce income.

Applying this formulation of matching to excess cleanup costs does not work, however, because there is no income produced by the excess cleanup costs. First, according to taxpayers commenting on the tax treatment of cleanup costs, such costs do not produce any economic benefit and businesses are capable of operating at full productivity without incurring the cleanup expenditures.[33] If what these taxpayers say is true, cleanup costs do not contribute to an increase in profit but reduce the net profit of a business. The conclusion that the excess portion of a cleanup expenditure does not produce income is supported by the fact that the costs did not have to be incurred concurrently with the income-producing activities that produced the pollution necessitating the cleanup. It is also supported by the fact that federal regulation has been needed to force taxpayers to take responsibility for cleaning up the ground and water polluted by their toxic dumping.[34]

Still, it may be possible to identify intangible economic benefits from cleaning up polluted property. For instance, the business may enjoy a public relations boost. In addition, it may be argued that complying with environmental regulations permits the business to continue operations, providing a survival benefit.[35] Even so, these long-term benefits are not consistent with a current deduction and instead support capitalization of the excess portion of cleanup costs.[36] Interestingly, most cases involving the question whether expenses imposed by government regulation are current or capital land on the side of capitalization.[37] It appears the courts have had difficulty identifying any income-production benefit other than a long-term survival benefit and therefore have refused to link the expenditures to income produced in any one year.

However, if the taxpayers are correct in claiming that environmental cleanup does not provide any economic benefit, a different way of looking at matching has to be conceived to make use of the concept at all. In fact, there are two possible approaches. Expenses could be matched to the income from the activity giving rise to the expense. In the alternative, expenses could be matched to the income from which the expense is to be recovered. The first approach to cleanup costs would match the expenses backward in time to the activities that created the pollution necessitating cleanup; the second approach would match the expenses into the future when they will be recovered from income of the taxpayer. (Taxpayers commenting on the cleanup issue focused on the first approach in arguing that a current deduction should be allowed as the next-best substitute for matching backward in time.)[38]

Neither of these alternative formulations of matching is justified by the goal of accurately measuring income. The first makes sense from a financial accounting perspective, where the goal is to provide investors with an accurate view of the profitability of the enterprise.[39] Income and profit, however, should not be synonymous. If an expense is a by-product of income production rather than an input to income production, it is a consumption expense and should not be allowed as a deduction on income measurement grounds. The second approach makes sense from a budgeting standpoint, where the goal is to make sure that the expense is affordable. Expenses and deductions, however, should not be synonymous. If an expense reduces profit without contributing to an increase in profit, it is a consumption expense and should not be allowed as a deduction on income measurement grounds.

In sum, there are at least three ways in which matching could be applied: matching expenses to the income they generate; matching expenses to the income from the activity giving rise to the expense; and matching expenses to the income from which the expense is recovered. Only the first formulation makes sense if the goal of matching is to determine what portion of income should be deducted as a recovery of capital. Yet, if commenting businesses are accurate in claiming that cleanup costs produce no economic benefit, the first formulation cannot be applied to the excess portion of those costs. Even if cleanup costs produce intangible public relations or survival benefits, they should not be deducted immediately but capitalized. The indeterminacy of applying the matching principle in this context reveals that cleanup costs, to the extent that they do not restore value to the related property, may be viewed as a form of consumption.

In contrast to cleanup costs, the link between excess expenditures and the production of income in the case of access costs is not difficult to identify. Again, no established tests help with the analysis, because traditional deduction analysis assumes that this kind of expense is personal and appropriately categorized as consumption. Access expenditures can be seen more readily as an input to income production for the wage earner, however, than cleanup expenses can be seen as an input to income production for the business. The link between the food a worker consumes and the physical and mental energy put into the labor by which she generates income illustrates most clearly why a portion of many personal expenses should be deductible as inputs to income. A similar, but less obvious, link can be made between the living circumstances of the laborer and her income. In order to work, the laborer must free up sufficient time and energy to meet the demands of her employer. In many cases the access expenditure will be a prerequisite to a disabled worker's income-producing activities. The need for the expenditure is not a by-product of work but is an input to work. Although this kind of expense will also likely serve a host of nonproductive functions, those should not negate the productive function of the expenditure. As with other expenses, such as food, shelter, education, commuting, child care, and clothing, there is undoubtedly a consumption component. There is, nonetheless, also an income production component. To deny any income measurement deduction for the productive element of access costs and other personal expenditures as cited above, is to deny the productive function of home and family.[40]

Administrative convenience does not explain the difference in treatment between cleanup and access costs. Application of a bifurcation analysis to access costs forces appraisal of the related property—the very result the realization doctrine is purported to prevent. Why should bifurcation be any more difficult or less desirable in the environmental cleanup context? It is the difference in the initial productivity presumption, rather than the inherent difficulty of line drawing, that explains the absolute denial of income measurement deductions in the personal realm but not in the business realm.

How Does Traditional Analysis Fail?

As we have seen, application of principles of economic income suggests that cleanup and access costs should be treated consistently for income tax purposes. Each expenditure should be bifurcated, with the portion adding value being capitalized and the portion in excess of added value being analyzed, in the case of cleanup costs, as a possible consumption expenditure, or, in the case of access costs, as a possible expense of producing income. Traditional deduction analysis, however, provides that cleanup expenditures may be fully deducted, including the portion causing an increase in value. In contrast, the investment portion of access expenses must be capitalized and only the excess portion can be deducted. Thus, for cleanup costs the deduction is allowed as a matter of income measurement and extends to the investment portion of the expenditure. For access costs the deduction is allowed as a matter of grace and does not extend to the investment portion.

If income measurement does not adequately explain the different approaches to the two expenditures, what does? One explanation may be the reliance on the personal/business dichotomy to distinguish between consumption and investment expenditures. In the absence of a personal benefit or motive, the traditional deduction analysis simply presumes that an expenditure by a business is invested to produce income and moves on to the timing or matching analysis. That means the starting point for analysis is different for business expenses than it is for personal expenses. Personal expenses are presumed to be for consumption and therefore can fail to be deductible at all. Business deductions are presumed to be for production of income, and the taxpayers that incur them risk only capitalization.

These initial presumptions carry through the entire traditional deduction analysis to lead to different outcomes for very similar expenses. Medical expenses are not considered deductible as a matter of justice in measuring income. They are personal and not associated with the production of income. Because allowing any deduction for access costs is constructed under the analysis as a subsidy, Congress and the IRS determined that it was reasonable to exclude from the deduction any expenditure causing an increase in the taxpayer's property. Even with that limitation, the taxpayer is viewed as having received a benefit from the government by being allowed a deduction for the excess portion. From this viewpoint, the tax result appears favorable to the taxpayer.

On the other hand, cleanup costs are business expenses providing no hint of personal benefit. The justification for business deductions is accurate measurement of income. They are not a subsidy from the government but a matter of right originating in the selection of income as the tax base. There is no doubt under traditional deduction analysis that a business incurring cleanup costs is entitled (under objective income measurement analysis) to a cost recovery allowance at some point in time for the entire expenditure and is further entitled to take a business deduction for the portion not adding value. The policy question addressed by Rev. Rul. 94-38 focused on whether the taxpayer should also be allowed to deduct the portion that added value to the property. To resolve this issue favorably for the taxpayer, the answer had to provide a current deduction for the entire expenditure. Requiring capitalization of either all of the expenditure or the portion that increased value would be viewed as an antitaxpayer result.

What would happen if instead we began the analysis for each type of expenditure with the same question—Is this expenditure for consumption or production of income? By identifying any income related to the expenditure and examining the nature and timing of the income/expenditure relationship, we may identify consumption elements in business transactions. Alternatively, we might find that the only reasonable link is to a long-term intangible benefit so that capitalization cannot be avoided. If we start from the possibility that a nonpersonal business expense could be nondeductible, we would lower the expectations of business taxpayers that they are entitled to deductions as matter of right. In turn, this starting point would give policymakers more flexibility in resolving complex interpretation problems. Asking the question in the context of personal expenses, we might find links between the expenditure and income production, revealing not only productivity in the personal realm but also the dependence of the business realm on the personal. Before exploring the question of why we persist in relying on the personal/business dichotomy to distinguish consumption from investment expenditures, the question of whether environmental policy explains the difference in treatment between cleanup and access costs must be addressed.

Environmental Policy

There is no doubt that cleaning up hazardous waste sites is, and should be, a major priority in this country. According to recent hearing testimony on the tax treatment of environmental cleanup costs, there are more than forty federal (and numerous more state) statutes requiring remediation of environmental contamination.[41] It has been estimated that there are as many as twenty-five thousand hazardous waste sites requiring remediation under the Comprehensive Environmental Response, Compensation and Liability Act of 1980 alone.[42] A report by the accounting firm of KPMG Peat Marwick concluded that the potential liability for cleaning up existing hazardous waste sites reached the trillion-dollar range by 1993.[43]

Given the magnitude of the problem, perhaps a full current deduction for cleanup costs can be justified as an incentive to clean up hazardous waste sites. Taxpayers commenting on the environmental cleanup issue uniformly argued that requiring capitalization of cleanup costs would undermine U.S. environmental policy, because it would create a disincentive to clean up by making those activities more expensive.[44] This argument seems misdirected given that tax regulators have neither the authority nor the expertise to devise environmental policy. Moreover, closer examination of the environmental policy issue suggests three reasons why environmental policy cannot explain the difference between the tax treatment of cleanup and access costs.

First, the tax law provides no incentive to clean up sooner rather than later. Under Rev. Rul. 94-38 a business can get a current deduction whether it cleans up annually or allows toxic waste to accumulate over a number of years into a massive remediation project. In fact Rev. Rul. 94-38 ensures a deduction for deferred cleanup costs where some uncertainty might have existed before, increasing the incentive to delay beyond what it was before the IRS began examining this issue. There is no reason to believe, based on their practices before the ruling, that businesses will begin cleaning up sooner or complete the task faster because of the deduction.

Second, allowing a current deduction in order to reduce the cost of pollution cleanup makes less sense if we consider a business's incentives before it engages in polluting activities. In a cost-benefit analysis of future operations, allowing a current deduction reduces the cost of pollution and may tip the scales in favor of polluting. In fact this concern has been used in defense of legislation to deny deductions for cleanup costs in other contexts, most notably the Exxon Valdez oil spill. "If corporate polluters can ruin the environment and then take a tax deduction if they get caught, why comply in the first place? . . . The current system encourages companies to take risks with the environment because ultimately they are not held responsible for the full costs of cleaning up their mess."[45] "[These bills denying a deduction for the costs of cleanup] state loud and clear that the costs of cleaning up pollution can no longer be passed off from polluters to general taxpayers. Those who pollute our water, our air, and our land must be held accountable."[46] (We could call this "tough love" for businesses, to extend the welfare reform rhetoric to the corporate welfare metaphor.)

By contrast, a tax rule that increased the cost of cleaning up pollution accumulated over a number of years relative to the cost of ongoing prevention and regular cleanup would more likely lead to environmentally responsible planning decisions. Furthermore, by denying a subsidy for environmental cleanup costs, we would ensure that investors, consumers, and others interested in the business fully internalize the costs of the business's activities in their assessment of profitability.[47] In fact, environmental regulation outside the tax area has moved in the direction of using incentives to prevent pollution rather than relying on cleanup efforts.[48]

Third, the effect of any environmental incentive may be related to the assumptions about tax entitlement, as illustrated by taxpayers' reaction to the congressional proposal to allow three- or five-year amortization of environmental cleanup costs. Had taxpayers believed that they ran a risk that cleanup expenses could be labeled nondeductible consumption expenditures, they may have lauded the amortization proposal as a welcome incentive to clean up pollution. Because they believed their choice to be current deduction or capitalization, however, the capitalization proposal seemed unenticing, even with relatively fast amortization. Thus, the starting point for analysis shapes the taxpayers' perception of whether they are being encouraged or discouraged, helped or harmed, by a tax policy proposal.

Perhaps, though, denying a deduction for cleanup expenses sends the wrong message about the responsibility of businesses for cleaning up the pollution they cause. Does identifying such expenses as consumption suggest they should not be incurred by for-profit enterprises? Perhaps this is just the kind of analysis that supports the view that cleanup is an externality. To the contrary, the myth that all expenditures by businesses are, and must be, productive may hinder internalization by businesses of costs that would otherwise be borne by others (e.g., the local community or the larger society) in the absence of governmental intervention. It is only due to the myth of productivity that consumption leaves off being descriptive and becomes value laden, taking on the taint of inefficiency. By acknowledging that businesses consume, we do shift the cost of some of their activities from the general taxpaying public to those interested in the business, but we also recognize that it is normal and expected for such activities to be undertaken by businesses.

Finally, and in contrast, it is worth noting that social welfare considerations support providing tax benefits to encourage taxpayers with disabilities to live productively and independently. "By almost any definition, Americans with disabilities are uniquely underprivileged and disadvantaged. They are much poorer, much less well educated[,] . . . have fewer amenities and have a lower level of self-satisfaction than other Americans."[49] Federal legislation over the past twenty-five years has reflected a policy of opening access to jobs and public places for persons with disabilities. In 1973 the U.S. Congress enacted section 504 of the Rehabilitation Act of 1973 in a "conscious effort to include individuals with disabilities as productive members of society."[50] Congress expanded this effort with the more comprehensive Americans with Disabilities Act of 1990, which prohibits discrimination against persons with disabilities in the areas of employment, public accommodations, public transportation, and telecommunications.[51] Allowing a full deduction for access costs would be consistent with these efforts to eliminate barriers to productivity for persons living with disabilities.

THE PERSISTENCE OF THE
PERSONAL/BUSINESS DICHOTOMY

If the personal/business dichotomy does not accurately capture the distinction between deductible and nondeductible expenditures and leads to anomalous results, why do we continue to rely on it in tax analysis? I would suggest that one reason it appears to be useful is that the dichotomy reflects deeply held beliefs about the differences between the personal and business realms and the prominence of the business realm. If I am right, then the next question to ask is How does the personal/business dichotomy maintain and perpetuate the personal/business hierarchy?

There are at least three ways in which the treatment of the personal/business dichotomy as an objectively accurate means of measuring ability to pay obscures the role of the tax law in creating and maintaining the hierarchy. The first is by shifting some of the burden of taxation from those who can take business deductions to those who rely on personal deductions, all under the guise of "fairness." The second is by reflecting and reinforcing the view that business activities are productive and therefore valuable and that personal activities are a drain on the economy and therefore trivial or even damaging. The third is by rationalizing deference on the part of the government toward the business realm while justifying regulation of the personal realm.

Shifting the tax burden on the basis of the personal/business dichotomy privileges businesses by awarding them tax benefits as a matter of right. The choice to tax income is said to be justified by fairness. Income purportedly measures the taxpayer's ability to pay. Whether the income tax achieves its aspiration, however, depends on the components of its definition. If the deductions allowed to reach taxable income are too generous for some taxpayers and too restrictive for others, then to that extent the burden of taxation will be shifted from the first group to the second and the goal of fairness will be undermined. By masking consumption in the business realm and ignoring investment in the personal realm, the personal/business dichotomy contributes to undertaxation of owners and managers of businesses while overtaxing workers and their families, at least to the extent the benefit of business deductions is not passed through to workers in the form of higher wages or lower prices. If the implementation of the income tax falls far enough short of an ideal measure of ability to pay, then the message that fairness explains the choice of the income tax base is a public relations scam ranking right up there with the message that a flat tax will make life simpler for working middle-class Americans.

The second way the personal/business dichotomy privileges business is by its unquestioning association of personal with consumption expenditures and business with investment expenditures. These linkages carry a potent message that cannot be dismissed as an innocent convenience. The dichotomy helps define the relative roles and values of families and businesses by perpetuating the myth that productive activity is limited to the business realm and the myth that the business realm is and should be only about productivity. In so doing, it reifies and insulates from scrutiny the business realm while marginalizing and exposing to scrutiny the personal realm.[52]

Who inhabits these realms? According to the personal/business dichotomy, the business realm is inhabited by those who invest, namely the owners of capital. The personal realm consists of those who consume, namely workers and their families, as well as the families of the owners. In other words, both class and gender divisions underlie the separation of the world into personal and business realms. In reality of course, both businesses and families are comprised of people with myriad goals and motivations, making it inevitable that businesses invest and consume and families consume and invest. Moreover, the relationship of the two realms to each other make the business and personal realms interdependent and interlocking.

The third way the personal/business dichotomy privileges business is by allowing the tax base to be determined by deference to business judgments. Just as the concept of privacy separates the world into a sphere that may validly be regulated (the public) and a sphere that is protected from governmental regulation (the private),[53] the personal/business dichotomy serves the function of carving out territory that should not be regulated, as that term is understood within the income tax system. Ironically, in the tax world, activities in the sphere of business are more protected from government intervention (regulation) than activities in the sphere of home. Deference is given to business judgments when characterizing expenses as deductible business expenses.[54] Critical examination of the privacy concept along with the tax law helps reveal that those who have power in the home and in the marketplace enjoy relative liberty in both spheres—they can invoke privacy notions to avoid regulation at home (e.g., allowing domestic violence to go unprosecuted) and public benefit notions (productivity) to avoid regulation in business and obtain benefits as a matter of right.

It is no coincidence that the IRS ruled favorably on the cleanup cost issue, which "affects nearly every taxpayer engaged in manufacturing, natural-resource extraction, transportation and related industries."[55] A powerful array of taxpayers stood their ground firmly in favor of a current deduction, holding the IRS hostage with thinly veiled threats to slow down remediation efforts if required to capitalize cleanup costs.[56] With the personal/business dichotomy on their side, they could insist that cleanup costs have nothing to do with the production of income, yet fear no result worse than capitalization. They could scoff at three- to five-year amortization. By contrast, the taxpayers affected by the bifurcation rule applicable to access costs wield little political or economic power.[57]

It is not enough to identify all the ways business activities provide personal benefit or are for personal purposes, although we could certainly use more work in that direction. It is the formulation of the issue as a contrast between personal and business expenses, rather than between consumption and investment expenses, that reifies the view that there are different realms with different goals and values. Without the unquestioning association of the different expenditures with the different realms, it would be harder to maintain the distinction at all.

LOOKING AHEAD

Diligence to the personal/business dichotomy is likely to continue unabated in any reform involving substantial reliance on a consumption tax. In reform discussions thus far, the problem of defining consumption remains virtually unexamined. For instance, the Armey-Shelby flat tax proposal[58] would allow a deduction against "gross active income" for "the cost of business inputs."[59] Cost of business inputs is defined as the amounts paid for "property sold or used in connection with a business activity" and "services . . . in connection with a business activity."[60] The act explicitly excludes from "business inputs" those "items for personal use not in connection with any business activity."[61] It thus maintains the distinction between business and personal expenses as a substitute for defining consumption. Furthermore, it allows immediate expensing of all business expenses[62] and denies any deduction to individuals for medical expenses,[63] widening the gap between cleanup and access expenditures.

Other consumption tax proposals similarly leave untouched the presumption that business expenditures by business taxpayers are for investment and expenditures by nonbusiness taxpayers are for consumption. The Nunn-Domenici Unlimited Savings Account Tax proposal allows businesses to deduct all their payments to other firms from their gross income from sales and services.[64] Individuals are allowed only designated deductions for savings and certain expenditures categorized as personal. The cash-flow consumption tax described in *Blueprints for Tax Reform* would leave in place the provisions of the current Code that create the personal/business dichotomy.[65] In sum, all the consumption tax proposals share this feature: they rely on the distinction between the business and personal realms to define consumption rather than defining it independently.

The purpose of this essay is not to persuade that cleanup costs are primarily consumption expenditures or that access expenditures are primarily for production of income. Rather its purpose is to question the soundness of the personal/business dichotomy and to reveal the role the dichotomy plays in privileging the business realm and in devaluing the contributions of workers and their families to our economy and society. Were our tax analysis to begin with the question whether the expenditure at issue is for consumption or for the production of income, without regard to whether the expenditure is personal or business, we would be led to acknowledge and value both the productive functions of the personal realm and the consumption functions of the business realm.

NOTES

1. Rev. Rul. 94-38, 1994-1 C.B. 35.

2. Priv. Ltr. Rul. 93-15-004 (Apr. 16, 1993).

3. *See, e.g., Letter from Donald C. Alexander to Assistant Secretary (Tax Policy) Fred Goldberg, in* 92 Tax Notes Today 198-36 (Sept. 30, 1992); William L. Raby, *Two Wrongs Make a Right: The IRS View of Environmental Cleanup Costs,* 59 Tax Notes 1091 (1993); Benjamin H. Shiao & Philip J. Holthouse, *Deductibility of Environmental Cleanup Costs: The Debate Continues,* 21 J. Real Est. Taxes 3 (1993); *ABA Tax Section Midyear Meeting: IRS's Carrington Defends Asbestos Abatement Ruling,* 58 Tax Notes 834 (1993); *Does the IRS Need to Clean Up Its Ruling on Cleanup Costs?* 59 Tax Notes 728 (1993); *Environmental Cleanup Ruling Gets Mixed Reviews,* 93 Tax Notes Today 99-12 (May 7, 1993).

4. Miscellaneous Revenue Proposals: Hearings Before the Subcomm. on Select Revenue Measures of the House Comm. on Ways and Means, 103d Cong., 1st Sess. 1445, 1470, 1475–76, 1604–46, 2513–17 (1993) [hereinafter Miscellaneous Revenue Proposals]; *see also* Staff of Joint Comm. on Taxation, 103d Cong., 1st Sess., Description of Current Revenue Proposals 72–74 (Comm. Print 1993).

5. Treas. Reg. § 1.213-1(e)(1)(iii).

6. *See, e.g.,* James J. Freeland et al., Fundamentals of Federal Income Taxation 483 (8th ed. 1994); Michael J. Graetz & Deborah H. Schenk, Federal Income Taxation: Principles and Policies 262–65 (3d ed. 1995); Sanford M. Guerin & Philip F. Postlewaite, Problems and Materials in Federal Income Taxation 449–50, 691–92 (4th ed. 1994); *see also* Marvin A. Chirelstein, Federal Income Taxation: A Guide to the Leading Cases and Concepts 90–91 (7th ed. 1994) (a popular study aid).

7. William A. Klein & Joseph Bankman, Federal Income Taxation (10th ed. 1994).

8. *Id.* at 523.

9. *Id.* at 474.

10. *See* Jonathan Barry Forman, *The Income Tax Treatment of Social Welfare,* 26 U. Mich. J.L. Ref. 785, 799–804 (1994); Stanley S. Surrey, *Tax Incentives as a Device of Implementing Government Policy: A Comparison with Direct Government Expenditures,* 83 Harv. L. Rev. 705, 706–13 (1970).

11. Klein & Bankman, *supra* note 7, at 25.

12. *See, e.g.,* Staff of Joint Comm. on Taxation, Estimates of Federal Tax Expenditures for Fiscal Years 1995–1999, 103d Cong., 2nd Sess. 3–5, 17–18 (1994).

13. Klein & Bankman, *supra* note 7, at 25.

14. *See* Richard Goode, The Economic Definition of Income, *in* Comprehensive Income Taxation 1, 15 (Joseph A. Pechman ed., 1977) [hereinafter Pechman].

15. *See* E. Cary Brown & Jeremy I. Bulow, *The Definition of Taxable Business Income, in* Pechman, *supra* note 14, at 241, 243 (accretion in net worth of the firm plus distributions, net of capital contributions, to owners).

16. *See, e.g.,* Goode, *supra* note 14, at 5–15.

17. *See, e.g., id.* at 15; David F. Bradford & U.S. Treasury Tax Policy Staff, Blueprints for Basic Tax Reform 28 (2d ed. rev. 1984).

18. Rev. Rul. 94–38, *supra* note 1.

19. Rev. Rul. 87–106, 1987–2 C.B. 67.

20. *See* Treas. Reg. § 1.213-1(e)(1)(iii).

21. Rev. Rul. 94–38, *supra* note 1.

22. Telephone conversation with Robert Kilinskis, tax specialist, Office of Tax Legislative Counsel, Department of Treasury (Oct. 28, 1993).

23. Henry C. Simons, Personal Income Taxation 50 (1938).

24. See Charlotte Crane, *Matching and the Income Tax Base: The Special Case of Tax-Exempt Income*, 5 Am. J. Tax Pol'y 191, 197 (1986).

25. See Goode, *supra* note 14, at 15.

26. See id. at 5 (summarizing theory of Sir John Richard Hicks).

27. See, e.g., Mary Louise Fellows, *A Comprehensive Attack on Tax Deferral*, 88 Mich. L. Rev. 722, 726–28 (1990); Gwen Thayer Handelman, *Acknowledging Workers in Definitions of Consumption and Investment: The Case of Health Care*, this volume.

28. Goode, *supra* note 14, at 15.

29. 39 T.C. 333 (1962).

30. See generally Crane, *supra* note 24.

31. See *Newark Morning Ledger Co. v. United States*, 113 S. Ct. 1670 (1993); *Indopco, Inc. v. Commissioner*, 503 U.S. 79, 84 (1992).

32. See *Indopco, Inc. v. Commissioner*, 503 U.S. 79, 87–88 (1992).

33. See, e.g., *Letter from Moshe Schuldinger (on behalf of electric industry) to Robert Kilinskis, Tax Specialist, Office of Tax Legislative Counsel, Department of Treasury*, 94 Tax Notes Today 42–43 (Feb. 8, 1994); *Letter from Joel E. Bassett of Arent Fox Kintner Plotkin & Kahn to Robert Kilinskis, Tax Specialist, Office of Tax Legislative Counsel, Department of Treasury*, 93 Tax Notes Today 178–17 (August 9, 1993); *Comments of Tax Executives Institute on the Proper Income Tax Treatment of Environmental Remediation Expenditures*, 93 Tax Notes Today 133–76 (June 15, 1993) [hereinafter the Executives Institute].

34. See John W. Bagby et al., *How Green Was My Balance Sheet? Corporate Liability and Environmental Disclosure*, 14 Va. Envtl. L.J. 225, 229–30 (1995).

35. See Miscellaneous Revenue Proposals, *supra* note 4, at 1698 (testimony of John W. Lee, professor of law, College of William & Mary).

36. See id.

37. *Teitelbaum v. Commissioner*, 294 F.2d 541 (7th Cir. 1961) (conversion from D.C. to A.C. current); *Woolrich Woolen Mills v. United States*, 289 F.2d 444 (3rd Cir. 1961) (construction of water filtration plant); *Jones v. Commissioner*, 242 F.2d 616 (5th Cir. 1959) (renovation of historic building to avoid condemnation); *Cerda v. United States*, 84–1 U.S. Tax Cas. (CCH) ¶9490 (N.D. Ill. 1984) (repairs to rental apartment buildings); *R.K.O. Theatres v. United States*, 163 F. Supp. 598 (Ct. Cl. 1958) (addition of exits and fire escapes); *Bloomfield Steamship Co. v. Commissioner*, 33 T.C. 75 (1959) (repairs to make former warships sea- and cargoworthy); *Hotel Sulgrave Inc. v. Commissioner*, 21 T.C. 619 (1954) (installation of sprinkler system); *Beaven v. Commissioner*, 6 T.C.M. (CCH) 1344 (1947) (installation of coal burning central heating system); *Home News Publishing Co. v. Commissioner*, 18 B.T.A. 1008 (1930) (replacement of wooden girders with steel girders); *I.M. Cowell v. Commissioner*, 18 B.T.A. 997 (1930) (hotel building alterations).

38. See sources cited *supra* note 33.

39. See William W. Pyle & John A. White, Fundamental Accounting Principles 69 (7th ed. 1975).

40. See generally Handelman, *supra* note 27 (demonstrating that worker health care expenses are "primarily directed to the activity of work" and criticizing the "false dichotomy between investment and consumption" that rationalizes the treatment of human capital investments as nondeductible personal expenses).

41. See Miscellaneous Revenue Proposals, *supra* note 4, at 1626, 1628 (testimony of Wayne Robinson, director of taxes at Gencorp, testifying on behalf of the Coalition for the Fair Treatment of Environmental Cleanup Costs).

42. See id.

43. *See* Marianne Lavell, *Deductions Mulled for Environmental Cleanup Expenses*, Nat'l L.J., Dec. 20, 1993, at 15, 18.

44. *See supra* notes 4, 33 and accompanying text.

45. *Studds Release on Deductibility of Sewer and Water Services*, 93 Tax Notes Today 131–18 (May 21, 1993).

46. *Friends of the Earth Release Backs Studds Bill to Eliminate Tax Breaks for Polluters*, 93 Tax Notes Today 135–79 (June 25, 1993).

47. *See* Bagby et al., *supra* note 34 *passim*.

48. *See id.* at 229; Robert L. Glicksman, *Pollution on the Federal Lands III: Regulation of Solid and Hazardous Waste Management*, 13 Stan. Envtl. L.J. 3, 3 (1994); Allison Rittenhouse Hayward, *Common Law Remedies and the UST Regulations*, 21 B.C. Envtl. Aff. L. Rev. 619, 619–20 (1994).

49. S. Rep. No. 116, 101st Cong., 1st Sess. 8 (1989) (citing Lou Harris polls).

50. Elizabeth Clark Morin, Note, *Americans with Disabilities Act of 1990: Social Integration through Employment*, 40 Cath. U. L. Rev. 189, 189 (1990).

51. Americans with Disabilities Act of 1990, Pub. L. No. 101–336, 104 Stat. 327 (codified at 42 U.S.C. §§ 12111–213).

52. *See* Nancy Chodorow, *Mothering, Male Dominance, and Capitalism, in* Capitalist Patriarchy and the Case for Socialist Feminism 83, *passim* (Zillah R. Eisenstein ed., 1979).

53. *See id.* at 90.

54. *See, e.g., Welch v. Helvering*, 290 U.S. 111, 113 (1933) ("We may assume that the payments to creditors of the Welch Company were necessary for the development of the petitioner's business, at least in the sense that they were appropriate and helpful. . . . He certainly thought they were, and we should be slow to override his judgement.").

55. Tax Executives Institute, *supra* note 33.

56. *See supra* notes 3–4, 33 and accompanying text.

57. *See supra* note 49 and accompanying text.

58. H.R. 2050, 104th Cong., 1st Sess. (1995).

59. *Id.* at § 102(a).

60. *Id.*

61. *Id.*

62. *See id.*

63. *See id.* at § 101(a).

64. S. 722, 104th Cong., 1st Sess. (1995).

65. *See* Bradford & U.S. Treasury Tax Policy Staff, *supra* note 17, at 101–28.

PART III

RETHINKING DEVELOPMENT: OLD PRACTICES, OLD RULES, NEW WORLD

8

BEVERLY I. MORAN

Economic Development

Taxes, Sovereignty, and the Global Economy

A New York state senator called on New York City . . . to cancel a
package of $234 million in tax breaks and subsidies awarded to
Chase Manhattan Corp. that was intended to create new jobs.

"Chase Manhattan Bank has gone from the largest recipient of
tax breaks in the city's history to the city's biggest corporate welfare
cheat," Leichter said in a statement. In addition to the $234 million
retention program, Chase has received more than $200 million in
tax exemptions from the New York City Industrial Commercial
Incentive Program, Leichter said. The city has given more than
$300 million in tax breaks since 1988 to four banks, including
Chase. The tax breaks were given in return for assurances that new
jobs would be created in the city and others would be kept.

The senator . . . noted Republican National Bank announced in
May that it would cut 850 jobs, less than a year after receiving a
$6.4 million tax incentive agreement from the city to create 1,100
new jobs. —Reuters

This essay assesses the present state of the American use of local government tax incentives as economic development
tools. In particular I focus on the use of government-provided tax
incentives to relocating businesses because I believe that these incentives portend serious future conflicts among sovereignty, taxation, and
economic development.

I have chosen to look at local, rather than federal or state, tax incentives for a number of reasons. First, I started my tax career in local government as a general counsel to a New York City board that granted tax
exemptions. At the time tax incentives seemed the wave of the future.
Yet, I felt uncomfortable with the massive giveaways I administered.
Second, I believe that tax policy analysts tend to ignore the significance
of local government practices in economic development even though
local tax policy plays a critical role in business and tax planning. Finally,

a study of local incentives is important because local initiatives have national impact.

This essay begins with a brief history of the use of tax incentives by local governments. It will demonstrate that the local incentive problem is not new. I then review social science literature on the effect of incentives on business relocation decisions. These studies reveal a contradiction: on the one hand they claim that incentives are not a major factor in business relocation decisions while at the same time they show an accelerating use of incentives by state and local governments. In subsequent sections I ask why localities continue to provide incentives, given the tremendous economic risks involved and, in addition, I examine the problems created by the use of tax incentives to encourage local investment. Finally, I look at the alternatives and offer a possible solution to the dilemma of ever-accelerating tax incentives.

HISTORY OF TAX INCENTIVES OF LOCAL GOVERNMENTS

As we will see below, the history of local government incentives is not a happy one. In the past local governments competed for business by diverting public revenues to relocating companies. This competition often led to crisis as companies enjoyed incentives without providing reciprocal benefits and then departed to other locales for even greater rewards. There are, however, two things that make today different from yesterday: the inability or unwillingness of state governments to restrict local government giveaways and the expansion of the world economy with its shift in markets from the regional to the national and the global.

American municipalities began using incentives to attract industry at least as early as the railroad era.[1] In that era towns offered railroads incentives in order to attract highly coveted railway stations. These incentives, which were mostly in the form of loans and grants rather than tax relief, often left localities bankrupt when railroads went under or otherwise failed to honor their obligations.[2]

In response to these bankruptcies, state legislatures sometimes passed constitutional amendments prohibiting localities from providing incentives.[3] At times state courts also stepped in and prohibited incentives to specific businesses or business communities.[4] Apparently, these restrictions, combined with the end of the railroad era, led to a decline in the use of financial incentives by localities as a means of attracting business relocations.

The next period of wide use of government incentives came on the federal level as part of the New Deal.[5] This use generated such projects as the Hoover Dam and the Tennessee Valley Authority. However, these federal incentives were different from the local incentives discussed here. The New Deal projects focused on regions rather than on an industry or a company. In contrast, modern local incentives are customized for targeted companies and uses.[6]

Government incentives began to change after World War II. Although the federal government continued some of its major projects, under the Nixon administration the emphasis shifted to block grants to the states followed by local administration of those grant funds. These projects were often based on the idea of rehabilitating a particular area rather than attracting a particular business. The progeny of these programs can be found in such federal programs as enterprise zones. In enterprise zones, particular areas are targeted for economic development. Any business that moves into these areas can expect to receive substantial tax benefits. In general, however, enterprise zones are not tailored to a particular business. Instead, they usually provide the same benefits to all businesses that relocate to the zone.[7]

As federal moneys began to dry up in the 1980s, localities were left to fend for themselves. With no state or federal financial assistance, there was a shift again to local incentives. With less cash available for direct grants, local governments began to emphasize tax benefits and other incentives as a means of attracting business.

Incentives in the 1990s

As localities feel a greater and greater need to control their own economic destiny, the variety and size of incentives grow. This is true even though business relocation studies assert that tax and financial incentives play a small, even nonexistent, role in attracting industry. The increasing use of incentives is not even diminished by well publicized fiascos in which companies take advantage of incentives and then leave their benefactors to garner additional funds from new locations. Even in the face of this practice, local incentives continue to proliferate both in the United States and abroad.

In the 1990s localities offer a wide variety of incentives to attract businesses. For example, Alabama is now famous for its 1993 "Mercedes" plan, which provided the Mercedes Benz Company with tax abatements, training expenses, and land worth between $250 million and $300 million, or about what the company expected to pay to build a plant in Tuscaloosa.[8] In South Carolina Aiken stole Beaulieu of America from Augusta, Georgia, by providing Beaulieu with $1,220,000 for infrastructure improvements, $400,000 in highway set-aside funds, property purchased by the county for $650,000, and a $100,000 contribution from the state electrical cooperative for site preparation.[9]

These practices are increasingly common. For example, all of the southeastern states have enacted or amended their economic development laws in the 1990s.[10] State and local jurisdictions now offer low-interest loans and grants for infrastructure improvements, utility lines, site clearing, landfills, road construction, grading, and water and sewerage lines.[11] Furthermore, as competition accelerates among the states, local property tax concessions often last for decades. Some states even allow companies to share in the state sales taxes they collect as a means of attracting these companies to their communities. As a result of these varied benefits, *Industry Week* reports that incentives are a buyer's market.[12]

Do Incentives Make a Difference? Beginning at least as early as the 1940s, social scientists began studying business relocation decisions. Almost uniformly, these studies show that the major attractions in a relocation site are transportation, access to markets, labor costs, and labor skills rather than taxes or financial incentives.[13] In fact, some studies have found that taxes and financial incentives have no effect at all on the relocation decision, while others indicate that taxes and financial incentives have a low impact on investment decisions when compared with other factors.

For examples:

In its survey of Fortune 500 companies, Deloitte and Touche found that taxes and financial incentives ranked fourteenth out of a possible seventeen factors in the relocation decision.[14]

In his study of high technology firms' decisions to relocate their research and development facilities, Samuel Rabino reports that political stability and the availability of skilled work forces is significantly more compelling than tax incentives or disincentives.[15]

In a review of relocation studies from the 1960s through the 1980s, John Blair and Robert Premus report that of the seventeen surveys they reviewed, only one ranked tax incentives as "primarily significant" in the relocation decision, and no survey ranked financial incentives as "primarily significant."[16]

Neal Schmitt and company found in their study that the actual location decision "seems to be driven primarily by labor and distance considerations."[17]

Incentives Overseas. As shown above, government incentives and their accompanying problems are not new. At several points in our history, local governments have emptied their pockets to attract business and have suffered for their largesse. What makes incentives more problematic today is that we are no longer in the post–World War II era in which production was centered in the United States because other locations were either destroyed or undeveloped. Today, American towns that once competed only with each other now compete in a world economy.

In the early 1900s a company's relocation choices were often restricted by transportation costs and access to skilled labor markets. In fact this restriction was so powerful that early relocation decision studies limited location variables to transportation costs between suppliers and markets.[18]

Today, some industries are difficult if not impossible to move. For example, farming and mining rely on particular attributes of specific lands, and accordingly, they are less likely to relocate than a semiconductor production business. By contrast, industries that seemed immovable in the early part of this century, such as automobile production and pharmaceuticals, now travel from country to country with regularity. For example, in the 1900s the garment industry was settled in New York City. Even as the trade moved from the northeast to the southeast, Mexico, Hong Kong, and New York City maintained some shops that handled rush orders for designer samples. Now that the garment trade has moved farther into Central America and into China, even New York City "sweatshops" have diminished, and the garment unions are disappearing. Given increasing global markets and decreasing transportation costs, garment production will continue to move from the United States to lower-cost labor sites.

As industry becomes more mobile, countries rely more on tax and financial incentives to attract and retain business. The resulting lost revenues have prompted the World Bank to recommend the elimination of tax incentives in developing countries' tax reform programs.[19] However, this appeal has not dampened the eagerness of many industrialized nations to provide these incentives.

EXPLAINING THE CONTRADICTION

How do we reconcile the studies that assert that incentives do not affect relocation decisions with the accelerating pace of state and local tax incentives? Why do localities, states, and countries all continue incentive programs when faced with businesses that exploit governmental resources for their sole benefit? What do the states know that the studies do not reveal? The states know that financial incentives work on the margin. That is, they work at the end, rather than the beginning, of the relocation process. In order to understand this concept, this section reviews the process of reaching a relocation decision.

A company goes through several steps in making a relocation decision.[20] The first step is forecasting future capacity requirements. If capacity is expected to grow, the next step is to decide how to handle the projected increase. There are several alternatives, including the use of subcontractors, increasing prices to decrease demand, and expansion at the present site. If these alternatives prove unsatisfactory, a company will begin to consider relocation.[21]

The first step in considering relocation is the formation of a site selection team, which generally comes up with two lists, a "must have" list, listing the factors that must be provided in any location and a "want" list, for each site.[22] The next step is information gathering. What locations can satisfy the "must have" list? At this stage those companies most likely to receive relocation incentives (i.e., large firms that can promise significant infusions of capital and jobs) focus on labor climate, proximity to markets, and to a lesser extent state and local taxes in making their choices. This focus narrows the company's choice to a few localities. [23]

Next the company begins to investigate these preselected localities. At this point the company also begins its contacts with local governments. Thus, companies first enter the "buyer's market" of tax incentives when their relocation choices are limited to a few locations.[24] This is also the first time that localities try to influence the relocation decision by offering incentives.

Localities and states know that companies look to more than incentives in making their relocation decisions. Accordingly, local governments start their economic development process by evaluating their strong points and packaging those points into promotional materials. As noted by *Industry Week*, "when it comes to economic development, not all places are created equal. And no amount of financial inducements can transform Gopher Gulch into Camelot."[25] However, what localities and states also know, and what recent literature shows, is that—once the field is narrowed down—companies expect and receive massive relocation incentives.

For example, when Steve Bergsman reports on the Deloitte and Touche survey discussed above, he finds that, although the surveyed companies did not consider tax and financial incentives in making their initial relocation decisions, 82 percent of them maintained that tax and financial incentives made a difference once their location choice was narrowed to between three and five locations.[26] Furthermore, in a review of fifty-seven studies on the effect of taxes on relocation decisions, Timothy Bartik argues that tax incentives influence relocation decisions especially when competing locations offer the same level of government services.[27] That situation almost always arises once a company narrows its list to a few locations with similar attributes.

Thus, we now know what the states know and what some later studies have shown: infrastructure and labor pool may be what first attracts a company, but tax incentives often close the deal.[28]

WHAT'S WRONG WITH INCENTIVES

If incentives do make a difference in business relocation decisions, then why should localities employ strategies to limit incentives? There are at least three reasons.

First, the social science research on incentives makes it clear that what really attracts business is a good business climate. Good business climate means different things to different industries, but at the very least it means a local government that can deliver services such as good schools and roads, trained workers, and access to markets. Although some of these factors are a matter of good fortune, most are paid for from tax revenues. Thus the irony of tax incentives is that the very things that attract companies to pick among three, four, or five possibilities are the things that companies avoid paying for by negotiating special deals.

The argument in favor of incentives, however, is that relocating companies do in fact pay their fair share, albeit indirectly, by providing jobs that in turn generate revenues in the form of taxes on salaries. However, this argument ignores at least two considerations.

Initially, there is the question of fairness. Is it fair that local citizens pay for their benefits directly while relocating businesses pay for their benefits indirectly through this type of "trickle down" approach? Localities should face this question directly rather than simply assume that business tax benefits translate into public benefits. After all, taxation is not only about raising revenues. It is also about how revenues are raised.

Second, even if localities decide that they have no moral problem allowing companies to pay for government services indirectly through their employees' payroll taxes rather than directly through business taxes, it is not clear that these new jobs can generate sufficient revenues to offset company benefits. According to one advocate of tax incentives for businesses, "[f]or a state or metropolitan area to permanently increase its employment by one job compared to what it otherwise would be, the state or metropolitan area would have to enact general business tax rate cuts that would reduce business tax revenues, from business activity that would have occurred even without the tax cut, by $1,906 to $10,800 per year, year after year."[29] Given that very few workers earn enough income to generate an additional $10,800 of local tax revenues each year, it is difficult to argue that relocating companies actually give back anything near what they receive, especially if other incentives are added to lost tax revenues.

Furthermore, the literature shows that the amount of tax incentives companies receive is increasing as competition becomes more heated. As a result, if companies continue to force localities and states into a "race to the bottom" of tax incentives, the essential government services that once made these localities attractive will be lost. Thus, in the long run, tax incentives may actually work against economic development by making localities less attractive location choices.

Third, even if tax incentives are set so that localities get back what they give, the payback can work only if the relocating companies stay in their new location. However, the unfortunate reality of the incentives game is that companies that receive attractive incentive packages sometimes prematurely leave the communities that gave so much to attract them. Perhaps the most well known example of this phenomenon occurred in Ypsilanti, Michigan, where the locality attempted to prohibit General Motor's relocation under a contract theory. The town and the state gave General Motors a series of incentives based on the company's projections that it would create jobs by placing its automobile plant in Ypsilanti. When General Motors threatened to leave the town, thereby reducing the number of promised jobs, a Michigan state court issued an injunction preventing the move.[30] However, the decision was later reversed by a higher court and the plant was allowed to leave.[31] This essay started with a quoted reference to another example that recently attracted press interest, the case of the Chase Manhattan Bank/Chemical Bank Corporation merger. That merger will cost thousands of jobs even though Chase received hundreds of millions of dollars from New York City to attract and retain those jobs.[32]

What makes these stories unique is not that the companies left, but that the localities publicly complained and tried to extract some relief. After all, a city or town that loses a large employer is not always eager to broadcast the news, particularly when there are other businesses to entice and these businesses may not like litigious local governments.

ATTEMPTS TO ADDRESS THE INCENTIVES PROBLEM

A number of institutions could step forward and try to control incentives. Yet, to date, there is no end in sight. In an attempt to understand why no one has stepped forward to meet the challenge, this section looks briefly at the role courts, government, and the markets play in controlling incentives.

Can courts control incentives? As noted earlier, attempts to enforce claimed contract rights have failed because courts have refused to find a contract even when a company made specific promises about jobs or capital investment. It is not surprising that American courts are unwilling to apply a contract theory in these situations, given that incentives may not be in written agreements. Perhaps because courts are unwilling to construct these contracts, few states or localities sue when they get less than they expected in return for their lost tax dollars.

Localities could better protect the interests of their communities by insisting on written contracts. Unfortunately, local governments have not used this approach as much as they could. A recent example comes from the many sports teams that received huge incentive packages but left for better locations. Furthermore, written contracts may not impede corporate flight because localities may be reluctant to use such costly methods. Further, contracts cannot cure bad deals. Although part of the problem is round robin relocation, the more prevalent problem is that incentives are so generous that they can never be repaid even if companies fully comply.

Localities could rely on the market to control, or limit, incentives. Reliance on market forces would depend on a belief that the market would result in the selection of the most efficient site by businesses without regard to tax incentives. Unfortunately, a review of how relocation decisions are made indicates that the market does not prevent incentive wars between localities. Instead, companies find the few places that meet their nonincentive requirements and then hold those localities hostage for the best incentive packages. So far the market has merely increased businesses' power. In other words, excessive tax incentives define the market, and so the market is not the cure.

State governments could step in and prohibit the use of incentives, as they did in the nineteenth century. However, rather than taking a neutral position, states are as eager as localities to enter the incentive market.

The federal government is also a potential player in this area. One recent proposal is that the federal government should strictly prohibit incentives. Arguments in favor of a federal limitation are:

The federal government's greater political insulation allows for more objective economic development decisions;

State legislatures have demonstrated limited ability to control competition by failing to act; and

Contract theory has failed to protect localities that have been misled in the relocation process.[33]

The problem with looking to the federal government is that business relocation is more than a national problem. Today, with transportation costs greatly reduced; with manufacturing giving way to high tech; and with the Pacific Rim, the Indian subcontinent, the rest of North America, South America, and Europe all providing skilled labor forces, business relocation is no longer merely a national concern. In fact there is a strong argument that a federal prohibition against relocation incentives would only increase the transfer of capital and labor opportunities overseas.

Furthermore, there is the question of sovereignty. Sovereignty is closely linked to the ability to tax. Thus states may be reluctant to transfer their right to tax (or, more appropriately, not to tax) to the federal government.

FUTURE POSSIBILITIES AND PREDICTIONS

Economic development and the competition for business are most likely here to stay. As the global manufacturing base declines and transportation costs between localities, states, countries, and even continents decrease, localities will face an economy in which there is a limited supply of jobs and capital investments. This is not merely a national trend. It is also a trend in Asia, Europe, and North America. The question is not whether or not states and nations will compete against one another for economic development. The question is whether localities will compete on businesses' terms or whether they will find a way to regain control over their own economic development without relinquishing sovereignty to the federal government.

The nature of the relocation decision suggests that cooperative action by localities may foster healthy economic development. As discussed above, incentives do not help a company identify its initial relocation choices, but they have a potentially large effect on the final location decision.[34] The fact that incentives do not play a role in a company's first, second, or even third choice means that localities are not competing with every other place in the world. Each locality will compete with a few others based on a similarity of attributes such as infrastructure, labor climate, and transportation costs. These competing location sites may be scattered worldwide, but they are not global in the sense of every locality competing against every other.

The fact that a locality can identify its competition is significant, because the ability to identify competitors is a prerequisite to the ability to enter into noncompetition agreements.[35] Furthermore, if competitors can join, they can shift power from a buyer's market to a greater state of equilibrium by limiting the incentives market. By collaborating, regions could more fairly set incentive levels so as to limit their own exploitation.

The cartels I suggest have several advantages. First, by identifying the competition and forming incentive cartels, localities retain the ability to compete. An inability to compete could very well result if the federal or state governments prohibited incentives in this country while other nations continued to offer whatever they can to attract business.

Second, localities maintain, and even increase, their sovereignty when they control their own tax systems without state or federal oversight. This is particularly important because location decisions are local decisions. They do not operate on a national, or even a statewide, level. When larger political bodies get involved in these local decisions, they are less likely to perceive or understand rapid changes in business climate. As a result of a lack of current information, larger governments are also less likely to make adjustments for those changes. Local governments, on the other hand, are well versed in local business conditions. They are also well aware of actual and potential competitors. The more control localities have, the more likely they are to put their superior information and interest to good, swift use.

Finally, the cartels I envision could provide the tailored incentives that companies prefer. The only difference between present-day incentives and the incentives of my projected future, is that, in my future, incentives are limited in conjunction with competitors rather than increased in an attempt to beat the competition.

This does not mean that my proposal is an easy or an obvious solution. Clearly, something has so far prevented localities from forming, or even conceptualizing, incentive cartels of this sort. For several reasons this failure seems odd because the basis for these cartels is well in place. First, there are no legal impediments to governments' joining forces.[36] Second, the competition is clearly identifiable, a major prerequisite to the creation of a cartel. Third, there is little chance that new competitors will enter the market because the sorts of things that localities sell (quality of life, transportation, labor climate, etc.) are difficult to replicate over short periods of time. Thus, once a cartel is formed, it would be difficult for an outsider to help destroy the agreement by undercutting the cartel. Fourth, countries, states, and localities have a history of joining together for other projects such as joint transportation facilities. Accordingly, mechanisms exist to facilitate communication between these competitors and to help them reach agreement. Yet, something keeps governments from joining together to protect themselves from this new and growing form of corporate raiding.

The classic explanation for the failure of governments to join together is the game theory story of the prisoners' dilemma. The classic prisoners' dilemma starts with a story. Two men have committed a crime, but there is not enough evidence to convict unless one of the two confesses. Logically, neither should confess because, without a confession, both will go free. However, the police have kept them separate from one another, and each is offered a deal—confess and go free while the other is convicted. In this situation the best solution for each individual is the worst solution for the group.[37]

Governments, however, are not in the same position as the prisoners in the game theory tale. The most dramatic difference between the two situations is that governments can, and do, get information on what companies demand and what they receive. Governments are simply not in the position of having some outsider keep them from getting the information they need to make good decisions.

A better way to understand the problem of incentive cartels is to look at the OPEC oil cartel, which took almost twenty years to form and which still has compliance problems. OPEC is an example of how difficult it is to form cartels. After all, there is always the chance that someone will cheat. Experience shows that trust must be built up over time. Furthermore, everyone in the cartel must be sure that everyone else is a repeat player because only repeat players have the incentive to collaborate today for benefits tomorrow. Using OPEC as an example, we might conclude that incentive cartels will form in the future once governments have a chance to understand the buyer's market they have created and the time to build the relationships that they need to make the cartel work.

Although it may seem unlikely, I think the "repeat player" problem is at the core of the failure of governments to join into cartels. This may seem an odd claim at first because governments are classic repeat players. They are not going anywhere, and they will always want as much business as they can handle. However, I believe the problem lies in the fact that although localities are repeat players, their representatives in their economic development offices are not. Instead, what happens on the economic development level is that localities employ young graduates of law, business, and public administration schools. These people make their reputations based on the big relocation deals they help negotiate, not on how these relocations work out. For these professionals, there is much more incentive to give away the store than there is to join with the competition.

In this way governments are very different from businesses. Young people come to businesses to make their career, whereas young people come to government to make their reputations and then move on to business careers. The fact that local governments' interests conflict with their employees' interests undercuts the repeat player perspective that is so important for cartels. Governments may have to change the way that they staff their economic development offices before they can fully exploit their natural advantages.

Greed, abandonment, frustration, and the demands of the new global economy have all helped to create a buyer's market in tax incentives.

Each day's newspaper brings more stories of growing business benefits and diminishing government return. In this new world where businesses cross boundaries with ease, the traditional regulators of the public good—federal and state government, the market, and the courts—have failed to right the imbalance between local governments and the businesses they try to attract.

Fortunately for local governments, social science research shows that, for business relocation decisions, each area competes with a few similar sites. The fact that each business requires particular amenities that, in turn, are found in particular places may provide localities with some relief. Local governments know what makes them attractive to business, and they know which other regions offer similar benefits. Because they have this knowledge, local governments also know their competition, that is, the few places with similarly attractive nontax attributes. Until now, businesses have forced these comparable districts to bid against one another in the tax incentive war. However, these governments could turn the tables by joining together with their competitors to cap benefits between them.

Of course, forming an incentive cartel is no easy thing to accomplish. One barrier I identify to a successful cartel is the repeat player problem. Successful cartels are based on a limitation of present benefit in contemplation of greater future reward. Because expectations concerning the future play such an important role in their formation, cartels are made up of repeat players. At first sight, governments seem the perfect repeat players because they are locked into a site and into the need to attract business to that site. However, where economic development is concerned, the differences between governments and their professional economic development teams may undercut their repeat player status.

Despite the challenges to their formation, local government-sponsored incentive cartels have some attractions over alternatives such as federal and state restrictions or reliance on the courts. The most significant benefit that I discuss is the strengthening of local government control and the concurrent increase in local sovereignty. Without incentive cartels, or some other form of intervention, I, along with others, predict an ever-increasing amount of local tax incentives that cannot pay for themselves.

NOTES

1. Mark Taylor, Note, *A Proposal to Prohibit Industrial Relocation Subsidies*, 72 Tex. L. Rev. 669 (1994).

2. *Id.* at 671–72.

3. *Id.*

4. *Id.*

5. *Id.* at 671–75.

6. Joseph F. McKenna, *Operator, Get Me Kansas City: Competition for Industrial Development*, Mar. 6, 1995, *available in* LEXIS, News Library, Indwk File.

7. For a description of federal enterprise zones, see Sidney Kess, *Empowerment Zone Incentives*, N.Y. L.J., Feb. 6, 1995, at 41.

8. James Krohe, Jr., *Relocation Reconsidered: Do These Incentives Sound Too Good to Be True?* Across the Board, Feb. 1995, at 41.

9. Steve Bergsman, *Incentives, Location, Quality of Life: All Figure into the Site Selection Equation*, Nat'l Real Est. Investor, Oct. 1993, at 158.

10. Frank Schaefer & Milette Shanon, *Size Up State, Local Tax Incentives before Making a Move*, Nov. 1994, *available in* LEXIS, News Library, Crcash File.

11. McKenna, *supra* note 6; James Rayball, *Ohio's Economic Development Strategy: Jobs and Taxes in a Global Economy*, Feb. 1995, *available in* LEXIS, News Library, Asap File.

12. McKenna, *supra* note 6.

13. For a review of relocation studies from the 1960s to the 1980s, see John P. Blair & Robert Premus, *Major Factors in Industrial Location: A Review*, 1 Econ. Dev. Q. 72, 77 (1987).

14. Bergsman, *supra* note 9.

15. Samuel Rabino, *High Technology Firms and Factors Influencing Transfer of R & D Facilities*, 18 J. Bus. Res. 195, 204 (1989).

16. Blair & Premus, *supra* note 13.

17. Neal Schmitt et al., *Business Climate Attitudes and Company Relocation Decisions*, 72 J. Applied Psychol. 622, 625 (1987).

18. Blair & Premus, *supra* note 13, at 72.

19. International Bank for Reconstruction and Development, Lessons of Tax Reform (1991).

20. Blair & Premus, *supra* note 13, at 74.

21. *Id.*

22. *Id.*

23. *Id.*

24. *Id.* at 75.

25. McKenna, *supra* note 6.

26. Bergsman, *supra* note 9, at 158.

27. Timothy J. Bartik, *The Effects of State and Local Taxes on Economic Development: A Review of Recent Research*, 6 Econ. Dev. Q. 102, 103–5 (1992).

28. *Id.*; Bergsman, *supra* note 9, at 158.

29. Bartik, *supra* note 27, at 106.

30. *Charter Township of Ypsilanti v. General Motors Corp.*, 506 N.W. 2d 556 (Mich. Ct. App. 1993).

31. *Id.*

32. *N.Y. Senator Urges Chase Tax Break Repeal*, Reuters, Aug. 30, 1989, *available in* LEXIS, News Library, Curnews File.

33. Taylor, *supra* note 1, at 694–701.

34. Krohe, *supra* note 8, at 44.

35. For a discussion of noncompetition agreements, see Steven D. Shadowen & Kenneth Voytek, *Economic and Critical Analyses of the Law of Covenants Not to Compete*, 72 Geo. L.J. 1425 (1984).

36. Sherman Antitrust Act, 15 U.S.C. §§ 1, 2 (1988).

37. Lola L. Lopes, *Psychology and Economics: Perspectives on Risk, Cooperation, and the Marketplace*, 45 Ann. Rev. Psychol. 197 (1994).

9

KAREN B. BROWN

Transforming the Unilateralist into the Internationalist

New Tax Treaty Policy toward Developing Countries

The U.S. international tax system of the 1990s is a relic[1] that largely reflects policy concerns of the early 1960s during President John F. Kennedy's tenure. The international tax rules generated during that period remain effective today. Those rules were designed to combat international tax avoidance or evasion at a time when U.S. enterprises were the primary players in the world economy. International tax policy at that time reflected serious concerns for the U.S. fisc. Given that U.S. businesses held a significant piece of worldwide wealth, the government mostly aimed to deter cross-border transactions that threatened to lower tax revenues and deplete the U.S treasury. The controlled foreign corporation provisions that reduced the ability of U.S. business owners to escape U.S. tax on foreign operations typify international tax legislation of the 1960s. The fear of unbridled manipulation of U.S. tax liability by the conduct of business transactions abroad also motivated U.S. tax treaty policy. Increasingly, the United States insisted on exchange of information provisions in bilateral income tax treaties as a means of policing cross-border deals.

To minimize interference with the business decisions of its constituents and to protect its revenues, the United States continued its commitment to the principle of capital export neutrality in its international tax system. Capital export neutrality is a subset of the broader goal of economic neutrality. It is a tax doctrine premised on the notion that capital is allocated most efficiently when tax considerations do not distort the choice of location of investment by multinational enterprises.[2] In the United States this meant that tax rules were designed to have no impact on the investment decisions of U.S. multinationals.[3] U.S. tax liability was identical whether operations were located at home or abroad. As a consequence capital could be invested where it was most efficiently employed, where it derived the greatest economic return.

The principle of capital export neutrality prevails in the United States today. A key component is elimination or reduction of double taxation that may result when more than one country taxes profits resulting from cross-border transactions. The tax credit available for income taxes paid to foreign countries insures neutrality by offsetting the U.S. tax otherwise imposed on the worldwide income of U.S. businesses. Some exceptions to the neutrality principle, such as the exclusion for certain income earned from services provided abroad, offer incentives to operate abroad in order to increase exports of U.S. goods and services. Others, like the limitation on the tax credit when the foreign tax rate exceeds that of the United States, protect the U.S. treasury.

The continued reliance of the United States upon capital export neutrality has impeded its ability to construct effective alliances with developing countries. The traditional mechanisms used by developing countries to attract investment, tax holidays (periods of no taxation for specified businesses) and low tax rates, do not interest the U.S. investor who will be taxed on all income, even income derived from outside the United States, at higher U.S. rates. If, for instance, a developing country taxed manufacturing profits at the rate of 5 percent, the rate reduction would not affect a U.S. corporation, which would owe additional tax at the rate of 30 percent to the U.S. government on those profits.[4]

The following example demonstrates this result. Assume a U.S. corporation derives $1,000 in taxable income from manufacturing operations in a developing country. That country imposes a tax of $50 (5 percent of $1,000). The United States imposes a 35 percent tax on the same profits, or $350, but allows a credit for the $50 paid to the developing country. The U.S. corporation pays $50 to the developing country and $300 to the United States ($350 minus $50). The lower rate of tax in the developing country is of no consequence to the U.S. corporation.

In contrast, capital import neutrality, the tax doctrine viewed as most compatible with the goal of encouraging investment in developing countries, has been rejected by the United States. That doctrine maintains that capital should be taxed under the rules of the location in which it is employed, regardless of its origin. Proponents of capital import neutrality would support an exemption from U.S. tax for profits generated abroad. Many industrialized countries other than the United States, including Canada, France, Germany, and the Netherlands, have accepted import neutrality as a means to assist development.[5] They believe that the stimulation of investment resulting from low taxes will increase worldwide competition and encourage economic activity that can only inure to the benefit of all multinational enterprises. The loss of revenue to an individual country is offset by the increment in worldwide growth created by increased production. As long as investment in a developing country is not stimulated by exploitative means (for example, by payment of subsistence wages to workers, by construction of environmentally hazardous production facilities, or by exporting unsafe products, such as cigarettes, to locales where product safety regulations do not reflect modern health concerns), both the industrialized and the developing economies may benefit from expanded production. Projected benefits include the spreading of costs of production worldwide and the expansion of exports.[6]

Considering the decline since the 1960s of the U.S. position in the world economy, devotion to the capital export neutrality principle is misplaced. From 1960 to 1990 the U.S. share of world gross domestic product dropped from 43 percent to 24 percent.[7] For the same period its share of high technology exports fell from 34 percent to 19 percent.[8] From 1975 to 1989 foreign investment in the United States increased from $220 billion to almost $2.1 trillion. At the same time U.S. investment abroad failed to keep pace and grew from $295 billion to only $1.4 trillion. As a result the U.S. net international investment position was *negative* $664 billion in 1989. The United States became a net debtor nation (foreign investors had more claims on U.S. assets than U.S. investors had abroad) for the first time in 1985.[9]

The trade position of the U.S. has eroded seriously. By 1990 its current account balance was *negative* $100 billion. That balance reflected a huge trade deficit (the excess of imports of goods and services over exports of goods and services) created primarily by an imbalance in merchandise exports. The U.S. trade deficit for 1995 reached $111.5 billion.[10]

Despite the decline in its economic prominence, the United States continues to assert hegemony in international tax politics. In the tax policy debate, it behaves like a unilateralist.[11] A unilateralist constructs international policy alone with regard primarily for its own asserted interests. Given the growing importance of other actors in the world economy, however, the United States should act in tax matters as an internationalist. An internationalist forms alliances, and it acts in partnership with those allies.[12] I argue in this essay that the United States should become an internationalist in the 1990s, because concerted action possesses the greatest potential to advance the interests of the United States and its partners.

The evolution of U.S. relations with developing countries must begin to reflect internationalist strategies. Creative use of tax treaties by the United States and developing country partners may advance economic goals significantly. Two important tax policy goals, efficiency and growth, may be achieved by the combined efforts of the United States and emerging partners, especially developing countries. The mechanism for change is the development of tax treaties that represent multilateral interests. Departing from the two-party tax agreements generated by the current regime, treaties that strengthen the economic position of a select group of trading partners could reform international tax strategy. If these agreements respect the interests of workers and local communities and the integrity of the environment, the enhanced business and investment opportunities in developing countries created by the multilateral treaties would inure to the United States and its partners. Accordingly, as discussed below, the transformative multilateral treaty proposed in this essay would withdraw treaty benefits from business arrangements that attempt to exploit the social and economic resources of the developing country.[13]

Developing countries are the preferred partners for the multilateral arrangement because they offer the greatest prospect for economic growth. The United States has not taken full account of the economic opportunities provided by partnerships with developing countries. Fear that every developing country is a tax haven that hopes to siphon U.S. revenues and careless assessment of development potential have caused the United States to neglect possibilities for collaboration.

Although the multilateral approach to treaty negotiation (one that values broad coalition and group interests) is new in the United States,[14] it has been employed successfully abroad. Examples of successful multilateral agreements are the tax directives relating to mergers, parent-subsidiary transactions, and transfer pricing implemented by the fifteen members of the European Union and the European Economic Agreement, extending tax and trade agreements to the Economic Free Trade Agreement nations.[15] The movement supporting establishment of free trade zones also demonstrates the timeliness of a collaborative model in tax matters.[16]

Construction of effective tax alliances should include provisions designed to assure fair working conditions and prevent environmental harm. Collaboration with a broad group of countries ultimately may offer the greatest benefits, but this essay considers the prospect for multilateral agreements with developing countries with significant populations of color. Development of a blueprint for cooperation with this group will furnish valuable guidance for future treaty negotiations by the United States with a wider group.

TRADITIONAL IMPEDIMENTS TO COOPERATION BETWEEN THE UNITED STATES AND DEVELOPING COUNTRIES

The United States is party to income taxation treaties with 57 countries.[17] Excluding Russia and Central and Eastern European nations, only eight treaties are with developing countries: Barbados, India, Indonesia, Jamaica, Mexico, Pakistan, People's Republic of China, and Trinidad and Tobago. Although the former treaty with South Africa, revoked in protest of the former apartheid regime, is under renegotiation, there are no treaties with African nations. Other than the treaty with Mexico, there are no treaties with Latin American or South American nations. The United States has entered into exchange of tax information agreements with Barbados, Bermuda, Costa Rica, Dominica, Dominican Republic, Grenada, Guyana, Honduras, Jamaica, Peru, St. Lucia, and Trinidad and Tobago. These agreements do not offer the typical investment incentives provided by tax treaties because they are limited to information sharing. Many developing countries conclude these agreements with the United States in order to become attractive sites for U.S. owners of foreign sales corporations. Of the Asian nations, the United States has concluded treaties only with the People's Republic of China, India, and Indonesia. Most treaties with developing countries are of recent vintage. The treaty with Mexico did not become effective until 1993. The treaty with China was ratified in 1986, and the treaties with India and Indonesia were ratified in 1990.

The absence of a mature treaty network with developing countries results in part from the xenophobia that characterizes international relations of the United States.[18] That xenophobia is particularly strong in the case of certain developing countries with substantial populations of color, as demonstrated by restrictive immigration policies for residents of Caribbean nations, especially Haiti and Cuba, Latin and South America, Mexico, and Africa.[19] This has caused the United States to ignore or reject these countries as viable partners for treaty strategies that will support economic growth.

Fear of political incompatibility has also impeded treaty partnerships with developing countries that have significant populations of color. With few exceptions, the United States has eschewed alliances with Marxist and other governments deemed faithful to leftist politics. The human rights records of some developing countries have also impeded coalitions.[20] Xenophobia, reaction to progressive politics, and human rights concerns have combined to create a stereotype for U.S. businesses and international tax policymakers according to which developing nations with significant populations of color become viewed as inferior players in the global market and undesirable partners for strategic development.

For other developing countries, however, xenophobia, political instability, and human rights violations have not prevented partnerships for economic development. Russia and many of the other former members of the Soviet Socialist Republic have entered into treaties with the United States. After the USSR dissolved, Russia entered into a new treaty with the United States, but the other former members of the USSR automatically remained parties to the former USSR-U.S. treaty. Most are negotiating expanded treaties with the United States. For example, Kazakhstan anticipates treaty ratification in the near future, after it solves problems with proposed information exchange provisions.[21] Treaties with Poland, Romania, Hungary, and the Czech and

Slovak Republics are in force. Much of the progress may be attributed to the demands of U.S. businesses for expanded development opportunities with central and eastern European countries.[22]

China, a country with a significant population of color, is an important example of a tax treaty partnership in which the stereotype of the developing country as an inferior business partner has not prevailed. In that case the United States has not allowed a communist government and egregious violations of human rights to impede a tax treaty alliance.[23] For China factors that have removed the usual obstacles to conclusion of a treaty with a developing country include its enormous population (nearly one-fifth of the world's population) and the willingness of U.S. industrialists and tax analysts to view China as a capable fiscal strategist. With the exception of Mexico, India, and Indonesia, however, the stereotype has held for other developing countries with significant populations of color and has prevented successful treaty negotiations with the United States.

The slim U.S. network with developing countries witnesses the inadequacies in international and tax treaty policy. In addition to the xenophobic reluctance to enter into partnerships with developing countries, there are three major impediments to successful treaty relations by the United States with these countries: the acceptance of the principle of capital export neutrality, the unilateral use of tax treaties to advance U.S. interests, and the underestimation of the capabilities of the economies of developing countries.

Capital Export Neutrality

Capital export neutrality is a primary obstacle to development of a vibrant treaty network with developing countries. Acting in accordance with the principle of capital export neutrality, the United States taxes the foreign income of its residents and citizens (U.S. taxpayers) in order to promote worldwide efficiency in the allocation of resources. U.S. taxpayers are taxed the same whether they derive income from domestic or foreign sources. The system avoids the double taxation that could result from taxation of worldwide income by allowing a credit (that decreases U.S. tax liability) for foreign taxes paid on income derived from operations abroad. If the tax rate applied by a foreign jurisdiction is less than that in the United States, however, the U.S. taxpayer does not benefit from lower rates. Instead it pays the excess over the foreign rate to the U.S. treasury. Thus, a U.S. business has no incentive to locate operations abroad unless the economic return (independent of tax costs) is higher.

The U.S. system of capital export neutrality is not perfect, however, because the United States does not extend the principle to a situation in which the tax rate in the foreign jurisdiction is higher than the U.S. rate. If it carried the efficiency goal underlying export neutrality to its logical conclusion, the United States would refund the taxes in excess of the U.S. rate to multinational enterprises. The refunds would assure that the issue of tax cost would be removed from the business judgment about the appropriate locale for investment or production activities. Capital export neutrality would demand that a multinational enterprise consider only the economic return from investment. If, for instance, a U.S. business were to conclude, based on a comparison of costs (other than taxes) and return on investment, that operations outside the United States were more profitable, then, under a neutral system, the United States would subsidize the higher tax rates of that foreign locale by refunding taxes in excess of the U.S. rate. Out of concern for its treasury, however, the United States limits the amount of creditable taxes to those that would result from a tax at the U.S. rate, and no credit is allowed for any excess.

This system provides an incentive to exploit the social and economic resources of developing countries. Because capital export neutrality removes the advantage of low tax rates, the developing country is forced to provide U.S. investors other incentives that lower barriers to entry into the developing economy. These include low wages for workers, worker safety and child welfare regulations that are less rigorous than those in the United States, and environmental protection laws less restrictive than those in the United States. These incentives attract U.S. investment by exacting severe costs on workers and the environment and by undermining construction of a healthy infrastructure upon which to develop the economy. Although no responsible government would voluntarily support economic policies that lead to the exploitation of its worker population (through payment of below subsistence wages and inhumane working conditions) and the depletion of natural resources, developing countries are forced to enter into exploitative partnerships in order to attract U.S. dollars.

The Mexican maquiladora demonstrates the social destruction wreaked by actions designed to attract U.S. investment. A maquiladora is a company that assembles components or conducts labor-intensive manufacturing operations on behalf of a foreigner to produce goods for export.[24] U.S. companies have found ownership of a maquiladora attractive in part because it offers production of goods to be sold in the United States at lower cost. The cost advantages derive from the ability to employ workers for wages far below that necessary for subsistence. In the clothing manufacturing industry, for example, workers in some plants earn no more than the equivalent of seventy cents for a long workday under conditions in which they are virtual prisoners with limited access to sanitary facilities and no possibility of exit before the end of the shift.[25] As demonstrated by the example of the maquiladora, capital export neutrality supports a system in which a U.S. investor's primary incentive for investment in a developing country is the possibility of exploiting resources to maximize return on investment. The consequence of export neutrality is that it forecloses the ability of a developing country to attract investment by targeted tax incentives that would offer rate reductions in exchange for commitments of resources designed to strengthen the social and fiscal infrastructure.

Serious examination of the U.S. international tax regime dispels the notion that the disincentive to invest in developing countries, and the exploitation of developing country resources that results from attempts to counter the disincentive, may be justified by a neutrality or efficiency norm. The U.S. system departs from the neutrality goal in situations that operate to advantage targeted activities. In an effort to encourage export of U.S. goods and services, the United States exempts from tax income derived by U.S. taxpayers from performance of services abroad.[26] To the extent that the subpart F provisions (requiring U.S. taxation of certain types of income of foreign affiliates) do not apply, the United States also exempts income derived from manufacturing or other sales operations conducted by U.S.-taxpayer-owned foreign corporations.[27]

The operation of the foreign tax credit itself allows circumvention of the neutrality principle. By manipulating the geographical source of income rules upon which the foreign tax credit depends, a taxpayer may inflate the amount permitted to offset U.S. tax liability. If, for instance, a U.S. seller of whiskey purchased abroad contracts with U.S.

purchasers to pass title to the goods abroad, the resulting sales income will be treated as foreign source income even if the seller has no economic connection to the foreign place of purchase.[28] If, as a result of the lack of economic nexus, the foreign locale fails to tax the whiskey sales income, the U.S. seller may nonetheless include the whiskey sales income in computing its credit for taxes paid to other foreign countries on other foreign source income. By simply contracting for passage of title in a foreign country, the U.S. seller may arbitrarily reduce its worldwide tax liability. The source rules provide that the source of income from sales of purchased inventory is where title passes. Passage of title may be provided by contract. The agreement of the parties is sufficient to determine passage of title and, hence, the source of income, unless there is a tax avoidance motive and the "substance of the sale" is not in a foreign country but rather is in the United States.[29]

If, for example, the seller has other income of a foreign source in the amount of $1,000, which was taxed by a foreign country at the rate of 50 percent, and $1,000 of whiskey sales income of a U.S. source, a foreign tax credit of only $350 (foreign source income [$1,000]/worldwide income [$2,000] x U.S. tax liability [$2,000 x 35 percent] of $700) would be allowed to offset the U.S. seller's U.S. tax liability of $700 ($2,000 of worldwide income x 35 percent). The foreign tax credit limitation of section 904(a) effectively limits the maximum credit against U.S. tax liability to the effective U.S. rate of tax on foreign source income.[30] The U.S. seller would pay $350 to the United States and $500 to the foreign country, for a total of $850 in tax liability. If, however, the whiskey sales income were of a foreign source and the foreign locale assesses no tax, a credit of $700 would offset U.S. tax liability of $700 (foreign source income [$2,000]/worldwide income [$2,000] x U.S. tax liability of $700 [$2,000 x 35 percent]. The U.S. seller would pay $500 to the foreign country, for a total of $500 in taxes. This example demonstrates that ability to manipulate the source of income rules to minimize worldwide tax liability converts the capital export neutrality principle supporting the current U.S. tax system into a myth.

The foreign tax credit rules also result in the marginalization of investment in developing countries. As suggested by the whiskey seller example, the foreign tax credit encourages strategies to permit blending of high-rate taxes paid in foreign countries, for which the maximum credit allowable may not exceed the 35 percent U.S. rate, with lower-taxed or exempt income derived from other sales transactions. If, for example, a U.S. taxpayer derives taxable income of $1,000 from operations in a foreign industrialized country that imposes a 50 percent tax and $1,000 from U.S. operations, the maximum credit against U.S. tax liability is $350 (foreign source income of [$1,000]/ worldwide income of [$2,000] x $700 [$2,000 x 35 percent]). The company pays $350 tax to the United States (U.S. tax liability of $700 [$2,000 of worldwide income x 35 percent] minus the foreign tax credit of $350) and $500 to the foreign country for a total of $850. If the company can shift $300 of profits to a no-tax jurisdiction, such as a developing country that does not tax sales income from manufacturing operations, or if it can arrange passage of title in a developing country that does not tax such sales if not attributable to permanent operations located within its jurisdiction, it may reduce its overall tax liability to $700 (versus $850) with the same return on investment ($2,000).[31]

Although the 1986 Tax Reform Act legislation established separate foreign tax credit limitations for discrete categories of income (known as foreign tax credit baskets) in an effort to limit the ability of multinationals to circumvent the foreign tax credit limitations by rate blending, these rules generally do not prevent the possibility of blending rates on income derived from manufacturing and sales operations. Unless it fits within the special categories for shipping or financial services income, business income from operations in different countries will be placed in the same category, the residual basket.[32]

The U.S. system, which allows manipulation of the geographical source of income rules and provides an incentive to blend higher-rate taxes with lower ones, encourages no meaningful investment in developing countries. Instead it facilitates abuse of the tax systems of developing countries by permitting U.S. companies to obtain tax benefits with no commitment of capital or other resources to support the economy. Under this system developing countries do not become magnets for investment by U.S. multinationals. Instead either they become pawns used primarily to subsidize operations in industrialized countries to which U.S. businesses have committed substantial resources or they become candidates for exploitative ventures that deplete the economy rather than build it.

Another impediment to fruitful relationships has been the refusal by the United States to allow the "tax sparing" credit that has formed a

cornerstone of tax policy in many developing countries. Many countries have cited this refusal as a major impediment to the successful
conclusion of a treaty with the United States. U.S. rejection of the tax
sparing credit was a major cause of the delay in the negotiation of
treaties with the People's Republic of China and India. It is the reason
there is no treaty between the United States and most African nations
or between the United States and Singapore. Although the United
States rejected the request of the People's Republic of China to include
a tax sparing credit, it agreed to incorporate such a provision if adopted
in any other U.S. treaty.[33]

The tax sparing credit would allow U.S. businesses the advantages of
low tax rates imposed in a developing country. In a tax sparing provision, the United States allows a credit in the amount of the U.S. tax rate
on developing country income, even if the developing country taxes
paid were lower than the U.S. rate.[34] The "tax spared" by the developing
country benefits the U.S. business because there is no additional tax
imposed by the United States on developing country income even
though U.S. rates are higher.[35] The failure of the United States to accept
the tax sparing credit has derailed many developing country treaty
negotiations.[36] Motivated by a concern for lost revenues, the United
States has not incorporated tax sparing agreements into its treaties,
even though they would encourage U.S. investment in developing
countries.

Tax Treaties—A Tool for Pursuing U.S. Interests

Traditionally, the United States has employed tax treaties to advance
its short-term interests but has neglected its long-term interests.
Notwithstanding that a treaty is a form of contract and the treaty
process reflects a give and take in which each party relinquishes some
rights in exchange for other privileges and benefits, the United States
maintains that the bargain struck may be changed unilaterally by subsequent legislation, by revocation of the treaty, or by promulgation of
administrative regulations.[37] Industrialized countries have condemned
the U.S. hegemonic stance but, nonetheless, feel compelled to conclude
an agreement because of the importance of the United States as a
source of relatively stable investment for their multinational enterprises.[38] In this case the decision to negotiate tax agreements with the

United States results from a conclusion that the benefits outweigh the burdens.

For developing countries, however, the conclusion of a tax treaty with the United States is not motivated merely by a cost-benefit analysis. The investment incentives provided by a tax agreement with the United States are key to their ability to attract significant investment by U.S. multinationals and to the stability of their economies. For a developing country, a tax treaty with the United States may provide an indirect sanction for investment by constituents of other industrialized countries. Consequently, if the United States is to become a responsible actor in the global economy, it must look beyond short-term interests and it must look forward to and create opportunities to collaborate with developing countries. The status of the United States as a superpower in foreign relations matters (including the civil wars in Bosnia, Haiti, Northern Ireland, and parts of Africa) dictates that it become a leader in advancing effective tax policy proposals that support the economic interests of developing countries.

Underestimation of Developing Country Economies

Since glasnost and the fall of communism, the United States has asserted a strong interest in constructing investment alliances with central and eastern European countries.[39] It has shown much less enthusiasm for economic partnerships with other developing countries in Latin and South America or Africa even though many of these nations have operated compatible political systems for a considerably longer period. This neglect of developing countries with substantial populations of color seems founded in the mistaken belief, held until just recently, that such countries do not offer significant investment opportunities.[40] Careful study, however, demonstrates the enormous promise these countries hold for substantial contribution to world economic growth.

Recent congressional hearings indicate, for example, that African nations offer the prospect of important trade and investment growth.[41] Sub-Saharan Africa has a population of 560 million, an amount expected to double in thirty years.[42] In the period from 1986 to 1993, African imports of U.S. goods grew by 50 percent, a growth rate faster than that of the European Union.[43] If demand for U.S. goods remains constant, exports of U.S. goods and services would amount to $50 billion.[44] In short, economic and political reforms in Africa coupled with significant investment promise to "transform the region into a leading growth market during the first half of the [21st century]."[45] Opportunities appear most promising in Ethiopia, Uganda, Tanzania, Kenya, Ghana, Senegal, Guinea Bissau, and South Africa.[46] As noted by a representative of AT&T, "[t]argeted investments in key technologies can help move Africa from an aid-based to a trade-based economy and into the mainstream of international economic prosperity—a benefit for everyone."[47] This testimony demonstrates that the time is now right for a change by the United States in its international tax strategy that will maximize the social and economic advantages to be gained by collaboration among the United States, Africa, and other developing countries with significant populations of color.

PROPOSAL FOR DEVELOPING COUNTRIES

The proposed change in strategy is that the United States begin to negotiate its future tax treaties on behalf of a block of nations with significant populations of color. Specifically, each new U.S. treaty would extend benefits to businesses organized in the developing country. The United States would implement this policy by expanding the "limitations of benefits" provisions of each treaty to encompass business enterprises in the developing country.

Limitations of benefits provisions typically restrict the availability of rate reductions on investment income or the availability of tax exemptions for business profits to residents (whether individuals or business entities owned in significant part by resident individuals) of the contracting parties.[48] Nearly all U.S. treaties are bilateral (involving only two parties), and benefits are rarely accorded residents of third countries. The bilateral approach safeguards the U.S. interest in meting out treaty benefits only in exchange for bargained concessions. This approach harms developing countries, perceived as having little to offer. Capital export neutrality and stereotypes together discourage U.S. businesses from demanding that the U.S. government negotiate the type of treaty (one featuring tax sparing) acceptable to developing countries. In addition, developing countries are excluded from the valuable benefits offered by two-party treaties. The sophisticated two-party treaty network is constructed apart from developing countries in a way that damages their interests. That harm can be rectified only if the United States becomes an internationalist that constructs treaties aimed at offsetting the disadvantages to developing countries already built into the U.S. international tax system.

The United States can counteract the distortions created by its current treaty strategies by adopting limitations of benefits provisions in treaties that encourage appropriate investment practices with businesses in developing countries that have significant populations of color. The most important innovation would be incorporation of treaty language that extends treaty benefits to enterprises owned in substantial part by residents of selected developing countries. An example of the type of provision needed is found in the U.S.-Mexico treaty, which automatically extends its benefits to third parties that become signatories to NAFTA as follows:

> [A] company which is wholly owned, directly or indirectly, by residents of any State that is a party to the North American Free Trade Agreement ("NAFTA") in whose principal class of shares there is [ ] substantial and regular trading on a recognized securities exchange; . . . and [ ] more than 50% owned, directly, or indirectly, by residents of either Contracting State [U.S. or Mexico] in whose principal class of shares there is such substantial and regular trading on a recognized securities exchange located in such State. . . .[49]

The suggested provision would extend benefits to companies owned at least in part by residents of the developing country. It would encourage formation of business ventures by multinationals in the United States and the third country with partners from the developing country. If the United States were to incorporate this type of provision into its next treaty with Canada, for instance, joint ventures formed with capital from the United States, Canada, and selected developing countries would benefit from the tax incentives offered by the treaty. As additional treaties are negotiated, an economic development block of nations, sharing treaty benefits with selected developing countries, would emerge.

Admittedly, this proposal contains weaknesses. From the perspective of the developing country, it is only second best, because it supports a treaty that lacks a tax sparing provision. As discussed above, many developing countries are not willing to become signatories in the absence of such a provision.[50] Given the reluctance of U.S. government policymakers to approve tax sparing agreements because of revenue concerns, it is not likely that a tax sparing arrangement will gain acceptance in the near future.[51]

The prime advantage of the proposed new treaty policy is that it may benefit developing countries, even if they are not willing to make concessions to the United States in the treaty negotiation process by becoming signatories to an agreement that does not feature a tax sparing arrangement. The benefit would result from the incentive given investors to form ventures with developing country businesses that would derive income eligible for preferential treatment. Without participation of the developing country as a signatory to the treaty, however, treaty benefits would go only to ventures reaping profits in the United States or the third country (for example, a joint venture owned by residents of the United States, Canada, and South Africa would enjoy treaty benefits only for investment income or profits from U.S. or Canadian sources), and they would not extend to ventures deriving profits or income from the developing country. The advantage to the developing country is that its businesses may gain without a corresponding drain on the nation's tax revenues or other resources. Although investors from industrialized countries have traditionally sought treaty benefits for activities in a developing country, the proposal reverses this dynamic. Developing country businesses would share in substantial returns from ventures abroad, find markets for local goods or services in industrialized markets, and invest profits in the local economy. The resulting expansion in economic development may ultimately convince U.S. policymakers that enactment of tax sparing provisions is affordable.

New international tax policy strategies are needed to correct the current U.S. international tax system that disfavors developing countries with significant populations of color. The proposal made by this essay is a first step toward development of a tax regime that does not harm developing countries. The goal is development of a broad coalition of countries that derive benefits from tax partnership. Investment and business opportunities will increase as participation increases. A network of countries connected through the multilateral tax treaty can offer only greater diversity of investment in a variety of locales. The partnership of a broad group of industrialized countries with a select group of developing countries would generate economic gain for all. The selected group would exclude developing countries in which governments have not rigorously protected human rights (including rights of workers) or the integrity of the environment. The most important aspect of the proposal is that it urges policy innovation that would provide growth opportunities for developing countries and avoid exploitation of their social and economic resources.

NOTES

The author wishes to acknowledge the support of the University of Minnesota Law School Faculty Summer Research Fund and the support, encouragement, and very helpful critique of the other contributors to this anthology who participated in Taxing America: A Conference on the Social and Economic Implications of Tax Reform, held November 3–5, 1995, at the University of Minnesota, especially Prof. Mary Louise Fellows, an incredible mentor (though a contemporary) and friend who has freely shared her insightful analysis.

1. Department of Treasury, International Tax Reform: An Interim Report v (Jan. 15, 1993) [hereinafter Interim Report].

2. Gary Clyde Hufbauer, U.S. Taxation of International Income: Blueprint for Reform 49 (1992).

3. Interim Report, *supra* note 1, at 3.

4. *See* I.R.C. §§ 901, 904(a).

5. Hufbauer, *supra* note 2, at 57.

6. *Id.* at 58.

7. Hufbauer, *supra* note 2, at 3 (table 1.1).

8. *Id.*

9. *See* Staff of Joint Comm. on Taxation, 102d Cong., 1st Sess., Factors Affecting the International Competitiveness of the United States 79–81 (Comm. Print 1991).

10. *Import Surge Drives Up Trade Deficit,* L. A. Times, May 18, 1996, at D1.

11. *See* David Fromkin, *We Can Go It Alone. We Shouldn't,* N.Y. Times, Sept. 29, 1995, at A17.

12. *See id.*

13. *See* John A. McLees et al., *Mexico Moves toward Resolution of Maquiladora Transfer Pricing Issues,* 11 Tax Notes Int'l 183 (1995).

14. *See* H. David Rosenbloom, *Derivative Benefits: Emerging US Treaty Policy,* Intertax (Feb. 1994), at 83.

15. *See* Dick G. Vliet et al., Tax and Legal Aspects of EC Harmonisation 147–95 (A. Peter Lier ed., 1993); John G. Goldsworth, *Tax Aspects of the European Economic Area Agreement,* 8 Tax Notes Int'l 1310 (1994).

16. *See* James Brooke, *U.S. and 33 Hemisphere Nations Agree to Create Free-Trade Zone,* N.Y. Times, Dec. 11, 1994, at 1.

17. Andre Fogarasi et al., *Current Status of U.S. Tax Treaties*, 24 Tax Mgmt. Int'l J. 480–81 (1995).

18. *See The Two Kinds of Immigration*, S. F. Chron., Dec. 5, 1995, at A22.

19. *See id.*

20. *See* Paul Beckett, *Shell Boldly Defends Its Role in Nigeria*, Wall St. J., Nov. 27, 1995, at A9; Nosa Igiebor, *A Regime's Offense/Nigeria Scoffs at Worldwide Rebuke*, Newsday, Nov. 25, 1995, A8.

21. *See Bank Secrecy Issue Holding Up U.S.-Kazak Treaty, Official Says*, Daily Tax Rep. (BNA), July 17, 1995, at G-5.

22. *See The Russian Market Takes on New Luster*, Wall St. J., July 11, 1994, at A1.

23. *See* Ken Brown, *Rights Issues Aside, Asia Deals Rise*, N.Y. Times, Aug. 1, 1994, at C1; A. M. Rosenthal, *History Is Today*, N.Y. Times, Feb. 7, 1995, at A11.

24. *See* Nicasio del Castillo & Manuel F. Solano, *Business Operations in Mexico*, 92 Tax Mgmt. Int'l Portfolios (BNA) at A-5 (Dec. 1993).

25. Bob Herbert, *Not a Living Wage*, N.Y. Times, Oct. 9, 1995, at A11; Ray Sanchez, *Taking on Guatemala Sweatshops, Organizers Risk Death by Trying to Launch Unions*, Newsday, Sept. 4, 1995, at A6.

26. *See* I.R.C. § 911; Charles I. Kingson, *A Somewhat Different View*, 34 Tax Law. 737 (1981); *see also* I.R.C. § 921 (exempt income from certain export activities of foreign sales corporations).

27. *See* I.R.C. §§ 951–64.

28. *See Liggett Group, Inc. v. Comm'r*, 58 T.C.M. (CCH) 1167 (1990) (basis for example in text); *see also Intel Corp. v. Comm'r*, 67 F.3d 1445 (9th Cir. 1995) (interpreting Treas. Reg. §1.863–3(b), which applies the source rule to transactions involving manufactured goods).

29. I.R.C. §§ 861(a)(6), 862(a)(6); Treas. Reg. § 1.861–7; *see also id.* at § 1.863–3(b) (source rule for manufactured goods).

30. *See* I.R.C. § 904(a) (establishing the following formula: foreign source taxable income/ worldwide taxable income x U.S. tax liability).

31. *See* Linda Galler, *An Historical and Policy Analysis of the Title Passage Rule in International Sales of Personal Property*, 52 U. Pitt. L. Rev. 521 (1991).

32. I.R.C. § 904(d)(1)(I).

33. *See* Joint Comm. on Taxation, Explanation of Proposed Treaty between the United States and the People's Republic of China, *in* Tax Treaties (WGL) ¶ 72,134, at 72,128 (1995).

34. Charles I. Kingson, *The Coherence of International Taxation*, 81 Colum. L. Rev. 1151, 1262 (1981).

35. H. David Rosenbloom & Stanley I. Langbein, *United States Tax Treaty Policy: An Overview*, 19 Colum. J. Transnat'l L. 359, 379 (1981).

36. Mary Bennett, *Policy Perspective—Reflections on Current U.S. Policy for Developing Country Tax Treaties*, 90 Tax Notes Int'l 698 (1990).

37. *See* H.R. Conf. Rep. No. 1104, 100th Cong., 1st Sess., pt. 1 (1988); Department of Treasury, Preamble to Conduit Arrangements Regulations, 59 C.F.R. 52,110 (1994).

38. *See* Richard Doernberg, *Legislative Override of Income Tax Treaties: The Branch Profits Tax and Congressional Arrogation of Authority*, 42 Tax Law. 173 (1989).

39. Richard W. Stevenson, *Russia's Arms Makers Try Change*, N.Y. Times, May 2, 1994, at C1.

40. *See* Ken Brown, *Taking Stock in Third World*, N.Y. Times, Nov. 11, 1995, at 17; John F. Burns, *India Now Winning U.S. Investment*, N.Y. Times, Feb. 6, 1995, at C1.

41. *See* Joint Hearing on Investment and Trade in Africa Before the Subcomm. on Africa and International Economics Policy and Trade of the House Comm. on International Relations, 104th Cong., 1st Sess., *available in* WESTLAW, 1995 WL 93664 (Mar. 9, 1995) [hereinafter Joint Hearing]

(testimony of John F. Hicks, Assistant Administrator, Bureau for Africa, U.S. Agency for International Development).

42. *Id.*

43. *Id.*

44. *Id.*

45. *Id.*

46. *See* Joint Hearing, *supra* note 41, at 1995 WL 93666 (testimony of General Motors Corp.); *id.* at 1995 WL 93668 (testimony of the Coca-Cola Co.).

47. *See* Joint Hearing, *supra* note 41, at 1995 WL 96023 (testimony of William B. Carter, President of AT&T Submarine Systems).

48. *See* William P. Streng, *"Treaty Shopping": Tax Treaty "Limitation of Benefits" Issues,* 15 Hous. J. Int'l L. 1 (1992).

49. *See* U.S.-Mexico Income Tax Treaty, art. 17(1)(d)(iii), *in* Tax Treaties, *supra* note 33, at ¶62,118, at 62,110 (1995); *see also* U.S.-Canada Income Tax Treaty, art. XXIX A, *in id.* at ¶22,075, at 22,100-Z.134 (1995) (extends tax rate reductions on investment income (royalties, interest, and dividends) to third party residents of countries having a comprehensive income tax treaty with the United States).

50. *See Treasury Will Not Hold Tax Treaty Talks with Brazil until Assurances Are Met,* Daily Tax Rep. (BNA), Oct. 16, 1995, at G-2.

51. *But cf.* National Comm. on Economic Growth and Tax Reform, Unleashing America's Potential: A Pro-Growth, Pro-Family Tax System for the 21st Century, *reprinted in* 70 Tax Notes 449 (1996) (recommending that Congress consider a territorial tax system imposing tax only on income generated within the borders of the United States, a change that would support tax sparing agreements).

10

LABRENDA GARRETT-NELSON

The Future of Deferral

*Taxing the Income of
U.S. Multinationals*

The U.S. international tax regime can be explained by reference to four goals: efficiency, competitiveness, compatibility with international tax norms, and preservation of the U.S. income tax base. *Efficiency* generally refers to the policy of minimizing tax considerations in investment decisions. In this regard U.S. tax rules tend to favor *capital export neutrality* or the imposition of an equivalent U.S. tax burden on income wherever it is earned. The general U.S. policy of taxing citizens and domestic firms on their worldwide income is intended to promote capital export neutrality.

Capital export neutrality is sometimes at odds with the goal of preserving the ability of U.S. taxpayers to compete in international markets. If capital export neutrality were the only policy at stake, U.S. policymakers might not concern themselves with whether domestic corporations earning income abroad are taxed on the same income by both the United States and a foreign country. Clearly, however, this sort of double taxation would disadvantage U.S. firms, relative to the many foreign firms organized in countries with territorial (*not* worldwide) tax systems.

The United States has sought to harmonize its tax laws with international tax norms, including the elimination of international double taxation. Consistent with the goal of avoiding double taxation, U.S. competitiveness is furthered by the deferral of U.S. income tax on the active business earnings of controlled foreign corporations (CFCs). Deferral allows U.S. multinational corporations to invest in a foreign country, on an equal footing with foreign competitors, without attracting current U.S. income tax.

In recent years U.S. policymakers seem to have elevated the goal of preserving the U.S. income tax base over all others. In principle this goal calls for clearly defining the tax base and limiting the extent to which U.S. rules operate to subsidize foreign governments. For example, the U.S. foreign tax credit (FTC) is provided to relieve taxpayers of international double taxation, but it is limited to the U.S. tax on foreign-source income.[1] Thus, no FTC is available to the extent that a foreign tax rate exceeds the U.S. tax on income included in the base. In addition to enacting FTC limitations and income source rules, legislators, in the interest of preserving the income tax base, have adopted antideferral rules that impose current U.S. tax on certain income earned through CFCs.

Obviously, the imposition of current U.S. income tax has the potential to increase the cost of doing business abroad through CFCs in contravention of the goals of advancing U.S. competitiveness and compatibility with international tax norms. On the other hand, both capital export neutrality and the goal of preserving the U.S. tax base argue for antideferral measures. Indeed, a rule allowing unlimited deferral would create an incentive to locate income-producing activities in low- or no-tax jurisdictions, and the unfettered allowance of FTCs would impair the domestic tax base if foreign tax payments could be used to shelter income from U.S. sources. The goal of preserving the U.S. tax base accounts for a plethora of exceptions to deferral and the awful complexity of the current rules limiting the use of FTCs.[2]

The balance that has been struck between competing U.S. tax goals may be revisited as a result of the political change that occurred after the 1994 midterm elections, giving Republicans control of both houses of the Congress for the first time in forty years. Another harbinger of change is the growing interest in fundamental tax reform that would replace the current income tax system with some form of a consumption-based tax.[3] Many of the issues presented by deferral will be obviated if the U.S. income tax is replaced (or augmented) by a consumption tax. This essay explores the factors relevant to (1) whether the Republican hegemony will set the stage for liberalizations that would lower the current U.S. tax on CFC operations, (2) the contravening implications of a fiscal environment in which the need for new sources of revenue could result in further cutbacks on deferral, and (3) selected issues relating to the significance of deferral in the event the United States adopts a consumption-based tax. At the least, the congressional focus on competitiveness and tax reform should facilitate a serious reexamination of the current U.S. tax policy that purports to advance capital export neutrality (and preserve the income tax base) by taxing a wide range of foreign investments.[4]

DEFERRAL—IN THEORY AND PRACTICE

Deferral of tax on the foreign business operations of domestic corporations results from the structure of the U.S. system that treats a corporation and its shareholders as separate taxpayers. The general rule is that a U.S. corporate parent of a CFC pays no U.S. tax on the CFC's foreign-source income, unless and until the CFCs earnings are repatriated (as dividends, gain on sale of the CFC, or otherwise).

The international tax norm of avoiding double taxation could be violated by the U.S. rules that tax the worldwide income of domestic corporations, including that derived from a foreign country. The United States bows to the international norm by allowing U.S. multinational corporations to reduce U.S. tax liability with FTCs, including credits for foreign taxes paid by a CFC but deemed paid by a U.S. parent corporation when income is distributed by the CFC. I.R.C. § 901 provides a dollar-for-dollar credit for taxes paid directly by a U.S. taxpayer, subject to the limitations of I.R.C. § 904. Where a U.S. corporation operates in a foreign country through a CFC, I.R.C. § 902 provides an indirect credit for taxes paid by a foreign subsidiary. It deems payment by the U.S. parent of foreign taxes paid by the CFC in respect of income distributed as dividends. I.R.C. § 960 also allows an indirect FTC for taxes paid by a CFC on income deemed distributed to a U.S. parent under the subpart F rules.[5]

In addition, the United States has entered into numerous bilateral income tax treaties that limit the taxation of U.S. multinational corporations by treaty partners. In theory, to the extent the United States cedes taxing jurisdiction to a foreign country with a comparable corporate income tax rate, no additional U.S. tax is payable when a CFC's earnings are taxed to a U.S. shareholder.

Prior to 1962 antideferral rules were limited to foreign personal holding companies (FPHCs) and generally imposed a current tax only where at least half of a foreign corporation's income was passive investment income.[6] Thus, before enactment of subpart F, U.S. multinational corporations enjoyed unlimited deferral of U.S. income tax on business profits earned abroad through CFCs. CFC status under subpart F is based on whether U.S. shareholders own more than 50 percent of the vote or value of a foreign corporation's stock, determined with the application of constructive ownership rules.[7] A U.S. shareholder is defined as one owning at least 10 percent by vote or value of the stock in a corporation. One consequence is that a U.S. shareholder is taxed currently on the CFC's "subpart F income," which includes investment income and certain business income earned by related parties in transactions deemed to suggest a tax avoidance motive.

Originally, subpart F was akin to the FPHC rules, focusing on income from passive investments. Indeed, subpart F trumps the FPHC rules where both could apply. Although certain active business income was subjected to current taxation, this generally occurred only where U.S. taxpayers employed the device of organizing foreign base companies to isolate business profits in low-tax jurisdictions. In a typical case a domestic firm would sell its exports to a CFC for resale abroad. The CFC would be organized in a foreign country in which little or no tax was imposed on income derived from resale to a third country. This enabled the U.S. parent to reduce tax on a portion of its foreign business profits. Over the last three decades, however, Congress has increased the number and expanded the scope of antideferral rules applicable to CFCs, imposing current U.S. tax even in the case of active business income derived through CFCs that were not organized to avoid tax.

The 1986 Tax Reform Act added the passive foreign investment (PFIC) rules[8] and amended subpart F to eliminate deferral for shipping and most activities of the financial services industry. Moreover, under legislation enacted in 1993, current income inclusions are required to the extent a CFC's passive assets exceed 25 percent of its gross assets.[9]

Prior to enactment of the PFIC rules, taxpayers could shelter passive income from current U.S. taxation by organizing foreign mutual funds with widely dispersed ownership because subpart F has no application where no U.S. shareholder (defined to mean at least a 10 percent shareholder) exists. The PFIC rules were intended to halt the use of U.S.-owned foreign mutual funds to defer U.S. tax on investments,[10] but in operation the PFIC rules can apply to CFCs engaged in bona fide business activities.

The enactment in 1993 of the I.R.C. § 956A tax on excess passive assets was justified on the ground that "deferral of U.S. tax on accumulated active business profits is not necessary to maintain the competitiveness of business activities conducted by [CFCs] where . . . held in the form of excessive accumulations of passive assets."[11] Treasury officials have defended this provision by reporting research results indicating that the average percentage of passive assets for all CFCs was just 13 percent at the time the provision was enacted and only 7 percent in non–tax haven countries.[12] Others, however, point to what has been described as a "perverse result" that encourages CFCs to make foreign (rather than domestic) investments in business assets, in order to remain below the 25 percent threshold.[13] Moreover, it has a disparate impact on certain U.S. businesses because the current statute makes no allowance for CFCs that might accumulate profits in excess of the average for legitimate business reasons (e.g., funding planned business expansions out of retained earnings).

THE CASE FOR COMPETITIVENESS AS A TAX POLICY GOAL

When subpart F was enacted in 1962, the Congress recognized that there are nontax business reasons for locating a U.S.-owned facility outside the United States (for example, reducing distribution, transportation, and customs costs). The validity of this premise is evidenced by the number of CFCs organized in countries such as the United Kingdom and France where corporate income tax rates are comparable to U.S. rates. The compromise reached in 1962 was intended to guard against the potential for abuse while protecting the ability of U.S. businesses to compete abroad.[14] In the past congressional Republicans have expressed dissenting views with respect to the breach of the 1962 compromise by antideferral legislation. Thus, one would expect a Republican-controlled Congress to reexamine post-1962 legislation that runs counter to the goal of promoting competitiveness.

When the House Ways and Means Committee reported on the 1993 bill that ended deferral for CFCs with excessive passive assets, the (then minority) Republican members of the committee opined that "[t]he area of U.S. taxation of international operations, already written off by most knowledgeable persons as a disaster, would be made significantly worse."[15] The Republicans further predicted, "U.S. corporations will be shackled with additional burdens, virtually assuring that they will fall behind in international competitiveness. Income of foreign subsidiaries earned in prior years and not repatriated to the United States will, in many cases, be subject to immediate taxation in what can only be called a retroactive tax change."[16]

The concern underlying the Republican dissent from the 1993 Ways and Means Committee bill is that the United States taxes outbound investments more heavily than other countries. Although the 35 percent U.S. corporate income tax rate is in the same range as that of our major trading partners,[17] countries such as Germany, the Netherlands, and France refrain from taxing foreign-source income. In contrast with a multinational organized under the laws of Germany or France, a CFC operation would result in residual U.S. income tax payments (after application of the FTC limitations) in addition to foreign income tax liability. Even countries that have enacted provisions that are similar to subpart F (including Germany, the United Kingdom, and Japan) generally limit current taxation to passive income.

FEDERAL BUDGETARY CONCERNS

Republican control of the Congress has spawned a concerted effort to balance the federal budget. This fiscal exercise may tend to restrain any efforts to reduce current tax payments on CFC operations.

The Revenue-Raising Potential of a Repeal of Deferral

Notwithstanding the pronounced antideferral bias of past legislation in this area, deferral continues to be the general rule for many CFCs (primarily, those engaged in manufacturing or other activities confined to a CFC's home country). Because the curtailment of deferral continues to be viewed as a source of potential revenue, the subject continues to surface in congressional debates. In 1992 the former chairman of the House Ways and Means Committee, Dan Rostenkowski, cosponsored a bill to eliminate deferral for CFC operations,[18] and as recently as May of 1995, the Republican chairman of the House Budget Committee, John Kasich, included the repeal of deferral on a list of corporate revenue raisers, estimating that the proposal would raise $26.4 billion over seven years. In July of 1995 the former chairman of the Senate Finance Committee, Robert Packwood, scheduled a hearing on the deferral of income tax of U.S. multinationals.

Rostenkowski's bill provided for repeal in the context of comprehensive international tax reform, a proposition that might be viewed as too expensive in today's budgetary environment. It is possible, however, that a stand-alone proposal to repeal deferral will arise, if at all, in the context of a search for revenue raisers. Thus, putting aside the many debates about tax policy considerations that such a proposal would engender,[19] the legislative prognosis for a simple repeal of deferral might turn, in large part, on estimates of the revenue effect. In this regard it is far from clear that a proposal to repeal deferral would generate the full amount of potential revenue. Rather, the potential revenue gain might well be reduced by the inclusion of transition or other remedial provisions. Moreover, there is a basic question about the magnitude of the potential revenue gain, in light of the availability of FTCs.

On a repeal of deferral, equity considerations would certainly suggest that U.S. parent corporations be allowed to include the results of a CFC's operations on their U.S. consolidated tax returns, particularly in light of the strong political opposition that repeal would generate. Indeed, Rostenkowski's 1992 bill coupled the repeal of deferral with an irrevocable election to treat a CFC as a domestic corporation. Alternatively, a repeal of deferral could be accompanied by a rule that treats CFCs as branch operations. In either case U.S. multinationals would then be permitted the use of foreign operating losses on their U.S. return, a result that would surely reduce any hope for revenue gain attributable to future taxable years.

Given the expected pressure to implement a repeal of deferral by allowing U.S. taxpayers to reflect CFC operating results on their U.S. return, it may be that the only way to turn repeal of deferral into a substantial revenue raiser would be to trigger tax on previously untaxed earnings (i.e., earnings that have escaped taxation under antideferral rules). The provision of transitional relief would not only reduce the revenue potential, but it would also increase the complexity of the law for those taxpayers who would then be required to account for results under both the old and new regimes. Nevertheless, this is exactly the way the Congress implemented the I.R.C. § 956A tax on passive assets in 1993,[20] and taxpayers would be sure to point to this precedent if faced with a serious attempt to eliminate deferral completely.

The Impact of FTC Limitations

Some have argued that the repeal of deferral would have no signifi-cant impact on the tax liability of CFCs, and thus no significant rev-enue effect, because the United States has one of the lowest tax rates among major industrial countries.[21] This view assumes that most CFC earnings would be fully sheltered by FTCs, ignoring the reality of the FTC limitations that operate to deny full credit for income taxes paid to foreign governments.

In addition to the overall FTC limitation, based on the U.S. tax on foreign-source income, there are nine (including the general) separate limitations or "baskets." The FTC baskets isolate the tax effects of par-ticular types of income, including:

passive income,
income from financial services,
income subject to high withholding tax, and
dividends paid by *each* foreign corporation that fails to qualify as a CFC because only 50 percent or less is owned ("noncontrolled foreign corporation basket").[22]

The higher rate of tax on foreign income of U.S. multinationals[23] can be attributed to the FTC limitations. The stated purpose of the separate FTC limitations is to prevent cross-crediting or averaging of foreign tax rates.[24] Consider a U.S. corporate taxpayer with $100 of foreign-source business income (on which foreign tax of $36 was paid) and $100 of U.S.-source income. The U.S. tax on the $200 of worldwide income would be $70, before allowance of any FTC: $200 worldwide income x

35 percent U.S. Tax Rate = $70 U.S. tax liability. Under the overall FTC limitation, the taxpayer's FTC would be limited to the U.S. tax on the $100 of foreign-source income: $100 foreign-source income / $200 worldwide income x $70 U.S. tax liability = $35 overall limitation. The taxpayer would have a $1 excess FTC (the $36 foreign tax payment, less the $35 overall FTC limitation), which could not offset U.S. tax. Suppose the taxpayer earned an additional $100 of foreign-source passive income, with respect to which no foreign tax was imposed? In this case the overall FTC limitation would be $70 (the U.S. tax on the $200 of foreign-source income): $200 foreign-source income / $300 worldwide income x $105 U.S. tax liability = $70 overall limitation. In a world without separate limitations, the $1 excess FTC generated by the $36 payment on the $100 of foreign-source business income would be available to offset a dollar of U.S. tax on the $100 of foreign-source passive income. Here, however, the application of the separate FTC limitation for passive income would apply to prevent the cross-crediting of the $1 against U.S. tax on the foreign-source passive income.

In operation, the FTC baskets can result in disparate treatment of income earned by a single CFC from the same business activity. For example, consider the case of a financial services CFC engaged in leasing and other financing transactions. Whether the CFC's income ends up in the general basket for business income or the passive basket will depend entirely on the mix of leasing income in any given year.[25]

Another basket that creates arbitrary results is the one for dividends from noncontrolled foreign corporations. Its limitation hinders the ability of U.S. multinationals to enter into joint ventures with foreign-owned enterprises because the U.S. venturer will always need more than 50 percent ownership to avoid placing income from the venture in a separate basket. In many cases, however, taxpayers are able to plan around this rule, for example, by entering into complex structures involving the use of a hybrid foreign entity that will be treated as a partnership (and *not* a corporation) for U.S. tax purposes.

PIECEMEAL (AND LESS COSTLY) REFORMS

Against this backdrop 1995 saw the introduction of a bipartisan bill (H.R. 1690) by the House Ways and Means Committee members, which proposes simplification with a modest revenue impact and liber-alization of the CFC regime.[26] Many of the provisions in the 1995 bill were adopted by Congress in 1992 legislation that was vetoed.[27] H.R. 1690 serves as a laundry list of some of the less defensible provisions of current law and may be a likely candidate for enactment. Its salient pro-visions are listed below.

Simplification of the Separate FTC Basket for Noncontrolled Foreign Corporations. H.R. 1690 would apply the "look through" rule that now applies to dividends from controlled foreign corporations and to dividends from noncontrolled foreign corporations when the information necessary to trace the source (or content) of a dividend is available.

Extending the Use of FTC Carrybacks and Carryforwards. The period during which excess FTCs could be carried back would be extended from two to three years, and the carryforward period would be changed from five to fifteen years in conformity with the domestic rules for net operating losses.

Simplification of Antideferral Regimes. The European Union (EU) would be treated as a single country, for purposes of subpart F, a change that would reduce the instances in which use of EU sub-sidiaries in cross-border transactions could trigger deemed applica-tion of the antideferral rule.

Restoration of Deferral for Financial Services. H.R. 1690 would restore the pre-1986 active business exception, as it applied to banks, insur-ance companies, and other financial services businesses.

Elimination of the PFIC/CFC Overlap. CFCs would be exempt from the PFIC rules.

Not surprisingly (given the Republican position on past legislation to curtail deferral), the 1995 House Budget Reconciliation bill not only incorporates several of the simplifications previously passed by the Congress, but it also proposes to repeal the I.R.C. § 956A tax on excess passive assets.[28] In addition to the proposed repeal of I.R.C. § 956A, the House Budget Reconciliation bill would eliminate the overlap between subpart F and the PFIC rules. Whatever the fate of this bill, the content indicates a retreat from the antideferral bias of prior years. Furthermore, the reality of budgetary constraints means that the scope of the House version of the 1995 Budget Reconciliation bill may represent the outer limits of a tax treatment of CFCs viewed by multinational business as more favorable.

OVERVIEW OF CONSUMPTION-BASED TAXES

The Republican focus on international competitiveness dovetails with the growing interest in consumption-based taxes, particularly because the United States is the only major economy of the G-7 (the group of nations that includes Canada, France, Germany, Italy, Japan, and the United Kingdom) without a value added tax (VAT).[29] A consumption tax can take the form of a retail sales tax, a consumed income tax, or a VAT, the common element being the exclusion of savings and investments from the tax base. Whatever the form of a consumption-based tax, it is likely that politics will dictate the allowance of exemptions or other mechanisms to introduce an element of progressivity. In Europe, for example, governments tend to use three rates: standard rates, which range from 12 percent in Luxembourg, Spain, and Turkey, to 25 percent in Ireland; lower rates, 0–17 percent, which are used to combat regressivity and usually cover items such as food, medical care, books, electricity, and so forth; and higher rates, usually over 30 percent, which typically apply to luxury items, such as automobiles, televisions, and VCRs.[30]

The real differences among the three basic forms of consumption taxes are the methods of collection. A retail sales tax is familiar to most taxpayers because state and local governments impose sales taxes on a broad range of goods and services. The point of collection of a retail sales tax is by businesses on sales to the ultimate consumers.[31] A consumed income tax may use a base identical to that of a retail sales tax, with the difference being that the tax would resemble (and be collected as) a personal income tax with savings excluded from the tax base. An example of a consumed income tax that uses this structure is the individual tax component of the Unlimited Savings Allowance (USA) tax, introduced by Senators Pete Domenici and Sam Nunn on April 25, 1995.[32] The USA tax, imposed at the rate of 11 percent on gross profits, defined as taxable receipts reduced by business purchases, would apply to businesses that sell or lease property or sell services in the United States. Gross receipts would not include amounts attributable to property or services exported from the United States.

A VAT is like a sales tax if it is collected along the production chain. A VAT is a consumption tax if purchases of capital goods are deducted immediately. Like a retail sales tax, a VAT is collected by businesses under one of three models: the subtraction and the addition methods (both of which rely on accounting records) and the credit invoice method (based on sales and purchase invoices). A consumption-based VAT may be structured as a broad-based tax on business activities, with businesses paying tax on gross receipts net of business purchases of goods and services, collected through the subtraction method. This is the gist of the 14.5 percent Business Activities Tax introduced during the 103d Congress by then senators John Danforth and David Boren (referred to herein as the Danforth-Boren Business Activities Tax).[33] The USA tax on businesses discussed above is also a subtraction-method VAT.

If the federal corporate income tax were replaced by a consumption-based tax (as would occur under the USA tax), most of the issues relevant to deferral would be obviated because gross receipts from exports would be tax exempt. In designing the consumption tax, however, it would be necessary to define the jurisdictional borders of the United States. In this regard, because U.S. multinationals would continue to have an incentive to structure CFC operations in a manner that minimizes worldwide tax liability, the concept of capital export neutrality would have continued relevance in defining jurisdictional borders.

Generally, consumption taxes are thought of as being territorial, that is, imposed only on goods consumed in the country imposing the tax, as under the USA tax. Indeed, as the staff of the Joint Committee on Taxation reported in 1991, "[v]irtually all present-day VATs are based on the destination principle. In order to implement the destination principle, exports must be relieved of the domestic VAT and the domestic VAT must be imposed on imports."[34] If the general rule under a consumption-based tax exempts export sales, one would not expect retention of any special rules to reach the foreign sales of CFCs. This result would be consistent with the current U.S. tax policy of equalizing the treatment of taxpayers that operate through CFCs and those that operate through branches.[35]

There are proponents, however, of a consumption tax based on origin. For example, both the House majority leader, Richard K. Armey, and Sen. Arlen Specter proposed flat-rate consumption taxes that would tax exports, not imports.[36] A tax based on origin might place U.S.-based companies at a competitive disadvantage, relative to foreign-based companies that could sell their products in the United States at a price that would not include the origin-based consumption tax. Thus, examination of anticompetitive consequences should accompany consideration of an origin-based VAT.

The move to a consumption-based tax might not resolve all of the competition issues identified under current law. For example, commentators have identified a concern about the international competitiveness of U.S. financial service companies under a VAT, if financial services are exempted (as they are under European VAT regimes).[37] Generally, this concern would be presented if financial services are exempt from tax *and* the seller is denied credit for (i.e., the ability to recover) taxes paid on purchases related to the sale. A competitive disadvantage to domestic providers (companies in the securities, insurance, banking, mutual fund, and leasing industries that have been hardest hit by cutbacks in deferral) may result if offshore financial service providers receive tax preference.

Generally, because the United States is a party to GATT, it is obligated to refrain from subsidizing exports. In practice, however, an "indirect tax" is excluded from this prohibition.[38] Thus, as is the case with the typical European-style VAT, an indirect tax can be adjusted at the border without running afoul of GATT. Proponents of moving the United States to a consumption tax often cite this "border adjustability" feature as one that would improve international competitiveness. With respect to any given form of consumption tax, however, the GATT legality of border adjustments will depend almost entirely on whether U.S. trading partners agree that a levy qualifies as an indirect tax.

A retail sales tax would automatically exempt imports because the tax would be imposed only on domestic consumers. A VAT could be structured to reach the same result by exempting export sales and allowing exporters to claim a credit for business purchases of goods and services, as was proposed in the Danforth-Boren Business Activities Tax and as is the case in most countries that have a credit-invoice VAT.[39] In any case a border adjustment scheme would have to be structured to avoid challenge as a GATT-actionable (or countervailable) export subsidy. Otherwise, U.S. exports benefiting from border adjustments could face penalties equal to the export subsidy.

Except in the case of a VAT, border adjustments generally are permitted only for taxes imposed on physically incorporated components of exported products. Export rebates of prior stage cumulative indirect taxes are considered subsidies, unless the tax was levied on goods that were physically incorporated into the exported product.[40] No adjustment would be necessary if exports were simply excluded from the base.

It is not known whether U.S. trading partners will agree that the GATT standards would be met by a consumption tax that resembles an income tax. For example, notwithstanding the economic similarity to a VAT, one might view the USA tax as an income tax (and not an indirect tax) because the tax is not computed on a transactional basis.

Tax policymakers who have considered replacing the income tax with a consumption-based tax have loosely described a transition that would involve grandfathering old investments but requiring future investments to be made under the new system.[41] This does not mean that CFCs with earnings accumulated before the effective date of a consumption tax would receive a windfall on repeal of the income tax. Presumably, unless special rules are included to deal with eventual repatriation of previously untaxed CFC profits, those earnings would be taxed as they are consumed in the United States. Alternatively, it has been suggested that transition could take the form of a final tax on capital and consumer goods,[42] which would present the issue whether a multinational's investment in stock of a CFC would be treated as subject to a final tax on capital.

CFCs UNDER A MIXED TAX SYSTEM

The United States would stand alone among the world's major economies if Congress opted for a wholesale replacement of the income tax with a consumption-based tax.[43] What is far more likely to occur, perhaps as a transitional approach, is the enactment of a consumption tax that would supplement income tax revenues. For example, the Danforth-Boren Business Activities Tax would overlay the current federal corporate tax. It is fair to assume that the subpart F regime and other antideferral rules would survive a move to a mixed system that combines income and consumption taxes. On the other hand, a new source of revenue, such as a consumption tax, would also loosen the budgetary constraints that have prevented policymakers from rationalizing some of the more severely criticized "glitches" under the current antideferral rules. If the income tax ceases to be the prime source of government revenues, the cost of simplifying amendments will also be less of an issue.

It is unlikely that this or any other Congress would withstand the onslaught of lobbying that would ensue in the event of a proposal to repeal deferral without other meaningful tax reform of the CFC regime. The fiscal movement to balance the federal budget will proscribe extensive protaxpayer changes in this area, but we are likely to see limited reforms around the edges.

Fundamental tax reform is a number of years away (and will certainly not happen until after the 1996 presidential elections); nevertheless, given the level of interest in moving in this direction, it would behoove multinationals and their tax advisors to begin to analyze the many issues that would be presented should a consumption-based tax become a reality. At the least, even if the Congress ends up adopting a mixed income/consumption tax system, another new source of revenue will take some of the pressure off of the current statutory rules that are designed to preserve the income tax base, with the result that tax policymakers might gain breathing room (in terms of revenue) to rationalize the CFC regime.

NOTES

1. I.R.C. § 904.
2. *See* Staff of Joint Comm. on Taxation, 99th Cong., 2d Sess., General Explanation of the Tax Reform Act of 1986, 861, 1023 (1987) [hereinafter 1986 Blue Book].
3. *See, e.g.,* Hearings on Flat Tax Proposals Before the Senate Comm. on Finance, 104th Cong., 1st Sess. (1995); The National Comm'n on Economic Growth and Tax Reform, Unleashing America's Potential: A Pro-Growth, Pro-Family Tax System for the 21st Century, *reprinted in* 70

Tax Notes 413 (1996) (commonly referred to as the Kemp Commission Report).

4. For a detailed discussion of the principle of capital export neutrality, see Staff of Joint Comm. on Taxation, Factors Affecting the International Competitiveness of the United States, 101st Cong., 1st Sess. (Comm. Print 1991).

5. I.R.C. §§ 951–64 (referred to as subpart F).

6. *See id.* at §§ 551–58.

7. *See id.* at §§ 957, 958.

8. *See id.* at §§ 1291–97 (the PFIC rules).

9. For a consideration of I.R.C. § 956A, see Melvin S. Adess et al., *The Erosion of Deferral: Subpart F after the 1993 Act,* 47 Tax Law. 933 (1994).

10. *See* 1986 Blue Book, *supra* note 2, at 1023.

11. Fiscal Year 1994 Budget Reconciliation Recommendations of the Comm. on Ways and Means, House Comm. on Ways and Means, 103d Cong., 1st Sess. 250, 254 (Comm. Print 1993) [hereinafter 1994 Budget Reconciliation Recommendations].

12. *See* Hearings on U.S. Taxation of Foreign Income Before the Senate Comm. on Finance, 104th Cong., 1st Sess. (July 21, 1995) (statement of Joseph H. Guttentag, International Tax Counsel, Department of the Treasury) (unpublished).

13. *See id.* (statement of Gary Hufbauer, Reginald Jones Senior Fellow, Institute for International Economics) (unpublished) [hereinafter Hufbauer].

14. *See* S. Rep. No. 1881, 87th Cong., 2d Sess. 78 (1962).

15. 1994 Budget Reconciliation Recommendations, *supra* note 11, at 383, 388.

16. *Id.*

17. *See* Perry D. Quick & Thomas Neubig, *Tax Burden Comparison: U.S. vs. the Rest of the G-7,* 65 Tax Notes 1409 (1994).

18. H.R. 5270, 102d Cong., 2d Sess. (1992) (Foreign Income Tax Rationalization and Simplification Act of 1992).

19. *Compare* Hearings on H.R. 5270 Before the House Comm. on Ways and Means, 102d Cong., 2d Sess. 358–76 (1992) (statement of Michael J. McIntyre, professor of law, Wayne State University Law School, on behalf of Citizens for Tax Justice) [hereinafter McIntyre] (supporting the repeal of deferral) *with* Hufbauer, *supra* note 13 (encouraging the adoption of territorial taxation).

20. *See* H. R. Conf. Rep. No. 213, 103d Cong., 1st Sess. 633, 637 (1993) (the conference agreement followed the Senate bill that applied only to earnings accumulated after Sept. 30, 1993).

21. *See, e.g.,* McIntyre, *supra* note 19.

22. I.R.C. § 904(d).

23. U.S. Gen. Accounting Office, 1988 and 1989 Company Effective Tax Rates Higher Than in Prior Years (1992).

24. *See* 1986 Blue Book, *supra* note 2, at 861.

25. *See* Treas. Reg. § 1.904-4(e)(3) (definition of a financial services entity).

26. H.R. 1690, 104th Cong., 1st Sess. (1995) (introduced by Rep. Amo Houghton and Rep. Sander Levine).

27. The 1992 legislation was derived from the Tax Simplification Act of 1991, H.R. 11, 102d Cong., 1st Sess., which was not enacted.

28. *See Language on Title XIII, Reconciliation Provisions Reported by the House Ways and Means Committee,* Daily Rep. for Exec. (BNA), Sept. 27, 1995, at Spec. Supp.

29. *See* Quick & Neubig, *supra* note 17, at 1417.

30. *See* Ken Militzer, *VAT: Evidence from the OECD,* 47 Tax Notes 207, 210 (1990).

31. See Hearings on Tax Reform Before the House Comm. on Ways and Means, 104th Cong., 1st Sess. (June 8, 1995) (prepared testimony of Sen. Richard Lugar) (unpublished).

32. S. 722, 104th Cong., 1st Sess. (1995). For a description of this tax, see *USA Tax System: Description and Explanation of the Unlimited Savings Allowance Income Tax System*, 66 Tax Notes 1482 (1995).

33. S. 2160, 103d Cong., 2d Sess. (1994).

34. Staff of Joint Comm. on Taxation, *supra* note 4, at 310.

35. *See* 1986 Blue Book, *supra* note 2, at 869.

36. The Freedom and Restoration Act of 1995, H.R. 2060, 104th Cong., 1st Sess. (1995).

37. *See* Peter R. Merrill & Harold Adrion, *Treatment of Financial Services under Consumption-Based Tax Systems, reprinted in* 68 Tax Notes 1496, 1497 (1995) (presented at a Kemp Commission hearing on Sept. 6, 1995).

38. General Agreement on Tariffs and Trade, opened for signature Oct. 30, 1947, 61 Stat. Pts. 5, 6, T.I.A.S. No. 1700, 55 U.N.T.S. 187 [hereinafter GATT], Annex I, Note Ad Article XVI (providing "[t]he exemption of an exported product from duties or taxes borne by the like product when destined for domestic consumption, or the remission of such duties or taxes in amounts not in excess of those which have accrued, shall not be deemed to be a subsidy").

39. Before Canada levied a VAT (effective Jan. 1, 1991) the twenty members of the Organization of Economic Co-operation and Development with VATs used the consumption type. *See* James M. Bickley, Value Added Tax in Canada: Background, Evaluation, and Implications for the United States, CRS Rep. No. 93-438 E, The Library of Congress 6 (Apr. 14, 1993).

40. Guidelines on Physical Incorporation, GATT, Basic Instruments and Selected Documents 32nd Supp. 156 (1985) ("Indirect rebate scheme can allow for exemption, remission or deferral of prior stage cumulative indirect taxes levied on goods that are physically incorporated (making normal allowance for waste) in the exported product"). *See also* Agreement on the Interpretation and Application of Articles VI, XVI, and XXIII of the General Agreement on Tariffs and Trade, Annex A, paragraph (h), n. 1 (1980) (the GATT Subsidies Code defines an "indirect tax" to include a sales, excise, or value added tax, whereas a "direct tax" would include taxes on wages and other forms of income).

41. *See Gramm Promises End to Estate Tax, Calls for Balanced Budget and Flat Tax,* Daily Rep. for Exec. (BNA), Oct. 18, 1995, at G-3.

42. *See Tax Reform: Gephardt Tells Kemp Commission He Expects Democratic Support for Tax Restructuring,* Daily Rep. for Exec. (BNA), Sept. 7, 1995, at G-6 (indicating suggestion in text was made by Wayne Angell, a former Federal Reserve governor now with Bear, Stern & Co.).

43. *See* Hearings on Tax Reform Before the Senate Budget Comm., 104th Cong., 1st Sess. (1995) (statement of Eric Toder, deputy assistant secretary for tax analysis, Department of the Treasury), *available in* 95 Tax Notes Today 36-29 (Feb. 23, 1995) (most of our trading partners now rely on a mixed tax system).

PART IV

IMPLEMENTING SUBSIDIES: TAX RELIEF FOR SAVERS AND FOR WORKERS

11

REGINA T. JEFFERSON

The American Dream
Savings Account

Is It a Dream or a Nightmare?

The general rule of federal income taxation is to tax all income as it is earned. However, since the establishment of the income tax in 1913, there have been exceptions to the general rule. Accordingly, income derived from certain sources and allocations of income to certain expenditures historically have received favorable tax treatment.[1] Typically, these exceptions attempt to encourage behavior that is believed to benefit not only individual taxpayers but also society as a whole.[2]

All taxpayers, including America's least wealthy taxpayers, subsidize the preferential tax treatment of these social programs. Everyone pays higher tax rates on the portions of their incomes that do not enjoy special tax treatment to compensate for revenues lost because of the social programs operated through the tax system. Although all taxpayers, rich and poor alike, subsidize the preferential tax treatment of these special programs, many critics of the federal income tax system have observed that most preferential tax treatments disproportionately benefit wealthy Americans.[3] Thus, some policymakers contend that it is grossly inequitable for the federal government to continue providing tax benefits to the wealthiest Americans without offering similar incentives to those with modest or little wealth.[4]

One of the country's costliest special tax programs is the private pension system. The private pension system is an employment-based savings program in which both participating employers and employees receive tax benefits. One tax benefit is that employer contributions are deductible by the employer when made, but they are not taxed until distributed to the employee.[5] This treatment is an exception to the general rule that an employer cannot take a tax deduction for salary-related expenditures as an ordinary and necessary business expense before the employee includes the payment in income.[6] Another tax benefit is that income earned on the accumulated contributions is not taxed until distributed. The nontaxability of investment income is the essence of the favorable tax treatment of qualified pension plans.[7] The cost of the national retirement program is estimated at $64 billion for 1996.[8] Notwithstanding the enormous cost of the private pension system, it was not designed to be a stand-alone program for individual retirement savings.[9] Instead, the private pension system was designed to supplement personal savings and Social Security old-age benefits.[10]

In addition to employment-based pension plans, the retirement system includes Individual Retirement Accounts (IRAs), which, on a more limited basis than employer-sponsored plans, provide individual workers with tax incentives to save for retirement.[11] Although in many respects IRAs resemble defined contribution plans, IRAs fall outside the qualified plan regime.[12] However, when defining the cost of the private pension system for the tax expenditure budget, estimates generally include the tax expenditure for IRAs.[13]

IRAs first were introduced in 1974 to provide a tax-preferred retirement savings arrangement for workers who were not covered by employer-sponsored plans.[14] Since that time, however, the IRA program has been expanded, so that it now allows individuals covered by employer-sponsored plans to establish and maintain IRAs.[15] An IRA can provide two distinct tax benefits to individuals. First, under certain conditions, individuals can deduct contributions made to an IRA from their gross income. Second, the investment earnings on the contributions made to an IRA are tax free until distribution.[16] In general, under present law, all workers are entitled to contribute annually up to two thousand dollars and to have investment income on the contribution accumulate tax free. However, taxpayers who are eligible to participate in employer-sponsored pension plans, or who have spouses who are eligible to participate in employer-sponsored plans, are subject to phase-out rules for the deductibility of their contributions.[17]

America's national savings rate is the lowest in the developed world.[18] This country's savings deficit contributes to a lack of domestic investment capital in the U.S. economy, and investment capital is essential for economic growth and prosperity. More national savings means more money available for both small and large businesses at a lower interest rate. In addition, increased personal savings benefits individual savers by providing a cushion to prevent them from living on the edge of an "economic precipice."[19] Thus, assisting individuals in saving for retirement accomplishes two important social goals: (1) aggregate individual savings increases, which creates greater national savings and investment capital for American economic growth; and (2) taxpayers who ordinarily may not be able to save adequately for retirement more likely can do so.[20] The accomplishment of both of these goals is desirable and necessary to ensure the well-being of both individual members of society and society as a whole.

Notwithstanding substantial federal income tax incentives to foster retirement savings, individual savings rates are declining in America.[21] Americans save only 4 percent of their after-tax income, as compared to 12 percent in Germany and France and 15 percent in Japan.[22] While it may not be surprising that the savings rate among low-income taxpayers is negligible, it is surprising that the savings rate among those in the middle class also is dangerously low.[23] In fact, the accumulated savings of middle-income Americans is so low that their savings are not expected to keep up with their projected future needs.[24] Thus, unless individual saving patterns change significantly, the bulk of the "baby boom" generation could experience retirement living standards significantly lower than their current standards.[25] Based on a "worst case" model, there is a risk that the baby boomers will not enjoy the same standard of living as their parents have during retirement.[26]

In an effort to raise the nation's dismal savings rate, and at the same time to respond to charges that too much is being done for the wealthiest taxpayers, the U.S. House of Representatives recently passed legislation that would reduce taxes substantially for middle-income Americans.[27] The Tax Fairness and Deficit Reduction Act of 1995 (1995 Act) is designed to provide $189 billion worth of tax relief mostly to middle-income taxpayers.[28] The figure of $189 billion is an estimate of the decrease in federal revenues that will occur over the five-year budget horizon from 1995 to 2000 resulting from changes in the tax law made by the 1995 Act.[29] However, budget watchers have raised concerns about the potential under the 1995 Act for substantial losses in revenues after the initial five-year budget period.[30] The 1995 Act also has caused much debate about whether the tax provisions actually will benefit the middle class.[31] Most of the argument centers on whether the benefits will go primarily to the wealthy or to the middle class, but few have bothered to define middle class. A general assumption appears to be that a household income level between $30,000 and $75,000 is middle income.[32]

The 1995 Act includes the American Dream Restoration Act under the Contract with America. As one method for providing relief to middle-income taxpayers, the American Dream Restoration Act creates the American Dream Savings Account (ADSA),[33] a more flexible retirement account than the traditional IRA. Investment earnings in ADSAs would accrue tax free subject to certain conditions, as they do in IRAs. A difference between the two plans is that taxpayers could continue to make contributions to ADSAs after the age of 70$^{1}/_{2}$.[34] Under traditional IRA rules, deductible contributions are available and distributions are taxed upon receipt.[35] If the taxpayer or the taxpayer's spouse is covered by an employer-sponsored plan, then the maximum deduction of $2,000 is phased out. The phase-out range is from $40,000 to $50,000 for joint returns and from $25,000 to $35,000 for single taxpayers.[36] In contrast, all contributions to an ADSA would be nondeductible and all distributions from it occurring after age 59$^{1}/_{2}$ would be tax exempt.[37] Distributions prior to age 59$^{1}/_{2}$ from an ADSA that had been open for at least five years would be also tax exempt, provided that the funds were used for the purchase of a first-time home, educational expenses, or medical expenses.[38] Distributions prior to age 59$^{1}/_{2}$ for nonqualified purchases would be subject to an early distribution excise tax.[39] In addition, for an interim period ADSAs would accept penalty-free rollovers from traditional IRAs.[40]

Thus, although there would be no immediate tax advantage when a taxpayer contributed money to an ADSA, that taxpayer ultimately could withdraw all of the investment buildup of the contributions tax free. ADSAs are referred to as *back-loaded* plans because their tax benefits would be deferred until distribution.[41] Conversely, traditional IRAs are referred to as *front-loaded* plans, because contributions are deductible when made, but all distributions are taxed upon withdrawal.[42]

Because taxpayers could use ADSA funds for qualified events, supporters of ADSAs contend that individuals ordinarily reluctant to save in traditional retirement savings arrangements for fear of losing access to their funds may be encouraged to save.[43] However, directing savings toward the goals of purchasing a first home, educating children, or paying for medical expenses raises numerous equity and policy concerns. As passed by the House, an ADSA has less restrictive distribution rules than a traditional IRA. Consequently, introducing ADSAs would redefine established pension policy substantially by shifting the focus from retirement saving to saving in general. To the extent that ADSAs would encourage individuals to contribute more to personal savings, they would be consistent with existing pension policy.[44] However, to the extent that they would cause individuals to save less for retirement, ADSAs could prove problematic.

Therefore, while it is important to assess the effectiveness of ADSAs in accomplishing congressional goals independently of other social programs, it is also important to determine whether these goals can be accomplished without undermining existing pension policy. To this end I describe and critique in this essay the objectives of ADSAs. I first place ADSAs into context by exploring the development of IRAs and describing how ADSAs differ from traditional IRAs. Then I analyze the potential social and economic effects of ADSAs' accomplishing their identified objectives. I conclude that the shift in pension policy made manifest by congressional enactment of ADSAs would have potentially dramatic implications for future retirement savings among middle- and low-income Americans.

THE DEVELOPMENT OF IRAS

Despite all of the attention recently given to numerous IRA proposals,[45] expanding the IRA is not a new concept.[46] Over the last twenty years, IRAs have become less restrictive and then more restrictive[47] in efforts to stimulate retirement savings equitably.[48] When Congress enacted the Employee Retirement Income Security Act of 1974 (ERISA), IRAs were limited to workers not covered by employer-sponsored plans. These individuals were permitted to contribute annually the lesser of fifteen hundred dollars or 15 percent of their compensation to an IRA. At that time, however, advocates for IRA expansion argued that because all workers needed supplemental retirement savings, all workers should have access to IRAs.[49] In response Congress in 1981 expanded the use of IRAs and allowed all workers to establish these accounts.[50] At the same time Congress raised the maximum contribution amount to the lesser of two thousand dollars or 100 percent of compensation. These two changes caused the number of IRA contributors to more than triple and the amount of IRA contributions to escalate fivefold in the early 1980s.[51]

The popularity of IRAs abruptly ended, however, when the Tax Reform Act of 1986 became law.[52] In 1986 15.5 million taxpayers claimed IRA deductions. In 1987, after the Tax Reform Act of 1986 became effective, only 7.3 million taxpayers claimed IRA deductions.[53] The 1986 Act substantially decreased individual marginal tax rates, which in part explains the sharp decline in IRA contributions. By lowering the marginal tax rates, Congress effectively reduced the benefits of tax deferral derived from IRA contributions.[54] Additionally, to help offset the revenue loss from lowering marginal tax rates, Congress widened the income tax base by limiting the deductibility of IRA contributions to workers and their spouses not participating in an active plan or workers who met certain income tests.[55] However, under the 1986 Act, just as under current law, regardless of a wage earner's tax deferral status,[56] she could make nondeductible contributions of up to the lesser of two thousand dollars or 100 percent of her current compensation and thereby avoid taxation on investment income until distribution.[57]

Congress made the 1986 changes because it determined that the expanded availability of IRAs had no discernible impact on aggregate personal savings levels. Congress also believed that the widespread availability of options to make elective contributions in cash or deferred arrangements (CODAs),[58] more commonly known as 401(k) plans, reduced its concern that individuals in employer-sponsored plans needed to save additional amounts for retirement. Another reason Congress made the 1986 changes was the indication by statistical studies that significant IRA participation was absent among low-income taxpayers and was present only among wealthier taxpayers, who presumably would have saved adequately for retirement even without the IRA incentives.[59]

Notwithstanding the findings and conclusions responsible for the 1986 limitations on the deductibility of IRA contributions, recently there have been numerous proposals to restore the benefits taken away from IRAs by the Tax Reform Act of 1986.[60] These proposals have as their rationale the need to increase national savings by increasing personal savings among middle- and low-income Americans. The ADSA is one of those proposals. By establishing a new retirement savings plan that does not incorporate the 1986 restrictions, enactment of the ADSA attempts to recreate the level of popularity that IRAs enjoyed in the early 1980s. Moreover, the ADSA would extend the available uses of the traditional IRA to nonretirement saving goals in its effort to improve the nation's saving level. By extending the flexibility of IRA usage beyond that of the pre-1986 period, proponents of the ADSAs hope to increase national savings by attracting greater numbers of low- and middle-income savers.[61]

THE ADSA

As passed by the House, contributions to an ADSA would not affect a taxpayer's eligibility to make contributions to traditional IRAs. Thus, taxpayers would be allowed to make contributions both to an ADSA and to a traditional IRA.[62] ADSA provisions also would allow all wage earners to contribute to an ADSA regardless of income or employer-sponsored plan participation status. Individuals could contribute up to $2,000 annually ($4,000 for married couples filing jointly) to an ADSA.[63] The 1995 Act also proposes to increase the $250 IRA contribution limit for nonworking spouses to $2,000 for the ADSA.[64]

For an interim period, from December 31, 1996, through January 1, 1998, ADSAs would accept penalty-free rollovers from existing IRAs.[65] However, the rolled-over amounts would be subject to an income tax at the time of transfer.[66] The tax would be assessed ratably over a four-year period starting with the taxable year in which the rollover was made.[67] Future earnings on rolled-over amounts would accrue tax free, and distributions from ADSAs resulting from these rolled-over amounts would be subject to the ADSA distribution rules.[68]

Several policy arguments exist for eliminating the 1986 restrictions on the tax deductibility of IRA contributions. One reason for lifting the restrictions is that denying tax-deferred status to employees covered by employer-sponsored plans assumes that all employer-sponsored plans provide adequate retirement benefits. Many retirement plans, however, provide relatively small benefits.[69]

Another reason for lifting the 1986 restrictions on the deductibility of IRA contributions is that denying tax-deferred status to employees covered by employer-sponsored plans assumes that all covered employees eventually will receive their accrued pension benefits. Some employees, however, will not receive their accrued pension benefits because of vesting rules. Employees who do not remain in their employer's service for the requisite time will not obtain vested rights in their accrued benefits and therefore will forfeit their retirement benefits when they terminate employment.[70] Thus, employees with short service histories are unlikely to receive sufficient retirement benefits.

Finally, the fact that individuals with no pension coverage are denied deductions for their IRA contributions simply because their spouses are covered by employer-sponsored plans ignores the reality that many marriages are not permanent.[71] The restriction on deductibility also fails to acknowledge that one spouse's retirement benefit may not be sufficient to support two retirees adequately.[72]

The ADSA legislation not only incorporates the expansive participation and eligibility rules that existed in the early 1980s when IRAs reached their greatest popularity, but it also introduces more flexible distribution rules.[73] Both the flexible distribution rules for ADSAs and the ability to roll over IRA funds to ADSAs radically change the underlying policy of federal pension law, which has been aimed at encouraging individuals who ordinarily would not be able to save to provide for retirement. Although there may be good reasons for lifting the 1986 restrictions, the expansion through ADSAs of the available uses of retirement savings would be potentially damaging to middle- and low-income Americans. Allowing nonretirement distributions from ADSAs would have a substantial impact on current pension policy and on future retirees because the distribution rules create disincentives to save adequately for retirement. Furthermore, it is unlikely that ADSAs would either benefit low- and middle-income taxpayers significantly or bring about the intended result of increasing aggregate personal savings among nonwealthy Americans.

Shift in Pension Policy. National leaders rank crime, health care, and welfare reform as the most pressing problems plaguing American society, but they identify inadequate savings as one of the leading problems of a second order of societal problems.[74] Low personal savings rates cross wealth and income lines. Interestingly enough, however, although overall national savings is down, more Americans save for retirement than for any other savings goal.[75] The relative popularity of retirement saving in general, and IRA saving in particular, has led to interest in increasing overall personal savings by using traditional retirement vehicles to direct saving toward other goals.[76] ADSA legislation relies upon this theory.

Historically, IRAs have been used exclusively for the purpose of retirement saving. The underlying purpose for the preferential tax treatment of retirement savings plans, including IRAs, is to encourage retirement saving, which in turn increases economic security in old age. To ensure that retirement funds actually are used for retirement purposes, Congress imposed restrictions on the use of retirement savings. Nonretirement use of retirement funds is discouraged by a 10 percent excise tax on the taxable portion of all early distributions from tax-favored retirement savings arrangements, unless the distributions are made on account of death or disability.[77]

Generally, distributions received before age $59^{1}/_{2}$ are considered early distributions. All early distributions from IRAs, as well as from employer-sponsored retirement plans, are subject to the early distribution excise tax.[78] Notwithstanding the penalty for early withdrawal, many individuals continue to take early distributions from their retirement savings, making those distributions available for current consumption. As a result some policymakers have argued that the early withdrawal penalty should be higher to ensure that individuals retain their retirement assets until retirement.[79] Therefore, to the extent that the ADSA distribution rules would allow funds otherwise earmarked for retirement purposes to be used for nonretirement purposes, existing pension policy would be undermined.

Some have speculated that the reason many who are eligible to utilize a tax-deferred IRA choose not to is that they are hesitant to put savings in a vehicle that places their assets beyond their reach for fear that they will need the funds before retirement.[80] The withdrawal rules of the ADSA address this concern by allowing penalty-free access to retirement funds after five years for qualified expenditures.[81] The less restrictive distribution rules undoubtedly would encourage greater contributions to ADSAs. However, these rules redirect the emphasis placed on saving for retirement to saving in general. This change of focus not only expands the concept of the private pension system, but it also de-emphasizes the importance of retirement saving, which effectively creates a new tax subsidy for current consumption.

Regardless of the restrictions placed on the nonretirement uses of an ADSA,[82] if retirement funds are spent for current consumption they will not be available at retirement.[83] It was for this very reason that Congress introduced the early distribution excise tax in 1986.[84] At the time, Congress believed it inappropriate to provide tax incentives for retirement saving if the savings were diverted to nonretirement uses.[85] Moreover, Congress generally provided for no exceptions to the early distribution rules, regardless of an individual's compelling need for the funds.[86] The ADSA therefore would violate congressional intent and fundamental pension policy by allowing individuals to use retirement funds for purposes other than retirement security. As a consequence, if the ADSA is established, millions of Americans, who previously were encouraged to save for retirement through the favorable tax treatment of retirement arrangements and discouraged from using those funds for current consumption by the 10 percent excise tax on early withdrawals, could choose to divert their retirement savings to nonretirement uses without penalty. The brunt of this policy shift would be borne substantially by middle-and lower-income Americans.

Dissavings for Retirement. ADSAs probably would be popular because they would allow taxpayers penalty-free access to their money before retirement for qualified purposes.[87] However, it is doubtful that contributions to ADSAs would result in an overall net increase in the savings of individual taxpayers because any projected increase in ADSA savings likely would be accomplished at the expense of retirement savings. For an interim period the ADSA, as passed by the House of Representatives, would permit the transfer of funds from existing IRAs to ADSAs without penalty.[88] Accordingly, prior contributions made to traditional IRAs, including lump-sum distributions from employment-based pension plans[89] previously rolled over into traditional IRAs, would be eligible for transfer to an ADSA.[90] Rolled-over contributions currently represent significant amounts of retirement savings.[91] From 1987 through 1990, for example, taxpayers made 11.2 million rollover contributions to traditional IRAs.[92] During that same period total IRA contributions reached $220 billion.[93] Therefore, if the ADSA is established, as much as $220 billion of current IRA retirement funds, if rolled over into ADSAs, would be available penalty free in five years for nonretirement purposes. Thus, not only does the ADSA legislation redefine present pension policy, but it threatens the success of the existing retirement savings program by allowing early, penalty-free withdrawals of current retirement funds for purposes other than retirement. This result could affect the retirement security of future retirees adversely by encouraging them to use funds earmarked for retirement savings for other purposes.[94]

Proponents of the ADSA likely will argue that spending for the permitted purposes is consistent with retirement policy goals and that these purchases serve to enhance future retirement income security.[95] In other words, they will maintain that purchasing a first home, educating children, and saving for medical expenses are all socially desirable goals consistent with pension policy and public interest. However, for individuals who currently use different types of savings vehicles for different savings goals, the limitations placed on the use of ADSA funds would prove effectively meaningless because the ADSA legislation allows taxpayers to shift their savings from traditional retirement savings arrangements to the more flexible ADSAs.

The following example illustrates this point. A taxpayer, some years ago, desired to save for retirement, to pay for a child's college education, and to purchase a new sports car. However, the taxpayer was forced to choose among these goals because of limited resources. The taxpayer, being a responsible parent, decided to forgo the sports car and to save for the payment of college tuition and retirement through mutual funds and traditional IRAs respectively. With the enactment of ADSAs, the taxpayer elects to roll over the entire balance of the IRA into an ADSA so that, if necessary, the funds will be available before retirement. By the time the rollover occurs, the retirement fund has grown to a level that easily could appear to be a comfortable nest egg. However, the appearance of saving adequacy may be misleading, given the uncertainty of future inflation, anticipated income increases, and expected investment performance.[96] Five years later the child enters college and tuition becomes due. Notwithstanding years of sacrificing to save for retirement security, because of a lack of awareness about the insufficiency of the retirement fund, the taxpayer decides to take a tax-free distribution from the ADSA to pay for the child's tuition. As a result of this decision, the funds in the mutual fund are now available to purchase the new sports car.

Effectively, by shifting savings goals and savings instruments, the taxpayer is indirectly able to use the ADSA funds, which have enjoyed tax-free earnings over several years,[97] to purchase a new sports car. Most people would agree that the purchase of the sports car would not be consistent with retirement income security or policy. Yet, the transfer of traditional IRA funds to the ADSA facilitates the purchase. Moreover, by shifting the funds, the taxpayer in effect is able to enjoy preferential tax treatment and a penalty-free early distribution for a nonqualified purchase. Absent the ADSA, the sports car purchase would not have been possible for the taxpayer without either incurring a substantial penalty[98] or forgoing the child's education. Absent the ADSA, the tax law would have encouraged the taxpayer to use the mutual funds for the child's education and the IRA for retirement purposes as originally planned. Thus, as this example illustrates, ADSAs not only would allow individuals to use money previously targeted for retirement for current consumption, but they actually would encourage them to do so.

Adverse Effects on 401(k) Plans. In addition to its negative impact on retirement savings in general, ADSAs ultimately would have an even more detrimental impact on employer-sponsored 401(k) plans. Under these plans the employee is given an option to have the employer make contributions to the plan from current wages.[99] Thus, the contributions are elective. Under existing law there is general consistency in the withdrawal rules for 401(k) plans and IRAs.[100] However, the more flexible distribution rules for the ADSA would give the ADSA a competitive advantage, which has the potential to cause contributions to employer-sponsored 401(k) plans to decline.[101]

If the ADSA legislation is enacted, some employees, especially low-paid employees, would prefer to save in ADSAs, where they could have penalty-free access to their funds earlier than they could if they saved in an employer-sponsored plan. Most employers already have trouble persuading low-paid employees to contribute to elective contribution plans.[102] Participation among low-paid employees is necessary to enable qualified plans[103] to meet ERISA's minimum participation and nondiscrimination standards.[104] The minimum participation standards limit discrimination in favor of highly compensated employees by requiring an employer who establishes a plan covering highly compensated individuals also to cover some individuals who are not highly compensated. The nondiscrimination rules ensure that the tax subsidy benefiting the highly compensated employees also provides some benefit to rank-and-file employees. Failure to meet these standards results in a plan's losing its preferential tax status.[105] If low-paid employees were to shift their retirement savings from 401(k) plans to ADSAs because of the less restrictive distribution rules, the maximum 401(k) plan contribution level of higher-paid employees would have to decrease in order for the plan to retain its qualified status. The availability of ADSAs, therefore, would be likely to cause the retirement savings among both lower-paid and higher-paid employees in 401(k) plans to decline.[106]

Ultimately, difficulty meeting the minimum participation standards could have a negative impact on the establishment and maintenance of employer-sponsored 401(k)s. Some employers may refrain from establishing or maintaining 401(k) plans on the assumption that employees would prefer to save in the more flexible ADSAs. This trend could prove problematic for future retirees because generally it is believed that 401(k) plans are more generous and offer greater retirement security than IRAs.[107] For example, 401(k) plans often have employer matching features as a way of encouraging participation. Under these options the employer matches a given percentage of every dollar of pay contributed by the employee to the 401(k) plan;[108] consequently, plan participants receive a greater return from their investments than they would if they saved in an IRA-type vehicle. Employer-sponsored 401(k) plans also offer the convenience of payroll deduction, whereas ADSAs would not. Most importantly, however, the typical employer-sponsored plan is professionally managed[109] and is designed to ensure maximum investment performance.[110] In contrast, the ADSA, like the traditional IRA, would require that investment decisions be made by individual ADSA holders, who may have little or no experience in financial management.

In sum, the ADSA could cause retirement dissavings among low-

and middle-income workers who would divert their retirement savings through ADSAs to current consumption uses. In addition, the ADSA could have an adverse impact on retirement savings among higher-income taxpayers to the extent that their contribution levels would be forced to decrease as low- and middle-income employees shift their retirement savings from employer-sponsored plans to ADSAs. Finally, ADSAs also could cause retirement dissavings if employers, operating under the assumption that employees would prefer the more flexible distribution rules of the ADSA, decided not to offer 401(k) plans.

Disproportionate Benefit to the Wealthy. ADSAs have been promoted as part of a middle-income American tax relief package.[111] However, most of the benefits from ADSAs would go to those who already are able to save. Therefore, although the proponents of ADSAs have targeted middle-class Americans as the primary beneficiaries of this reform, in reality upper-income taxpayers would receive the greatest benefits.[112]

The most obvious reason ADSAs would benefit wealthier Americans disproportionately as compared to middle- and low-income Americans is the tax system's progressive tax rate structure. The applicable tax rate increases as individuals earn more income. That means that the advantage of tax deferral increases as an individual's marginal tax rate increases. Thus, the incentive to save in a tax-deferred account and the amount of the tax subsidy creating that incentive is greater for higher-income than for lower-income taxpayers.[113]

ADSAs raise other related questions of fairness concerning the merits of a savings program based solely on tax incentives. For example, giving preferential tax treatment to first-home buyers adds to the large tax subsidies already available to homeowners, which include the failure to tax imputed income and the deductibility of interest paid for qualified mortgages.[114] Put more succinctly, the ADSA increases the disparity between individuals who can afford to purchase their own homes and those who are forced to rent. The inequity of this situation affects not only low-income Americans but millions of middle-income Americans who, notwithstanding tax incentives, are unable to purchase their first home. Similarly, the offering of a tax-advantaged method of funding education and medical expenses must be balanced against the adequacy of public education and health funds for lower-income individuals.[115]

Another reason wealthy Americans will benefit more from the ADSA is that, unlike 401(k) plan contributions, which are made by a cross section of the population, households that contribute to IRAs tend to be wealthy.[116] The primary reason given by nonwealthy wage earners for not establishing IRAs is lack of money.[117] More than 40 percent of low-income, non–IRA owners reveal that after meeting the cost of their necessities and basic expenses, nothing is left to contribute to an IRA.[118] Approximately one-third of Americans are convinced that, notwithstanding the need to save, they cannot save more because they do not have extra money. Seventy-four percent of households with an income less than forty thousand dollars do not save at all because of inadequate income.[119] Therefore, unless Americans earn more in wages, they will continue to lack sufficient disposable income to take advantage of ADSAs or, for that matter, any other savings program.

Contrary to the expectations of proponents of ADSAs, increased savings limits are not likely to increase total saving among low- and middle-income individuals. This prediction can be more fully understood by looking at current IRA contribution patterns. Under existing law IRA contributions are limited to $2,000. In 1987 only 5 percent of households earning between $10,000 and $20,000 made IRA contributions. These households were eligible to make fully deductible contributions of $2,000 to their IRAs.[120] Presumably, low IRA participation is primarily attributable to low earnings.[121] Thus, to the extent that low earnings are the reason for low participation, increasing the contribution levels for ADSAs for one-wage-earner couples from $2,250 to $4,000 will have no effect. Couples who cannot afford to contribute $2,250 under current law to an IRA will not be able to contribute $4,000 to an ADSA. Similarly, allowing all wage earners to make contributions up to the $2,000 limit (or $4,000 for couples) is not likely to motivate individuals who currently have little disposable income to save.

Thus, the principal beneficiaries of ADSAs will be those who already save and require no additional incentive to do so—the wealthy. They will benefit substantially from ADSAs because they will receive additional tax benefits for first-home purchases, education, and medical care expenditures which currently enjoy preferential tax treatment.[122]

Increase in Savings Unlikely. If the objective of enacting ADSAs is to increase savings in general, then a fair question to ask is whether taxpayers would be likely to use ADSAs for saving.[123] The Joint Committee on Taxation estimated that 73 percent of all taxpayers with earned income were eligible for full tax deferral of their 1991 IRA contributions and 9 percent were eligible for partial deferrals. Yet, only 2 percent of the eligible population made contributions to IRAs in 1991.[124] Furthermore, during the height of IRA participation in the early 1980s, IRA contributions never accounted for more than 1 percent of disposable income. Therefore, the IRA's history of limited participation suggests that it is unlikely that the ADSA would do much to bridge the personal savings gap between America and other countries.[125]

One of the most controversial features of the ADSA is that it is back loaded.[126] Accordingly, taxpayers choosing an ADSA over a traditional IRA must be willing to pay current taxes on funds not available to them in reliance on a future tax benefit. If tax rates remain constant, back-loaded and front-loaded savings arrangements provide the same tax benefits.[127] An example can illustrate this point. A one-wage-earner couple has $4,000 to invest in retirement saving at a 5 percent rate of return. The couple's marginal tax rate is 28 percent, and they plan to retire in fifteen years. If the couple invests in a back-loaded ADSA, they would pay an initial tax of $1,120, which leaves $2,880 to invest. At the end of fifteen years their account balance would be $5,988 and would be free from tax.

In contrast, if the couple invested $4,000 in a front-loaded IRA, they would pay no taxes initially, leaving the entire $4,000 to invest at 5 percent. At the end of fifteen years their account balance would be $8,316. A 28 percent tax would apply when the funds were distributed, leaving the couple again with $5,998 for their retirement.[128] If tax rates were expected to increase, however, the back-loaded feature would encourage increased ADSA savings.[129] Conversely if tax rates were expected to decrease, taxpayers would find it more advantageous to invest in traditional IRAs. Thus, the back-loaded feature of ADSAs would present a calculated risk for prospective ADSA savers.

The possibility of an income tax repeal presents a similar set of risks, especially for savers who may expect a future consumption tax.[130] Thus, the anticipation of income tax reform could discourage or encourage a taxpayer from paying taxes initially in reliance on future tax benefits. Taxpayers should rely on future tax benefits only if they are convinced that the current income tax system will be in place in the future, or at least that its replacement will provide equally favorable future tax benefits. It is therefore ironic that ADSAs, which create a tax incentive based on the present value of future tax benefits, are being introduced at the same time that the chairman of the House Ways and Means Committee is urging a total repeal of the current income tax system.[131] Moreover, even if the federal income tax system is not repealed and the income tax retains its current structure, years from now the rules for ADSA distributions could be amended. When one considers the increasing budget deficit, it is not difficult to imagine a taxpayer's reluctance to incur current tax liability in reliance on future tax benefits.

Even in the absence of the possibility of marginal tax rate changes, a repeal of the federal income tax system, or distrust of continued preferential tax treatment, the back-loaded feature of ADSAs alone may make them ineffective as a saving incentive. ADSAs may have less appeal than traditional IRAs simply because ADSAs do not reduce a taxpayer's tax liability immediately. During the early 1980s the IRA program was much more popular than it is today, particularly among middle-income taxpayers. Once IRAs were restricted and the tax deductible feature was eliminated for most workers, however, many taxpayers discontinued their contributions.[132] Just as the elimination of the immediate deduction contributed to the sharp decline in IRA participation in 1986,[133] the absence of an immediate deduction for ADSAs may minimize their investment appeal today.[134] An additional reason ADSAs may not have much appeal is the currently low marginal tax rates. IRAs were most popular before the Tax Reform Act of 1986, which lowered tax rates. Lower tax rates diminish the value of a tax-free buildup, making it less appealing to sacrifice spending flexibility for a future tax benefit. On the other hand, relatively low rates might encourage some taxpayers to invest in ADSAs and incur current tax liability because the risk of higher tax rates in the future is greater.

Administrative Difficulties and Adverse Budgetary Implications. ADSAs introduce significant administrative complexity. If the House version of the ADSA is enacted, it will be necessary to educate taxpayers about the differences between front-loaded and back-loaded tax programs. ADSAs also will be administratively burdensome to taxpayers and the IRS. Accounting for and accurately measuring the five-year holding period necessary for tax-free distributions for qualified purchases may become cumbersome. Many taxpayers will have both traditional IRAs and ADSAs, which could cause great confusion about the disparate distribution rules of the two types of accounts. As a result, taxpayers will incur additional reporting requirements, and the treasury will incur additional costs for the administration of ADSAs and the enforcement of their regulations.

A further issue is the cost to the treasury of ADSAs. Budgetary estimates indicate that if Congress enacts the ADSA as passed by the House, net revenue losses will be substantial.[135] For the interim period that taxpayers are allowed to roll over funds from traditional IRAs to ADSAs, the ADSAs would produce revenue because these transactions would be subject to an income tax. The income tax would be paid on the rolled-over amounts over a four-year period, beginning with the tax year in which the transfer was made. Thus, the conversion of traditional IRAs to ADSAs initially would increase revenue.[136] However, as individuals became eligible for tax-free distributions after the first five years, the ADSA would produce revenue losses that would increase exponentially. As a result, over time, rather than increasing national savings, ADSAs, by increasing the federal deficit, could actually decrease national savings.[137]

Various estimates project very different figures about the amount of revenue ADSAs would generate in the short run as well as the amount of revenue they would lose in the long run.[138] For example, the Joint Committee on Taxation estimates that ADSAs would raise $2.2 billion over the first five years through taxation of IRA rollovers but would lose $23.9 billion over the second five years.[139] The treasury offers different figures. It estimates that over the first five years ADSAs would raise close to $5 billion but would lose $22.7 billion in revenue over the second five years.[140] Budget experts may not be in accord on the revenue produced or the cost incurred in connection with the ADSA, but many experts do agree that the ADSA could be a fiscal nightmare rather than an American dream.[141]

ADSAs represent a dramatic movement away from the existing tax policy of providing incentives to save for retirement security rather than for current consumption. This shift in policy has potentially dramatic implications for future retirement saving. In particular, the shift in pension policy would discourage retirement saving among middle-and low-income individuals who previously have been encouraged to save

THE AMERICAN DREAM SAVINGS ACCOUNT 271

for retirement. Additionally, because the 1995 Act establishing ADSAs allows taxpayers to roll over funds from traditional IRAs to ADSAs, taxpayers would be encouraged to shift their assets from one savings vehicle to another. The ability to roll over funds that can be used only for retirement purposes to an arrangement that permits penalty-free nonretirement usages, may cause some individuals to shift their saving goals to accomplish favorable tax treatment of nonqualified expenditures. Furthermore, to the extent that ADSAs would adversely affect the establishment of employer-sponsored pension plans, they could have a negative impact on overall retirement saving. Finally, because the ADSA is backloaded, taxpayers would be required to risk paying taxes today in anticipation of future tax benefits. Thus, the success of the ADSA program in increasing savings ultimately would depend on how risk averse taxpayers are. Therefore, despite its potentially disruptive effect on current pension policy and its adverse budgetary implications, the establishment of ADSAs is unlikely to be successful in accomplishing its goal of increasing aggregate personal savings among nonwealthy Americans. Even worse, the establishment of ADSAs could be responsible for decreased retirement security among millions of middle- and low-income future retirees who currently are encouraged to save for retirement by the existing retirement program.

NOTES

I am grateful to Prof. Daniel I. Halperin for his comments on an earlier draft. I also wish to thank Peter Nikos Koufos and Elizabeth Diane Soscio for their extremely valuable research assistance.

1. *See, e.g.*, I.R.C. §§ 163(a), (h)(1)–(3) (allowing a deduction for "qualified residence interest"), 170(a)(1) (generally allowing "a deduction [for] any charitable contribution").

2. *See* Joseph M. Dodge et al., Federal Income Tax: Doctrine, Structure and Policy 244–46, 256–60 (1995).

3. *See, e.g.*, Camilla E. Watson, *Machiavelli and the Politics of Welfare, National Health, and Old Age: A Comparative Perspective of the Policies of the United States and Canada*, 193 Utah L. Rev. 1337, 1356 (1993).

4. *See generally* Regina T. Jefferson, *The Earned Income Tax Credit: Thou Goest Whither? A Critique of Existing Proposals to Reform the Earned Income Tax Credit*, 68 Temp. L.Q. 143, 143–45 (1995) (noting that the earned income tax credit (EITC) is designed to lessen overall regressivity within the federal tax system).

5. *See* I.R.C. §§ 402(a)(1), 404(a)(1)–(3); Regina T. Jefferson, *Defined Benefit Plan Funding: How Much Is Too Much?* 44 Case W. Res. L. Rev. 1, 2 (1993).

6. *See* Jefferson, *supra* note 5, at 2.

7. *See* I.R.C. § 72(t)(2); Daniel I. Halperin, *Interest in Disguise: Taxing the "Time Value of Money,"* 95 Yale L.J. 506, 519–22 (1986); Jefferson, *supra* note 5, at 2.

8. *See* Celia Silverman et al., EBRI Databook on Employee Benefits 19–23, table 2.5 (Carolyn Pemberton & Deborah Holmes eds., 3d ed. 1995).

9. *See* Jefferson, *supra* note 5, at 40–41.

10. *See, e.g.,* Senate Subcomm. on Labor of the Comm. on Labor and Public Welfare, 94th Cong., 2d Sess., Legislative History of the Employee Retirement Income Security Act of 1974, 1693 (Comm. Print 1976) [hereinafter History of ERISA] (noting that Social Security can only supplement pension and personal savings); 119 Cong. Rec. 16,824 (1973) (statement of Sen. Roth) (noting that Social Security can only hope to supplement income derived from pensions and personal savings).

11. *See* History of ERISA, *supra* note 10, at 3554 (statement of Senator Schneebeli) (stating that an IRA "allows the fellow who . . . is not covered by a pension plan to contribute to a retirement account"), at 4809 (noting that for the first time the millions of employees not covered by any pension plan will "be allowed to set up their own tax-free retirement plans"); Staff of Joint Comm. on Taxation, 104th Cong., 1st Sess., Description and Analysis of Tax Proposals Relating to Individual Savings 2–6 (Comm. Print 1995) (describing and comparing the tax incentives associated with IRAs and qualified plans).

12. *See* John H. Langbein & Bruce A. Wolk, Pension and Employee Benefit Law 51 (2d ed. 1995); *see also id.* at 41–52 (discussing plan types).

13. *See* Silverman et al., *supra* note 8, at 19–23, tables 2.4, 2.5.

14. The Employee Retirement Income Security Act of 1974, Pub. L. No. 93-406, 88 Stat. 829 (ERISA) (codified as amended in scattered sections of 29 U.S.C.).

15. Economic Recovery Tax Act of 1981, Pub. L. No. 97-34, 95 Stat. 172 (ERTA) (codified as amended in scattered sections of 26 U.S.C.).

16. *See* I.R.C. § 219.

17. *See id.* § 219(g).

18. *See* Bruce E. Thompson, Jr., *Time to Tackle Our Savings Deficit,* Wash. Times, Apr. 4, 1995, at A19.

19. *See id.*

20. *See id.*

21. *See id*; *see also* Joseph S. Coyle, *How to Beat the Squeeze on the Middle Class,* Money, May 1, 1995, at 106, 109 (quoting DeeLee, a financial planner, as saying "[t]he middle class does not postpone its pleasures any more").

22. *See* Coyle, *supra* note 21, at 109.

23. *See id.*

24. *See* Research Division, American Ass'n of Retired Persons, Aging Baby Boomers: How Secure Is Their Economic Future? 4 (1994) [hereinafter AARP Report].

25. *See* Douglas Bernheim, *Adequacy of Savings for Retirement and the Role of Economic Literacy, in* Retirement in the 21st Century, Ready or Not 73, 73–78 (Dallas L. Salisbury & Nora Jones eds., 1994). *But see* AARP Report, *supra* note 24, at 20 (stating that baby boomers may not be able to maintain their working life standards in retirement but may be better off than their parents will be in retirement).

26. *See* AARP Report, *supra* note 24, at 20.

27. H.R. 1215, 104th Cong., 1st Sess. (1995) (Tax Fairness and Deficit Reduction Act) [hereinafter H.R.1215]; *see also* Cheryl Wetzstein, *House Approves GOP Tax-Cut Plan, 246-188: Passage of "Crown Jewel" Completes "Contract,"* Wash. Times, Apr. 6, 1995, at A1 (discussing the House's passage of the Act).

28. *See, e.g.*, Wetzstein, *supra* note 27, at A1.

29. *See* Joint Committee on Taxation Staff Preliminary Revenue Estimates of Tax Provisions in Republican Contract with America (H.R. 6, H.R. 8, H.R. 9, & H.R. 11) (1995), *reprinted in* Daily Tax Rep. (BNA), Feb. 2, 1995, at L-1.

30. *See, e.g.*, Albert J. Davis, *Budget Implications of the Contract with America Tax Cuts* 67 Tax Notes 827, 827 (1995) (noting that in the following five-year period, 2000–2005, the U.S. Treasury Department estimates the revenue losses will increase to $452 billion and that this will seriously hurt efforts to balance the budget).

31. *See, e.g.*, 141 Cong. Rec. H4213-02-73 (daily ed. Apr. 5, 1995) (debating the Tax Fairness and Deficit Reduction Act of 1995).

32. *See, e.g.*, 141 Cong. Rec. S9356-01, S9363 (daily ed. June 29, 1995) (debate between Senators Murray and Dodd on the Budget Conference Report).

33. H.R. 1215, *supra* note 27, at §§ 6101–4.

34. *Id.* at § 6103.

35. *See* I.R.C. § 219(g)(1)–(3).

36. *Id.*

37. H.R. 1215, *supra* note 27, at § 6103 (proposed addition to I.R.C. § 408A, at (c)(1), (d)(2)(A)(I)).

38. *Id.* (proposed addition to I.R.C. § 408A, at (d)(2)(B), (e)).

39. *Id.* (proposed addition to I.R.C. § 408A, at (d)(1)(B)).

40. *Id.* (proposed addition to I.R.C. § 408A, at (c)(5)(B), (d)(3)).

41. *See* Clay Chandler, *GOP Contractors' 'Dream' Bill Has Deficit Hawks Losing Sleep*, Wash. Post, Dec. 9, 1994, at A27.

42. *See id.*

43. *See* Office of the House Majority Leader, H.R. 1215: The Tax Fairness and Deficit Reduction Act: Facts, Figures, and Sources for the Tax Bill Debate, H.R. Doc. No. 3572, 104th Cong., 1st Sess. 14–17 (1995) [hereinafter Tax Bill Debated].

44. *See* Gene Epstein, *The Coming Changes in IRAs Will Be Popular, but They Won't Make Americans Save More*, Barron's, Jan. 16, 1995, at 51 (noting that the purpose of IRAs is to provide a saving incentive).

45. *See, e.g.*, Vivian Marino, *This Could Be the Year of the IRA*, Assoc. Press, Feb. 28, 1995, *available in* WESTLAW, 1995 WL 4364689.

46. *See supra* notes 14–15 and accompanying text.

47. *See supra* note 14.

48. *See infra* notes 56–57 and accompanying text.

49. *See, e.g.*, H.R. Rep. No. 807, 93d Cong., 2d Sess. 521 (1974), 1974-3 C.B. Supp. 236 (comparing original IRA proposal submitted by the Nixon administration with the IRA proposal adopted by ERISA; noting that the administration's proposal was broader in coverage, because it would have allowed employees covered by employer plans with low benefit levels to establish IRAs; quoting statement of Rep. Broy Hill).

50. *See* James R. Storey, CRS Issue Brief: Individual Retirement Account Issues and Savings Account Proposals 1 (1995).

51. *See id.* at 2.

52. *See id.* at table.1.

53. *See id.*

54. *See* Stephen B. Cohen, Federal Income Taxation: A Conceptual Approach 10 (1989) (explaining progressive income tax structure).

55. *See* I.R.C. § 219(g).

56. *See* Storey, *supra* note 50, at 3.

57. *See* I.R.C. § 408(o).

58. *See infra* notes 99–110 and accompanying text.

59. *See* Staff of Joint Comm. on Taxation, *supra* note 11, at 16–17; Storey, *supra* note 50, at 5–6.

60. *See* Marino, *supra* note 45.

61. *See* Tax Bill Debated, *supra* note 43, at 13–15; *see generally* Hearings on the Contract with America Before the House Comm. on Ways and Means, 104th Cong., 1st Sess. (1995).

62. *See* Tax Bill Debated, *supra* note 43, at 13–15.

63. H.R. 1215, *supra* note 27, at § 6103 (proposed addition to I.R.C. § 408A, at (c)(2)).

64. *Id.* at § 6104 (proposed amendment to I.R.C. § 219(c)).

65. *Id.* at § 6103 (proposed addition to I.R.C. § 408A, at (c)(5)).

66. *Id.* (proposed addition to I.R.C. § 408A, at (d)(3)).

67. *Id.*

68. *See supra* notes 33–40 and accompanying text.

69. *See* Langbein & Wolk, *supra* note 12, at 137.

70. *See* I.R.C. § 411.

71. *See* Storey, *supra* note 50, at 5.

72. *See id.*

73. *See supra* notes 33–41, 62–68, and accompanying text.

74. Steve Farkas & Jean Johnson, Promises to Keep: How Leaders and the Public Respond to Saving and Retirement 8 (1994) (a report from Public Agenda in collaboration with Employee Benefit Research Inst.).

75. *See id.* at 9.

76. *See* Marino, *supra* note 45.

77. *See* I.R.C. § 72(t); Langbein & Wolk, *supra* note 12, at 349.

78. *See* I.R.C. § 72(t).

79. *See* Storey, *supra* note 50, at 6.

80. *See* Kathy Stokes Murray & Paul Yakoboski, *Congress Considers IRA Expansion*, EBRI Notes, Apr. 1995, at 1 [hereinafter EBRI].

81. *See id.*

82. *See supra* note 43 and accompanying text.

83. *See* Langbein & Wolk, *supra* note 12, at 342.

84. *See* Tax Reform Act of 1986, Pub. L. No. 99-514, 100 Stat. 2085 (1986).

85. *See* H.R. Rep. No. 426, 99th Cong., 1st Sess. 728–29 (1985).

86. I.R.C. § 72(t).

87. *See* EBRI, *supra* note 80, at 3.

88. *See supra* notes 65–68 and accompanying text.

89. I.R.C. § 402(c).

90. EBRI, *supra* note 80, at 2.

91. *See id.* at 4; Hearings on Proposal to Boost Savings and Investments Before the House Comm. on Ways and Means, 104th Cong., 1st Sess. (1995) (testimony of Martin Jaffe, CFP president, International Association for Financial Planning), *available in* WESTLAW, 1995 WL 35220 [hereinafter Jaffe].

92. *See* EBRI, *supra* note 80, at 4.

93. *See id.*

94. *See* Storey, *supra* note 50, at 8.

95. *See* EBRI, *supra* note 80, at 5.

96. *See* Cohen, *supra* note 54, at 198–99.

97. *See supra* notes 5–7 and accompanying text.

98. *See* I.R.C. § 72(t); *see also supra* notes 77–81 and accompanying text (describing the 10 percent excise tax for early withdrawals).

99. *See* Langbein & Wolk, *supra* note 12, at 251–52.

100. *See* I.R.C. § 72(t).

101. *See* Christine Philip & Vineeta Anand, *401(k)s Safe from New Competition*, Pension & Investment, Mar. 20, 1995, at 3.

102. *See* Gordon Williams, *Pensions Piranhas*, Fin. World, May 23, 1995, at 82.

103. *See* I.R.C. § 401(a)(4), (5).

104. *See id.* § 411.

105. *See id.* § 401(a).

106. *See* Williams, *supra* note 102, at 82.

107. *See* Philip & Anand, *supra* note 101, at 3.

108. *See* Langbein & Wolk, *supra* note 12, at 252; *see also* I.R.C. § 401(m) (explaining the nondiscrimination rules); Langbein & Wolk, *supra*, at 253 (analyzing the section 401(m) nondiscrimination rules for matching contributions).

109. *See* Philip & Anand, *supra* note 101, at 3; *see also* Regina T. Jefferson, *Rethinking the Investment Risk of Defined Contribution Plans* (on file with author) (explaining the advantages of professional management of pension assets).

110. *See* Philip & Anand, *supra* note 101, at 3.

111. *See* Chandler, *supra* note 41, at A27.

112. *See* Gary Belsky, *Why Most of the Rich Will Get Richer*, Money, May 1995, at 134; *see also* Chandler, *supra* note 41, at A27 (noting that expanded IRA-type programs only encourage asset shifting among those who are already high savers).

113. *See* Storey, *supra* note 50, at 2.

114. *See id.* at 8; *see also* I.R.C. § 163(h) (allowing a deduction for the interest on a purchase of a qualified residence).

115. *See* Storey, *supra* note 50, at 8.

116. *See* R. Glenn Hubbard & Jonathan S. Skinner, *The Effectiveness of Saving Incentives: A Review of the Evidence* 17 (July 12, 1995) (unpublished manuscript on file with author).

117. *See* Research Dep't, Inv. Co. Inst., IRAs: The People's Choice 31 (1985).

118. *See id.*

119. Farkas & Johnson, *supra* note 74, at 14.

120. *See* Storey, *supra* note 50, at 5 (noting that 8 percent of those earning over $50,000 made contributions).

121. *See* Staff of Joint Comm. on Taxation, *supra* note 11, at 52–55.

122. *See, e.g.*, I.R.C. §§ 127(a) (providing an exclusion of up to $5,250 for educational assistance provided by an employer), 163(h) (allowing deduction for interest on a qualified residence), 213(a) (providing a deduction for medical expenses exceeding 7.5 percent of adjusted gross income).

123. *See* EBRI, *supra* note 80, at 3.

124. *See* Storey, *supra* note 50, at 2–3.

125. *See supra* notes 21–22 and accompanying text.

126. *See supra* notes 41–42 and accompanying text.

127. *See* Hubbard & Skinner, *supra* note 116, at 12–13.

128. *See id.*

129. *See id.*

130. *See, e.g.,* Peter Passell, *Spending It: The Tax Code Heads into the Operating Room,* N.Y. Times, Sept. 3, 1995, at C1.

131. *See* David E. Rosenbaum, *Chairman Proposes Redefining Tax Code,* N.Y. Times, June 7, 1995, at A22.

132. *See* Jaffe, *supra* note 91.

133. *See supra* notes 52–57 and accompanying text.

134. *See* Staff of Joint Comm. on Taxation, *supra* note 11, at 64; Robert D. Hershey, Jr., *Toiling to Reduce Taxes in a Changing Environment,* N.Y. Times, Feb. 26, 1995, at C11.

135. *See* Chandler, *supra* note 41, at A27.

136. *See id.*

137. *See* Staff of Joint Comm. on Taxation, *supra* note 11, at 70–80 (explaining the relationship of national savings and the federal deficit, defining national savings as private savings plus public savings; public savings is positive when the government runs a surplus; public savings is negative when the government runs a deficit).

138. *See* H. Jane Lehman, *IRA Proposals Could Aid First-Time Buyers: Congress Weighs Waiving Withdrawal Penalty,* Wash. Post, Feb. 11, 1995, at E1.

139. *See id.*

140. *See* Alissa J. Rubin, *Tax Cuts, 10 Years down the Road,* Cong. Q. Wkly. Rep., Feb. 4, 1995, at 345.

141. *See* Chandler, *supra* note 41, at A27.

12

JONATHAN BARRY FORMAN

Simplification for Low-Income Taxpayers

Some Options

What can be done to simplify the federal tax system for low-income individuals? Some of the more promising alternatives include statutory and regulatory changes that could both reduce the number of low-income individuals required to file tax returns and simplify the return-filing process for those low-income individuals who must file returns.

According to the Census Bureau, more than thirty-six million Americans live in poverty.[1] The principal federal taxes affecting these low-income individuals are the individual income tax and the Social Security taxes. Once the earned income credit is taken into account, relatively few low-income individuals actually have a net federal tax liability at the end of the year. Nevertheless, the current federal tax system requires virtually all low-income individuals to file income tax returns, if only to recover refunds of their overwithheld taxes. Simplification of the federal tax system can alleviate the heavy costs and burdens imposed by the current system on both low-income individuals and the Internal Revenue Service (IRS). Such changes hold the promise of achieving significant economic and equitable gains. It may not be possible to simplify the federal tax system for all individuals, but it should be possible to simplify it for low-income individuals.

CURRENT FEDERAL TAX TREATMENT
OF LOW-INCOME INDIVIDUALS

The Individual Income Tax. The federal income tax is imposed on a taxpayer's taxable income. In general, the taxable income of a low-income individual is equal to the individual's adjusted gross income less a standard deduction and personal exemptions. A low-income individual's preliminary tax liability (if any) is equal to 15 percent of taxable income. The amount that the individual must pay with the return or, alternatively, the amount of the refund, is equal to the individual's preliminary tax liability minus allowable credits. Other than the credit for withheld income taxes, the principal credits used by low-income individuals are the dependent care credit and the earned income credit.

Each year, the U.S. Department of Treasury adjusts the standard deduction amounts, the personal exemption amounts, the earned income credit, and the income tax rate tables to reflect the prior year's change in the Consumer Price Index.[2] For 1996 the basic standard deduction amounts are $6,700 for married couples filing jointly and surviving spouses, $5,900 for heads of household, $4,000 for unmarried individuals, and $3,350 for married individuals filing separately. Aged or blind individuals generally are entitled to claim additional standard deduction amounts of $800, except that aged or blind unmarried individuals can claim additional standard deduction amounts of $1,000.

The personal exemption amount for 1996 is $2,550. The rate tables have also been modified so that for 1996 the 15 percent marginal tax rate extends to all taxable incomes up to $40,100 for married couples filing jointly and surviving spouses, $32,150 for heads of households, $24,000 for unmarried individuals, and $20,050 for married individuals filing separately. For taxable incomes above those amounts, marginal tax rates of 28, 31, 36, and 39.6 percent are applicable. The maximum earned income credit amounts for 1996 have also been increased. Individuals with one qualifying child are entitled to an earned income credit of up to $2,152. Individuals with two or more qualifying children are entitled to an earned income credit of up to $3,556. Individuals without children are entitled to an earned income credit of up to $323;

however, childless individuals under age twenty-five or over age sixty-four are not eligible for any earned income credit.

Individuals file income tax returns as married couples filing joint returns, as surviving spouses, as heads of household, as unmarried individuals, or as married individuals filing separately. Some 115 million individual income tax returns were filed for the 1994 tax year.[3] Of these, about 68 million were on Form 1040, 23 million were on Form 1040A, and 19 million were on Form 1040EZ.

Typically, about 70 percent of individuals claim the standard deduction in lieu of itemizing their deductions. For example, for 1993 roughly 81 million individuals claimed the standard deduction, and the remaining 33 million itemized their deductions.[4] An even greater percentage of low-income individuals claim the standard deduction: more than 90 percent of taxpayers with adjusted gross income of $30,000 or less claimed the standard deduction in 1993.[5]

Some low-income families also claim the dependent care credit. This is a credit of up to 30 percent of the employment-related expenses incurred to care for one or more children under the age of thirteen or for certain disabled spouses or dependents. Because the credit is nonrefundable, however, it is generally of little or no value to low-income families. For 1992 only about 15 percent of the benefit from the credit accrued to families with adjusted gross income of less than $20,000.[6]

Finally, many low-income workers claim the earned income credit. Of particular importance, the credit is refundable; that is, if the amount of the credit exceeds the taxpayer's income tax liability, the excess is payable to the taxpayer as a direct transfer payment. To claim the earned income credit, an individual must file a tax return, and individuals with children must attach Form EIC. Almost nineteen million families are expected to claim the earned income credit for 1996, and their claims are expected to total more than $25 billion.[7] Of that amount, $4 billion will offset preliminary income tax liabilities, and the remaining $21 billion will be refunded as direct transfer payments to these families. Virtually all of the benefits of the earned income credit go to families with adjusted gross incomes of $30,000 or less.

Social Security Taxes. Social Security taxes are levied on earnings from employment and self-employment covered by Social Security, with portions of the total tax allocated by law to each of the Old-Age and Survivors Insurance trust fund (OASI), the Disability Insurance trust fund (DI), and the Medicare Hospital Insurance trust fund (HI). For 1996 employees pay Social Security taxes of 7.65 percent of the first $62,700 of wages and 1.45 percent of wages over $62,700.[8] Employers pay a matching Social Security tax of 7.65 percent of up to $62,700 of wages of each covered employee and 1.45 percent of wages over $62,700. Similarly, self-employed workers pay an equivalent Social Security tax of 15.3 percent of up to $62,700 of net earnings from covered self-employment and 2.9 percent of net earnings over $62,700. In 1992 almost 118 million civilian workers were subject to Social Security taxes.[9]

THE IMPACT OF FEDERAL TAXES ON LOW-INCOME INDIVIDUALS

Because of standard deductions, personal exemptions, and the earned income credit, relatively few low-income individuals pay any income taxes. On the other hand, because the Social Security tax system has no standard deductions or personal exemptions, many low-income individuals are required to pay Social Security taxes. Fortunately, the earned income credit offsets the Social Security tax liabilities of most low-income individuals. Consequently, not many low-income workers owe any federal taxes at the end of the year.

Table 12.1 compares the combined income and Social Security tax thresholds (i.e., net federal tax thresholds) of various family units with their poverty income guidelines. For example, consider the tax treatment of a typical family of four in 1995—a married couple with two children. Assuming that the couple's income consisted entirely of wages or salaries, the couple owes no federal taxes unless they earned more than $18,370. Basically, the couple's $6,550 standard deduction and four $2,500 personal exemptions together sheltered $16,550 from the income tax, and the couple's earned income credit offset the rest of their income and Social Security tax liability. By way of comparison, the poverty level for a family of four in 1995 was just $15,150.[10]

Table 12.1 shows that many (if not most) low-income individuals had no net federal tax liability for 1995. In particular, low-income married couples with one, two, or three children generally received welfare-

Table 12.1. POVERTY LEVELS AND NET FEDERAL TAX THRESHOLDS
AFTER THE EARNED INCOME CREDIT IN 1995, BY FAMILY SIZE,
IN DOLLARS

	FAMILY SIZE					
	1	2	3	4	5	6
Poverty levels	7,470	10,030	12,590	15,150	17,710	20,270
Simple income tax threshold (before earned income credit)	6,400	11,550	14,050	16,550	19,050	21,550
Income tax threshold after earned income credit	7,357	11,550	19,386	22,360	23,425	24,490
Social Security tax threshold	0	0	0	0	0	0
Combined income and Social Security tax threshold (i.e., net federal tax threshold)	4,100	4,100	15,547	18,370	19,245	19,350

The table reflects assumptions that all family income consists of wages or salaries earned by a single worker, that families of two or more include a married couple (rather than an unmarried head of household with one or more dependents), that all family members are under age 65 and not blind, and that all family units are eligible for the earned income credit (for example, childless workers are between the ages of 25 and 65). Also, only the employee's portion of Social Security taxes is considered.

Sources: U.S. Department of Health & Human Services, Office of the Secretary, Annual Update of the Poverty Income Guidelines, 60 Federal Register 7772 (1995) and author's computations.

like subsidies from the federal tax system, through earned income credit refunds in excess of any withheld income or Social Security taxes. For example, a family of four with a poverty-level income of $15,150 received a net federal transfer of $1,171 from the federal government.[11] Many other low-income families were entitled to refunds for 1995.

On the other hand, some low-income childless individuals, childless couples, and large families had net federal tax liabilities for 1995. For example, a married couple with four children (family of six) who earned more than $19,350 had a net federal tax liability. Similarly, a childless individual who was eligible to claim the earned income credit had a net federal tax liability if she earned more than $4,100 in 1995.

An analysis of family units headed by unmarried individuals (i.e., heads of household) would show results similar to those in table 12.1.

For example, consider a single parent with two children and income equal to the poverty level. She owed no federal taxes until she earned more than $17,216 in 1995.[12] Her $5,750 standard deduction and three $2,500 personal exemptions together sheltered $13,250 from the income tax, and her earned income credit offset the rest of her income and Social Security tax liability. Moreover, a single parent with two children and a 1995 poverty-level income of $12,590 received a net federal transfer of $1,884 for 1995.[13]

In contrast, an analysis of low-income childless individuals and couples who are ineligible for the earned income credit (e.g., because they are under age twenty-five or over age sixty-four) would show slightly greater tax liabilities. For example, for 1995 a twenty-one-year-old childless individual owed Social Security taxes from her very first dollar of earned income; she owed income taxes once her earnings exceeded her $6,400 simple income tax threshold; and she has a net federal tax liability of $732 if she earned a poverty-level income of $7,470.[14]

Thus, in large part because of the earned income credit, relatively few low-income families with children owed any federal taxes for 1995. The earned income credit is especially important to single parents, who are most likely to be women. In that regard almost 64 percent of earned income credit beneficiaries in 1993 were heads of household.[15] The earned income credit also protects many childless workers and couples from regressive Social Security taxes.

Unfortunately, even though relatively few low-income workers owe federal taxes, most must file income tax returns and fill out Schedule EIC to recover their overwithheld taxes and their refundable earned income credits. For example, for the tax year 1993 almost 25 percent of the 114.6 million individual income tax returns filed showed no income tax liability.[16] That is roughly 28 million returns, and many of those were filed by low-income workers. Indeed, that year more than 12 million low-income workers received earned income credit refunds in excess of their income tax liabilities.[17]

Moreover, millions of Americans need help preparing their income tax returns. More than 56 million taxpayers used paid preparers for their 1993 tax returns.[18] That is about half of all individual taxpayers. Even more astonishing, more than 1.5 million taxpayers paid private preparers to help them fill out 1040EZ forms, and more than 5.8 million taxpayers paid preparers to help them fill out 1040A forms.

Furthermore, half of earned income credit recipients use paid preparers.[19] At twenty dollars or more per return for preparation, plus additional fees for electronic filing and refund anticipation loans, that amounts to millions of dollars going from low-income workers to private preparers. All in all, filing returns is burdensome and expensive for low-income workers and for the IRS.

OPTIONS FOR SIMPLIFICATION

Complexity is a major problem for the federal income tax system. Complexity erodes voluntary compliance with the tax laws, creates a perception of unfairness for the system, and results in high compliance costs for taxpayers and the IRS.[20] Simplification of the tax system is in order.

Simplify the Return-Filing Process

Recently, the IRS has implemented a variety of alternative tax methods that have helped reduce burdens on many low-income individuals.[21] Forms 1040A and 1040EZ were themselves efforts to reduce the burden on individual taxpayers. Also, volunteer programs such as Volunteer Income Tax Assistance (VITA) and Tax Counseling for the Elderly have helped millions of taxpayers. More than three million taxpayers received volunteer assistance with their 1993 returns.[22]

Newer alternatives include electronic filing, telephone filing (Telefile), 1040PC, and 1040EZ-1. Electronic filing allows IRS-approved tax preparers to send tax returns over telephone lines directly to the IRS service center computers. Telefile allows taxpayers to file 1040EZ returns using touch-tone phones. The 1040PC program allows taxpayers to prepare tax returns on their own personal computers. Finally, Form 1040EZ-1 is a simplified form of the 1040EZ. A taxpayer answers a few questions, attaches any W-2s, and signs the form. The IRS then figures the tax liability and sends the taxpayer a refund or a notice of tax due, together with an explanation of how the tax was figured.

So far, the most important of these alternatives is electronic filing. After a tax return is sent directly to the IRS service center's computer system, the information is automatically edited, processed, and stored. A refund can even be electronically deposited in an individual's account at a bank or other financial institution. Moreover, through so-called refund anticipation loans, taxpayers can usually get spending money even earlier than they can get their refunds. The IRS started accepting electronically filed income tax returns in 1986, and by the year 2001 the IRS hopes to convert some 80 percent of all taxpayers to electronic filing.[23] Of note, the IRS recently announced plans to allow taxpayers to file electronically through the Internet.[24]

Low-income taxpayers especially benefit from the IRS's efforts to simplify the individual income tax system, and the IRS should continue with those efforts, including (1) working to simplify its forms and publications, (2) developing and expanding its taxpayer assistance programs, and (3) exploring and expanding alternative filing methods. In particular, measured expansion of the electronic filing program and Telefile should result in significant simplification for both low-income taxpayers and for the IRS.

Another reform would be to allow the IRS to prepare returns for individual taxpayers. The IRS believes that it is barred from preparing tax returns by Office of Management and Budget (OMB) Circular A-76.[25] Promulgated by the Reagan Administration, that ruling was designed to prevent government agencies from competing with private-sector businesses. Modifying that circular, or at least the IRS's restrictive interpretation of it, would enable the IRS to help individual taxpayers prepare their returns.

It would make sense especially to allow the IRS to prepare returns for those low-income taxpayers who claim the earned income credit. Virtually all welfare programs help individuals apply for benefits, and the earned income credit provides a welfare-like benefit. Why not allow the IRS to prepare returns so that eligible low-income individuals can get their earned income credit refunds?

Simplify Returns

Increase the Standard Deduction and Personal Exemption Amounts and Repeal or Curtail Certain Itemized Deductions. Raising the standard deduction and/or personal exemption amounts would raise the income tax thresholds and would mean that fewer taxpayers would be required to file income tax returns. Of course, this would greatly simplify the tax system for those individuals and for the IRS. Raising the standard deduction would also decrease the number of taxpayers who itemize their deductions; there would then be fewer complicated tax returns for taxpayers to file and for the IRS to process.

Repealing any of the many itemized deductions would also reduce the number of individuals who itemize and so simplify their returns. Admittedly, relatively few low-income taxpayers itemize their deductions. Still, if the deductions for mortgage interest, state and local taxes, and charitable contributions were repealed, virtually no low-income taxpayers would end up itemizing their deductions. Moreover, because these itemized deductions are used primarily to reduce the tax liabilities of middle- and high-income taxpayers, repeal of these deductions would make the income tax more progressive.

Simplify or Replace the Earned Income Credit. Over the years the earned income credit has become both more generous and more complicated. For example, in 1996 a qualifying taxpayer with two children may claim an earned income credit of up to $3,556, but a low-income worker must file a tax return and workers with children must attach Schedule EIC to receive the credit. Not surprisingly, taxpayer compliance and participation in the program have become major concerns. In that regard recent studies have shown that the earned income credit reaches only 80 percent of its target population.[26] Moreover, over 20 percent of taxpayers who claim the credit mistakenly claim too large a credit or are completely ineligible for the credit. Consequently, it might make sense to simplify or replace the credit with an alternative program for distributing benefits to low-income workers.

At the outset it should be noted, however, that the earned income credit is a whoppingly successful program that, at least until recently, has enjoyed broad bipartisan support. Largely because of the earned income credit, millions of American workers pay no federal taxes. Furthermore, the credit provides important income assistance for millions of low-income workers, especially single-parent, female-headed households. And the earned income credit has lower administrative costs than any other welfare program, just 1 percent of program costs, according to the General Accounting Office.[27]

Simplify the Earned Income Credit. One reform idea would be to modify the 1040 Forms so that workers with children would no longer have to file a Schedule EIC in order to claim the credit. It would also make sense to simplify some of the earned income credit eligibility requirements. For example, it might be reasonable to simplify the definition of *qualifying child* and to better coordinate it with the definition of *dependent*. In order to claim another person as a dependent for purposes of the personal exemption, the taxpayer must generally show (1) that the other is related to the taxpayer (relationship test), (2) that the taxpayer has provided more than half of the support for the other (support test), (3) that the other's gross income does not exceed the amount of the exemption (gross income test), and (4) that the other does not file a joint return (joint return test). Different tests apply to claiming a person as a qualifying child for purposes of the earned income credit: (1) the taxpayer must have a child (relationship test), (2) the child must be under the age of nineteen or a full-time student under the age of twenty-four (age test), and (3) the child must have the same principal place of abode as the taxpayer for more than one-half of the year (residence test). It is no wonder that so many low-income taxpayers pay to have their tax returns prepared, because it takes the Code, a dictionary, and a tax advisor to figure out conditions such as these. Obviously, significant simplification could be achieved by conforming the definition of *qualifying child* to that of *dependent*.

Another reform would be to simplify the definition of *earned income* that is used to determine the amount of an individual's earned income credit. The current definition of earned income includes several items that are excluded from gross income and that are not reported on IRS W-2 or 1099 forms. Most taxpayers eligible for the credit have none of these items, but both taxpayers and the IRS must try to keep track of them. Consequently, one simplification would be to base the credit directly on items actually appearing on W-2 and 1099 forms. For example, it would make sense if an employee could compute her earned income credit directly from the *wages* entry on her Form W-2.

It might also be good to limit the earned income credit for self-employed workers to the amount of their self-employment taxes. Under current law the high level of earned income credit benefits available can actually provide an incentive for low-income individuals to report fictitious amounts of earnings. Such fraud is relatively difficult for wage earners because the IRS can match the employee and employer W-2 forms. Because only a portion of self-employment earnings shows up on 1099 forms, however, it is easy for self-employed workers to overstate their earnings. Consequently, limiting the credit available to self-employed workers may be an appropriate way to curb abuse (although, admittedly, such a limit would create an inequity between wage earners and self-employed workers).

Another improvement might be to simplify or repeal the so-called advance payment option. Under current law eligible individuals can claim a portion of their earned income credit during the year through increases in their weekly paychecks. To receive these advance payments, individuals must provide their employers with a completed IRS Form W-5, Earned Income Credit Advance Payment Certificate, but less than 1 percent of eligible individuals bother to file it.[28] Moreover, despite extensive outreach efforts by the IRS and by nonprofit organizations such as the Center on Budget and Policy Priorities, participation in the advance payment option remains dismal. Redoubling outreach efforts and incorporating Form W-5 into the standard Form W-4, Employer's Withholding Allowance Certificate, might increase the use of the advance payment option. On the other hand, it might be better to eliminate the advance payment option altogether.[29]

Replace the Earned Income Credit. Given the complexity of the earned income credit, it is worth considering some alternative approaches for distributing similar benefits to low-income individuals. One approach would be to replace the earned income credit with alternative tax provisions that could provide similar benefits directly to low-income workers.[30] Much of the complexity of the current system results from imposing Social Security taxes on every dollar of earned income and then using the earned income credit to offset those taxes for low-income workers. Because of that relationship, would it not be simpler if the federal tax system did not collect Social Security taxes from low-income workers in the first place?

One alternative would be to add a $5,000 or $10,000 exemption to the Social Security tax system.[31] Unlike the earned income credit, a Social Security tax exemption would reach 100 percent of low-income workers, and it would be less complicated than first collecting Social Security taxes and then using the credit to refund them. Also, unlike the earned income credit, which most workers collect around April 15 of the year following their work, a Social Security tax exemption would result in extra money every paycheck. This would be a powerful work incentive. For example, a $5,000-per-worker Social Security tax exemption for employees would leave $382.50 in the hands of every worker in America ($382.50 = $5,000 x 7.65 percent). Moreover, economic theory suggests that most of the benefit of a $5,000-per-worker Social Security tax exemption for employers should pass through to workers in the form of relatively higher wages.

Most importantly, neither low-income workers nor the IRS would have to bother with tax returns to get the Social Security tax exemption: millions of low-income workers would simply no longer need to file returns. According to the Joint Committee on Taxation, replacing the earned income credit with a Social Security tax exemption could eliminate more than ten million tax returns annually and free IRS resources for other, more productive work.[32] Moreover, the paperwork burdens for many employers could also be reduced.

Some might be concerned that a Social Security tax exemption would require a concomitant reduction in Social Security benefits.[33] But there would be no reason to reduce Social Security benefits; the revenue lost from a Social Security tax exemption could easily be made up by raising Social Security tax rates on earnings above the exempt amount or by raising income tax rates.[34] In any event, the earned income credit has already decoupled any real link between Social Security taxes and benefits. A Social Security tax exemption would just be a more efficient way of offsetting Social Security taxes for low-income workers.

Of course, much of the benefit of the current earned income credit seems to be geared to providing income assistance to families with children. But it would be simpler to provide that type of family benefit through a refundable child tax credit like the $1,000-per-child tax credit recently proposed by the bipartisan National Commission on Children.[35] Congress could start by making the $500-per-child tax credit in the House-passed tax bill refundable.[36] A portion of the needed revenue could come from the current earned income credit.

A second alternative would be to replace the current earned income credit with a tax benefit that reaches low-income workers through their employers.[37] For example, a tax credit could be provided to the employers of low-wage workers. Again, economic theory suggests that the benefits of such an employer tax credit would pass through to the low-wage workers in the form of relatively higher wages. Consequently, an employer tax credit could end up helping most of the same low-income workers targeted by the current earned income credit. Yet, an employer tax credit would be significantly easier to administer than the current earned income credit, if only because there are far fewer employers than low-income workers.

Another approach would be to combine the earned income credit with other welfare programs such as food stamps, Aid to Families with Dependent Children (AFDC), and Supplemental Security Income (SSI).[38] The multiplicity of these federal welfare programs has resulted in complexity, inequity, and high administrative costs. Consequently, it might make sense to combine the earned income credit and other federal welfare programs into a single, comprehensive program that could be administered by a single agency. That agency might even turn out to be the IRS, although the Department of Health and Human Services or the Social Security Administration might be more appropriate. Alternatively, the revenues now used for the earned income credit could be bundled together with the appropriations for other welfare programs and revenue-shared out to state welfare agencies. In any event the administrative savings that would result from combining the earned income credit with other welfare programs could be passed on to beneficiaries in the form of higher benefits.

Create a $500-per-year Exclusion for Interest, Dividends, Gains, and other Miscellaneous Items of Income. Another way to simplify income tax returns for low-income individuals would be to add an exclusion for some modest amount of noncompensation income. It just does not make sense to require millions of individuals to report negligible amounts of interest, dividends, gains, state tax refunds, and other miscellaneous items of income and then make the IRS dispute returns that miss a few dollars of such income. One option would be to let taxpayers exclude from gross income up to $500 per year of interest, dividends, gains, state tax refunds, and other miscellaneous items of income. The benefits of such an exclusion could result in a windfall to those middle- and high-income taxpayers who are more likely to have such miscellaneous items of income, but minor tinkering with the rate structure could easily recapture the lost revenue.

Classify More Workers as Employees Rather Than as Independent Contractors. Low-income workers face several problems because of the federal tax distinction between *employees* and *independent contractors.*

At the outset, some low-income workers may have difficulty in properly determining whether they are employees or independent contractors
for tax purposes. Many analysts have offered recommendations about
how to clarify IRS worker classification rules; such clarification could
help simplify the tax system for low-income individuals, employers,
and the IRS. But being classified as an independent contractor causes
two far more significant problems for low-income workers. First, low-
income independent contractors (e.g., taxi drivers) often find it difficult to save enough money during the year to meet their income and
Social Security taxes the following April 15. Second, the tax returns of
low-income independent contractors are generally far more complicated than those of low-income employees (e.g., they must file IRS Form
1040 and Schedules C and SE).

One solution would be to change the IRS worker classification rules
so that virtually all low-income workers are classified as employees. That
would make their compensation subject to the ordinary wage withholding rules. They would then avoid the financial hardship that often
results from the absence of withholding, and they would be able to file
relatively simpler tax returns as employees. Another alternative would
be to require that taxes be withheld from payments to low-income
workers who act as independent contractors.[39] Although low-income
independent contractors would still have to file relatively complicated
returns, at least they would avoid the financial hardship that can result
from underwithholding.

Simplify Definitions. Low-income individuals can also have difficulty determining the number of dependents they can claim and whether
those dependents are qualifying individuals for head of household status, surviving spouse status, the earned income credit, and the dependent care credit. Many analysts have therefore recommended simpler
definitions of such terms as *child* and *dependent.*[40] These individuals
may find the filing status terms perplexing. A person must first determine her marital status. Only then can she determine which of five filing statuses is applicable: married filing jointly; married filing separately; surviving spouse; head of household; or single. Much of the
complexity in the individual income tax could be eliminated if these
determinations were simplified. Still more simplification could be
achieved by having each individual, married or unmarried, with or
without children, file as an individual under a single tax rate schedule.[41]

Fundamentally Revamp the Current System

Integrate the Income and Social Security Taxes into a Comprehensive Income Tax. A more fundamental reform would involve better integrating the income and Social Security taxes. As previously mentioned, one approach would be to allow each worker to exempt the first $5,000 or $10,000 of earnings from Social Security taxes. Another would be to add standard deductions and personal exemptions to the current Social Security tax system.

An even more substantial reform would be to combine the individual income and Social Security taxes into a single, comprehensive income tax.[42] Individuals with incomes below some poverty threshold would be exempt from tax, and tax rates could be increased in order to raise the same amount of revenue. In effect there would be a single, higher-yield income tax instead of the current bifurcated tax system, and millions of low-income individuals would no longer have to file returns. For example, an integrated tax system might be designed to impose no tax on income below some poverty threshold, a 25 percent tax rate on income from that threshold up to $100,000 of income, and a 40 percent tax rate on income over $100,000.

Move to a Flat Tax. Another alternative would be to replace the current income tax with some form of flat tax.[43] The underlying tax base could be either income or consumption. The key is that above a certain threshold, a single tax rate would apply. To keep the single rate low, most flat tax plans would get rid of many, if not all, itemized deductions.

For example, Rep. Richard K. Armey (R-Texas) recently proposed replacing the current income and Social Security taxes with a flat tax on earned income.[44] Under his proposal a taxpayer would total her earned income, subtract a large personal allowance, plus a deduction for each child, and then pay a flat 17 percent rate on the remainder. Proponents of flat taxes are fond of saying that most individuals would be able to file their tax returns on a postcard.

Move to a Return-Free System. A return-free tax system would be another possibility.[45] Under the return-free tax system envisioned by the IRS, most Form 1040EZ and Form 1040A filers and a few Form 1040 filers, some fifty-five million taxpayers in all, could elect to have the IRS compute their tax liabilities and prepare their returns. Starting in January of each year, a taxpayer would initiate the process by submitting a signed postcard containing the basic information needed to process a return (such as name, address, Social Security number, filing status, and number of dependents). The IRS would then prepare a tax return based on information and withholding reports received from employers and other taxpayer income sources. Starting in early March, the IRS would begin mailing returns to taxpayers, along with a refund or a bill. If the taxpayer disagreed with the amounts shown on the return, he could return it to the IRS for adjustment. All taxpayers would remain responsible for the validity of their returns.

For a variety of reasons, the IRS concluded that it was not feasible to implement this return-free system. In truth the IRS system would not really be return-free; rather, at a taxpayer's election, the burden of preparing the return would shift from the taxpayer to the IRS. Taxpayers would save some time filing their returns (ten minutes for a 1040EZ filer and thirty minutes for a 1040 filer), but many would have to wait longer to get their refunds. Also, the program would increase the burdens on the IRS and on employers and other filers of information documents. To generate tax returns, the IRS would need to receive timely, verify, and post 970 million wage and information documents. The IRS estimated that it would cost over $1 billion and require about 17,000 additional staff to implement the program. Moreover, the program would burden employers and other payers; they would have to file their information returns with the IRS by January 31, rather than February 28.

With ever-expanding IRS computer capabilities, it may become feasible for the IRS to move to a return-free system in the future, and further consideration is merited. The return-free tax system envisioned by the IRS, however, would increase the agency's work load just when the goal should be to reduce the number of tax returns processed.

Move to a Final Withholding System. An even more fundamental change would be to move to a so-called final withholding tax system. Final withholding tax systems are similar to return-free systems, except that they rely more heavily on withholding.[46] Under a final withholding system, the amount withheld by employers and other income sources is the tax, thus eliminating the need for many taxpayers to file tax returns. More than thirty foreign countries use some form of final withholding, including Great Britain, Japan, Germany, and Argentina.

In Great Britain the income tax is withheld by employers under the British Pay as You Earn (PAYE) final withholding system. When an individual first becomes potentially subject to tax, an initial return must be filed so that the Inland Revenue can determine how much the employer should withhold. Thereafter, individuals with simple incomes and modest earnings are normally required to file a return only about once every five years. In 1991, for example, more than twenty-three million of the twenty-six million taxpayers eligible for PAYE did not file tax returns.

Would a final withholding system work in the United States? A final withholding system could significantly reduce burdens on both taxpayers and the IRS. In its analysis of the issue, the General Accounting Office concluded that most taxpayers who now file 1040EZ returns (about nineteen million in 1994) and many of those who now file 1040A returns (about twenty-three million in 1994) could be served by a final withholding system.[47] Most of these people would no longer have to gather information, become familiar with tax laws, or prepare and file returns. The burden on the IRS would also be greatly reduced.

Millions of low-income Americans have no net federal tax liabilities, yet they are required to file income tax returns to recover refunds of their overwithheld taxes. Millions more have to keep records and file unnecessarily complicated tax returns to pay relatively little federal tax. I have proposed a number of ways to restructure the federal tax system to help low-income taxpayers and the IRS.

In many ways the federal tax system is at a crossroads. Will it move toward having virtually every individual file a tax return, or will it move in the opposite direction and reduce the number of individuals who must file returns? On the one hand, the repeated expansion of the earned income credit has obliged more and more individuals to file returns, if only to collect their earned income credit refunds. On the other hand, technological changes, such as information reporting and electronic filing, could enable the federal tax system to move away from having so many individuals file returns. But whichever direction the tax system goes next, there will be opportunities to simplify the system for low-income taxpayers and for the IRS. It is my hope that the next round of tax reform will seize those opportunities.

NOTES

This essay is adapted from Jonathan B. Forman, *Simplification for Low Income Taxpayers: Some Options*, 57 Ohio St. L. J. 145 (1996) and from Jonathan B. Forman, *How to Reduce the Compliance Burden of the Earned Income Credit on Low-Income Workers and on the Internal Revenue Service*, 48 Okla. L. Rev. 63 (1995).

1. U.S. Dep't of Commerce, Economics and Statistics Admin., Bureau of the Census, Statistical Abstract of the United States 1994: The National Data Book 475 (1994).

2. *See, e.g.*, Rev. Proc. 95-53, 1995-52 I.R.B. 22.

3. Internal Revenue Serv., Selected Historical and Other Data, 14 Stat. Inc. Bull. 139, 189 (Fall 1994).

4. Internal Revenue Serv., Selected Historical and Other Data, 15 Stat. Inc. Bull. 141, 202 (Fall 1995).

5. Author's computations are based on data found *id.* at 144.

6. Staff of the House Comm. on Ways and Means, 103d Cong., 2d Sess., Overview of Entitlement Programs: 1994 Green Book: Background Material and Data on Programs within the Jurisdiction of the Committee on Ways and Means 707 (Comm. Print 1994) [hereinafter Green Book].

7. *Id.* at 702–4.

8. U.S. Dep't of Health & Human Serv., Social Sec. Admin., 1996 Cost-of-Living Increase and Other Determinations, 60 Fed. Reg. 54,751, 54,753–54 (1995).

9. Green Book, *supra* note 6, at 80.

10. U.S. Dep't of Health & Human Serv., Office of the Secretary, Annual Update of the Poverty Income Guidelines, 60 Fed. Reg. 7772 (1995).

11. *See* Jonathan B. Forman, *Simplification for Low Income Taxpayers: Some Options*, 57 Ohio St. L. J. 145, 153 (1996).

12. *Cf.* note 10.

13. Because her $12,590 poverty-level income is below her $13,250 simple income tax threshold, she has no preliminary federal income tax liability. She owes $963 in Social Security taxes ($963 = 7.65% x $12,590), but her $2,847 earned income credit more than offsets her Social Security tax liability ($2,847 = $3,110 - .2022 [$12,590 - $11,290]). Consequently, she will get a net refund of $1,884 (-$1,884 = $963 - $2,847).

14. *See* Forman, *Simplification for Low Income Taxpayers, supra* note 11, at 157.

15. Hearings Before the Senate Comm. on Finance, 104th Cong., 1st Sess. 6–31 (1995) [hereinafter 1995 Finance Comm. Hearings] (statement of Margaret Milner Richardson, Commissioner of Internal Revenue) [hereinafter Richardson Statement].

16. Internal Revenue Serv., *supra* note 4, at 197–98.

17. *Id.* at 144.

18. *Id.* at 217.

19. U.S. Gen. Accounting Office, Earned Income Credit: Targeting to the Working Poor 31 (1995).

20. *See* Tax Div. of the Am. Inst. of Certified Pub. Accountants, Blueprint for Simplification (1992); Federal Income Tax Simplification (Charles H. Gustafson ed., 1979).

21. U.S. Gen. Accounting Office, Internal Revenue Service: Opportunities to Reduce Taxpayer Burdens through Return-Free Filing 37 (1992).

22. Internal Revenue Serv., *supra* note 4, at 217.

23. *See* Rita L. Zeidner, *TSM: How the Service Plans to Move into the 21st Century*, 63 Tax Notes 1239, 1241 (1994).

24. Ryan J. Donmoyer, *IRS Plans to Take Cyberplunge, Allow Returns Filing Via Internet*, 68 Tax Notes 1534 (1995).

25. U.S. Office of Management & Budget, OMB Circular No. A-76 (Rev.), Performance of Commercial Activities, 48 Fed. Reg. 37,110 (1983).

26. *See* Richardson Statement, *supra* note 15; John Karl Scholz, *The Earned Income Tax Credit: Participation, Compliance, and Antipoverty Effectiveness*, 47 Nat'l Tax J. 63 (1994); George K. Yin et al., *Improving the Delivery of Benefits to the Working Poor: Proposals to Reform the Earned Income Credit Program*, 11 Am. J. Tax Pol'y 225 (1994).

27. *See* 1995 Finance Comm. Hearings, *supra* note 15, at 35–37 (statement of Lynda D. Willis, Associate Director, Tax Policy and Administration Issues, GAO).

28. U.S. Gen. Accounting Office, Earned Income Tax Credit: Advance Payment Option is Not Widely Known or Understood by the Public 3 (1992).

29. Yin, *supra* note 26, at 274–75.

30. *See* Regina T. Jefferson, *The Earned Income Tax Credit: Thou Goest Whither? A Critique of Existing Proposals to Reform the Earned Income Credit*, 68 Temple L. Rev. 143 (1995); Yin, *supra* note 26, at 279–94.

31. *See* Yin, *supra* note 26, at 280–86.

32. Staff of Joint Comm. on Taxation, 104th Cong., 1st Sess., Present Law Issues Relating to the Earned Income Credit 19 (Comm. Print 1995).

33. *See, e.g.*, Nancy J. Altman, *The Reconciliation of Retirement Security and Tax Policies: A Response to Professor Graetz*, 136 U. Pa. L. Rev. 1419, 1432–34 (1988).

34. Yin, *supra* note 26, at 280–82.

35. U.S. Nat'l Comm'n on Children, Beyond Rhetoric: A New American Agenda for Children and Families 80–88 (1991); Jonathan B. Forman, *Beyond President Bush's Child Tax Credit Proposal: Towards a Comprehensive System of Tax Credits to Help Low-Income Families with Children*, 38 Emory L.J. 661 (1989).

36. H.R. 1215, 104th Cong., 1st Sess. § 101 (1995) (Tax Fairness and Deficit Reduction Act of 1995).

37. *See* Yin, *supra* note 26, at 286–94.

38. *See* Forman, *Simplification for Low Income Taxpayers*, *supra* note 11, at 186; Jonathan B. Forman, *How to Reduce the Compliance Burden of the Earned Income Credit on Low-Income Workers and on the Internal Revenue Service*, 48 Okla. L. Rev. 63, 73 (1995).

39. *See* U.S. Gen. Accounting Office, Tax Administration: Approaches for Improving Independent Contractor Compliance 4-5 (1992).

40. *See, e.g.*, Deborah H. Schenk, *Simplification for Individual Taxpayers: Problems and Proposals*, 45 Tax L. Rev. 121 (1989).

41. *See* Marjorie E. Kornhauser, *Love, Money, and the IRS: Family, Income Sharing, and the Joint Return*, 45 Hastings L.J. 63 (1993); Edward J. McCaffery, *Taxation and the Family: A Fresh Look at Behavioral Gender Biases in the Code*, 40 UCLA L. Rev. 983 (1993); Lawrence Zelenak, *Marriage and the Income Tax*, 67 S. Cal. L. Rev. 339, 342 (1994).

42. *See* Jonathan B. Forman, *Promoting Fairness in the Social Security Retirement Program: Partial Integration and a Credit for Dual-Earner Couples*, 45 Tax Law. 915 (1992); Joseph A. Pechman et al., Social Security: Perspectives for Reform *passim* (1968).

43. *See* Robert E. Hall & Alvin Rabushka, The Flat Tax (2d ed. 1995).

44. H.R. 2060, 104th Cong., 1st Sess. (1995); *see also* The National Comm'n. on Econ. Growth and Tax Reform, Unleashing America's Potential: A Pro-Growth, Pro-Family Tax System for the 21st Century (1996), *reprinted in* 70 Tax Notes 413 (1996).

45. *See* Internal Revenue Serv., Current Feasibility of a Return-Free Tax System (1987); U.S. Gen. Accounting Office, *supra* note 21.

46. *See* U.S. Gen. Accounting Office, *supra* note 21, at 22–23.

47. *Id.* at 25; Internal Revenue Serv., *supra* note 3, at 139, 189.

13

GEORGE K. YIN

The Uncertain Fate of the Earned Income Tax Credit Program

A largely unknown element of the federal safety net for many years, the earned income tax credit (EITC) program has suddenly burst onto the scene as a highly controversial part of the nation's tax and transfer systems. Rarely a day goes by without the president, a leader in Congress, or some other important national figure or group voicing objection to or support for one or more possible changes to the program. The partisan division regarding the program seems as stark and unyielding as that concerning Medicare, Medicaid, or other major aspects of the federal budget. In this essay I discuss the evolution of the EITC program, how it came to be so controversial, and why current "reform" efforts, though perhaps well-intentioned, are largely misguided. Instead, I prescribe a major overhaul of the program in which the bulk of its benefits are delivered through the transfer system rather than the tax system.

ORIGINS OF THE EARNED INCOME TAX CREDIT PROGRAM

The EITC program provides cash assistance to certain low-income workers.[1] As originally enacted in 1975, the program was primarily designed to relieve eligible beneficiaries of their obligation to pay Social Security taxes.[2] Congress decided that workers should not be taxed into poverty. But instead of simply exempting low-income workers from the payment of Social Security taxes, which (unlike the income tax) are imposed on the first dollar earned, Congress created a small transfer program, administered by the income tax system, to reimburse those workers for the taxes paid. Like a negative income tax, the program provided a cash benefit, equivalent to a negative tax, to eligible recipients. Unlike a negative income tax, however, being poor was not enough to entitle one to the benefit; the recipient also had to be working and have requisite family responsibilities.

From the beginning the program enjoyed widespread, bipartisan support.[3] By providing income assistance to *low-income families with children,* but only if headed by one or more *workers,* the program offered a strong appeal to liberals and conservatives alike. Also, like a negative income tax, the program held out the possibility of being a highly efficient transfer mechanism. Government benefits could be delivered to eligible recipients without the administrative burden and cost of an elaborate bureaucracy.[4] The income tax system could provide "one-stop shopping": in one transaction, taxpayers could both settle up their tax obligations with the government and receive from it any net benefits to which they might be entitled.[5]

During its first ten years the program remained quite small and was not closely scrutinized. Nevertheless, there were early, inconclusive indications of potential problems with it. For the most part the difficulties were attributable to the incongruity of having a government transfer program for the poor administered by the tax system. Here, it is important to understand how the tax system is able to function with relatively low administrative costs to the government: the system achieves that outcome by shifting much of the burden of such costs onto taxpayers and the private sector. The self-assessment system forces taxpayers to determine their own tax liabilities and to file appropriate reports of their liabilities with the government in the form of annual tax returns. Taxpayers spend tens and hundreds of hours each year, as well as hundreds and thousands of dollars, "voluntarily" complying with their self-assessment obligations. The government then spends just a small fraction of that cost overseeing and reviewing the efforts undertaken by taxpayers to insure the accuracy and completeness of the reports.[6]

For many working Americans, tax withholding and information reporting relieve much of the burden of the tax system. Withholding insures that taxes are paid in a timely and relatively effortless fashion, and information reporting, typically supplied by the taxpayer's employer, facilitates much of the rest of the task. Thus, for many taxpayers, the burden of voluntary compliance is fairly modest in terms of both time and money. Of course, for those taxpayers with sizable amounts of capital income and more complicated economic lives, the burden is considerably heavier. Yet those same taxpayers, either because of their more favorable economic circumstances or their greater familiarity with tax arcana, may be more able to bear that added cost. In short, just as the income tax is a levy on one's "ability to pay," the voluntary compliance system might be thought of as largely a tax on one's "ability to comply."

These broad generalizations get turned on their head when the tax system also tries to administer a government transfer program for the poor. To obtain a government benefit through the tax system, a beneficiary must likewise incur the "voluntary compliance" expense of that system: the beneficiary must first be aware of the existence of the benefit and his or her potential eligibility for it and then must maintain the necessary records and understand and complete the necessary forms in order to obtain it. Furthermore, the burden cannot easily be reduced through withholding or information reporting.[7] As a consequence, a sizable portion of the administrative cost relating to the EITC program falls on the beneficiary of the program, who may have neither the economic resources nor the educational background to bear that burden without considerable difficulty. Moreover, many beneficiaries would not need to deal with the tax system at all but for the EITC, thus making a mockery of the notion of "one-stop shopping."[8] Finally, implementing a transfer program through the tax system produces one other quirky outcome: the concept of "self-assessment" becomes instead one of "self-certification." Individuals certify themselves as eligible for the government benefit and obtain it without having to encounter any person face to face.

As might be expected from the foregoing description of the program, there were early indications (based on limited available data) of problems in making eligible beneficiaries aware of the program and getting them to participate in it.[9] In addition, the rate of erroneous claims on the part of those who did participate seemed unacceptably high.[10] As indicated below, these and other areas of concern became more prominent as the program experienced a dramatic increase in growth.

GROWTH OF THE PROGRAM (1986–96)

Congress approved three major expansions of the EITC program in 1986, 1990, and 1993, with the last expansion phased in over the period 1994 through 1996. The changes increased the size and scope of the program in five principal ways. First, Congress raised substantially the level of benefits available from the program—to a maximum amount of $3,556 expected in 1996[11] —so that for many beneficiaries the EITC represents much more than mere relief from the payment of Social Security taxes. Second, Congress extended eligibility for the program to families with greater amounts of income. If the 1993 changes are fully implemented, families with incomes of up to $11,610 will be eligible to receive full benefits, and those with incomes of up to $28,495 will be eligible to receive some benefit in 1996.[12] Third, Congress provided increased benefits to EITC claimants with responsibility for two or more qualifying children. Fourth, it permitted certain childless low-income workers to receive a small EITC benefit calculated to equal an exact rebate of their Social Security taxes. Finally, it indexed all eligibility amounts to keep them up with inflation.

Table 13.1 provides some indication of the overall effect of these expansions by comparing the growth in total federal expenditures for the major means-tested, income-support programs between 1986 and 1996, assuming the 1993 EITC changes are fully phased in. The table indicates that since 1986 the EITC program has grown far faster than all of the other major means-tested, income-support programs, with the nominal growth in the EITC program between 1986 and 1996 projected to be *more than 1,000 percent*. According to these figures, by 1996 federal spending for the EITC program will be over $25 billion per year, or more than one and one-half times as much as the federal share of the AFDC program.[13]

There are a number of reasons for this phenomenal rate of growth.

Table 13.1 GROWTH IN FEDERAL EXPENDITURES FOR MEANS-
TESTED, INCOME-SUPPORT PROGRAMS, 1986–96

	TOTAL FEDERAL EXPENDITURES AND GROWTH RATES				
Program	1986 spending	1993 spending	1986–93 increase	1996 spending (proj.)	1986–96 increase (proj.)
EITC	2.0	13.2	560%	25.1	1,155%
SSI	9.5	20.3	114%	27.0	184%
food stamps	12.5	24.8	98%	n/a	n/a
AFDC	9.2	13.8	50%	14.8	61%

Source: U.S. House Comm. on Ways and Means, 103d Cong., 2d Sess., Overview of Entitlement
Programs: 1994 Green Book: Background Material and Data on Programs within the Jurisdiction
of the Committee on Ways and Means 262 (table 6-25), 389 (table 10-21), 704 (table 16-13), 782
(table 18-11) (Comm. Print 1994). All spending figures are in billions of nominal dollars.

Certainly, the core attributes of the EITC program—its assistance
directed toward the poor who work and who have young children
living in the home—continued to be extremely appealing to a broad
range of legislators. In addition Congress determined that other, related
objectives could be served by the EITC program. For example, during
the late 1980s there was considerable interest in developing a new federal subsidy for child care expenses, including the costs of health insurance for children. Rather than create one or more new federal programs, Congress and the Bush Administration eventually channeled
this interest into an expansion of the EITC program.[14]

But the growth of the program during this period cannot be
explained merely on the basis of its desirable programmatic elements.
After all, the 1986–96 period was marked by continued huge federal
budget deficits each year, with persistent efforts to curtail the rate of
federal spending on all sorts of potentially worthwhile programs.
Instead, two budget policy features of the EITC program no doubt
enhanced its attractiveness to policymakers.

One feature concerns how the cost of the EITC program is "scored"
for budget accounting purposes. In both 1986 and 1990 the cost of the
increases to the program were treated as *revenue reductions* for budget
purposes.[15] This characterization applied not only to the portion of the
program that in fact reduced taxes otherwise owed by program beneficiaries, but also to that portion representing an actual outlay of funds
by the government. In other words, *increasing the size and scope of the*

EITC program was treated for budget purposes as a tax cut, not an increase in spending. During a period when "no new taxes" was practically a mantra for certain of our nation's leaders, with tax cuts therefore being viewed in a positive light and spending increases in a negative one, this characterization gave the EITC program a critical, competitive advantage over other direct spending programs for the poor.

Of course, the same characterization can have the opposite effect where the objective is to restrain the growth in the program instead of continuing its rapid expansion. Such an effort could be characterized by its opponents as a tax increase rather than an attempt to control federal spending. Sadly, we have seen exactly that level of rhetorical debate in recent times. Those seeking to curb growth in the program have emphasized how they are "controlling spending," whereas those opposed to such moves have labeled them as "tax increases on the working poor."[16]

Of greater importance than the budget scoring issue is the treatment of EITC program changes in estimating the *distributional effect* of government actions. Here, one needs to recall the importance policymakers have placed of late on the distributional impact of tax changes: whether they disproportionately benefit or disadvantage certain income classes. Proponents of the Tax Reform Act of 1986, for example, included a pledge to maintain distributional neutrality: to enact changes that would continue the same relative tax burden across the entire income spectrum.[17] The same issue arose prominently in 1993 when the Clinton Administration offered as one of its tax proposals a broad-based consumption tax on energy. At that time the Administration sought out progressive proposals to offset the regressive impact of the proposed energy tax on lower- and middle-class Americans.[18]

In general, official distributional analyses utilized by lawmakers do not take account of the distributional impact of government transfer programs.[19] For example, enactment of a tax on the beneficiaries of the Head Start program to pay for an expansion of that program would have a neutral distributional impact because there would be no shift of the benefits and burdens of government action from one income class to another. Yet, under current policies the changes would be treated as regressive because the distributional effect of the expansion of the Head Start program would be disregarded. Rather, all that would be counted for distributional purposes would be the tax on the Head Start beneficiaries, a regressive change if viewed in isolation.

Although distributional analyses generally disregard the effects of government transfer programs, the EITC program is an important exception. Changes to the EITC program, apparently because it is part of the "tax" system, *are* taken into account in making distributional estimates.[20] In other words, if the tax on Head Start beneficiaries were used to pay for an expansion of the EITC program, the changes would be treated for budget purposes as distributionally neutral. Similarly, in contrast to an increase in, say, the food stamp program or AFDC, expansion of the EITC program in 1993 served as a progressive offset to the Administration's regressive energy tax proposal. Little wonder, then, that the EITC program has increased so much more than the other two. Indeed, this budget policy characteristic of the EITC program was perhaps the single most important reason that federal spending patterns for the poor have tilted so far in its favor in recent years.

COMPLEXITY, PARTICIPATION, AND COMPLIANCE

As the size and the scope of the EITC program have increased, so too have its problems. One problem is complexity, the bane of any program but particularly a program like the EITC in which the burden of administration falls on beneficiaries with relatively low levels of formal education and familiarity with applicable rules. Complexity in that type of program tends to deter participation and invite errors.

Compared with many aspects of the tax system, the EITC program is not that complicated. But surely that is not the right comparison. The fact that the EITC is implemented through a simplified Rube Goldberg scheme is of no solace to those who find any such scheme a complete puzzle. A better indication of complexity is the length of instruction booklets (thirty-two pages in recent years), the clarity of expression contained in those booklets, and the number and length of forms and worksheets that must be gathered and completed in order to file a proper claim. Based on those factors, most observers would agree that the EITC program is unacceptably complex.[21] True, many beneficiaries probably obtain professional assistance in preparing and filing their claims, but the cost of that help reduces the net benefit provided to the beneficiary by the program.[22] It also interferes with the work incentive effect of the program, as described shortly.

There are many reasons why the program has become so complicated, but the two most important are probably the desire for targeting and the presence of the program in the tax system. Targeting involves the creation of eligibility conditions to insure that only "deserving" claimants are entitled to the benefit. The more precise the definition of who is deserving, the more complicated the rule structure for all participants. Implementation of the EITC program through the tax system means that the program's rules need to mesh to some extent with existing tax rules.[23] Yet tax law is not the paradigm of simplicity. If one can imagine an irregular, multisided figure needing to fit into a hole with many highly irregular sides and crevices, one can get a little feel for the difficulty of the task.

To illustrate the problem, consider first the condition that EITC recipients must have the requisite family responsibilities, generally intended by Congress to mean responsibility for a minor child. But what do *responsibility* and *minor child* mean? For example, does responsibility refer to daily care and nurturing, monetary support, or something else altogether? Would a child over the age of majority qualify if disabled or a student? Does the child have to have a certain relationship with the EITC claimant and if so, what relationship?

Assuming appropriate definitions can be developed, who should be treated as meeting the condition when two or more persons have responsibility for the same child or children? Here, the tax laws help a bit by generally treating a married couple as one person. Thus, a married couple (acting as a single EITC claimant) or a single person with responsibility for a minor child both meet the condition.[24] But suppose the persons with shared responsibility are not married? Examples of such arrangements include an intergenerational household (for example, a grandmother, a mother, and a child living together), two adult sisters with responsibility for the child of one of them, or an unmarried couple living with their children. If those with shared responsibility in each of these examples are all treated as meeting the condition, then unless some type of formula is mandated for splitting the EITC, two or more benefits might be awarded for the same child or children, a result not intended by Congress.

Early on, Congress defined the EITC family responsibility condition in terms of the tax filing status of the claimant: to be eligible for the EITC, a claimant had to qualify either as a "surviving spouse," a "head of household," or a married couple with a child who is a tax "dependent" of the couple.[25] These categories were chosen because they establish the meaning of family responsibility for other, related purposes in the tax system. They also provide "tiebreaker" rules in the event of shared responsibility. Finally, the categories were selected because they were familiar ones in the tax system and therefore were thought to facilitate the filing task of the claimant and the review responsibility of the Internal Revenue Service (IRS).

Problems with these categories soon became evident. For one thing, they meant that EITC claimants had to satisfy *different* family responsibility conditions depending upon the nature of the family unit. A single-parent claimant, for example, was required to provide over half the costs of maintaining the household in which the child resided (one of the requirements for "head of household" status), whereas a married claimant had to meet other criteria, including providing over half the support of the child (one of the tests for a tax dependent).[26] In addition, the conditions themselves proved to be quite cumbersome in application. For example, "support" provided by the claimant did not include welfare benefits or child support,[27] so that an EITC claimant caring for a child with too much of either of those sources of funds unwittingly became ineligible for the credit. For these and other reasons, erroneous claims were commonplace.[28]

Congress responded to these problems by adopting a uniform definition of family responsibility: a claimant must have a child of a certain age and relationship who resides with the claimant for more than half the year.[29] And Congress then specified additional tiebreaker rules to apply when two or more potential claimants meet that test for the same child.[30] But these requirements represented new ones for the tax system, adding some complexity to the claims process and making verification by the IRS more difficult. Furthermore, by focusing only on the presence of shared residence, they arguably mistargeted the benefit in favor of parents who do not provide the bulk of support for their children. In short, it is difficult to implement a family responsibility condition, particularly if the condition must conform to some extent to existing tax rules and if the determination and certification of compliance with the condition are to be undertaken by the beneficiaries on their own.

As another example, consider the condition that an EITC claimant must be poor. This aspect of the EITC program would seem most easily administered by the income tax system because of that system's determination of a taxpayer's level of income. And indeed, the initial design of the EITC program calculated benefit levels based on the amount of income reported by the claimant for tax purposes.[31]

But matters did not stay that simple for long. There are important differences between the concept of income used for tax purposes and an economic concept of income, with many items of economic income, such as the value of certain fringe benefits, not being treated as taxable income. Congress decided early on to condition EITC eligibility based on a broader notion of income, not just taxable income, and therefore required a whole host of nontaxable items to be included in the base for determining whether a claimant is poor.[32] During the past year Congress has gone even further by implementing a form of wealth test for EITC eligibility[33] and by proposing to add even more nontaxable items into the claimant's income base. The Balanced Budget Reconciliation Act of 1995 expands the definition of income for EITC purposes to include tax-exempt interest, nontaxable Social Security benefits, nontaxable pension and IRA distributions, and certain child support payments, and to disregard certain losses.[34]

In theory, all of these modifications may be perfectly justified. After all, poverty is an economic condition, not some technical tax concept. The problem is that the tax system is not equipped to make those economic determinations. More often than not, if an item of economic income need not be included in taxable income, there is little or no paper trail of the item to assist the claimant in filing a proper EITC claim and to help the IRS in verifying the accuracy of the claim. As a result, the claims process becomes extremely burdensome to the claimant, with resulting adverse effects on program participation levels, and there is no effective way to protect against errors and omissions of the claimants.[35] The assumed advantage of using the tax system to administer the EITC program is lost if the program does not utilize the existing tax concepts at its disposal.[36]

FRAUD

We have seen how complexity in the EITC program may be an important source of inadvertent claimant error. Of course, claimant error may also be intentional. Specifically, the self-certification feature of the EITC program provides the opportunity for fraudulent misrepresentations of one's family responsibilities, income level, and working status in order to maximize the size of benefit available. "Curbing fraud in the EITC program" is now one of the rallying cries of those in favor of restraining growth of the program,[37] and although data is limited, there does appear to be a significant fraud problem in the program.[38]

No one, of course, favors fraud, but should fraud in the EITC program be any more a concern than tax fraud generally?[39] Some might argue in the affirmative, based on a moral and philosophical distinction between stealing someone else's money and stealing back what was originally one's own. A counter view, however, is that those who commit fraud in the EITC program may be less well off economically, and therefore somehow more sympathetic cases, than those who perpetrate tax fraud generally; it is difficult to develop much sympathy for the Leona Helmsleys of the world.

If the moral and philosophical element is set aside, there are still reasons for special concern about EITC fraud. For one thing, one senses that the IRS may not be able to devote full effort to tracking down erroneous $2,000 and $3,000 EITC claims, whether resulting from fraud or not; surely the agency has bigger fish to fry than that. But if the EITC program is to be largely unmonitored, it would seem especially important to design a program well insulated against possible fraud. In that regard current proposals to add EITC eligibility conditions that are not part of the normal income tax system increase the program's susceptibility to fraud by making it more likely that a fraudulent disregard of the law will go undetected.[40]

Another reason to be concerned about EITC fraud involves a relatively unique feature of the program: up to some level, it actually awards *greater* amounts of benefits to claimants who report higher levels of income. The program was designed in this manner to enhance the work incentive for very low-income workers, a topic discussed in the next section. But from a fraud standpoint, it means that there are incentives for claimants to *over*state their income levels.

The IRS is, and will be, hard pressed to deal with this type of fraud, should it occur. The tax laws and administrative procedures are all designed to ferret out income *under*statement cases, not the reverse situation. For example, information reporting creates a record to help prevent taxpayers from fraudulently omitting an item of income from their tax return. But if taxpayers voluntarily choose to report income amounts in excess of those reflected in their records, the IRS is ordinarily in no position to rebuff such assertions.[41]

What can be done to prevent EITC fraud? If monitoring efforts are to be minimal, the answer must lie in reducing opportunities and incentives to commit fraud. To reduce opportunities, the key step is tying eligibility conditions to easily verifiable items. Thus, it might be appropriate to consider only taxable wage and salary income provided by an employer as evidence that the claimant worked during the year and may therefore be eligible for the EITC. The presence of such income can be verified through information reporting provided by the employer. To reduce incentives for fraud, one could shrink the size of the maximum benefit awarded. In the income overstatement situation, for example, the reporting of income carries with it certain liabilities such as employment taxes due. Hence, if the size of the EITC benefit were tailored merely to offset the claimant's income and employment tax liabilities, there would be no incentive to overstate income and commit fraud in the process.[42]

WORK INCENTIVE OR DISINCENTIVE?

One major source of controversy surrounding the EITC program is its labor supply effect. Proponents argue that by increasing the return from work, the program favors work over leisure. Those who are currently not working, such as welfare recipients, would receive an unambiguously positive incentive from the program to begin work.[43] Others note that the benefits provided by the program permit a recipient to achieve desired consumption levels with less work. This "income effect" of the program therefore discourages work. Furthermore, once income levels of a beneficiary become high enough to cause a gradual loss of EITC benefits, additional work actually reduces the return from work. Thus, for those beneficiaries in the income range where benefits are level or being phased out, there is an unambiguously negative effect on work.[44]

A few studies have attempted to measure the impact of the EITC program on hours worked, but they have found a small, almost negligible, overall effect.[45] Needless to say, many questions remain about the program's net labor supply effect as well as its impact on categories of work and subpopulations. For example, what types of work are encouraged and discouraged by the program: does it result in an overall increase in national product? Relatedly, how much of the work encouraged by the program is already taking place "off the books" in order to avoid tax and other consequences of "on-the-books" activity? *Who* is being encouraged and discouraged to work more or less? Are current welfare recipients being encouraged to work, are secondary earners of two-earner married couples being discouraged from doing so, and would those results be desirable from a policy standpoint? Lastly, what are the labor supply effects on those who must finance the cost of the program through higher taxes?[46]

Some contend that it is inappropriate to measure the value of an antipoverty program like the EITC on an efficiency scale, such as whether it increases national product, because the program is a redistributive one, which is trying to achieve other goals. Under this view any program that shifts benefits from the more to the less well-off may have an adverse labor supply effect. Rather, the appropriate scope of comparison is with other alternatives that attempt to accomplish the same wealth transfer. Applying that test, some argue that the EITC program has a more favorable effect on labor supply than do pure welfare or other programs for the poor.[47]

But perhaps comparing a program tied to work, such as the EITC, with a program not tied to work, such as pure welfare, is also a false test. The proper question is whether a redistributive program linked to work effort should be administered through the tax or transfer system. In that regard the existing program carried out by the tax system would seem to have two big strikes against it. First, despite considerable efforts to encourage recipients to receive the EITC benefit little-by-little in each paycheck, as is permitted under current law, almost all current recipients obtain the benefit just once a year, in the form of a lump-sum check received at tax time.[48] Second, as previously mentioned, many recipients likely utilize a paid intermediary—an income tax return preparer—to obtain their EITC benefit, and the intermediary may well convey little or no information regarding the critical link between work effort and benefit obtained. Both of these aspects of the existing EITC program—a once-a-year check and the presence of an uncommunicative intermediary—would seem to mute any significant influence the program might have on the work decision. The EITC check from the government might well be perceived as an income tax refund, a product of the tax return preparer's ingenuity, or simply a pure windfall, and not a reward for work and work effort.[49]

IMPACT ON THE MARRIAGE DECISION

Consider two individuals whose income levels and family responsibilities entitle each of them to a maximum EITC benefit of over $3,000 apiece. Under current law, if the two individuals were to get married, they would not be entitled to aggregate their respective EITC awards to produce a total benefit of over $6,000. Rather, as a married couple, they would be entitled to a total EITC of only approximately $1,000. In other words, by getting married, the two individuals would suffer a "marriage penalty" of approximately $5,000, or more than 80 percent of their premarriage entitlement.

Why would the individuals suffer such a loss of benefits if they decided to get married? The reason is that as a married couple, their pooled incomes make them appear less needy, and therefore less deserving of the EITC benefit. Hence, they would experience a reduction in the size of their award. The existing benefit structure could be, and perhaps should be, modified a bit to lessen the size of the marriage penalty, but at some point the shift in benefits from single heads of households to married couples would be unacceptable. To illustrate, if the marriage penalty were to be completely eliminated in the initial example, a married couple earning twice the amount of a single head of household would have to receive not merely the same amount of EITC benefit but *twice* the size of the single person's benefit. It is difficult to see how a need-based program like the EITC could justify such a disparity in awards.

The marriage penalty in the EITC program is thus caused by the choice of household unit utilized to determine need.[50] Current law treats a married couple and a single head of household exactly alike for that purpose. If the couple and the household head have the same amount of income, they are treated as equally needy and entitled to the same size EITC benefit. Therefore, if two single household heads with equal amounts of income get married, they appear for EITC purposes to be twice as well off as their individual premarriage situations, and therefore not entitled to receive a benefit even as large as either of their premarriage awards.

One method for achieving marriage neutrality would be to disregard the existence of marital status in the award structure. The relevant unit for determining need would be the individual; the economic situation of the claimant's spouse, if the claimant were married, would be ignored. Although this approach would eliminate all marriage penalties, it would presumably not be a satisfactory solution. It would potentially allow, for example, a low-income spouse of a millionaire to receive the EITC.[51]

Most antipoverty programs move in the opposite direction and broaden the definition of the relevant unit beyond merely single heads of household and married couples.[52] One might, for example, treat all of the members of the same household as the appropriate unit for purposes of determining need. Thus, if the two individuals in the initial example had been members of the same household even prior to their marriage to one another, their decision to marry would not affect the amount of their EITC award. Both prior to and following marriage, they would be treated alike for EITC purposes. But this solution simply shifts the penalty to some earlier stage in their relationship, when they were not yet sharing a household but were contemplating doing so. The decision to become members of the same household would trigger the penalty. In addition, defining "household" for this purpose would be a formidable task and could make the IRS's review function in this area extremely intrusive.[53]

In summary, the EITC program creates fairly sizable marriage penalties, but they are largely unavoidable if the present general design of the program is retained. Perhaps the one positive comment one can make is that the decision to marry is very complex, and therefore maybe not heavily influenced by the existence of marriage penalties in the tax and transfer systems.[54]

THE EITC AND CONSUMPTION TAXES

There seems to be greater and greater interest each day in adoption in this country of a broad-based consumption tax to replace the existing income tax. We are told that the income tax (along with the IRS) is going to be torn out of the tax system by its roots and disposed of completely. That scenario raises an interesting thought: how would the EITC program fare in a pure consumption tax world?

Not very well, one suspects. But not because the program wouldn't be needed. Indeed, even proponents of broad-based consumption taxes advocate the continuation and expansion of EITC-type programs to offset the fact that a consumption tax would be more regressive than the existing income tax.[55] Because the poor consume a greater proportion of their income than the wealthy, it is believed that a change from taxing income to taxing consumption would shift some of the tax burden from the wealthy to the poor. The analysis is actually more complicated than that, but the conclusion is reasonably accurate as a short-term forecast.[56]

Thus, an EITC-type program might be needed as a policy tool in a consumption tax world, but how would such a program be designed and implemented? Here, we come up against a stark reality: although *income* for present tax law purposes is a number of steps short of the concept of *economic income,* the amount of one's consumption is even further removed from that concept. Yet, as discussed earlier, economic income is the appropriate measure for entitlement to a benefit such as the EITC; it measures need for the need-based benefit. Therefore, by enacting a consumption tax and completely repealing the existing income tax, lawmakers would make it even more difficult to ascertain economic income levels and entitlement to need-based benefits. Put more simply, the EITC program is designed to help the poor, but *in a pure consumption tax world, one would not know who the poor would be.*[57] A person who consumes very little, and therefore pays very little consumption tax, may nevertheless have ample amounts of income and wealth and should not benefit from a need-based program like the EITC. But how would we know who should benefit?

PRESCRIPTION FOR CHANGE

I have described how obscure budget accounting policies largely explain the recent, phenomenal growth of the EITC program and why it is now such an important part of the nation's tax and transfer systems. With the growth and resulting increased public scrutiny, however, has come the realization that this program, trapped in the tax system, faces very significant problems. As the ETIC is presently designed, it will be difficult if not impossible for the program to be as targeted as Congress apparently desires, to maintain high levels of participation and compliance, to serve as an effective work incentive, to be neutral toward the decision to marry, and to avoid unacceptable levels of fraud. Furthermore, the outlook for the program is not brightened by the possible switch to a broad-based consumption tax.

Thus, there is ample cause for concern on the part of policymakers interested in improving the effectiveness of the program. Unfortunately, though the current level of rhetoric about the program is high, the degree of serious debate and analysis by lawmakers is extremely low. This state of affairs is reflected in current 'reform' proposals that seem certain at this time to make the program only harder to administer. Among the ideas presently being considered are further efforts to target the benefit more precisely and to create differential treatment of various subgroups of the EITC population.[58] Although many of the ideas may be well-intentioned, the net effect will surely increase the complexity of the program, with resulting adverse impact on participation, compliance, and efforts to curb fraud.[59]

The problems are extremely difficult but perhaps not completely intractable. The following four points provide a blueprint for reforming the manner in which benefits are provided to the working poor. They assume a policy determination that a redistribution of a certain amount of benefits in favor of low-income workers is desirable.

1. One straightforward suggestion is to return at least a part of the EITC program to its roots and to exempt the first $5,000 or $10,000 of wages of a worker from the payment of Social Security taxes.[60] As described earlier, the EITC originated in part as an effort to rebate to low-income workers the Social Security taxes collected from them. Instead of collecting such taxes and then trying to return those amounts to workers in the form of the EITC, it would make much

more sense simply to refrain from collecting the payroll taxes in the first place.

The appeal of this idea is its simplicity: an exemption could be easily administered by employers through an adjustment to the Social Security tax withholding tables. Claimants would not need to file claims to get the benefit—the ultimate simplification for them—so participation levels would be extremely high. Furthermore, the link between work and reward would be more evident because the benefit would appear in each paycheck rather than as a lump sum at the end of the year. Each individual could be treated separately, thereby eliminating marriage penalty problems. Finally, compliance could be expected to be very high because of the simplicity of the system and because there would be no net cash benefit transferred by the government back to the beneficiaries. Hence, the incentive to commit fraud to obtain the benefit would not be nearly as strong as under the current program. In addition, taxpayers who try to qualify fraudulently for multiple Social Security tax exemptions by reporting fictitious earnings from several different jobs would quickly face adverse *income* tax consequences as a result.

To be sure, many in Congress might be fearful of tampering with the Social Security system. They might object to a proposal that decouples the link between Social Security taxes and benefits. The reality, however, is that for low-income workers the EITC program has *already* decoupled the link between taxes and benefits. Such workers ostensibly pay Social Security taxes and thereby become entitled to Social Security benefits, even though the EITC payment completely reimburses them for their Social Security contributions. In effect they pay *no* Social Security taxes yet are entitled to receive Social Security benefits. This proposal simply accomplishes exactly the same result but in a direct fashion, by not collecting the Social Security taxes in the first instance. The proposal would make the exemption available to *all* workers, those with high and low incomes, and then would raise Social Security tax rates on wages above the exempt level to help pay for the exemption and, in effect, to "recapture" the value of the exemption from workers with higher earnings.

2. If a Social Security tax exemption is not viable, either because of political reluctance or because it is believed to be not sufficiently targeted to the poor, a *small* benefit paid through the tax system to reflect a

rebate of Social Security taxes up to some level of income would be an adequate alternative. To be successful, however, this alternative would need to be much simpler than the existing EITC program. Specifically, there should be *no* attempt to implement a family responsibility condition: if the goal of this small program is to avoid having Social Security taxes push low-income workers into poverty, it should make no difference whether the worker has responsibility for young children. (As described shortly, special benefits for children could be provided separately.) In that regard current proposals to do away with the small EITC now available to childless low-income workers are ill-advised.[61] It might also be appropriate to require that this small benefit be paid out in each paycheck, rather than as a lump sum at the end of the year, in order to maximize the work incentive effect of the benefit.

3. Either of the first two suggestions would accomplish a portion of what the EITC program is trying to do in a more effective manner. But what about the rest of the program? *All remaining benefits should be delivered through the transfer system and not the tax system.* One natural suggestion would be to utilize the rest of the EITC money to help finance the work component of welfare reform. The appropriate work programs could be administered by the federal government or by the states if the welfare system is converted into a block grant. If a principal objective of the EITC program is to provide work incentives for welfare recipients, that goal should be addressed directly.

Our twenty-year experiment with the EITC has demonstrated the inability of the tax system to administer a transfer program for the poor in an effective and efficient manner. The tax system simply cannot target benefits precisely enough for policymakers without the creation of a rule structure that is impenetrable to claimants and unadministrable by the IRS. Furthermore, so long as the EITC program resides in the tax system, there is an undesirable duplication of bureaucratic expense in the tax and transfer systems, a division of budget responsibility with other related poverty programs, and a potential distortion in the budget accounting treatment of the program, as evidenced by the budget policies that triggered the growth in the program. Finally, there is at least a credible case that a redistributive program linked to work effort would have a more desirable effect on work incentives if the program were administered by the transfer rather than the tax system.[62]

Sad to say, what is needed to administer a program like the EITC effectively is a bureaucrat: a person who can explain rules and choices to potential beneficiaries, use discretion in difficult cases, and monitor the direction of the government's funds. The notion that the tax system somehow saves in bureaucratic costs is misguided. For a program like the EITC, those costs are not avoided but incurred by the beneficiary, probably the person least likely to bear such costs in an efficient manner. There really is no free lunch; if policymakers want to maintain a benefit program for the working poor, they must be willing to fund the costs of administration.

Some might contend that the EITC is in some way a structural part of the tax system and therefore should remain part of it. That position is based on a meaningless distinction. Rather, the tax and transfer systems constitute an integrated tool to effect public policy, and provisions in favor of the poor may be implemented with *either* negative taxes or positive transfers. There is no structural barrier to using either system to accomplish the policy goals. The question is which system is designed to achieve in a more expedient fashion the desired objective of delivering the prescribed benefits.

Finally, supporters of the EITC program might be concerned that the current political climate will not likely permit adoption of a major new spending initiative for the benefit of the poor. They would argue that it is therefore better to retain the EITC program in the tax system, even if that system is a poor delivery mechanism. But that concern, in a sense, is exactly the reason for the proposed reform. Lawmakers ought to be able to evaluate policy initiatives side-by-side with other programs designed to achieve similar objectives. Programs should not be hidden in the tax system and therefore be subject to a lower level of scrutiny. If as a transfer program the EITC would not garner a sufficient level of political support to remain viable, there is no reason that it should continue to exist in the tax system and in the process be administered inefficiently.

4. If lawmakers are unwilling to shift the bulk of the EITC program to the transfer system and insist upon relying on the tax system, then there are two remaining options. One choice would be to use the balance of the EITC money to help fund a refundable child credit. Both parties in Congress seem intent upon enacting a credit that would award families with $500 for each child in the family, and the Clinton Administration appears generally supportive of that effort.[63] But there

is disagreement over the refundable nature of the credit. A nonrefundable credit means that low-income families without income tax liabilities would receive no benefit at all. A better use of the EITC money, though not as desirable as the earlier suggestions, would be to provide such families with an equal-sized benefit. A refundable child credit would be easier to administer than the EITC and would deliver benefits to the same general population.[64]

The second option would be to provide the balance of the EITC benefit to low-income workers through their employers.[65] For example, a tax credit could be awarded to the employer of certain qualifying workers. The theory is that the same general transaction—the hiring and compensation of a qualifying worker—can be subsidized by providing a direct benefit to *either* the employer *or* the worker in the transaction if the benefit is capitalized in the compensation arrangement. The extent of capitalization will depend upon the competitive nature of the labor market.

Once again, the advantage of this idea would be to simplify administration of the program. It would be easier to administer because of the far smaller number of employers than workers. Further, employers are more used to dealing with the IRS than are low-income workers, so that at least noncompliance due to unintentional errors should be reduced. Finally, the greater dollar amounts involved per employer than per worker would make IRS enforcement efforts more cost effective. In a sense, this idea would convert part of the EITC program into a mini–block grant program to be administered by the business community rather than by the federal government.

True, the experience with a similar employer tax credit, the targeted jobs tax credit (TJTC),[66] has not been very positive. But a number of features unique to the TJTC program—its start and stop history, the limited duration of the subsidy to a portion of first year wages, the highly targeted nature of the subsidy directed toward individuals like ex-convicts who are undoubtedly the subject of negative stereotyping, to name a few—may help to explain that program's ineffectiveness. In contrast, a broadly applicable, employer-based subsidy program that is permanent has the potential for avoiding many of the TJTC's pitfalls.[67]

Lawmakers interested in real reform of the EITC program should give serious consideration to its major overhaul. Although there are no perfect solutions, replacement of the program with a Social Security tax exemption and delivery of remaining benefits through the transfer system would go far to effect a distinct improvement.

NOTES

1. I.R.C. § 32.

2. S. Rep. No. 94-36, 94th Cong., 1st Sess. 32–33 (1975).

3. *See* Jeff Shear, *The Credit Card*, 27 Nat'l J. 2056, 2057 (1995).

4. *Cf.* U.S. Gen. Accounting Office, Earned Income Credit: Noncompliance and Potential Eligibility Revisions 7–8 (1995) [hereinafter GAO Noncompliance Statement] (cost to the government to administer the EITC program much less than for comparable welfare programs).

5. *See* Milton Friedman, Capitalism and Freedom 191–93 (1962).

6. *See* Marsha Blumenthal & Joel Slemrod, *The Compliance Cost of the U.S. Individual Income Tax System: A Second Look after Tax Reform*, 45 Nat'l Tax J. 185 (1992); Joel Slemrod & Nikki Sorum, *The Compliance Cost of the U.S. Individual Income Tax System*, 37 Nat'l Tax J. 461 (1984).

7. *See* I.R.C. § 3507 (permitting advance payment of the EITC, a form of negative withholding); *see also* U.S. Gen. Accounting Office, Earned Income Tax Credit: Advance Payment Option Is Not Widely Known or Understood by the Public (1992) (less than one-half of 1 percent of those eligible and claiming the EITC in 1989 received an advance payment); George K. Yin et al., *Improving the Delivery of Benefits to the Working Poor: Proposals to Reform the Earned Income Tax Credit Program*, 11 Am. J. Tax Pol'y 225, 247 n.75 (1994) (according to IRS data, by early 1993 only about 16,000 taxpayers had reported obtaining an advance payment of the EITC during tax year 1992, or less than one-third of 1 percent of the 5.5 million taxpayers who had received a lump-sum EITC benefit by that time).

8. *See* I.R.C. § 6012; Rev. Proc. 95-53, 1995-52 I.R.B. 22, 24–25 (Dec. 26, 1995) (for 1996 a married couple with two children and income of up to $16,900 will not need to file a federal income tax return).

9. *See* John Karl Scholz, *The Earned Income Tax Credit: Participation, Compliance, and Antipoverty Effectiveness*, 47 Nat'l Tax J. 63 (1994); John Karl Scholz, *The Participation Rate of the Earned Income Tax Credit* (Institute for Research on Poverty Discussion Paper No. 928-90, University of Wisconsin, Madison) (1990) (roughly 30 percent of eligible beneficiaries did not participate in 1984); Yin et al., *supra* note 7, at 244–45 (estimated EITC participation rate in 1990 of between 75 percent and 86 percent, meaning that between 1.4 million and 2.5 million eligible families failed to participate).

10. *See* Yin et al., *supra* note 7, at 247–48, 253 (reporting IRS TCMP data indicating 30 percent to 40 percent EITC error rates during 1982–88 period, compared with 6 percent to 7 percent error rates for AFDC and food stamps). Noncompliance problems seem to have persisted despite (or perhaps because of) a number of changes to the program. *See* Hearing Before the Senate Comm. on Finance on the Earned Income Tax Credit, 104th Cong., 1st Sess. 76–77 (1995) (statement of Margaret Milner Richardson, commissioner of internal revenue) (based on small study of electronically filed returns during first two weeks of 1994, there was an excessive EITC claim rate of about 26 percent (by dollars excessively claimed) and 38 percent (by number of excessive claims), compared to an underclaim rate of about 1 percent (by dollars) and 6 percent (by claims)).

11. *See* I.R.C. § 32(a),(b); Rev. Proc. 95-53, 1995-52 I.R.B. 22, 24.

12. I.R.C. § 32(a),(b).

13. Barring statutory change, the program is projected to cost over $30 billion by the end of the decade. *See* Janet Holtzblatt et al., *Promoting Work through the EITC,* 47 Nat'l Tax J. 591, 591 (1994).

14. *See* Janet Holtzblatt, *Administering Refundable Tax Credits: Lessons from the EITC Experience,* 1991 Proceedings of the 84th Ann. Conf. on Tax'n of the Nat'l Tax Ass'n–Tax Inst. of Am. 180, 180.

15. *See* H.R. Rep. No. 99-841, 99th Cong., 2d Sess. II-866, table A.2 (1986); Staff of Joint Comm. on Taxation, 101st Cong., 2d Sess., Budget Reconciliation (H.R. 5835)—Revenue Provisions as Reported by the Conferees (Comm. Print 1990).

16. Shear, *supra* note 3, at 2059.

17. *See* Office of U.S. President, The President's Proposals to Congress for Fairness, Growth, and Simplicity 8 (1985).

18. *See* Elizabeth Drew, On the Edge: The Clinton Presidency 71–72 (1994).

19. *See* Staff of Joint Comm. on Taxation, 103d Cong., 1st Sess., Methodology and Issues in Measuring Changes in the Distribution of Tax Burdens 2–3 (Comm. Print 1993); Michael J. Graetz, *Paint-by-Numbers Tax Lawmaking,* 95 Colum. L. Rev. 609, 657 (1995).

20. Graetz, *supra* note 19, at 660; *see* Staff of Joint Comm. on Taxation, 101st Cong., 2d Sess., Summary of Distributional Effects, by Income Category, Budget Reconciliation (H.R. 5835)—Revenue Provisions as Reported by Conferees 46–90 n.1 (Comm. Print 1990).

21. *See* Lawrence S. Haas, *Fear of Filing,* 23 Nat'l J. 2415 (Oct. 5, 1991); J. Andrew Hoerner, *SOS on the EITC: Complex Rules Likely to Thwart Low-Income Filers,* 52 Tax Notes 1336 (1991); David Wessel, *Paved with Good Intentions, Tax Writers' Road to Help the Working Poor Turns into a Maze,* Wall St. J., June 11, 1991, at A16; James E. Williamson & Francine J. Lipman, *The New Earned Income Tax Credit: Too Complex for the Targeted Taxpayers?* 57 Tax Notes 789 (1992).

22. *See* Holtzblatt et al., *supra* note 13, at 600–601 (over 50 percent of EITC claimants utilize a tax return preparer).

23. *See* Anne L. Alstott, *The Earned Income Tax Credit and the Oversimplified Case for Tax-Based Welfare Reform,* 108 Harv. L. Rev. 533, 564–89 (1995).

24. I.R.C. § 32(d) (a married couple filing separate tax returns is not eligible for the EITC).

25. *Id.* at § 32(c)(1)(A) (prior to 1990 Amendment).

26. *See* Holtzblatt, *supra* note 14, at 181–82.

27. *See* Deborah H. Schenk, *Simplifying Dependency Exemptions: A Proposal for Reform,* 35 Tax Law. 855, 863–66 (1982).

28. *See supra* note 10 (estimates of EITC error rates).

29. I.R.C. § 32(c)(1)(A), (c)(3).

30. *See id.* at § 32(c)(1)(C) (in general, claimant with higher adjusted gross income is entitled to the credit).

31. *See id.* at § 43(c)(2)(B)(i), as enacted by Tax Reduction Act of 1975, Pub. L. No. 94-12, § 209(b), 89 Stat. 26, 35; H.R. Rep. No. 19, 94th Cong., 1st Sess. 30 (1975).

32. *See* Yin et al., *supra* note 7, at 255.

33. *See* I.R.C. § 32(i), as added by Self-Employed Health Insurance Act, Pub. L. No. 104-7, § 4(a), 109 Stat. 93 (1995) (denial of EITC to any taxpayer with aggregate investment-type income for the year of over $2,350); H.R. Rep. No. 104-92, 104th Cong., 1st Sess. 18 (1995); Cherie J. O'Neil & Linda B. Nelsestuen, *The Earned Income Credit: The Need for a Wealth Restriction for Eligibility Determination,* 63 Tax Notes 1189 (1994).

34. *See* Seven-Year Balanced Budget Reconciliation Act of 1995, H.R. 2491, 104th Cong., 1st

Sess. § 13205 (1995) (vetoed by President Clinton)[hereinafter 1995 Balanced Budget Bill]; Message Returning without Approval to the House of Representatives Budget Reconciliation Legislation, 31 Weekly Comp. Pres. Doc. 2140 (Dec. 6, 1995).

35. *See* U.S. Gen. Accounting Office, Earned Income Credit: Targeting to the Working Poor 30–31 (1995) [hereinafter GAO Targeting Report].

36. *See* Alstott, *supra* note 23, at 570–76.

37. *See* Shear, *supra* note 3, at 2058.

38. *See* GAO Noncompliance Statement, *supra* note 4, at 6 (intentional error rate 13 percent); George K. Yin, *Reforming the Earned Income Tax Credit Program,* 67 Tax Notes 1828, 1829 (1995) (intentional error rate as high as 25 percent of dollars claimed and 32 percent of total claims).

39. *See* GAO Noncompliance Statement, *supra* note 4, at 6 (self-employed as a group underreport 64 percent of income).

40. *See* 1995 Balanced Budget Bill, *supra* note 34, at § 13205(b) (inclusion of child support payments to determine eligibility); GAO Targeting Report, *supra* note 35, at 32–33.

41. *See* C. Eugene Steuerle, *The IRS Cannot Control the New Superterranean Economy,* 59 Tax Notes 1839 (1993); Yin et al., *supra* note 7, at 259–60.

42. *See* Yin, *supra* note 38, at 1832–33.

43. *See* Jane G. Gravelle, *CRS Report for Congress, The Earned Income Tax Credit (EITC): Effect on Work Effort, reprinted in* 95 Tax Notes Today 181-39 (Aug. 30, 1995).

44. *See id.;* Marvin H. Kosters, *The Earned Income Tax Credit and the Working Poor,* Am. Enterprise, May/June 1993, at 64.

45. *See* U.S. Gen. Accounting Office, Earned Income Tax Credit: Design and Administration Could Be Improved (1993); Saul D. Hoffman & Laurence S. Seidman, The Earned Income Tax Credit: Antipoverty Effectiveness and Labor Market Effects 37–51 (1990); Edgar K. Browning, *Effects of the Earned Income Tax Credit on Income and Welfare,* 48 Nat'l Tax J. 23 (1995); Stacy Dickert et al., *The Earned Income Tax Credit and Transfer Programs: A Study of Labor Market and Program Participation, in* 9 Tax Policy and the Economy 1 (James M. Poterba ed., 1995); Nada Eissa & Jeffrey B. Liebman, *Labor Supply Response to the Earned Income Tax Credit* (Nat'l Bureau of Econ. Res. Working Paper No. 5158) (June 1995).

46. *See* C. Eugene Steuerle, *The Future of the Earned Income Tax Credit (Part 2),* 67 Tax Notes 1819 (1995).

47. *Cf.* Hoffman & Seidman, *supra* note 45, at 55; Eissa & Liebman, *supra* note 45; Steuerle, *supra* note 46; George K. Yin, *Summary of EITC Conference Proceedings,* 11 Am. J. Tax Pol'y 299, 310–11 (1994) (statement of Gary Burtless).

48. *See supra* note 7.

49. *Cf.* Hearing on the Earned Income Tax Credit Before the Senate Comm. on Finance on the Earned Income Tax Credit, 104th Cong., 1st Sess. 55 (1995) (statement of Robert Greenstein) (uncertain understanding by EITC claimants regarding connection between EITC benefit levels and work effort); Staff of Joint Comm. on Taxation, 104th Cong., 1st Sess., Present Law and Issues Relating to the Earned Income Tax Credit 11 (Comm. Print 1995) (same); Eissa & Liebman, *supra* note 45 (same); Holtzblatt et al., *supra* note 13 (same); Lynn M. Olson, *The Earned Income Tax Credit: Views from the Street Level* (Working Paper Series, Center for Urb. Aff. and Pol. Research, Northwestern University) (Mar. 1994) (survey of thirty low-income working women making the transition from welfare to work found very little knowledge about relationship between EITC and work levels); Yin, *supra* note 38, at 1831.

50. *See* Lawrence Zelenak, *Marriage and the Income Tax,* 67 S. Cal. L. Rev. 339, 398–401 (1994).

51. *See* Alstott, *supra* note 23, at 563–64.

52. *See* 7 U.S.C. §§ 2012(i)(2), 2014(a) (1994) (food stamps); 42 U.S.C. §602(a)(38),(39)

(1994) (AFDC); U.S. House Comm. on Ways and Means, 103d Cong., 2d Sess., Overview of Entitlement Programs: 1994 Green Book: Background Material and Data on Programs within the Jurisdiction of the Committee on Ways and Means 762–63 (Comm. Print 1994).

53. *See* Boris I. Bittker, *Federal Income Taxation and the Family*, 27 Stan. L. Rev. 1389, 1398–99 (1975).

54. See James Alm & Leslie A. Whittington, *Income Taxes and the Marriage Decision*, 27 Applied Econ. 25 (1995); David L. Sjoquist & Mary Beth Walker, *The Marriage Tax and the Rate and Timing of Marriage*, 48 Nat'l Tax J. 547 (1995).

55. *See* USA Tax Act of 1995, S. 722, 104th Cong., 1st Sess. (1995); Congressional Budget Office, Estimates for a Prototype Saving-Exempt Income Tax 23 (1994); Sen. Pete V. Domenici, *The Unamerican Spirit of the Federal Income Tax*, 31 Harv. J. on Legis. 273, 296–97 (1994).

56. *See* George K. Yin, *Accommodating the "Low-Income" in a Cash-Flow or Consumed Income Tax World*, 2 Fla. Tax Rev. 445, 458–61 (1995).

57. *Id.* at 474.

58. *See* 1995 Balanced Budget Bill, *supra* note 34, at §§ 13201–5.

59. *See* GAO Targeting Report, *supra* note 35, at 30–31.

60. *See* George K. Yin & Jonathan Barry Forman, *Redesigning the Earned Income Tax Credit Program to Provide More Effective Assistance for the Working Poor*, 59 Tax Notes 951, 957–59 (1993); Yin et al., *supra* note 7, at 280–82, 284–86.

61. *See* 1995 Balanced Budget Bill, *supra* note 34, at § 13202.

62. *See* Yin, *supra* note 38, at 1829–31.

63. *See* 1995 Balanced Budget Bill, *supra* note 34, at § 11001(a) (adding new §23, a $500 per child tax credit).

64. *See* Yin & Forman, *supra* note 60, at 959–60; Yin et al., *supra* note 7, at 283.

65. *See* Yin et al., *supra* note 7, at 286–94.

66. I.R.C. § 51.

67. *See* Yin et al., *supra* note 7, at 291–92.

14

MARY L. HEEN

Welfare Reform, the Child Care Dilemma, and the Tax Code

Family Values, the Wage Labor Market, and the Race- and Class-Based Double Standard

Although federal work requirements have been imposed on welfare recipients for nearly thirty years, recent welfare reform proposals emphasize more stringent time limits on benefits without work and impose such requirements on mothers with younger children.[1] The shift in the welfare paradigm toward mandatory wage work for mothers with young children has not been accompanied, however, by universal child care. Historically, federal welfare and labor policies have impeded women's access to the wage labor market through the lack of affordable child care.[2] Tax policies have contributed to the problem.[3] Efforts to improve women's access to the wage labor market have clashed with policies aimed at reinforcing traditional family values, and with race- and class-based double standards in the treatment of child care by both the income tax and the income transfer (welfare) systems.

In requiring wage work of mothers with young children, policymakers assume that in-home care welfare mothers provide their own children does not constitute work at least equivalent in value to the wage work available to welfare recipients (including child care they may provide to other people's children);[4] alternatively, they assume that the wage work required of welfare recipients will produce long-term benefits greater than the intervening cost of providing (or not providing) substitute child care for their children.[5] At best those assumptions evidence an underestimation of the cost of quality substitute child care. At worst they reveal an entrenched race- or class-based devaluation of the care provided by welfare recipients to their children. Without the provision of adequate substitute child care, the work requirements represent an attempt to shift welfare mothers into poorly paid service positions while tacitly expecting that their child care responsibilities will be met by friends and relatives, including the aunts, siblings, and grandmothers of the children now receiving welfare. In any event the largely unstated assumptions suggest disturbing race, gender, and class stereotyping at work, along with a return to certain preentitlement era approaches to poor relief.[6]

Tax policies have historically evidenced a tension between reinforcing traditional family values and improving the access of women to the wage labor market. Congress has articulated various reasons for the tax allowance for work-related child care; it has analogized work-related child care to other business-related costs of producing income and at the same time has treated it as a hardship allowance for families disrupted by the death or disability of the primary breadwinner (usually the husband and father) or the death or disability of the primary caregiver (usually the wife and mother). In the early 1970s Congress linked the child care deduction to welfare-related work programs and expanded the deduction to encourage the employment of welfare recipients in household service positions.[7] Policymakers also have periodically addressed child care issues by providing additional or alternative tax allowances for families with children through increased exemption amounts for dependents or by advocating refundable or nonrefundable per child tax credits.[8] These tax adjustments are sometimes described as promoting traditional family values because they do not tie eligibility for the tax allowance to the parents' work outside of the home. Child tax credit proposals directed at the middle class are now receiving renewed political support.[9]

The juxtaposition of current welfare and tax policies suggests an apparent race-and class-based double standard. On the one hand tax policies favor the in-home provision of child care and household services by mothers in certain "traditional" two-parent households and facilitate the employment of child care providers if the single parent or secondary wage earner (usually the wife) can earn enough after taxes in the wage labor market to pay for child care and other household services. On the other hand welfare policies reject the in-home provision of child care for poor mothers. Low-income families are generally unable to afford adequate child care without additional government subsidies or the modification of current tax provisions. The interrelationship of tax and welfare policies thus creates a classic double bind for poor families.

The implications of the double standard applied to the poor through the tax system are troubling and worthy of further examination. I begin here a preliminary exploration of the interrelationship between tax and welfare double standards. In the welfare context a double standard historically has been applied by making race-based distinctions between the "deserving" and the "undeserving" poor. Although the discriminatory denial of welfare benefits largely ended as a result of major reforms achieved by the welfare rights movement in the 1960s,[10] current welfare reform proposals would eliminate the structural "entitlement" to benefits on which those reforms were built. In the tax context a family values double standard may be identified through the close correlation between an individual's race or gender and his or her family income or wealth.[11] Traditional family values are reinforced through the tax code; nevertheless, access to the wage labor market has been improved for middle- and upper-income women through offsetting tax allowances for work-related child care. Those adjustments are not generally available, however, to low-income working families. The double standard may be eliminated only through offsetting adjustments or more comprehensive changes in the income tax system.

WELFARE, WORK AND THE MOTHERS OF YOUNG CHILDREN

The Historical Race-Based Double Standard

Federal work requirements for welfare recipients represent a shift away from the origins in 1935 of the Aid to Dependent Children (ADC) program, which developed from "mothers' pensions" or "mothers' aid" programs.[12] Such programs were intended by social reformers to enable widows and certain other "deserving" mothers with "suitable homes" to care for their young children without being compelled to work outside of the home.[13] Local welfare offices, particularly those in the South, used the "suitable home" and other rules to deny assistance to African American children and their families.[14] In addition, long before the federal government imposed work requirements, some states used "employable mother" rules to deny welfare assistance to women with children, especially nonwhite women, on the ground that they should work.[15] The first employable mother rule was adopted by Louisiana in 1943, refusing ADC assistance to families during times when the mothers and their older children were needed to work in the cotton fields.[16] Georgia adopted a similar rule in 1952, denying assistance to mothers with children over three years of age where "suitable" employment (at any wage) was deemed to be available.[17] Thus, local welfare policies coincided with local labor market demands by keeping nonwhite women in seasonal agricultural and other labor pools.[18] As late as 1966 New Jersey notified Aid to Families with Dependent Children (AFDC) recipients that their grants would be cut because seasonal farm work was available.[19]

Federal work requirements were first imposed on welfare recipients by the Work Incentive Program (WIN) in 1967. WIN was not very effective, however, due to weak funding and enforcement.[20] Although potentially subject to the original WIN work requirements, mothers with preschool children were determined by many states to be "inappropriate" for job training or work and thus exempt from the work requirement.[21] As amended in 1971, WIN II required participation by mothers with children six years of age or older.[22]

The WIN program was replaced by the Job Opportunity and Basic Skills Program (JOBS), which was established by the Family Support Act of 1988.[23] The Family Support Act mandated improved procedures for child support enforcement and the establishment of paternity; guaranteed federal assistance for child care during participation in education, training, and employment (AFDC-related child care); and provided transitional eligibility for a year of extended child care and medical assistance for former AFDC recipients who become ineligible for AFDC because of increased income from employment (transitional child care).[24] All AFDC recipients, except those exempted by law, are required to participate in JOBS.[25] Mothers caring for a child under six years of age are required to participate in JOBS only if child care is guaranteed and participation is limited to twenty hours per week.[26] Those caring for children under three years of age are exempt from participation, unless required to participate under state option.[27] Most states, however, have exempted caretakers of children under the age of three from the work requirements.[28]

The shift in welfare policy toward work requirements occurred as the welfare population expanded and as more African American and other women of color and their families were added to the rolls.[29] The shift also coincided with the trend of increased labor market participation by women with young children.[30] Although AFDC mothers have been reported as participating in the labor market at significantly lower levels than their nonwelfare counterparts,[31] studies conducted by the Institute for Women's Policy Research show more comparable labor-force participation levels: "[A]bout forty percent of poor mothers receiving AFDC are also working in paid employment, and they work approximately half time, about as much as all mothers."[32] On average, mothers "work in paid employment about half time, devoting the other half of the 'normal' work week as well as the 'second shift' to child and family care."[33] Like many of their counterparts in the labor market, AFDC mothers do not earn enough on their own to support themselves and their children; many need both their welfare benefits and their earnings to survive. Because AFDC is not otherwise structured to encourage work effort, the paid work of welfare recipients has sometimes been driven underground.[34]

The Current Work Programs and the Cost of Child Care

As discussed above, the JOBS program was created in the last round of welfare reform during the late 1980s. The JOBS program is funded through a capped entitlement under which states are partially reimbursed (pursuant to a federal matching rate) for each dollar spent on JOBS until they reach the maximum amount allocated to them.[35] Federal funds for guaranteed JOBS-related child care are separately provided as open-ended entitlement matching funds to partially reimburse (at the Medicaid matching rate) state expenditures for AFDC and transitional child care.[36] As of the end of fiscal year 1993, states had claimed only about 70 percent of the allotted $1 billion in federal JOBS funds.[37] State budget constraints as well as the cost of guaranteed child

care were among the reasons identified for the less-than-full implementation of the JOBS program. In many states the same amount was
spent on JOBS-related child care as on the JOBS program itself.[38]

The At-Risk Child Care Program provides federal matching funds
for states to provide child care services for low-income families who are
"at risk" of becoming welfare recipients if they do not receive work-
related child care.[39] Families are required to contribute to the cost of
care on a sliding fee schedule based on the family's ability to pay.[40]
Low-income families also receive child care assistance through various
federal block grant programs. The Child Care and Development Block
Grant (CCDBG) program currently provides funding for child care
services to low-income families as well as for efforts to improve the
quality and supply of child care in general.[41] Federal funds are distributed to states under a formula, and no matching funds are required. In
addition to the CCDBG program, some child care funds are currently
available through the Social Services Block Grant Program of Title XX
of the Social Security Act.[42] Title XX block grants operate as a capped
entitlement, with no state matching requirement, under which states
are allocated funds pursuant to a formula based on their relative population. Most states spend some portion of their block grants on child
care services, and some, but not all, states determine eligibility for child
care services based on income standards.[43]

Under current federal funding levels (totaling approximately $2
billion per year),[44] the states have been unable to meet the need for
child care assistance for low-income families.[45] Between 5 percent and
6 percent of the AFDC caseload receive AFDC child care subsidies,[46]
and only about one out of three JOBS participants receive JOBS-related
child care.[47] About 20 percent of those eligible receive transitional
child care assistance for the first year after leaving welfare for work.[48]
Families that have used up their one year of guaranteed transitional
assistance after leaving welfare have to compete with other low-income,
non-AFDC families for child care assistance. Surveys conducted in
1993 and 1994 found that most states either had lengthy waiting lists
for child care assistance or had stopped accepting new applications.[49]
In addition the competition for slots resulted in the shifting of scarce
state child care funds from low-income working families to families
receiving AFDC.[50]

Programs with low reimbursement rates and retroactive reimbursement tend to steer families toward informal child care.[51] A recent study concludes that children who are in the care of family and relatives are receiving substandard care from providers who are "taking care of children to help out the mothers and not because they want to care for children."[52] The study's authors recommend that low-income families receive a child care subsidy sufficient to pay for higher quality care.[53] In addition they do not recommend requiring welfare recipients to become family child care providers and they urge states to screen all welfare-to-work recipients for interest, commitment, and aptitude before they become providers.[54]

The "devolution" approach to welfare reform recently considered by Congress would repeal entitlement programs such as AFDC and AFDC-related child care and would substitute capped federal block grants to the states, giving the states the freedom to impose their own requirements or restrictions without the necessity of applying for waivers of federal requirements.[55] Under the House version of welfare reform some of the federal budgetary savings from the elimination of entitlement programs would have been reallocated to a revised Child Care and Development Block Grant Program (CCDBG). Although the reallocation would have kept child care funding at 1994 levels, total funds available for child care would have been cut over a five- to seven-year period through elimination of the future growth of entitlement funding.[56] The Senate and conference substitute proposals added limited amounts over current funding levels for work-related child care.[57] Each of the proposals would have cut overall welfare spending over the next five to seven years[58] and would have increased the number of children in poverty.[59] Whether Congress and the President will be able to reach a compromise that will result in the enactment of major welfare reform legislation remains to be seen. Nevertheless, without substantially increased federal or state support of work-related child care, new work requirements may be programmed for failure, or worse, they may result in the endangerment of children.

If low-income families must pay the full cost of child care themselves, they face a major obstacle in their transition from welfare to work. In general the type of child care purchased and the amount spent on care varies by the family's economic situation and the type of care used. Lower-income families spend on average about 23 percent of their incomes on child care even though they spend significantly less, in absolute terms, on child care than families with higher incomes.[60] Without subsidized child care, low-income families will likely rely on lower-quality child care or informal arrangements and relative-provided care. Those who pay for relatives to care for their children pay the lowest average weekly costs, with increasingly higher weekly average costs for family child care, center care, and in-home care by a non-relative.

The family and relative care received by children from low-income families and the center-based care for very young children have raised developmental concerns. A recent study of children in family child care and relative care concluded that "regardless of maternal education, the lower the child's family income, the lower the quality of the child care home in which he or she is enrolled."[61] That finding differed from findings from research on center-based care, in which low-income children in subsidized care often were in better-quality arrangements than middle-income children.[62] In center-based care, the lowest quality care is received by toddlers and infants, with about 40 percent of those studied receiving below a minimally adequate level, although little difference in fees was found for centers providing high- or low-quality care.[63]

TAXES AND WORK: FAMILY VALUES AND ACCESS TO THE WAGE LABOR MARKET

History of Congressional Approaches

Congress has combined at least two or three notions in its approach to work-related child care costs for income tax purposes. Although it has treated child care expenses as comparable to an employee business expense, it has also targeted the deduction or credit to hardship situations and used the allowance as part of an overall effort to develop jobs for household workers, including former welfare recipients.[64]

Congress first provided a tax adjustment for employment-related child care costs in 1954,[65] as a type of working expense deduction targeted to those in hardship situations such as widows, widowers, and low-income families.[66] Over the next two decades, Congress increased the statutory dollar amounts and expanded the coverage of the child care provision but retained the basic structure of a child care deduction.

In the 1970s the rationale for the deduction shifted to include a job development purpose in addition to its continued function as a type of employee business expense in hardship situations.[67] When the deduction was significantly expanded in 1971, the Senate committee report identified it as a "job development deduction for household services and child care" and discussed it immediately following its description of a proposed tax credit for salaries paid welfare recipients under the WIN program.[68] When discussing the proposed WIN tax credit, the committee observed that the WIN program "has not been as successful as had been hoped, largely because persons have been placed in institutional rather than employment-based training."[69] The expanded child care deduction was intended to provide an incentive for the employment of household workers by giving large numbers of welfare recipients "the opportunity to perform socially desirable services in jobs that are vitally needed," while also helping "to remove these individuals from the welfare rolls and reduce the cost of providing public assistance."[70]

In 1976 Congress changed the child care deduction to a nonrefundable tax credit by repealing the deduction provision and adopting the predecessor of the current I.R.C. § 21.[71] The change to a tax credit was adopted as a way to reach taxpayers who elected the standard deduction and as a simplification measure.[72] Although the family income limitation amounts were eliminated and eligibility requirements were somewhat broadened, the credit otherwise retained the basic design of the earlier provisions with regard to determination of qualified expenses.[73] The credit was changed again in 1981, resulting in the current child care tax credit structure.[74] Although the Senate version of the credit included refundability, the conference agreement rejected making the credit refundable.[75] The credit was redesignated as I.R.C. § 21 in 1984,[76] and Congress did some fine-tuning to curtail perceived abuses or to make technical adjustments in 1987[77] and again in 1988.[78] No major changes have been made to the credit since 1981.

The Income Tax Work-Related Child Care Provisions

The Internal Revenue Code provisions specifically addressing child care expenses are I.R.C. § 21, the child and dependent care tax credit, and I.R.C. § 129, the exclusion from income for certain employer-provided child care benefits. The child care tax credit and the exclusion for employer-provided child care are estimated to reduce federal revenues by about $2.7 billion and $.7 billion, respectively, in fiscal year 1996.[79] Although not specifically aimed at the child care expenses of working parents, the earned income tax credit, I.R.C. § 32, provides a refundable tax credit for certain low-income working families with children. In addition, the personal exemption deduction for dependents, I.R.C. § 151, provides an adjustment in computing taxable income to account for the added household costs for those taxpayers supporting children.[80] I.R.C. §§ 21 and 129 provide tax benefits to all working parents, but upper- and middle-income taxpayers utilize them the most, for the reasons explained below. The following section describes in greater detail how the child care credit and employer-provided child care exclusion provisions work and how the current design of these provisions makes it difficult for low-income taxpayers to benefit from them.

How the Child Care Tax Credit Works. I.R.C. § 21 provides a nonrefundable tax credit, the amount of which is equal to an "applicable percentage"[81] of the eligible employment-related child care expenses[82] paid by the taxpayer during the year.[83] The applicable percentage, which ranges on a sliding scale of 20 percent to 30 percent, varies with adjusted gross income. The amount of child care expenses that may be taken into account depends upon the number of children[84] included in the household maintained by the taxpayer. Eligible expenses are limited to $2,400 per year for one child and $4,800 per year for two or more children.[85] A taxpayer with adjusted gross income of $10,000 or less receives a credit of 30 percent of employment-related expenses. The credit percentage declines by one percentage point for each $2,000 (or fraction thereof) in adjusted gross income above $10,000, but in no case is the applicable percentage reduced below 20 percent.[86] For taxpayers with adjusted gross incomes greater than $28,000, therefore, the applicable percentage is 20 percent. For taxpayers with adjusted gross income of $10,000 or less, thus qualifying for the highest applicable percentage of 30 percent, the maximum credit is $720 for one child and $1,440 for two or more children. For taxpayers with incomes in excess of $28,000, thus qualifying for the lowest applicable percentage of 20 percent, the maximum credit is $480 for one child and $960 for two or more children.

The amount of the dependent care credit and the applicable percentage income phase-down schedule have not changed since 1981.

Income tax thresholds, however, have substantially increased since then.[87] Thus, although I.R.C. § 21 appears to target low-income taxpayers, the relationship between the credit percentage income phasedown and current income tax thresholds makes it unlikely that poor taxpayers receive any benefit from the credit. The Tax Reform Act of 1986[88] removed about six million poverty level families from the income tax rolls[89] by increasing standard deduction[90] and personal exemption amounts,[91] and adjusting those amounts on a yearly basis for inflation.[92] In 1996, for example, a family of four (two parents and two children) would owe no taxes on up to $16,900 of adjusted gross income,[93] which is above the federal poverty threshold for a family of four.[94] A single head of household with one child would owe no taxes up to $11,000 of income,[95] which is above the poverty level for a family of two.[96] Although both families could be entitled to a child care tax credit, they would have no income tax liability to offset through use of the credit. The current thresholds for tax liability,[97] combined with the nonrefundability of the credit, thus make it unlikely for poor families to benefit from the child and dependent care tax credit.[98]

The Exclusion for Employer-Provided Dependent Care Assistance Programs. I.R.C. § 129 provides an exclusion from the gross income of employees of amounts up to $5,000 paid by the employer under a dependent care assistance program.[99] The dependent care assistance program must be a separate written plan of the employer for the exclusive benefit of employees[100] and must meet certain other requirements.[101] The amount of the exclusion may not exceed the lesser of the earned income of the employee or the earned income of the employee's spouse.[102] Payments for child care made to the employee's spouse or certain other related individuals (another child of the employee, for example) are ineligible for exclusion.[103]

Employers most frequently provide the dependent care assistance benefit through reimbursement accounts, sometimes referred to as flexible spending accounts, which may also cover other types of expenses, such as out-of-pocket health care expenses.[104] Up to $5,000 may be paid into a dependent care assistance account (through a salary reduction plan) from which child care expenses of the employee are reimbursed. The effect of such a program is that the employee may pay child care expenses (or out-of-pocket health care expenses) with pretax dollars. Thus, the I.R.C. § 129 exclusion operates as a complete adjustment, offsetting the tax costs of up to $5,000 of child care expenses, regardless of the taxpayer's marginal tax rate. About one-third of full-time employees at large and medium-sized private firms were eligible for such accounts in 1991, compared to nearly one-tenth of such workers who were eligible for child care benefits provided by the employer in the form of child care facilities provided at or near the workplace or through direct reimbursement of employee expenses.[105]

Generally, taxpayers choose whether eligible child care expenses will be claimed under the I.R.C. § 21 credit or the I.R.C. § 129 exclusion. Double dipping is not permitted.[106] For most middle- or upper-income taxpayers, the I.R.C. § 129 exclusion will provide the most benefit.[107] For example, for taxpayers subject to the highest marginal tax rate of 39.6 percent, the I.R.C. § 129 exclusion is worth $1,980 (maximum amount allowed of $5,000 x 39.6 percent), compared to the maximum I.R.C. § 21 credit of $480 for one child or $960 for two or more children.

Tax Theory: The Implications of Viewing a Child Care Allowance as a Subsidy or as a Cost of Producing Income

As discussed above, Congress has never really decided whether to conceptualize the child care credit as a cost of earning income, as a hardship allowance for child care, or as a job development program for household workers. Tax theorists have also disagreed about the proper treatment of such expenses. If child care expenses are a legitimate cost of producing income, they should be deductible regardless of the amount or the taxpayer's income level.[108] But if child care costs are personal consumption expenditures, they should not be deductible —just as expenditures for the costs of food or shelter are nondeductible.[109] Any special tax allowance for personal consumption expenditures may be viewed as a tax expenditure[110] and thus equivalent to a direct subsidy for child care. The conclusion one reaches with regard to these theoretical issues may have as much to do with one's view of the family, and the role of women within the family, as with one's understanding of tax policy.[111]

The following sections consider whether an adjustment to income to reflect child care costs can be justified under the tax norms of ability to pay and neutrality. I conclude that an income tax adjustment for child care costs should not be viewed as a subsidy because it reflects a taxpayer's ability to pay taxes. Even if it were viewed as a subsidy or equivalent to a direct expenditure, however, there are arguments in favor of retaining or expanding an income tax adjustment for child care expenses. Such an adjustment should be tolerated as a "second best" solution because it offsets other tax nonneutralities between wage work and household labor. Eliminating the "subsidy" would exacerbate already serious allocative inefficiencies involving participation by women in the labor market.

The Ability-to-Pay Norm. The ability-to-pay norm derives from the idea that taxpayers should contribute to the government according to the relative amount of material resources they control above subsistence amounts. Ability to pay may be understood in both horizontal and vertical equity terms. Questions concerning the normative underpinnings of the traditional tax policy equity analysis have recently provoked much commentary, and several theorists have emphasized that if two taxpayers pay different amounts in tax, the difference must be consistent with an appropriate theory of distributive justice.[112] Analysis under the traditional tax norm of horizontal equity, under which similarly situated taxpayers should be similarly taxed, tends to be conclusory because of the lack of a tax-determined method of identifying similarly situated taxpayers. For example, the conclusion reached with regard to horizontal equity may depend upon whether one begins with a worker with or without children and how one views one-earner versus two-earner working families.[113] Thus, the prior question of how taxpayers with equal incomes are identified determines the outcome of the horizontal equity analysis.

The application of the ability-to-pay norm generally does not favor deductions unless they relate to minimum subsistence amounts, certain nondiscretionary expenditures,[114] or legitimate costs of producing income. Child care costs reduce the taxpayer's ability to pay taxes only if one concludes that child care fits within such a category of expenditures. If so, a deduction or a credit would be justified based on the taxpayer's reduced capacity to pay taxes.

Debate about the tax treatment of child care costs generally centers on whether such expenses are personal or business expenses, that is, whether to treat such expenses as a cost of producing income or as a personal consumption expenditure. Although the business/personal boundary is difficult to delineate when the expenses involve additional costs of being employed, child care has been analogized to nondeductible personal expenses, such as commuting costs and higher clothing expense where the person "already at work" marks the boundary between business and personal expenses.[115] Some have argued that child care costs may contain elements of either personal or business expenditures or a mixture of both,[116] and at least one commentator has suggested that a limit in the amount of deductible expenses may be appropriate as a means of restricting the personal consumption element for middle- or upper-income taxpayers.[117]

Arguably, however, child care costs (up to some generally recognized standard amount for quality care) are legitimate costs of producing income, and a child care deduction properly reflects a working parent's ability to pay taxes. A caretaker is required if single or dual parents work outside of the home, and the tax code should recognize child care as a deductible work-related expense. But those who view child care costs as a personal expense would conclude that an income tax adjustment constitutes a subsidy. Under such a view the neutrality norm becomes more important because an adjustment to income cannot be justified on the basis of a working parent's relative ability to pay taxes.

The Neutrality Norm. The neutrality norm derives from the notion that taxes should influence allocation of resources in the economy as little as possible; otherwise, economic inefficiencies may result. Under the neutrality norm subsidies are suspect and should be discouraged. For those who view child care costs as a personal consumption expense, an income adjustment for such costs would constitute an income subsidy violating the neutrality norm. The neutrality norm, however, is tempered by several other theories.

First, under the theory of optimal taxation, nonneutrality does not result in economic distortions when taxes do not affect consumer or other allocative choices (that is, where there is a low degree of elasticity or substitutability of behaviors).[118] Accordingly, because economic distortions are a function of elasticity, higher taxes may be imposed on inelastic commodities without creating allocative inefficiencies. Second, under the Pigouvian theory of taxation, departures from the neutrality norm may be justified to correct market failures; when free markets do not work, through the presence of externalities or information failures, taxation may legitimately correct the failure.[119] For example, an observed market failure of parents or society to invest adequately in children's human capital[120] could provide theoretical justification for a tax incentive to correct such market failure. Third, the theory of the "second best" suggests that tax nonneutralities should not necessarily be corrected if allocative inefficiencies would be aggravated because of the existence of other nonneutralities.[121]

The theory of the second best provides a justification for a tax allowance for work-related child care because of the existence of the tax nonneutrality between wage work and household labor.[122] The tax system generally favors nonmarket production by failing to tax imputed income from services taxpayers perform for themselves or their households.[123] For example, no income tax is imposed on the value of services such as vegetable gardening, meal preparation, or hair cutting provided by taxpayers to members of their own households. However, for those taxpayers who hire others to perform such services, no deductions from income are generally allowed for the cost of the services. Unless each taxpayer earns more than the value of the services plus taxes, the tax system encourages taxpayers to provide the services on an in-kind basis (assuming that they have or can develop the skill to perform the services). A deduction for market-purchased services would eliminate the tax incentive for home production. Alternatively, nonneutrality could be eliminated by including the imputed income from the in-kind family-provided services in gross income. Inclusion of imputed income would be quite problematic, however, due to the administrative difficulties of valuation and enforcement.

Child care expenses arguably should be treated differently from other types of nondeductible household expenses because of the necessary relationship between child care and access to the labor market.[124] The need for a child care deduction or credit to offset the current tax incentive for a parent to provide child care at home is typically advanced in the context of a constellation of other social and economic factors discouraging women from full labor force participation.[125] Studies suggest that labor force participation of secondary workers responds to changes in tax rates,[126] and thus tax nonneutrality between wage work and household labor may result in allocative inefficiencies. The second best solution of a tax adjustment for work-related child care achieves special force in a setting otherwise discouraging women from entering or staying in the labor market.

The Double Standard Applied to Low-Income Taxpayers

As argued above, the tax treatment of child care expenses cannot be evaluated in isolation from the Code's taxation of the family in general. Even if one concludes that the child care credit cannot be justified under the ability-to-pay norm, analysis under the neutrality norm suggests that a tax allowance for child care costs could be justified as a second best solution to currently existing nonneutralities between wage work and household labor. I.R.C. §§ 21 and 129 offset, at least partially, the effects of certain policy trade-offs made in connection with taxation of the family. Thus, the child care allowances should be understood as serving important structural functions within the tax system. As I have argued elsewhere, because of the structural role played by these provisions as an offset to other nonneutralities involving taxation of the family, the child care tax credit should not be phased out for middle- and upper-income taxpayers as a means of redirecting benefits to low-income families. Instead, revenues should be reallocated from other sources to extend the benefits of such offsets to low-income families.[127]

The Policy Trade-Offs Creating Nonneutralities in Taxation of the Family. Conflicts among the competing tax policy goals of marriage neutrality, progressivity, and the policy of taxing equal-income married couples equally[128] have forced inescapable trade-offs in the taxation of the family. As many analysts have pointed out, it is mathematically impossible to accomplish all three goals at the same time, and given a progressive rate structure, nonneutralities may result.[129] The tax system has shifted the balance among these goals over time as Congress has responded to changes in social patterns, distributive goals, and prevailing perceptions of the role of the family in society.

The I.R.C. § 21 child care tax credit and the I.R.C. § 129 exclusion for employer-provided child care serve an important function as an offset to current nonneutralities between married and unmarried earners given the following features of the current tax structure: (1) the phase-out percentages of the earned income tax credit for low-income workers,[130] (2) a progressive rate structure, and (3) a joint filing regime for married taxpayers. Unless these features of the tax structure are altered, the child care tax provisions should be retained or expanded as a second best solution.

How the Nonneutralities Affect Low-Income Taxpayers. At low income levels, tax costs make working to cover child care expenses an inherently losing proposition. Although tax costs of working in the wage labor market are somewhat offset by I.R.C. §§ 21 and 129 for middle- and upper-income taxpayers, low-income taxpayers receive little or no benefit from those provisions. Thus, the low-income mother generally is better off staying at home to care for the children unless she earns more than it costs to purchase adequate child care or can rely on unpaid relatives or low-cost providers for child care.

As has been pointed out by Prof. Edward McCaffery, the tax costs result from a combination of the 15 percent marginal income tax rate on earned income above the tax threshold amounts, the 7.65 percent employee portion of social security taxes, and the phase-out percentage of the earned income tax credit.[131] The earned income tax credit is structured to benefit low-income working families. The amount of the credit initially increases with earnings, then remains constant as earnings increase, and then decreases with earnings until it is fully phased out. In 1996, unless scheduled increases are repealed by Congress,[132] the maximum benefit for a family with two or more qualifying children will be $3,556 (equal to 40 percent of the earned income amount of $8,890). The maximum benefit applies to incomes between $8,890 and $11,610 and declines thereafter. A phase-out percentage (21.06 percent) applies to adjusted gross income (or, if greater, the earned income) in excess of $11,610. Thus, the benefit is fully phased out at $28,495 of adjusted gross income for a taxpayer with two or more qualifying children.[133] In 1996, for example, the marginal income tax rate (15 percent), the employee portion of social security tax rates (7.65 percent), and the earned income credit phase-out rate (21.06 percent) equal a combined tax rate of 43.71 percent, without taking into account state taxes and the incidence of the employer portion of social security taxes.

The earned income tax credit phase-out percentages have the effect of increasing the marriage penalty for families at low-income levels; in addition, they make the marginal tax rate very high for low-income families earning at levels within the phase-out range.[134] A possible offsetting adjustment to these nonneutralities would be to make the child care tax credit refundable and to increase the applicable percentage to at least 50 percent of an increased level of eligible child care expenses.

Alternatively, I.R.C. § 129 programs could be made available to all employees.

The tax double standard as applied to low-income families operates at cross purposes to current welfare reform proposals and creates a double bind for welfare mothers. The problem could be partially addressed by delivering increased child care benefits through the tax system or through direct assistance programs, or some combination of the two. More comprehensive tax policy reforms would require revisiting the policy trade-offs regarding the use of the joint return, the goal of taxing equal earning families equally, and the nontaxation of imputed income from household labor. In the absence of more comprehensive tax reforms, the policy clash between welfare reform goals and the tax code will require increased attention by policymakers to the effects of the family values double standard as applied to low-income families.

NOTES

As this volume was going to press, President Clinton signed into law a modified version of welfare reform legislation that he had vetoed earlier in 1996. *See* Personal Responsibility and Work Opportunity Act of 1996, Pub. L. 104-193, 110 Stat. 2105. Some related portions of this essay were published by The Yale Law and Policy Review, Inc., Mary L. Heen, *Welfare Reform, Child Care Costs, and Taxes: Delivering Increased Work-Related Child Care Benefits to Low-Income Families,* 13 Yale L. & Pol'y Rev. 173 (1995) (examining the current federal child care programs, describing the need for increased assistance, and addressing the issue of whether additional federal child care assistance to low-income families should be provided through a transfer payment system, through the tax system, or through some combination of the two systems). Lisa Barnett, Dax Olsher, and John M. Ramey III provided research assistance, and the University of Richmond School of Law summer research fund provided financial support for this project.

1. Personal Responsibility and Work Opportunity Act of 1995, H.R. 4, 104th Cong., 1st Sess. (1995) (vetoed by President Clinton on Jan. 9, 1996); H.R. Conf. Rep. No. 430, 104th Cong., 1st Sess. (1995) (describing the House welfare reform bill, the Senate amendment, and the substitute agreed to in conference). The conference report was agreed to by a vote of 245 to 178 in the House, 141 Cong. Rec. H15533 (daily ed. Dec. 21, 1995), and by a vote of 52 to 47 in the Senate, 141 Cong. Rec. S19181 (daily ed. Dec. 22, 1995). *See also* Work Opportunity Act of 1995, H.R. 4, 104th Cong., 1st Sess. (1995), 141 Cong. Rec. S13802 (daily ed. Sept. 19, 1995) (passed by a Senate vote of 87-12); Personal Responsibility Act of 1995, H.R. 4, 104th Cong., 1st Sess. (1995), 141 Cong. Rec. H3790 (daily ed. Mar. 24, 1995) (passed by a House vote of 234-199).

2. *See* Sylvia A. Law, *Women, Work, Welfare, and the Preservation of Patriarchy,* 131 U. Pa. L. Rev. 1249 (1983).

3. *See* Edward J. McCaffery, *Taxation and the Family: A Fresh Look at Behavioral Gender Biases in the Code,* 40 UCLA L. Rev. 983 (1993).

4. *See* Gwendolyn Mink, *Welfare Reform in Historical Perspective*, 26 Conn. L. Rev. 879, 881–83 (1994); Dorothy E. Roberts, *The Value of Black Mothers' Work*, 26 Conn. L. Rev. 871, 873–75 (1994).

5. *See* Lance Liebman, *Evaluating Child Care Legislation: Program Structures and Political Consequences*, 26 Harv. J. on Legis. 357, 360–61 (1989) (questioning whether it is important that single mothers work even if child care costs more than their short-term earnings); *see also* Martha L. Fineman, *Images of Mothers in Poverty Discourses*, 1991 Duke L. J. 274 (observing that the primary objective of welfare reform legislation is to link poverty with the lack of a work ethic and critiquing mandatory work requirements, the substitution of governmental support with support from fathers, and the stigmatizing of single mothers).

6. *See* Mimi Abramovitz, Regulating the Lives of Women: Social Welfare Policy from Colonial Times to the Present 341 (1988); Linda Gordon, Pitied but Not Entitled: Single Mothers and the History of Welfare 1890–1935, 289–99 (1994); *see generally* Theodore R. Marmor et al., America's Misunderstood Welfare State: Persistent Myths, Enduring Realities 23–24 (1990) (describing the behaviorist vision of social welfare policy in which the poor are induced to behave "in a more socially acceptable manner").

7. *See infra* discussion in section titled *History of Congressional Approaches.*

8. *See* C. Eugene Steuerle & Jason Juffras, A $1,000 Tax Credit for Every Child: A Basis of Reform for the Nation's Tax, Welfare, and Health Systems 3–4 (Urban Inst. Changing Domestic Priorities Series 1991); *see also* Jonathan B. Forman, *Beyond President Bush's Child Tax Credit Proposal: Towards a Comprehensive System of Tax Credits to Help Low-Income Families with Children*, 38 Emory L.J. 661, 693–96 (1989) (proposing a $1,000 refundable children's allowance tax credit).

9. H.R. 2491, 104th Cong., 1st Sess. Title XI, Subtitle A, §11001 (1995) (House and Senate conferees agreeing to a $500 per child tax credit, phasing out the credit at adjusted gross incomes above $110,000 for joint returns and $75,000 for unmarried individuals); *see generally* Lawrence Zelenak, *Children and the Income Tax*, 49 Tax L. Rev. 349 (1994) (discussing various proposals for change).

10. *See* Frances Fox Piven & Richard A. Cloward, Regulating the Poor: The Functions of Public Welfare 248–340 (1971).

11. For a discussion of this correlation, see Dorothy A. Brown, *The Marriage Bonus/Penalty in Black and White*, this volume; john a. powell, *How Government Tax and Housing Policies Have Racially Segregated America*, this volume.

12. *See* Abramovitz, *supra* note 6, at 181–206, 315–19; Winifred Bell, Aid to Dependent Children 3–75 (1965); Gordon, *supra* note 6, at 37–64, 253–85.

13. *See* Alice Kessler-Harris, Out to Work: A History of Wage-Earning Women in the United States viii, 16–19, 119–27 (1982); Piven & Cloward, *supra* note 10, at 3–41, 123–45.

14. *See* Bell, *supra* note 12, at 174–94.

15. *See* Piven & Cloward, *supra* note 10, at 138.

16. *See id.* at 134; Bell, *supra* note 12, at 46 (noting that "[i]n one parish, the policy extended to children as young as 7 years of age).

17. *See* Piven & Cloward, *supra* note 10, at 134–35.

18. *See* Bell, *supra* note 12, at 46, 107, 141.

19. *See* Abramovitz, *supra* note 6, at 333.

20. *See* Joel F. Handler & Yeheskel Hasenfeld, The Moral Construction of Poverty: Welfare Reform in America 141–42 (WIN I), 156–58 (WIN II) (1991).

21. *See* Abramovitz, *supra* note 6, at 341 (attributing the exemption to limited funding, a lack of child care, and an excess of welfare recipients over WIN slots).

22. *See* Handler & Hasenfeld, *supra* note 20, at 154.

23. Pub. L. No. 100-485, Title III, 102 Stat. 2343 (codified as amended at 42 U.S.C. § 602 (1988)).

24. *See* H.R. Conf. Rep. No. 998, 100th Cong., 2d Sess. 1 (1988).

25. 42 U.S.C. § 602(a)(19)(B)(I) (1986).

26. *Id.* at § 602(a)(19)(C)(iii)(II).

27. *Id.* at § 602(a)(19)(C)(iii)(I).

28. *See* Staff of House Comm. on Ways and Means, 103d Cong., 2d Sess., Overview of Entitlement Programs, 1994 Green Book, table 10-4, at 344–48 (Comm. Print 1994) [hereinafter 1994 Green Book] (listing eight states exempting only those caretakers with children under age one, and four states and the Virgin Islands exempting those with children under age two).

29. *See* Piven & Cloward, *supra* note 10, at 341, App. Source, table 1, 4.

30. *See generally* Martha Minow, *The Welfare of Single Mothers and Their Children*, 26 Conn. L. Rev. 817, 826–31 (1994) (rejecting the argument that "work requirements for mothers on welfare simply reflect the changing social expectations of all women").

31. *See* 1994 Green Book, *supra* note 28, at 404 n. 2 (reporting that in 1992 16.1 percent of AFDC mothers or other caretakers were at school or training, 2.2 percent worked more than thirty hours per week, and 4.2 percent worked fewer than thirty hours per week); *see also* Ann L. Alstott, *The Earned Income Tax Credit and the Limitations of Tax-Based Welfare Reform*, 108 Harv. L. Rev. 533, 546–47 n. 52 (1995) (stating that data typically show that few AFDC recipients work and citing other studies indicating that a majority of women work at some point while receiving welfare). In comparison, about 56.8 percent of married women whose youngest child is under six participate in the labor force. *See* Minow, *supra* note 30, at 827 n. 53 (citing figures based on census data from 1987); *see also* Lucy A. Williams, *The Ideology of Division: Behavior Modification Welfare Reform Proposals*, 102 Yale L.J. 719, 745 n. 173 (1992) ("Of women with children under the age of six, 64 percent worked at some time during the year, although only 25 percent worked full-time year-round").

32. Heidi Hartmann & Roberta Spalter-Roth, *Reducing Welfare's Stigma: Policies That Build upon Commonalities among Women*, 26 Conn. L. Rev. 901, 908 (1994).

33. *Id.*

34. *See id.*

35. 1994 Green Book, *supra* note 28, at 342, 789.

36. 42 U.S.C. § 602(g)(3). *See* 1994 Greenbook, *supra* note 28, at 342.

37. *See* 1994 Green Book, *supra* note 28, table 10-5, at 349.

38. *See* Hearing on the Job Opportunities and Basic Skills Programs: Views from Participants and State Administrators Before the Subcomm. on Human Resources of the House Comm. on Educ. and Labor, 103d Cong., 2d Sess. 80 (1994) (statement of Raymond C. Scheppach, Executive Director, National Governor's Association); *see also* 1994 Green Book, *supra* note 28, table 10-5, at 349 ($646.6 million total federal funds expended on JOBS in 1993 compared to $582.5 million in JOBS-related child care); *id.* at 553, table 12-11 (estimated that about $668 million would be expended on AFDC child care and transitional child care in fiscal year 1994).

39. *See* 42 U.S.C. § 603(n)(2)(B) (Supp. IV 1992) (the program is authorized as a capped entitlement at $300 million annually).

40. 42 U.S.C. § 602(i)(3)(A) (1986).

41. 42 U.S.C. §§ 9858, 9858a–q (Supp. V 1993).

42. 42 U.S.C. §§ 1397 (1992), 1397a–f (1992 & Supp. 1995) (Social Services Block Grant Program of Title XX of the Social Security Act).

43. For a discussion of these programs, see Mary L. Heen, *Welfare Reform, Child Care Costs,*

and Taxes: Delivering Increased Work-Related Child Care Benefits to Low-Income Families, 13 Yale L. & Pol'y Rev. 173 (1995).

44. *Id.* (excluding amounts expended on programs such as Head Start and the Child and Adult Care Food Program).

45. *See* Ann Collins & Barbara Reisman, *Child Care under the Family Support Act: Guarantee, Quasi-Entitlement, or Paper Promise?* 11 Yale L. & Pol'y Rev. 203 (1993).

46. U.S. Gen. Accounting Office, Child Care: Working Poor and Welfare Recipients Face Service Gaps 4–5 (May 1994) (based on preliminary fiscal year 1992 data reported to the Department of Health and Human Services by the states).

47. *See* The Impact of Welfare Reform on Children and Their Families: Hearings Before the Senate Comm. on Labor and Human Resources, 104th Cong., 1st Sess. 211 (1995) (statement of Sandra L. Hofferth, University of Michigan Institute for Social Research) (citing reports published in 1991 and 1992).

48. *See id.* (based on transitional care data from twenty states).

49. Children's Defense Fund, The State of America's Children Yearbook 42 (1995) [hereinafter 1995 Yearbook] (finding that eight states had at least ten thousand children on the child care assistance waiting lists); Children's Defense Fund, The State of America's Children Yearbook 32 (1994) [hereinafter 1994 Yearbook] (finding that thirty-one states and the District of Columbia had waiting lists).

50. *See* U.S. Gen. Accounting Office, *supra* note 46, at 15; 1995 Yearbook, *supra* note 49, at 41–42; 1994 Yearbook, *supra* note 49, at 34.

51. *See* 1994 Yearbook, *supra* note 49, at 35.

52. Ellen Galinsky et al., The Study of Children in Family Child Care and Relative Care: Highlights of Findings 5, 97 (1994).

53. *Id.* at 97.

54. *Id.*

55. *See supra* note 1; Daniel Patrick Moynihan, *The Devolution Revolution,* N.Y. Times, Aug. 6, 1995, at D15.

56. *See* H.R. Conf. Rep. No. 430, *supra* note 1 (describing the House version of H. R. 4, which authorized states to use up to 30 percent of their family assistance block grants for other purposes, including for Title XX and Child Care and Development Block Grant programs, and provided $2.09 billion per year for child care block grants).

57. *See id.* (describing the Senate version of H. R. 4, which authorized states to use up to 30 percent of their family assistance grants for Child Care and Development Block grant activities, required the states to maintain 80 percent of historic state expenditures for five years, including child care expenditures, set aside funds to improve the quality of child care, and provided slightly increased federal funds for child care over a five-year period; and describing the conference substitute, later vetoed, which provided modest increases in federal child care funds over a seven-year period).

58. *See GOP Agrees on Cutting Welfare by $80 Billion,* L.A. Times, Nov. 11, 1995, at A21.

59. *See* Alison Mitchell, *Greater Poverty Toll Is Seen in Welfare Bill, but White House Says It May Be Forced to Accept Senate Measure,* N.Y. Times, Nov. 10, 1995, at A27.

60. *See* 1994 Green Book, *supra* note 28, at 540–41; Sandra L. Hofferth, et al., National Child Care Survey, 1990 119–96, 198–99 (1991) (defining child care as care provided while the mother is at work, and including care provided by fathers, mothers, and children themselves); Hearings, *supra* note 47, at 202 (in 1990, only 27 percent of the working poor paid for child care; the working poor who paid for child care spent about 33 percent of their incomes on child care, compared with 13 percent for working-class and 6 percent for middle-class families).

61. Galinsky et al., *supra* note 52, at 90.

62. *See id.* at 91.

63. *See* Cost, Quality & Child Outcomes Study Team, Economics Dept., U. of Colorado at Denver, et al., Cost, Quality, and Child Outcomes in Child Care Centers: Executive Summary 2, 5 (Apr. 1995) (finding also that the average center in the study expended $95 per week, per child for full-time care).

64. For a more detailed discussion of the legislative history of the child care tax credit and its predecessors, see Alan L. Feld, *Deductibility of Expenses for Child Care and Household Services: New Section 214,* 27 Tax L. Rev. 415 (1972); Heen, *supra* note 43, at 211–14; John B. Keane, *Federal Income Tax Treatment of Child Care Expenses,* 10 Harv. J. Legis. 1, 2–7 (1972); William A. Klein, *Tax Deductions for Family Care Expenses,* 14 B.C. Int'l & Comp. L. Rev. 917, 919–32, 936–37 (1973); *see also* Wendy Gerzog Shaller, *Limit Deductions for Mixed Personal/Business Expenses: Curb Current Abuses and Restore Some Progressivity into the Tax Code,* 41 Cath. L. Rev. 581, 606–9 (1992) (describing the § 129 exclusion for dependent care assistance).

65. Internal Revenue Code of 1954, Pub. L. No. 591-736, 68A Stat. 70 (codified at I.R.C. §214, repealed in 1976).

66. *See* H.R. Rep. No. 1337, 83d Cong., 2d Sess. (1954), *reprinted in* 1954 U.S.C.C.A.N. 4019, 4055; Detailed Discussion of the Technical Provisions of the Bill, *reprinted in* 1954 U.S.C.C.A.N. 4137, 4197–98.

67. *See* S. Rep. No. 437, 92d Cong., 1st Sess. 13–14, 59–62 (1971), *reprinted in* 1971 U.S.C.C.A.N. 1918, 1929, 1966–68.

68. *Id.* at 1928–29.

69. *Id.* at 1928.

70. *Id.* at 1929.

71. Pub. L. No. 94-455, Title V, § 504(a)(1), 90 Stat. 1563 (1976) (codified at I.R.C. § 44A) (amended in 1978 and 1981 and redesignated in 1984 as I.R.C. § 21).

72. *See* H.R. Rep. No. 658, 94th Cong., 2d Sess. 147–48 (1976), *reprinted in* 1976 U.S.C.C.A.N. 2897, 3040–41; S. Rep. No. 938, 94th Cong., 2d Sess., pt. I, 132–33 (1976), *reprinted in* 1976 U.S.C.C.A.N. 3439, 3565–66.

73. Pub. L. No. 94-455, *supra* note 71 (codified at I.R.C. § 44A(c)).

74. Economic Recovery Tax Act of 1981, Pub. L. No. 97-34, § 124, 95 Stat. 172, 197–201 (codified at I.R.C. §§ 44A, 129).

75. *See* H.R. Conf. Rep. No. 215, 97th Cong., 1st Sess. 195, 200–201 (1981), *reprinted in* 1981 U.S.C.C.A.N. 285, 290–91.

76. Deficit Reduction Act of 1984, Pub. L. No. 98-369, § 471(c)(1), 98 Stat. 494, 826.

77. Omnibus Reconciliation Act of 1987, Pub. L. No. 100-203, § 10101, 101 Stat. 1330–84 (codified at I.R.C. § 21(b)(2)(A)).

78. Family Support Act of 1988, Pub. L. No. 100-485, § 703, 102 Stat. 2343, 2426–27; Technical and Miscellaneous Revenue Act of 1988, Pub. L. No. 100-647, § 2004, 102 Stat. 3342, 3598.

79. Staff of Joint Comm. on Taxation, 104th Cong., 1st Sess., Estimates of Federal Tax Expenditures for Fiscal Years 1996–2000 (Comm. Print 1995), *reprinted in* Daily Tax Rep. (BNA), Sept. 6, 1995, at L-1, L-9, L-12 [hereinafter 1995 JCT Tax Expenditure Estimates].

80. *See* I.R.C. § 151(d)(3) (1986) (providing for the phaseout of personal exemptions for taxpayers with adjusted gross incomes above certain threshold amounts); Deborah H. Schenk, *Simplification for Individual Taxpayers: Problems and Proposals,* 45 Tax L. Rev. 121, 127–49 (1989); Zelenak, *supra* note 9.

81. I.R.C. § 21(a)(2).

82. *Id.* at § 21(b)(2).

83. *Id.* at § 21(a)(1).

84. *Id.* at §§ 21(a) (refers to "qualifying individuals" rather than children), 21(b)(1) (defines "qualifying individuals" as including three categories of individuals: (1) a dependent under the age of thirteen, (2) a dependent who is physically or mentally incapable of self-care, or (3) the spouse of the taxpayer, if physically or mentally incapable of self-care).

85. *Id.* at § 21(c); *see also id.* at § 21(d)(1), (2) (the amount of the employment-related expenses may not exceed the lower of earned income of the taxpayer or that of the taxpayer's spouse; however, if the taxpayer's spouse is a full-time student or incapable of self-care, a monthly amount of income is deemed to be earned by the spouse in the amount of $200 (if the $2,400 limit applies) or $400 (if the $4,800 limit applies)).

86. *Id.* at § 21(a)(2).

87. *See* Forman, *supra* note 8, at 686.

88. Pub. L. No. 99-514, 100 Stat. 2085 (1986).

89. *See* Michael J. Graetz & Deborah H. Schenk, Federal Income Taxation Principles and Policies 428 (3d ed. 1995).

90. I.R.C. § 63(c)(2).

91. *Id.* at § 151(b), (c).

92. *Id.* at §§ 63(c)(4) (requiring inflation adjustments to the standard deduction amounts beginning after 1988), 151(d)(4) (requiring inflation adjustments to the $2,000 personal exemption amount for tax years beginning after 1989).

93. See Rev. Proc. 95-53, 1995-52 I.R.B. 22 (for 1996 the inflation-adjusted standard deduction amount for a married taxpayer filing a joint return is $6,700; the inflation adjusted personal exemption amount is $2,550; thus, a family of four claiming a standard deduction ($6,700) and four exemptions (4 x $2,550 = $10,200) would pay no tax on up to $16,900 of income).

94. *See* Notice, Annual Update of the HHS Poverty Guidelines, 61 Fed. Reg. 8286 (1996) (the federal poverty guideline for a family of four is $15,600 for 1996).

95. Rev. Proc. 95-53, *supra* note 93, at §§ 3.04, 3.08 (for 1996 the inflation-adjusted standard deduction for a single head of household is $5,900; the inflation adjusted personal exemption amount is $2,550; the standard deduction ($5,900) plus two personal exemptions ($5,100) equals $11,000).

96. *See* Notice, *supra* note 94 (for 1996, the federal poverty income for a family of two is $10,360).

97. *See* Jonathan Barry Forman, *Simplification for Low-Income Taxpayers: Some Options*, Table 12.1, this volume.

98. *See* 1995 JCT Tax Expenditure Estimates, *supra* note 79, at 23, table 3, at L-12 (the staff prepares estimates by income class for the child and dependent care credit; the estimates illustrate the concentration of benefits in the middle and upper income ranges).

99. I.R.C. § 129(a).

100. *Id.* at § 129(d)(1).

101. *Id.* at § 129(d)(1)–(8) (including requirements that contributions to the plan not discriminate in favor of highly compensated employees, *id.* at (d)(2), and that employees be notified of the terms and availability of the program, *id.* at (d)(6)).

102. *Id.* at § 129(b)(1); *see also id.* at § 129(b)(2) (incorporating by reference the provisions of §21(d)(2), the statute applies the same rules that are applicable to the child and dependent care tax credit for determining a deemed amount of earned income for a student spouse or a spouse incapable of self-care).

103. *Id.* at § 129(c).

104. See 1994 Green Book, *supra* note 28, at 708 (citing U.S. Department of Labor, Bureau of Labor Statistics, Employee Benefits in Medium and Large Firms, 1991 (May 1993)).

105. *See id.*

106. *See* I.R.C. § 21(c) (providing that the amount of employment-related expenses claimed for purposes of the credit shall be reduced by the amount excludable from gross income under § 129 for the taxable year).

107. *See generally* 1994 Green Book, *supra* note 28, at 708 (". . . the credit generally is less valuable than the exclusion for taxpayers who are above the 15-percent tax bracket").

108. *See* Grace Blumberg, *Sexism in the Code: A Comparative Study of Income Taxation of Working Wives and Mothers*, 21 Buff. L. Rev. 49, 64–66 (1971).

109. *See Smith v. Commissioner*, 40 B.T.A. 1038 (1939), *aff'd without opinion*, 113 F.2d 114 (2d Cir. 1940) (denying a business expense deduction for child care costs on the basis that child care was one of the basic functions of family living and thus was a "personal" concern).

110. *See* Stanley S. Surrey & Paul R. McDaniel, Tax Expenditures 3 (1985) (explaining that departures from the normal tax structure are tax expenditures or special preferences and are viewed as equivalent to direct government outlays).

111. *See* Boris I. Bittker, *Federal Income Taxation and the Family*, 27 Stan. L. Rev. 1389, 1463 (1975).

112. *See* Thomas D. Griffith, *Personal Deductions in the Income Tax*, 40 Hastings L.J. 343, 385–94 (1989); Paul R. McDaniel & James R. Repetti, *Horizontal and Vertical Equity: The Musgrave/Kaplow Exchange*, 1 Fla. Tax Rev. 607 (1993).

113. *See* Klein, *supra* note 64, at 937–40; Brian Wolfman, *Child Care, Work, and the Federal Income Tax*, 3 Am. J. Tax Pol'y 153, 167–74 (1984).

114. *See* Klein, *supra* note 64, at 941; *see generally* Boris I. Bittker, *Income Tax Reform in Canada: The Report of the Royal Commission on Taxation*, 35 U. Chi. L. Rev. 637, 638–45 (1968) (discussing the commission's conclusion that a taxpaying unit's ability to pay taxes is measured by its discretionary economic power).

115. *See* Marvin A. Chirelstein, Federal Income Taxation: The Leading Cases and Concepts ¶6.01(a) (7th ed. 1994); Keane, *supra* note 64, at 30–35.

116. *See* Feld, *supra* note 64, at 429; McCaffery, *supra* note 3, at 1005–10; Daniel C. Shaffer & Donald A. Berman, *Two Cheers for the Child Care Deduction*, 28 Tax L. Rev. 535, 535–36 (1973).

117. Wolfman, *supra* note 113, at 190–93.

118. For a more detailed discussion of optimal income taxation, see Joseph Bankman & Thomas Griffith, *Social Welfare and the Rate Structure: A New Look at Progressive Taxation*, 75 Cal. L. Rev. 1905, 1919–29 (1987); McCaffery, *supra* note 3, at 1035–46.

119. A. C. Pigou, A Study in Public Finance (3d ed. 1947); *see* McCaffery, *supra* note 3, at 1046–53.

120. For the view that in economic terms, child care costs are an investment by parents in their children's human capital, see Lynn A. Stout, *Some Thoughts on Poverty and Failure in the Market for Children's Human Capital*, 81 Geo. L.J. 1945 (1993). *But see* Bittker, *supra* note 111, at 1447–48 (noting that the concept of children as the "poor man's capital," or as an informal social security system, has made little headway in the analysis of American society); *accord* Klein, *supra* note 64, at 940 n. 1189; *see generally* Joseph M. Dodge, *Taxing Human Capital Acquisition Costs—or Why Costs of Higher Education Should Not Be Deducted or Amortized*, 54 Ohio St. L. J. 927, 948–61 (1993).

121. *See* R. G. Lipsey & Kelvin Lancaster, *The General Theory of the Second Best*, 24 Rev. Econ. Stud. 11 (1956). For more general use of the term *second best solution* to refer to solutions to prob-

lems that take into account existing imperfections and tolerate compensating imperfections, see Boris I. Bittker, *A "Comprehensive Tax Base" as a Goal of Income Tax Reform*, 80 Harv. L. Rev. 925, 983–84 (1967); Dodge, *supra* note 120, at 941–43.

122. *See generally* Schaffer & Berman, *supra* note 116, at 537–43 (discussing the nonneutrality between wage work and house work).

123. *See* Wolfman, *supra* note 113, at 175–81.

124. *See* Schaffer & Berman, *supra* note 116, at 543–45 (distinguishing child care from other self-provided services because of the necessary, although not sufficient, relationship between the expense and the income earned).

125. *See* Rachel Connelly, *The Effect of Child Care Costs on Married Women's Labor Force Participation*, 74 Rev. Econ. & Stat. 83, 90 (1992).

126. *See* Bankman & Griffith, *supra* note 118, at 1925–27 (discussing studies).

127. *See* Heen, *supra* note 43, at 210–17.

128. For a discussion of the "fiction" of marital unity underlying the policy of taxing equal earning families equally, see Lily Kahng, *Fiction in Tax, this volume.*

129. *See* Bittker, *supra* note 111, at 1395–97.

130. *See infra.*

131. McCaffery, *supra* note 3, at 1015–16.

132. Omnibus Budget Reconciliation Act of 1993, Pub. L. No. 103-66, § 13131, 107 Stat. 312, 433 (increasing benefits through 1996).

133. *See* I.R.C. § 32(b); Rev. Proc. 95-53, *supra* note 93, at § 3.03; Alstott, *supra* note 31, at 541–44; Regina T. Jefferson, *The Earned Income Tax Credit: Thou Goest Whither? A Critique of Existing Proposals to Reform the Earned Income Tax Credit*, 68 Temp. L. Rev. 143, 145–52 (1995); George K. Yin et al., *Improving the Delivery of Benefits to the Working Poor: Proposals to Reform the Earned Income Tax Credit Program*, 11 Am. J. Tax Pol'y 225, 230–60 (1994).

134. *See* Alstott, *supra* note 31, at 549–50, 559–64; Dorothy A. Brown, *The Marriage Bonus/Penalty in Black and White*, this volume.

CONTRIBUTORS

Jennifer J. S. Brooks earned her undergraduate degree from Wake Forest University and her J.D. from Catholic University. After graduation she practiced tax law at the Washington, D.C., law firm of Covington and Burling, where she was strongly influenced by John B. Jones, Jr. In 1983 Brooks joined the faculty of the William Mitchell College of Law in St. Paul, Minnesota. She obtained her LL.M. from Harvard Law School, writing a thesis under the guidance of William D. Andrews. A member of the American Bar Association's Tax Section, from 1989 to 1990 Brooks served as chair of the Corporate Tax Committee, from 1991 to 1995 as secretary, and from 1995 to 1996 as a member of the council. She is currently co-chair of the Committee on Integration of the Corporate and Individual Taxes and a sponsor of the Tax and Social Policy Forum.

Dorothy A. Brown is associate professor of law at the University of Cincinnati College of Law. She received her J.D. from the Georgetown University Law Center and her LL.M. in tax from New York University. Before entering the legal academy, Brown practiced law and worked as an investment banker on Wall Street. She regularly publishes in the state and local and tax areas. Her most recent publication, *Invisibility Factor: The Limits of Public Choice Theory and Public Institutions,* will appear in the Washington University Law Quarterly in 1996. She is currently completing an article, *The Invisibility of Black Women in Tax Jurisprudence,* that examines the tax treatment of black women.

Karen B. Brown is professor of law and associate dean for academic affairs at the University of Minnesota. She was appointed Julius E. Davis Professor of Law for 1995–96. In keeping with her interest in the impact of the changing world economy on the U.S. system of taxation of income from international transactions, Brown has written numerous articles on corporate and international taxation and has coauthored a treatise on international transactions.

Before joining the Minnesota faculty, she was a professor at Brooklyn Law School. A graduate of Princeton University, she earned her J.D. and LL.M. in taxation from the New York University School of Law.

Charlotte Crane teaches tax and local government law at Northwestern University School of Law. She clerked for Judge Wade H. McCree on the Court of Appeals for the Sixth Circuit and for Justice Harry A. Blackmun on the Supreme Court of the United States. Before joining the academy, Crane practiced primarily in tax for four years in Chicago. Her recent research interests include questions not only regarding the appropriate tax base but also about the role of legal institutions in the design and implementation of such bases.

Jonathan Barry Forman has been a faculty member at the University of Oklahoma College of Law since 1985, where he teaches tax and social welfare courses. Previously, he served as tax counsel to U.S. senator Daniel Patrick Moynihan (1983–84), as a trial attorney for the U.S. Department of Justice, Tax Division, Northern Civil Trial Region (1979–83), and as a law clerk for Judge Robert J. Yock of the U.S. Claims Court (1978–79). Forman received his J.D. from the University of Michigan School of Law in 1978 and has M.A. degrees in economics from George Washington University and in psychology from the University of Iowa. He is admitted to practice in the District of Columbia and is active in the American Bar Association's Section of Taxation and in the Association of American Law Schools' Sections on Taxation and on Poverty Law. Forman's recent articles include *Reconsidering the Tax Treatment of the Elderly* and *The Income Tax Treatment of Social Welfare Benefits.*

LaBrenda Garrett-Nelson began the practice of tax law in 1978 as an associate at a major New York law firm. Later she joined the staff of the Joint Committee on Taxation, serving as counsel during the five-year period that saw enactment of the Deficit Reduction Act of 1984. Garrett-Nelson also had significant responsibility for major portions of the 1986 Tax Reform Act. For four years she taught corporate and foreign tax courses as adjunct professor in the graduate division of the Georgetown University Law Center. Garrett-Nelson has served on several committees of the American Bar

Association's Tax Section and on the Board of Advisors of the Journal of International Taxation. She has lectured extensively for continuing legal educational programs and before professional and trade organizations. Garrett-Nelson joined Washington Counsel, Inc., in 1996. She holds an undergraduate degree from John Jay College of Criminal Justice, City University of New York, and a J.D. and an LL.M. in taxation from New York University School of Law.

Gwen Thayer Handelman received a B.A. and a J.D., magna cum laude, from the University of Michigan. In law school she was an editor of *The Michigan Law Review.* Following graduation, she served as a law clerk to Patricia M. Wald of the United States Court of Appeals for the District of Columbia Circuit and as special assistant to Joseph A. Califano in his capacity as special counsel for the House Committee on Standards of Official Conduct. She was also an associate with the law firm of Covington and Burling in Washington, D.C. In 1986 she joined the law faculty of Washington and Lee University in Lexington, Virginia. Handelman teaches courses in federal income taxation, employee benefits law, and professional responsibility. She has authored a number of articles and has lectured widely on ethical issues and tax-related subjects. Active in the American Bar Association, Handelman co-chairs the Ethics Subcommittee of the Section of Labor and Employment Law Employee Benefits Committee and is chair of the Section of Taxation Committee on Standards of Tax Practice.

Mary L. Heen is associate professor at the University of Richmond School of Law. She previously taught at the New York University School of Law as acting assistant professor in the graduate tax program, where she also served as assistant editor of the *Tax Law Review.* She received an LL.M. in Taxation from New York University School of Law, a J.D. from the University of California at Berkeley (Boalt Hall), and a B.A. from Yale University. Before joining the faculty at Richmond, Heen practiced as a tax attorney at Patterson, Belknap, Webb and Tyler in New York City and as a national staff counsel for the Women's Rights Project of the American Civil Liberties Union. She has published a book chapter and articles on gender discrimination in addition to law review articles on tax and social policy issues.

Regina T. Jefferson is assistant professor of law at the Catholic University of America Columbus School of Law, where she teaches courses on federal income taxation, partnership taxation, and ERISA. Jefferson is an expert in the area of ERISA. She was a tax law specialist at the national office of the Internal Revenue Service in the Employee Plans Division from 1987 through 1990. Her publications include *Defined Benefit Plan Funding: How Much Is Too Much?* published in the Case Western Reserve Law Review, and *The Earned Income Tax Credit: Thou Goest Whither?* which appeared in the Temple Law Review. She was a speaker at the Teaching Taxation Section of the annual May meeting of the ABA Taxation Section, May 1994. Jefferson was a graduate Teaching Taxation Fellow in the Graduate Teaching Program for Future Law Professors at the Georgetown University Law Center. She has a B.S. in mathematics from Howard University (1981), a J.D. from George Washington University (1987), and an LL.M. from Georgetown University (1992).

Lily Kahng is associate professor at Cornell Law School. She previously taught at the New York University School of Law. She teaches and writes in the fields of federal income taxation and federal estate and gift taxation. Before entering law teaching in 1991, Kahng practiced tax law at the New York City firm of Simpson Thacher and Bartlett and was a vice president at Salomon Brothers. Kahng received her B.A. in philosophy from Princeton University in 1980, her J.D. from the Columbia University School of Law in 1984, and her LL.M in taxation from the New York University School of Law in 1991.

Beverly I. Moran is professor of law at the University of Wisconsin Law School. She has dedicated a large part of her career to increasing the number of minority professors in legal education. In addition to creating and coordinating a number of conferences for minority law professors, Moran has been instrumental in changing the direction of tax scholarship through her various speeches and publications emphasizing the social, race, and class aspects of taxation. She is a graduate of Vassar College, the University of Pennsylvania Law School, and the New York University Law School. She lectures widely on various tax issues in the United States, Canada, Hong Kong, the People's Republic of China, Ethiopia, and Eritrea.

john a. powell is professor of law at the University of Minnesota Law School and executive director of the Institute of Race and Poverty. He received his B.A. from Stanford University and his J.D. from the University of California, Berkeley (Boalt Hall). Before joining the faculty at Minnesota, Professor powell served as national legal director of the American Civil Liberties Union (ACLU). He has also taught at the Columbia University School of Law, Harvard Law School, the University of Miami School of Law, and the University of San Francisco School of Law. He is widely published in both the popular and the scholarly press. Professor powell also serves on the board of directors of the Poverty and Race Research Action Council and is a member of the ABA Commission on Homelessness and Poverty.

Denise D. J. Roy is associate professor at William Mitchell College of Law in St. Paul, Minnesota. She teaches feminist jurisprudence and a variety of J.D. and LL.M tax courses. Before becoming a law teacher, Roy served as tax counsel to the U.S. Senate Finance Committee under Chairman Lloyd Bentsen, practiced law at Long, Aldridge and Norman in Atlanta, Georgia, and clerked for Judge Thomas A. Clark on the U.S. Court of Appeals for the eleventh Circuit. Roy received her J.D. degree from Yale Law School. She is currently writing a book on tax law for family lawyers.

George K. Yin is Harrison Foundation Research Professor of Law at the University of Virginia, where he teaches primarily in the tax area. He previously taught law at the University of Florida and has been a visiting professor at the University of Pennsylvania, Brigham Young University, the University of Virginia, and the Joint Committee on Taxation in Washington, D.C. Before becoming a law professor, he served as tax counsel to the Senate Finance Committee and practiced law in Washington, D.C. He has written a number of articles in the tax field and is presently the reporter to the ALI tax project on the taxation of pass-through entities. He is a member of the board of trustees of the American Tax Policy Institute.

INDEX

Ability, as aspect of human capital income, 66–67
Ability-to-pay norm: and child care expenditures, 334–35, 337
ADSA. See American Dream Savings Account (ADSA)
Aid to Dependent Children program, 324
Aid to Families with Dependent Children, and child care, 325–28
American Dream: tax law and, 1–2
American Dream Savings Account (ADSA), 253–71; administrative complexity of, 269–70; back-loaded feature of, 256–57, 268–69; benefit to wealthy, 266–67; budgetary implications of, 269–70; class bias of, 266–67; compared with Individual Retirement Account, 256–57, 265; and consumption, 262; cost to U.S. Treasury of, 270; distributions from, 256, 260; effect on 401(k) plans, 264–65; effect on retirement savings, 257, 262–64, 265–66, 270–71; fairness of, 266–67; and low-income taxpayers, 260, 266–67; as part of Tax Fairness and Deficit Reduction Act of 1995, 256; provisions of, 259, 260, 262; regressivity of, 3; and retirement savings disincentives, 257, 260, 262–66; rollovers from Individual Retirement Account, 259, 262–63; social and economic impact of, 260–70; and U.S. savings rate, 259, 261–62, 267–68, 271. See also Individual Retirement Account (IRA); Private pension system
Americans with Disabilities Act of 1990, 186
Andrews, William, 121
Armey-Shelby flat-tax proposal, 125–26, 245; as alternative to income tax, 291; and consumption, 190
At-Risk Child Care Program, 327

Back-loaded feature, of American Dream Savings Account, 256–57, 268–69. See also American Dream Savings Account (ADSA)
Balanced budget, U.S., 238
Bankman, Joseph: on nondiscrimination rules, 139
Benefits, employee. See Employee benefits

Bentham, Jeremy: on legal fiction, 25
Bittker, Boris, 38, 121
Blair, John, and Rover Premus: business relocation studies by, 201
Border tax adjustments, 245–46
Bradford, David, 121; and consumed-income tax proposal, 128; on consumption tax and human capital, 165
Business: and government tax incentives, 197; privileged in personal/business dichotomy, 187, 189, 190
Business expenses: child care expenditures as, 334–35; and consumption, 177, 182; employee benefits as, 129–30; and entrepreneurial expenditures, 135; and environmental cleanup costs' nondeductibility, 173, 183; health expenditures as, 130; personal aspects of, 177; and personal expenses, 171; and productivity, 171–73, 177; tax deductibility of, 171, 172, 183, 189; worker training costs as, 135. See also Personal/business dichotomy
Business relocation, 197–211; from cities to suburbs, 95; Deloitte and Touche survey on, 200; John Blair and Rover Premus studies on, 201; Neal Schmitt study on, 201; problems with, 204–5; and property tax incentives, 200; reasons for, 200–201; Samuel Rabino study on, 201; tax incentives for, 200–203

Capital export neutrality: defined, 215; and developing countries, 215–16, 220; as economic neutrality goal, 215; and efficiency, 233; and maquiladora, 222; as myth, 223; and preservation of U.S. tax base, 234; and U.S. international tax policy, 214–16, 220–25, 227, 233, 234; as treaty obstacle, 220–25, 227. See also International tax policy, U.S.; Treaties, U.S. international tax
Capital gains preferences: as tax benefit of home ownership, 93
Car ownership: and racialization, 96
Cartels, government: for tax incentives, 208–10
Cash or deferred arrangements. See 401(k) plans

Independent contractors *(Continued)*
workers, 289–90; and nondiscrimination
rules, 139; reclassification as employees,
289–90
Individual Retirement Account (IRA), 254–55;
compared with American Dream Savings
Account, 256–57, 265; distribution restrictions of, 261–62; effect of Tax Reform Act
of 1986 on, 258–59; and Employee
Retirement Income Security Act of 1974
(ERISA), 257; history of, 257–59; and low-
income taxpayers, 258; rationale for, 261;
rollovers to American Dream Savings
Account, 259, 262–63; tax benefits of, 254,
258, 260. *See also* American Dream Savings
Account (ADSA); Private pension system
Institute for Women's Policy Research study of
welfare recipients' work patterns, 326
Internal Revenue Code: bias in favor of marriage, 46; on child care expenditures,
330–33; on environmental expenditures,
170; personal/business dichotomy in,
171–72; on tax deferral, 237; and U.S.
income tax, 148
Internationalism: defined, 217
International tax policy, U.S., 214–30; and capital export neutrality, 214, 215–16, 220–25,
233; competitiveness as a goal of, 233, 237;
and consumption tax, 243–47; and developing countries, 215–17, 219–30; and economic neutrality, 222; and foreign tax
credit, 222–24, 234; and General
Agreement on Tariffs and Trade (GATT),
245; goals of, 233–47; and human rights,
219; and investment, 224; and limitations-
of-benefits provisions, 227–29; multilateral
treaties, 217–18; and race, 219, 227; reform
of, 241–43; and tax sparing credit, 224–25,
229; treaties and, 217–20; unilateralism of,
217, 225–26; and value-added tax, 243. *See
also* Treaties, U.S. international tax
International tax treaties. *See* Treaties, U.S.
international tax
International trade deficit, U.S., 216–17
Inverse tax: defined, 74; and material capital,
74
Investment: and consumption, 158–60, 162,
170, 176–81, 190; and consumption expenditures, 174; and consumption tax,
146–47; and developing countries, 226–27;
disability access expenditures as, 177–78;
environmental expenditures as, 177; foreign, and Tax Reform Act of 1986, 236; and

income tax, 152, 158; and international tax
policy, 224; and tax reform, 120; and value,
177–80; and workers, 120
Investment and consumption: dichotomy
between, 134, 152, 175

Job Opportunity and Basic Skills Program
(JOBS), 325–27; and child care, 326–27
Joint Committee on Taxation: personal/busi-
ness dichotomy and, 173; on Social
Security tax exemption as alternative to
earned income credit, 288

Kalleberg, Arne: on part-time workers, 139
Kaplow, Louis: on consumption tax, 75,
160–61; definition of wealth, 59; on Haig-
Simons ideal tax base model, 59–60; on
human capital income, 58; on leisure, 66,
69; on wage-measured human capital, 65
Kasich, John: and tax deferral repeal, 239
Klein, William, and Joseph Bankman: on per-
sonal/business dichotomy, 172

Labor participation. *See* Work force participa-
tion
Legal fictions: criticism of, 25–26; defined,
25–26; Henry Maine on, 26; Jeremy
Bentham on, 25; John Chipman Gray on,
26; Lon Fuller on, 26; in tax, 26. *See also*
Economic neutrality; Marital unity fiction;
Tax objectivity
Leisure: as aspect of human capital, 66–67,
69–76; defined, 59; and human capital
income, 69; Louis Kaplow on, 66, 69
Lendors, and redlining, 91
Levittown, N.Y.: racial segregation in, 91
Limitations-of-benefits provisions: defined,
227; and developing countries, 228–29; of
tax treaties, 227–29
Low-income taxpayers: and American Dream
Savings Account, 260, 266–67; and child
care, 323, 327–28; and child care costs, 338;
and child care tax credit, 337; and dependent care credit, 278–79; and earned
income credit, 278–79; and earned income
tax credit, 287; effect of earned income tax
credit on, 280–83; effect of Social Security
taxes on, 280–82; income exclusion for,
289; and income tax forms, 284; and marriage penalty, 47; net federal tax on,
280–83; and private pension system, 259;
and retirement savings, 265, 267; and
Social Security taxes, 280–82, 287, 314–15;